ary,
and Pap

C000166100

2.

... many years apart,
... us are one at heart.

...ngle roof again
...seasons wax and wane.

... come, the years will go,
...larts, we cannot know,

...Ms, piecemeal and sincere,
... March, for one more year.

On Balance

to Anne — with best wishes
and thank you for your
warm
hospitality.

On Balance

An Autobiography

Leila

_19. 6. 2006_

Leila Seth

PENGUIN
VIKING

VIKING

Penguin Books India (P) Ltd., 11 Community Centre, Panchsheel Park,
New Delhi 110 017, India
Penguin Books Ltd., 80 Strand, London WC2R 0RL, UK
Penguin Group Inc., 375 Hudson Street, New York, NY 10014, USA
Penguin Books Australia Ltd., 250 Camberwell Road, Camberwell,
Victoria 3124, Australia
Penguin Books Canada Ltd., 10 Alcorn Avenue, Suite 300, Toronto,
Ontario, M4V 3B2,Canada
Penguin Books (NZ) Ltd., Cnr Rosedale and Airborne Roads, Albany,
Auckland, New Zealand
Penguin Books (South Africa) (Pty) Ltd, 24 Sturdee Avenue,
Rosebank 2196, South Africa

First published in Viking by Penguin Books India 2003

Copyright © Leila Seth 2003

All rights reserved

10 9 8 7 6 5 4 3 2 1

For sale in the Indian Subcontinent only

Typeset in *Adobe Garamond* by SÜRYA, New Delhi
Printed at Ajanta Offset & Packaging Ltd., New Delhi

To Premo
who gave me the space to grow
and
to Nandini
who is our future

It is perhaps as difficult to
write a good life as to live one.

Lytton Strachey

Contents

PART THREE: A SENSE OF FREEDOM

A Word of Thanks

Many relatives, friends and others helped me while I was writing this book. I mention those I remember—please forgive me if I have forgotten to include your name, but I thank you all.

Bina Aranha, Aloka and Gautam Chakravarti, Devkisan Chetwani, Maja Daruwala, Dayita Datta, Pradip Krishen, Siddhartha Mehta, Kuldip Nayar, Rajindar Sachar, Kamlesh Sharma, Kuldip Sood, Sheila and Trishna Tandon and Mohan Lal Varma for helping me with your expertise in diverse fields.

Christine Cipriani, Poulomi Chatterji, David Davidar, Peter Launsky-Tieffenthal and Aradhana Seth, Meenakshi Mukherjee, Ruma Pal, Gitanjali and Shantum Seth, Sashi and Usha Seth, Premo Seth, and Shanti Varma for reading the manuscript and so generously contributing your time, ideas and comments; as you read this book, each of you will recognize your particular contributions and realize how much your suggestions have helped to make *On Balance* a better and more cohesive book.

Kamini Mahadevan and Vikram Seth, my two editors: I shall always be grateful to you; and whatever I say in words will not be adequate. You Kamini, for prodding and probing to get me to jog my memory and put things down on paper and for then giving these some semblance of sense and sequence; and you, Vikram, for painstakingly correcting the English and grammar that I taught you almost fifty years ago, for helping me recall facts about the family, and for giving the book a more coherent structure. You have both made what was ordinary into what means something special to me.

Ravi Kumar Khattar, better known at Penguin India as Ravi Auto: for carrying, in the early morning and late at night, the draft pages for correction and typesetting between me, Kamini and the excellent typesetter, Rajinder Ganju, who carefully and speedily incorporated every semi-colon and full-stop.

Granville Austin, for allowing me to use material from your book *Working a Democratic Constitution: The Indian Experience* and to quote from it; Graciela Iturbide, Robert Lamar and Tejbir Singh for letting me use some wonderful family photographs taken by you; Bena Sareen for designing the book jacket so beautifully; V.K. Karthika for carrying the heavy manuscript in the hope it is widely marketed and Hemali Sodhi for helping to sell it.

Once again, I thank you, in legal parlance, both jointly and severally.

Preface

Why do I write? I wonder. Is it because I am over seventy and want to look back on my life? Not really, because I prefer looking ahead; there is still so much to be done, experienced and enjoyed. Now and then I have toyed with the idea of a memoir. Over the years, several young women have asked me what it was like when I started to practise law in 1959, and that too in a place like Bihar. They felt that my experiences would give them and others the courage and confidence to go ahead. Many young parents also asked me how I had brought up my three children to be such interesting young people. None of them do a nine-to-five job but they are all happy and successful. Others wanted to know how I balanced my home and my work.

Early in 1992 David Davidar of Penguin Books India came to stay with me in Shimla for over a week. He wanted to read my son Vikram's novel *A Suitable Boy* that ran into over 2,500 pages in manuscript. While David was there, both Vikram and he came up with the suggestion that when I retired in October, I should write about my life. But after retirement I was always far too busy. And somehow, at that stage, I was not inclined to look back at all. Perhaps this was for the best, as I had many interesting experiences thereafter, from which I learnt a great deal.

At the end of August 2000, I was due to complete my term as a member of the 15th Law Commission of India. But early that month I met with an accident at a Penguin book launch. It was a merry occasion at which cartoonist R.K. Laxman's book *The Best of Laxman: The Common Man in the New Millennium* was being released. Though for fifty years the Common Man had been silent, his creator had with his insightful comments on the social and political scene kept his readers wonderfully amused.

Like many others, I bought the book and got him to sign it. I was feeling very pleased with myself until I tripped over a microphone wire lying loose on the carpet. I was in utter agony. I had a multiple fracture of the left ankle and needed surgery, steel plates and screws, and plaster. I would have to be out of circulation for a minimum of thirteen weeks. I was contemplating suing somebody for this negligence. But whom could I sue? The delightful and distinguished Mr Laxman, my good friend David Davidar, or the Taj Mahal Hotel, or the lot? But considering the odds, and knowing the vagaries and slow pace of the law, I decided against any action. It would probably take thirty years for a suit in tort to come to fruition. I was unlikely to reach the age of one hundred, so like the Common Man I decided to remain silent and assume a quizzical expression.

The forced rest gave me time to reflect. And Penguin India's senior editor, Kamini, came to visit me and insisted I start writing. 'Now is the time,' she said.

I still prevaricated, being painfully aware of my limitations, and feeling embarrassed to project myself into the public eye.

Eventually, it was the birth of my granddaughter Nandini, four days after our fiftieth wedding anniversary, that propelled me into taking the plunge. I wanted her to know about our life, and I realized that I might not be around to tell her about it personally.

So, slowly and silently, I decided to get on with it; hopefully, this book will be published in time for my husband Premo's eightieth birthday.

NOIDA,
15 August 2003

part one

&

My Early Years

My Mother's Tongue

It was 20 October 1930, the day of Diwali. The eaves of my maternal grandfather's single-storied bungalow on 14 Jopling Road in Lucknow, set amidst a sprawling garden, were delineated with earthern oil lamps, shining brightly on the darkest night of the year. It was 8 p.m., and much to the joy of my parents, a girl had just been born.

The nurses and others were also excited and thought that I should be named Lakshmi after the goddess of wealth who was worshipped on that auspicious day. The doctor suggested that I should be called Raj Lakshmi, as my father's name was Raj Behari Seth. And for a few days I was Raj Lakshmi, the presiding goddess of prosperity. But my father did not want such a grandiloquent name. He favoured something shorter and decided that I should be called Meera. My mother, Chanda, objected strongly to that name, pointing out that the legendary Meerabai had deserted her husband. Even though it was for the love of Lord Krishna, my mother thought this behaviour unacceptable. As a compromise I was named Leila, the playful one, engaged in the play of universal energy.

Seventy-three years ago it was quite unusual for parents in

India—or indeed in most countries—to be so delighted about the birth of a girl. (Even these days it isn't always the case.) But my parents were different, exceptional and progressive. They had been influenced by western culture and education. My father was in the Imperial Railway Service run by the British government, and my mother, born in 1906, had studied at a missionary school. They already had two sons, Raj Kumar (or Michi) and Sushil Kumar (or Sashi) but were longing for a daughter to complete their family. (They believed in both family planning and equity.) I was told that my father had boldly announced at my birth that he had no intention of giving his baby girl a dowry when she got married, and that when she grew up she would have to stand on her own two feet.

My parents gave me love and care and also taught me to think for myself. They treated me no differently from my brothers and gave all of us the greatest gift, a good education. They also taught us to stand up and be counted when we believed in something.

My mother and father came from different backgrounds. Dr Raghunandan Lal (Mehra), my mother's father, Babujee to all of us, was a strict disciplinarian. He had dropped the surname Mehra in the interests of promoting a casteless society. He was handsome, well-dressed though short, and westernized. He excelled at medical studies and ultimately established and headed the Department of Radiology at the King George's Medical College in Lucknow. My grandfather never failed to remind us that he had had the occasion to meet Pandit Jawaharlal Nehru and to x-ray his wife Kamala, who was suffering from tuberculosis. His own father had been a stationmaster, who, though he had earned only ninety-nine rupees a month at the end of his career, had managed to put his son through medical college.

My maternal grandmother died young, in the great

influenza epidemic of 1918 that swept across India. My mother, who was born when her father was eighteen and her mother fifteen, was the eldest child. The burden of looking after her younger siblings, Shivnandan, Brijnandan, and Tara fell on her, an eleven-year-old. I wonder if it was a coincidence that the elder sister was a moon (Chanda) and the younger a star (Tara). Indeed, one was as beautiful as the full moon and the other was a singing star. It was difficult for Babujee to manage the family, especially after Chanda's marriage in early 1921. So his sisters persuaded him to remarry. The girl they chose for him was not beautiful, but educated and young. Everybody except Babujee called her Bhabhijee. Her name was Ratan Bai Uppal and she came from Navashahar, Doaba, near Jullunder in Punjab. They were married in 1924. In January 1928 they had a daughter, whom they named Sheila. She is our aunt, but is two years younger than my eldest brother, Michi bhai, who was born in December 1925. Bhabhijee herself was only two years older than my mother. And there was a gap of sixteen years between the spouses, which was not uncommon in those days.

In fact, when my parents were married, my mother was fourteen and my father was twenty-seven, a difference of thirteen years. Having studied at Isabella Thoburn School, she had all kinds of woolly thoughts about being westernized, calling her son-to-be 'Sonny' and decorating her home with Victorian furniture. At school she had been constantly admonished by her teachers when she spoke in Hindi. They would insist she should 'speak in English, think in English and dream in English.' Despite their efforts, I don't think they succeeded in making her do so.

My father, came from a more Indianized background. He belonged to the village of Biswan, near Sitapur in eastern U.P., where his father, Manorath Prasad, ran a small shop selling kitchen utensils or bartans. From the shop and the produce of his farmland he could afford to educate my father in the village school. My grandfather died when my father was very young. It was a difficult time for my father's mother. She wasn't educated and she was pregnant. She was worried that soon she would have seven children to look after. Though she knew that they would not starve because of the joint family system, she was anxious about their education. As a widow she had no income.

Wisely and willingly she pawned the only big piece of gold jewellery that she had, a waist belt or tagri, so that at least my father's education would not suffer. After Daddy got a job, one of the first things he did was to retrieve this tagri. My grandmother gave this to my mother on her marriage and it remained a very precious possession. My father had to really struggle even after joining government service, as he then had to look after three younger brothers, Achal, Brahma, and Shanti, who was a posthumous child, and his elder sister, who was a child widow. He also had to arrange the marriages of his two other sisters, Mangla and Kalyani.

My father had gone on a scholarship to the Thomason College of Civil Engineering, Roorkee, and there he came into his own. He was very good at mathematics. But when he took his final examinations, which involved not only mathematics but also drawing, he failed the drawing paper by three marks. In mathematics, he stood head and shoulders above the other students, having secured a mark of 98 per cent. The examiners at Roorkee decided to take away twelve marks from his mathematics score and give him three marks in drawing instead, so that he could pass. Despite this juggling, my father stood first in the college and was awarded the gold and silver medals for 1917 and 1918.

After that, it was an easy walk into the Imperial Railway Service—which is where he remained until his death in 1942 in Calcutta. His early bosses were Englishmen, and it certainly influenced his way of thinking. When my parents socialized at the club or at official functions with Westerners, my mother would smile and joke and carry on a conversation with them. She would even shake hands with them if they extended theirs, something unheard of for a young Indian woman—so much so, that this disgraceful behaviour was reported back to her mother-in-law. 'Imagine holding hands in public with a man—and a white man at that!' went the gossips.

In 1933 my parents went to Europe, as my father had a six-month assignment there. Sashi bhai and I were left in Banaras (or Varanasi) with my father's younger brother, Achal Behari Seth, who was a doctor. Michi bhai had been left in Lucknow with Babujee. I fell seriously ill and started vomiting and purging. The diagnosis was cholera; I did not respond to treatment. Sashi bhai, who was just four and half at the time, sensed the danger and watched over my cot like a little hawk. My uncle was very worried: he did not know how he would face his brother and sister-in-law if something happened to me. He also feared that Babujee, the radiologist, who was westernized, would accuse him of negligence and inadequate hygiene. So Achal Chacha out of desperation decided to give me a double dose of the medicine, accompanied by fervent prayers and puja. It worked and I survived, but I was left very weak and very dark complexioned.

In Europe, apart from work, my parents ice-skated and skied, spent time with my father's youngest brother, Shanti, who was studying in Berlin, and did a lot of sight-seeing and museum-gazing. When they returned to India, they could barely recognize me.

As I grew up, Daddy, who was a great tease, told me that I had in fact died; and that Achal Chacha, who did not know how to face my mother and him, decided to buy a girl child from Ramu Chamar, the local tanner, who gladly parted with her. Chacha then dressed the child in my clothes and presented her to his brother and wife as their Leila. Daddy told me this story so often that I started believing I was a changeling and one day went very tearfully to my mother for confirmation. She took me in her arms and reassured me, 'Look at me carefully, don't we look like each other? It's a story totally made up by your father to let you know that he doesn't believe in caste and class and would love you even if you were a chamar's daughter.' She also scolded my father for joking about something so serious as his relationship with me.

★

In the thirties, the years of my birth and childhood, it seemed that the British Raj in India would continue forever and that the sun would never set on its Empire. True, nationalist feelings were running high. Gandhi, Nehru and Bhagat Singh were already well-known figures. But our little lives moved on undisturbed. Macaulay's English, the language of the rulers, still held sway and people were eager to learn it. Western education was much sought after; Christian missionaries ran some of the best schools, and that was where we went to study. All the lessons were in English and it became our language.

I write in English because English is the only language I know well. It is the language in which—unlike my mother— I think and dream.

English was favoured in my immediate family even when the Quit India movement of 1942 started and there was a great surge to boycott everything English, even the language. However, my grandfather, Babujee, who was quite anglicized and spoke good English, insisted that all of us now speak pure Hindi so that we were not known as firanghis, a disparaging term for foreigners. So every day at tea time during our winter holidays in Lucknow, we were forced to converse only in Hindi, without using a single English word, though the odd Urdu phrase was allowed. The whole exercise was made to appear like a game and anyone who spoke in the forbidden language had to pay a fine of one paisa per word. Many paisas were collected, especially from my brothers and me.

At my school in Loreto Convent, Darjeeling, the nuns were Irish and the medium of instruction, needless to say, was English. But there was also an elderly Hindi teacher for us Indian students. We youngsters treated him, an Indian, very badly and played truant from his class most of the time. Like English children, I called my parents Daddy and Mummy. It was only after my father died and the Quit India movement was in full swing that Mummy became Ma.

After Independence in 1947, and later in life too, I used to be embarrassed that I always thought in English, and was reluctant to acknowledge this fact. I took my B.A. Honours degree in English from Calcutta University. But as it was soon after Independence, the politically-correct attitude was that Indians must study and know an Indian language, preferably Hindi. In fact, we were required to pass in Hindi to get the graduate degree. Some of my friends managed to get an exemption, either because they had studied abroad for a few years or because they had a parent who was not Indian or some other 'valid' reason. But despite my best efforts I was not able to get out of sitting the exam, especially as I belonged to the United Provinces (now Uttar Pradesh), where the language spoken was Hindi.

When the B.A. results came out, my name was not on the list of those who had passed. I was distraught, especially since I had been a very good student and had stood first in the whole of Bengal in the Senior Cambridge examination of 1946. Upon inquiry I learnt that I had got very high marks in my English Honours papers but had failed in Hindi by three marks and consequently had a so-called 'compartment' in it: I was permitted to sit for the Hindi exam again after about three months and if I passed, I would be treated as an ordinary graduate—but would lose my Honours.

I greatly regretted not being more proficient in Hindi and other Indian languages when I started practising law in earnest in late 1959 in Patna, Bihar. Quite often the evidence from the lower courts would be written in Hindi and sometimes even in the local dialect, Kaithi. I would then spend sleepless nights struggling through the evidence, reading it slowly and carefully, as a mere word or two could make all the difference between winning and losing a case. Even today, how I wish I was equally fluent in Hindi and English.

There is a funny story about English in our family. My eldest son Vikram, aged eight, was asked by Mr Janácek, the chief accountant of Bata Shoe Company, India, where my husband worked, 'What is your mother tongue?' He replied in English, 'My mother tongue is Hindi—but my mother's tongue is English.' He then proceeded to check out Mr Janácek's knowledge of the language. He asked him, 'If there is no food in a country, what is that called?' Mr Janácek, a stateless Czech refugee, who prided himself on his knowledge of English, replied confidently, 'Famine'. Vikram then pressed on and asked what the word was if there was no water. Mr Janácek was stumped and Vikram gleefully stated, 'Drought'.

Because my parents, like most parents, were anxious that we do well in school, they spoke to us in English even at home, so that we became confident and fluent in the language.

★

One of the most important contributions of British rule in India was the large railway network criss-crossing the country which they established beginning with the Bombay-Thane line in 1853. Of course, it was intended to serve their economic interests since it helped them to move goods across the country and to consolidate their political, military and economic hold. After all, the East India Company had come to India as traders almost a hundred years earlier. But the railways did help to unite the people of the country as well. My father was transferred and posted to various places and travelled to others in the course of his work. As he was in the North Western Railway and later in the East Bengal Railway we lived in towns like Rawalpindi, Ferozepur, Delhi, Lahore, Calcutta and Darjeeling and visited many towns in the North and East. So we came to have a good sense not only of the United Provinces, which was our home state, but also of Punjab and Bengal.

We also lived in small towns like Paksi, now in Bangladesh, where there was no electricity and petromax lamps gave us light at night. We often sat outside in the darkness, watching the magical twinkling light of the glow-worms. As a treat, we were sometimes allowed to go along with my father when he went on an inspection of the railway track. We would sit on an open trolley that ran along the track and was pushed by four trolley-men. The ride was exhilarating once the trolley gathered momentum, with the air brushing our faces and rippling through our hair.

Life in the small railway towns or the railway colonies in bigger towns was marked by camaraderie. It was like one big railway family. In Rawalpindi and Ferozepur, there were sprawling bungalows with wide verandahs all around; when a private tailor was called in he would sit in the verandah and stitch our clothes. We used to roller-skate in the verandahs and cycle freely around the colony. A teacher used to come to the house and teach me to dance in the Kathak style, much to the delight of my brothers, who made fun of him by copying his gestures and words, 'Tha, Tha, Thai, Thai'. My mother was also very keen that I learn how to sing even if she herself could not. (Her sister Tara sang very well.) Ma even learnt the sitar when she was expecting me in the hope that I would be born musical. But she was to be sorely disappointed, as the singing teacher asked to be excused after giving me just a few lessons. He said, 'Madam, your daughter *may* one day learn how to recite but she will *never* learn how to sing.'

In Lahore we lived in tents in Mayo Gardens, a railway colony. We children loved the tent house. It was a proper house unit, with three bedrooms and bathrooms and a drawing room and dining room and kitchen. There was a brick floor and we had proper wooden beds, cupboards and other furniture in the house. We didn't even have to bend to get into the house because there was a full-size door. It was quite a novelty for us to live in a tent house and we managed to make many of our school friends jealous of us. Each of us had our own 'thunder box'; these varied in size as we did, and a sweepress used to come through a back entrance and clean them at regular intervals. My mother had taught Tejju, the servant or 'bearer', how to curl my straight hair; and every night he would roll it very tightly into many small ringlets with paper curlers and ribbons, to satisfy my mother's vicarious vanity. It was very uncomfortable to sleep with these knots, but there was no way out.

My parents had an active social life. Sometimes they entertained at home; our cook, Mohanlal, made the most fantastic cakes and pastry. I still remember the taste of the delicious sponge and honey cake in the shape of a violin which he made for Michi bhai's 12th birthday—as well as the individual sugar baskets with fruits inside. He liked parties because it gave him an opportunity to make some extra money by charging my mother more than he paid for the ingredients he bought from the bazaar. Ma loved having flowers in the house and a dinner party gave her an excuse to fill the rooms with flowers. Daddy loved sports, and almost every day Mummy and he would play tennis in the early evening at the club and bridge afterwards.

I remember vaguely when I was four going on a car journey with my parents and brothers. There were seven of us in an old Dodge. We had gone to Ambala for a few days and it had been great fun. We were returning to Delhi; from there we were to catch the train to our final destination, Calcutta. My father was driving, my mother sat next to him, and my baby brother, a little over a year old, sat in between. (My brother Vijay Kumar, or Tuttu, had been born on 4 December 1933: a mistake, my mother claims, despite contraception.) Michi bhai, Sashi bhai and I sat at the back with Mohanlal. I was wedged between my brothers. We were cruising along when suddenly my father swerved the car to avoid a pedestrian, and we struck a tree. My mother was seriously injured, her beautiful face was scarred on one side. Michi's hand was fractured and Sashi had many bruises. Tuttu, the baby, had an ear injury and my father was badly shaken up. But there was not a scratch on me! We were brought to 7 Rajpur Road, Delhi, where Daddy's best friend Ganesh Pershad lived with his family. My mother had to be hospitalized for some time but they looked after us wonderfully.

The accident made my mother very apprehensive about cars. She could no longer bear any noise and suffered acute headaches. Because of this, my father, who was employed at the time as Government Inspector of the East Bengal Railway, decided to rent a house in Darjeeling, a quiet hill station. Though Daddy was posted in Calcutta, his job required him to travel and inspect the railways for six months of the year and to draft a report during the other six months. Daddy would come to Darjeeling when it was time for him to work on his report.

Our house was called Craig Mont. Like most houses in

hill stations, it had a sloping tin roof, so that the rainwater could flow off easily. But the roof was painted green, whereas most of the other houses had red roofs. We were proud of the distinction. It also had a glorious view of the snow-capped Himalayas, including Kanchenjunga and the ever-elusive Everest. We would often watch the sunrise on the mountains and the changing colours of the dawn sky. After we returned from school, my father sometimes read aloud to us in the very early part of the evening. While my father liked travel and other edifying books, my mother loved reading and reciting poetry. Two of her favourite poems were 'Casabianca' and 'The Blind Boy'. She loved the drama and the tragedy in the portrayal of the obedient child in the first poem, and sympathized with the blind boy in the second one.

> The boy stood on the burning deck
> Whence all but he had fled;

Ma idolized the boy's heroic obedience to his dead father's wishes, though today his lack of initiative might be thought rather stupid.

★

Michi bhai, my eldest brother, joined St Joseph's School, Darjeeling, as a day-scholar and my brother Sashi and I went to the sister school, Loreto Convent. (Boys were allowed in the lower classes.) As was normal in the hills, we walked to school every day, though it was quite a distance. One day when Sashi and I had almost got to school, he pushed me down the hillside from the Cart Road. I went rolling down the khud-side and landed on the school road, badly bruised and missing one shoe. When brought to task about his action, Sashi stated that he had done this because I was the only one who had not been hurt in the car accident and that that was very unfair.

Sashi, who was born on 1 April 1929, was a year and a half older than me. We were very close, so this was a big shock to me. Babujee, who was staying with us at the time, wanted Sashi punished. He gave him two options. The first was to walk to school without shoes so that everyone would know what he had done. The other was to be caned. Sashi chose the latter. Eventually, after profuse apologies and the intervention of Bhabhijee, things were patched up.

While we were at Craig Mont, my parents went regularly in the evenings to play bridge at the Union Club. It was a small, quiet place and, my father thought, better for my mother than the posh, elitist and stylish Darjeeling Gymkhana Club, especially since now she was reluctant to go out much because of her facial injuries. She was very conscious of her disfigurement and would cover her head with her sari so that the scarred side of her face was not visible. At the Union Club my parents came in close contact with Mr and Mrs S.K. Dutt. The Dutts, in the course of time, were to play a huge role in the life of our family. They were keen bridge players. He was the Municipal Engineer of Darjeeling and she was the niece of Sir Jagdish Chandra Bose, the famous scientist. They were much older than my parents. Their daughter Meera was only a couple of years younger than Ma. They took Ma under their wing. When Daddy was travelling, we even spent a few nights in their home. Naturally, we came under their influence as well.

They belonged to the Brahmo Samaj and were westernized; their outlook was severely rational. But also, being Victorian and puritanical in their views, they were going through a terrible trauma as their own only child, Meera, was contemplating divorce. Divorce in those days was considered something horrific and a matter of great shame. It was a word alien to the vocabulary of their circle of friends. They feared that their young grandson, Sanjoy, would be tossed in turmoil between his parents; they were distraught at the whole idea.

My mother's calm presence and closeness to their family seemed to them like a boon. They tried to use her good offices to persuade Meera to rethink matters. When Meera Aunty arrived in Darjeeling with her son, who was about the same age as me, there was great excitement. Sanjoy and I got on wonderfully. Meera Aunty looked so astonishingly smart. Though my mother was beautiful and spoke English fluently, she never used any lipstick or make-up. She dressed only in saris and wore her hair long, knotted traditionally in a bun. Always smiling gently and sincerely, she was the quintessential quiet beauty. She was a vegetarian and a teetotaler. Meera Aunty, on the other hand, had short hair and dressed in slacks. She wore bright red lipstick, plucked her eyebrows and used an eye pencil. She drank and smoked through a long and chic cigarette holder, spoke and laughed loudly and argued with her parents about her divorce and her right to choose her way of life. She was fascinating.

I was a docile and submissive child, brought up in my mother's shadow and under the all-pervading influence of a Roman Catholic Convent school of the thirties. I would hear the wrangling and raised voices between Meera Aunty and her parents and, though no one said anything to me, I began to believe that a woman who used lipstick, smoked and wore western clothes was 'bad'. The fact that she was contemplating divorce made matters worse. As a result, even when I went to a fancy dress party at the age of eight, I refused to let my mother apply rouge and lipstick on me. But despite their differences in style, my mother and Meera Aunty got on well, as Meera Aunty was very generous and warm-hearted. But Ma could not persuade her to change her mind. Meera was in love with her husband's best friend and wanted to marry him. She now found her own husband dull and boring. So that was that.

Uncle Dutt, who doted on his daughter, was torn between his love for her and his own fixed ideas. Aunty Dutt, too, was in a dilemma. What would her relations and friends say about the whole affair? She and Uncle Dutt threatened to disinherit Meera. They tried to intercept her love letters and appeal to her lover, but to no avail. Both Uncle and Aunty Dutt vehemently condemned her actions. But ultimately, mother-love won out over puritanical values. Ma tried to influence Uncle Dutt to look at matters a little differently and forgive Meera. But he was adamant and determined not to have anything to do with her. He fumed that if Aunty Dutt forgave her daughter he would have nothing to do with her either!

One day I overheard Aunty Dutt say to Uncle, 'Since I have to choose between my husband and my daughter—I have decided after much contemplation to choose my daughter.' She then promptly packed a small attaché case with some belongings and went off to the house of Sir Jagdish Chandra and Abla Bose, her maternal uncle and aunt. Uncle Dutt was totally unnerved and did not know what had hit him, since he had suddenly lost the two most important women in his life. My mother, however, persuaded him to accept matters, and love won the day. Despite the divorce, Meera remained the apple of his eye, albeit a bit bruised.

★

In 1939, my parents went trekking to Sikkim on the way to Tibet. (My elder brothers were at boarding school, and my younger brother and I were left with the Dutts.) They had hired two mules, one to carry their luggage, and the other to ride on, by turns if they were tired. But they both enjoyed walking and kept offering the mule to each other, as a result of which neither rode it much. I think Daddy must have unwittingly strained his heart, owing to both the altitude and the long trek. When the Second World War broke out on 3 September 1939, my parents had reached Gyantse and were on their way to Lhasa; they had to return immediately to Darjeeling.

Uncle Dutt was an active man physically. He was very fond of playing tennis; also, as the Municipal Engineer of Darjeeling, he used to inspect the city on horseback. I remember him as a tall, dark, handsome man in breeches, feeding the dark-brown horse every morning with sugar cubes before mounting and putting his feet into the stirrups. He carried a short leather whip. In his official capacity, he had been allotted a beautiful English-style house called Struan Lodge. The best thing about it was the garden. It even had a rockery with stone steps for climbing up and down and up again, with lilies, daffodils, narcissi, crocuses and snowdrops sprouting here and there. Aunty Dutt was a keen gardener, passionately fond of flowers. She insisted that I too should take an interest in gardening. Of course, one never wants to do what one is forced to by anyone. But Aunty was strict and never let me off my task. A patch was kept aside in the garden for me to try out my skills. In retrospect, I am very glad she didn't let me have my way in this matter. I owe my love of gardening, flowers and trees to her; for this I will always be grateful. I remember there used to be a lovely white camellia tree in the centre of her garden. I loved the delicate fragrance and the velvety petals of its blooms which I thought resembled a girl's tender breasts.

Uncle and Aunty were great disciplinarians and believed that the correct way to bring up children was not to spare the rod or the lashing of the tongue. They also felt that children should be taught how to sacrifice for the sake of the family, society and nation. When the War came closer to home, Aunty told us we had to do something to make our contribution. We were quite bewildered as to what we children could do. She told us that we were not to waste food—waste not, want not—and must eat whatever was put before us. We had to eat squash, gourd and cabbage, vegetables which we detested. But we were also given treats like asparagus and artichokes from time to time. Nothing was to be bought in the black market, and all rations had to be shared, especially sugar. Though all our friends continued to have sugar and sweets as usual, we were given a jar each with our fortnight's ration of sugar and told that we could choose either to finish it all in one day, or spread it out, or contribute a portion for puddings.

I was also made to knit for the troops. Some of the foreign soldiers came to Darjeeling to recoup and for a vacation. I was terrified of the 'tommies': they tried to be friendly, but I had been brought up in a conservative manner.

If we went to the cinema, we had to relate the whole story when we returned, which rather took the fun out of movies. I was mainly allowed to see Shirley Temple films and only in the Capital Cinema hall nearby. Uncle and Aunty talked to me about the poetry of Tagore, Michael Madhusudan Dutt and Toru Dutt. They also idolized Subhas Chandra Bose. But I was a Gandhi-Nehru lover and exhorted people to join the Congress party because Gandhiji was so wonderful and Pandit Nehru so good-looking.

I sometimes used to go with Aunty Dutt to visit Sir Jagdish Chandra Bose. He was a kindly gentleman and, knowing of his fame, I was very reverential towards him. Aunty Dutt often quoted his words to us: 'Not in matter, but in thought, not in possessions, but in ideals, lie the seeds of immortality.'

★

Loreto Convent had children from different countries. It was a boarding school and there were just a few day-scholars like me. The day-scholars were mainly Indians, Nepalese and Tibetans, whereas the boarders were English, Irish, Italian, French, Chinese, Burmese, Czechoslovak and of course, Anglo-Indians and Indians. Our class had thirteen children—three English, two Anglo-Indians, one Italian, one Burmese, one Indo-French, one Chinese, and four Indians. We were a truly cosmopolitan group, though most of the girls in our class were Roman Catholics. Church-going and an awareness of the Church and its ways was a part of the local environment. We all studied the Bible as a subject and the Hindu students usually stood first. The Catholics went for catechism classes, while the non-Catholics were taught moral science.

We were taught that love is the greatest force in the world. I remember reading *The Count of Monte Cristo* and enjoying it very much. I told my friend, Yolande Paul (she was half-Indian—originally 'Pal' I presume—and half-French and born on the same day and year as me) about it. The novel was not in the school library and so I lent her my copy. Unlike me, she was a boarder. When the nuns discovered the book, they were very annoyed; they confiscated it and took me to task. I could not understand what was wrong with the book and why Yolande should not be reading it. Ultimately, it emerged that it was not suitable because it glorified revenge, which was the antithesis of love and forgiveness.

We had to do three good deeds a day: for example, helping someone, or doing something that we didn't like doing without grumbling. After they were done, one was meant to feel good, as if one had earned a place in Heaven. But Heaven could not be attained by a non-Catholic. For that, one had to be part of the flock.

Conversion was very much in the air; the missionary influence was most evident at the time of our Retreat or

during Corpus Christi and other such Christian religious
functions. Day-scholars went to school at nine and left
immediately after classes; they were not subjected much to
Christian teachings. But boarders had to partake of all the
church-going and Christian festivities. Some nuns were more
zealous and committed in trying to convert children than
others. Among them was Mother Claude, who was always
looking for soft targets. I remember having many discussions
with her. But it was difficult to stand up to her logic.

Mother Claude told us that all those who were not
Catholics and not baptized would go to HELL and burn
forever after death. Children born of Catholic parents, but
who died before they could be baptized, went to purgatory—
even they had to forfeit heaven. But heathens like us had no
chance of even going to purgatory—we were destined for fire
and brimstone. When I asked her how God could be so
unjust as to punish me for no fault of mine, she would
respond that because he was so good and kind he had given
me a chance to convert. If I didn't grasp it, I would have to
suffer the consequences: I would be guilty of a sin of
omission. In my mind I could never reconcile a just God with
such behaviour.

My father died when I was almost twelve, but I continued
as a day-scholar. It was only when I was fifteen years old that
I became a boarder, as my mother had to go to Khulna to
keep home for Michi bhai, who had started a small rice mill
there. Life as a boarder was very different and my friend
Yolande Paul initiated me into its intricacies. The nuns were
very watchful and never liked the girls to become too friendly.
They objected to us chit-chatting in the toilets. When one of
the very nice girls from our class was asked to leave boarding
and become a day-scholar, we were all very intrigued. Looking
back now, I realize that it was because the nuns thought she
was a lesbian.

In general, we had a very strict routine. Before breakfast, all the older children went to church. We would sing hymns with lines like:

> O come, let us adore him,
> O come, let us adore him,
> O come, let us adore him,
> Christ the Lord.

We were repeatedly told that love is His law and God loves us so much that he sent His only begotten son to live and die for us.

The church was beautifully decorated. The altar was draped with embroidered white linen and fine lace, and adorned with fresh flowers and lit candles glowing in silver candlesticks. Organ music resonated in the nave. The service was in Latin chant, which we could not understand, but it added to the mystical air of the place. On the walls were icons of the Stations of the Cross; we kneeled and prayed before each of them.

One morning, while I was kneeling and praying, I keeled over and fainted. I was rushed to the school infirmary, warmed up, and given something to drink. After a few days it happened again. And a few days later, yet again. The other girls started believing that I was going into a trance. They thought I should become a Christian and a nun. Everyone in the school started talking about this and I became quite a celebrity. Shortly thereafter, I took part in a Retreat, where Christian teachings were given and silence was observed for the day. I had begun to feel with all this church-going that I was missing out on something, as only Catholics could receive the body and blood of Christ. I wondered what magic there was in the priest placing the sliver of bread, dipped in wine from the shining chalice lifted off the altar, on the tongues of the believers. I longed to receive Holy Communion.

One day I decided to become a Catholic and, furthermore, to take holy orders as a nun. It was soon after the Retreat. I must have been influenced by the religious teachings and meditation, the peace and quiet of the convent, Mother Claude and her impassioned speeches about the tragedy of my omission, the fact that the remedy for it would give me credit—also the fact that I did not want to burn in perpetual fire after death. This fear was very real, and I wondered what was happening to my Hindu father, who had died a few years earlier.

Here was my chance for salvation, and I grabbed it. It was a message from Jesus Christ and his much-adored mother, the Blessed Holy Virgin Mary. I also felt that just becoming a Catholic was not sufficient: I should become a nun as well. It would be less complicated for my family and for my future life: marriage would be out, for a start. I loved the nuns, and admired and looked up to them for guidance, especially to Mother Joseph Loreto, my class teacher. She was young and understanding. I believe she had tuberculosis, as she was often unwell. But despite her illness, she was very spirited and always smiling and calm. I wanted to be like her. I imagined myself in the long black habit that the nuns wore with a white veil while they were sisters, to be replaced by a black veil when they made the grade to motherhood. I wondered whether the nuns had their heads shaved or just cut their hair short: we could not even get a glimpse of it under the stiff white band that rested on the forehead and held the veil in place. I imagined the white collars around their necks were so starched that they hurt, while the large rosaries (complete with solid brass crucifix) hanging from their belts weighed them down. In the hot summer of the plains, the nuns wore white robes, but the colour of the veil still depended on their status.

I hoped that I would receive my training in the novitiate

in Darjeeling because I was familiar both with the nuns there and the convent itself. It was a beautiful place with gardens and a lovely Gothic church, with Christ on the Cross as the centrepiece inside, and outside a statue of Mary on the pediment below the spire. There were elegant halls, parlours, classrooms, music rooms, a skating rink, even a grotto with 'Our Lady' in it halfway down to the quiet cemetery. I was used to saying 'Hail Mary' and 'Our Father', as we often had to repeat these prayers in lieu of other punishments. When we behaved well, we were presented holy pictures as a reward.

Once I had expressed my desire to become a Catholic, Mother Claude was very keen that I be baptized quickly. It was my last year of school and she felt that once I left, the effect of the environment would wear off. So when my mother came from Khulna to see me in school, I told her about my intentions. Ma was devastated. She was a widow and there was really no one with whom she could share such a disaster. She took me home to the Dutts for the weekend and, wailing and hitting her head against the wall, asked me what was so special about being Catholic that I wanted to change the religion of my birth. 'Tell me, tell me,' she cried in desperation, 'if it is so wonderful, I will also become a Catholic.' But I had no logic to persuade her with; I just wanted to convert and was adamant.

Michi bhai told my mother that it was 'summer moonshine' and would pass. I wondered what that meant. As for me, I had made a commitment to the nuns and was determined to see it through. Ma was so upset with my decision, in fact, so desperate, that she even toyed with the idea of trying to get me married off to a Mr Bakshi, who was twenty-six years old and working at the Oxford Bookshop. On further reflection, she decided to take me out of school in Darjeeling and let me study at home in Khulna. She told me that when I attained majority I could take my own decisions.

I was a good student and Mother Joseph Loreto was very reluctant to let me go. She said, 'Your decision to become a Catholic must be very hard for your mother and you must think about it carefully.' It was my last year of school; apart from being very disturbed, I was also worried about my studies. My mother, however, persuaded the school to let me sit for my final examinations at the end of the year and told them she would bring me back in October as a day-scholar.

In Khulna, I was very depressed. It was my Senior Cambridge year but there were no teachers. Michi bhai helped me with Mathematics, but he was a very stern and angry teacher and the whole experience was traumatic. He berated me constantly and told me that I knew nothing. According to him, my teachers in Darjeeling didn't know the first thing about teaching mathematics, and in particular our teacher of Higher Mathematics, Mother Claude, was useless. Every time I got a sum wrong, he would become so furious that he would score it out with a finely-sharpened pencil, tearing many pages in my exercise-book and often breaking the lead as well. These lessons were a nightmare.

I studied history, geography and English by myself. My mother taught me Hindi and she too would lose her temper when I failed to respond correctly. She repeatedly told me that I was a disgrace and deserved to drown in a cup of water—literally a palmful, in Hindi. She was very angry at having to take me out of school and to have to remain in Khulna, where we had no friends or amenities. So she took out her frustration on me and would slap me across the face. Having done that, she would immediately burst into tears and beg my forgiveness.

The only joy in my life at that time were letters from Mother Joseph Loreto. She wrote to me regularly, sending me questions and problems pertaining to my studies in French, to which she expected written replies. She would promptly correct my answers and send them back, giving detailed explanations. It was time-consuming work, and truly an act of love on her part. She also kept me abreast of what was going on in my other subjects at school. So when I did well in the School Certificate Examination of Cambridge University, standing first in the whole of undivided Bengal, she felt really rewarded.

1946 was the centenary year for Loreto Convent, Darjeeling. I felt deprived at not being in school and thus missing most of the celebrations. I also missed Darjeeling and my friends, especially Bella Jabbar, who lived two houses up the hill from the Dutts' own house, Sanjoy Bhawan. Bella was dark and strikingly beautiful (in an era when being fair was everything), had large, lucent eyes and a soft, tinkling, bell-like speaking voice. Her family was very well-to-do and owned a large number of tea gardens. Quite often, rather than trudging home up the hill, with Kanchi, the maid, running after me, I would get a lift part of the way in Bella's car. After changing quickly out of my uniform, a blue pleated skirt and blazer, and having some tea, I would rush to Bella's house. I would spend an hour or two there before returning to do my homework at 6 p.m. Hers was a large, rambling house on top of the hill where our activities were not under constant scrutiny—all this was very different from the severe quasi-parental regime of Uncle and Aunty Dutt. We used to surreptitiously play planchette. We would sit around a round table with her older sisters, hands joined with both palms outstretched downwards on the table. Her elder sisters were the initiators and instructors. The eldest, Ajmeri, summoned the spirits, and Lily was the 'medium' who held the pencil and paper. I was a non-believer, but the whole idea of calling spirits and conversing with them somehow seemed forbidden, thrilling and dangerous. I even tried calling my father's spirit once, and often wondered what my life would have been like had he not died so prematurely.

Memories of Father and a Home

When I was ten years old I got minor chorea. In Darjeeling, nobody had heard about this malady, so it took a long time before it was diagnosed. I gradually lost control of the left side of my body. My left hand and foot would not respond to my instructions. If I was carrying a cup, I would suddenly drop it. If I was trying to tie a knot, my left-hand fingers would stall and I would have to pull the string with my teeth. When walking, my left foot would go awry. My mother thought I was being disobedient and careless, and scolded me. But when she discovered I was ill, she smothered me with care and affection. The disease was also known as Saint Vitus's dance, because the affected limbs went on a frolic of their own.

My parents took me out of school in Darjeeling for the year, and I stayed with them in Calcutta. My mother tried to get me into school in Loreto House, Calcutta, but without success. So I studied at home with a teacher. The good thing about this unexpected move was that I got an opportunity to spend time with my father and to get to know him. Thank

God for that. Little did I realize that a year later he would be dead.

My father was a lot of fun and tried to cheer me up. He had given me a statue of the three monkeys: see no evil; hear no evil; speak no evil. It is one of my very special possessions. He referred to me as his little monkey, part of his Bandar Log. In fact, he made up a poem for me, which I later pasted into my autograph book:

Pyare, Pyare, Bandar Log,
Rahté Ghar Ke Andar Log,
Mewa, Mithai Lagate Bhog,
Tum ho puré Bandar Log.

With lots of love to Leila Bandarwa

(Dear little monkeys,
Always staying at home;
Nuts and goodies are your treat.
You are perfect little monkeys.)

But he also treated me like an adult and we would discuss many things. He taught me Pelmanism as a way to improve my memory. We went for early morning walks together—just the two of us—in the Horticultural Gardens near the Belvedere Railway Colony where we lived. He told me about positive thinking and what an effect it had in overcoming illness. He complained that whenever he criticized Ma, she burst into tears rather than meeting the criticism with discussion, and he advised me, if I didn't agree with something, to try and persuade the other person with logical arguments. Tears were not the answer, he felt; in fact, they irritated him.

My father had a very bad temper and would lose it easily. But he would quickly forget what he had said and later be surprised that the other person nursed a grudge. He had a lovely sense of humour and when he was home, the house was full of jokes and laughter. He was very fair and handsome and had twinkling brown eyes; in fact, he looked like an Englishman until he spoke. His thin crop of hair was soft and slightly silvered. But he was not very tall—about five feet five inches. Ma, by contrast, was tall for an Indian woman; she was five feet four inches, had fairly broad shoulders and was big-boned. She was round-faced like her name, the moon, had large black eyes and an aquiline nose and was altogether lovely. On the left side of her chin she had three black moles, arranged like the mathematical abbreviation for 'therefore', which set off her face. My parents were a good-looking couple.

Daddy loved books and taught me to love them too. But he always wanted us to read two books at any given time— one of fiction or light reading and the other something serious. He said reading light novels one after the other was like eating too many sweets, which was bad for the teeth and the stomach. A balanced diet was necessary, so that you not only enjoyed yourself but also learnt something. He often repeated the phrase, 'Books are one's best friends and are the lifeblood of a master spirit.'

Daddy used to work very hard and was always short of time. But he wanted to give us something of himself. He taught us our multiplication tables and we had to repeat them to him while he shaved in the morning. He would suddenly interrupt us and ask, 'What is 3 x 16?' and we would have to reply promptly to gain his praise.

Despite his Hindu upbringing, he did not believe in observing rituals or doing puja daily—but he taught us the Gayatri Mantra and told us to recite OM instead of counting sheep when we couldn't sleep. We also celebrated our festivals with gusto, especially Holi and Diwali.

We were taught that a smiling face was a beautiful face. Each morning we were with Daddy a mirror was passed around and we had to look into it and smile and see the difference. Having worked on our beauty, we were then given a spoonful of honey with four almonds that had been soaked overnight and peeled, to enhance our digestion and intelligence.

One day, while Daddy was at the office, a man came to our house with a great many glittering gifts and even some toys. My eyes were shining just looking at them. But my mother refused to take anything and told him to go away. He was very unhappy, and requested her not to insult him and at least accept a token gift of a pair of blue papier-mâché vases, painted with a design of flowers and peacocks. As they were clearly not very expensive, my mother agreed to keep them. I wondered what the man had meant about feeling insulted.

When my father came home in the evening, all hell broke loose. He was furious with my mother for having kept even those two vases. According to my father, the man had some business dealings with the railways and what he had given amounted to a bribe, however small. My mother and I could not understand how such a paltry gift could be interpreted as a bribe. But my father said that, whereas on a grey or black sheet many marks might go unobserved, on a white sheet even a speck of grey would show. He reminded my mother of the one and only time he had allowed her to take her young sister with them in the railway saloon-car without a ticket, and there had been a check.

Much later, in the seventies, I shifted to Delhi. I used to drive myself to the Supreme Court and High Court and around the city. One day I saw the old Tilak Marg Railway Bridge being knocked down. I was attached to the bridge, as I had heard that my father was the superintendent engineer when it was built, and felt sad that it was to go. But when the workmen complained about the difficulty they were having in bringing down the bridge because it was so strong, bonded together with pure cement and tough to destroy, I felt extremely proud. It seemed to me to symbolize my father's reputation.

When my father was Senior Government Inspector of Railways, we often spent our holidays touring with him in his white saloon-car. The saloon was a little home in itself and consisted of a drawing-cum-dining room, two bedrooms, a bathroom, a toilet and a kitchenette. It would be connected to a train and then disconnected at a station where Daddy had to work. Since we were not allowed to cook while the train was moving, for fear of fire, my mother carried a lot of tinned food, fruit and biscuits to keep us happy and well-fed. It was like a perpetual picnic. We sang songs loudly and tunelessly, played Monopoly with great enthusiasm, and engaged in Blind Man's Buff and pillow fights. There was no refrigerator in the saloon in those days and we had to make do with an icebox in which the butter and cheese were preserved. Drinking water was carried in surhais and we had a special wooden stand with a handle for ours, so that the surhai didn't wobble and topple over. It would be refilled at the station from a tap marked 'Hindu Water'. There was no air-conditioner either, but trays with slabs of ice would be brought into the compartment and the fan put on 'full', to make the place delightfully cool.

After my father died, we suddenly had to travel in Inter class or third class as we could not afford to travel first or second. This was quite a come-down for us who had always travelled by train in a saloon or at least on a first-class pass. My mother was very unhappy at this sudden change. She was used to travelling in style and now there were only hard wooden berths, and our co-passengers were not of the same class as us. She wept bitterly the first time she had to take us in a third-class, overcrowded compartment, with people spitting and shouting all around us. She tried to keep her brood together and clean up the area we were all squashed in. It was truly hard for her. Daddy had told us never to use the toilet when the train was standing at a station, as it created problems of hygiene. So when we saw other passengers going to the toilet when the train was stationary, we tried to stop them—but they laughed at us in scorn.

When Daddy died, Ma was about thirty-six years old. Michi bhai was sixteen, Sashi bhai was thirteen and Tuttu was only eight. I was just shy of twelve. Ma was not qualified to earn any money. The Imperial Railway Service for which Daddy had worked was not a pensionable service at that time, so there was only a small provident fund. Even after his own marriage, Daddy had spent money for the wedding of his younger sister Kalyani and educated his youngest brother, Shanti, in Germany to become a dentist. So there were no real savings and it was difficult for my mother to know how to manage things. At first she thought she would go and live with Babujee in his large house on Jopling Road in Lucknow.

That winter in Lucknow, I was very ill. It was diagnosed as the infectious and deadly diphtheria. My mother was desperately upset; she had just lost her husband, and she was now faced with the loss of her daughter. Babujee was distraught: his colleagues had told him that there was no medicine available in India for this illness. A film had started forming across my throat, and it was difficult and painful for me even to swallow my own spittle. Once the membrane covered the entire opening, it would be the end.

Babujee made inquiries about how to get the medicine from England. One of the doctors who came to see me told him that he had recently treated a young girl for diphtheria. Her parents had managed, with great difficulty and at great expense, to get the medicine from England, but the girl had died before it arrived. The family might still have the medicine in their refrigerator. But it was hard to know how to approach them in their present sorrow. In the event, the doctor did speak to them; they willingly gave him the medicine and would not accept any payment, saying: 'We couldn't save our daughter, but we would be happy if the medicine saves someone else's.'

Babujee loved us, but was very strict. Bhabhijee was kind, but didn't show her emotions. Sadly, things did not work out well between her and my mother owing to misunderstandings created by Ma's sister-in-law. But where could Ma go? We had no home and hardly any money or income. She wrote to the Dutts about her problems in Lucknow. They immediately invited her to come and live with them in their home in Darjeeling.

Michi bhai had finished school at St. Paul's, Darjeeling. He was now invited by the school to come and teach there for a term. Mr Goddard (called 'Pa' by the boys), who was the Rector of the school, realized my mother's financial predicament; this was his way of helping out. My elder brothers were very good students and had been an asset to the school. My younger brother Tuttu, though only eight, was showing signs of promise. St. Paul's was a boarding school and the fees were high, so Ma was thinking of withdrawing Sashi bhai and Tuttu and putting them in a day school, though she was loath to do so. But even if she did, where would they live? How could four of us live with the Dutts? It was an unbearable burden to impose on them in terms of both space and money.

While my mother was desperately wondering what to do, she suddenly received a letter from the Rector informing her that a substantial scholarship would be available for the education of Sashi and Tuttu, and expressing the hope that she would decide to keep them in school till they finished their studies. This was a huge relief, and we therefore returned to Darjeeling—the boys to St. Paul's and my mother and I to stay with the Dutts. We were full of gratitude to them for their affection and their offer of protection.

★

When Daddy died after a prolonged illness, I was in Darjeeling with the Dutts. As usual I was staying with them when my mother was away. Aunty Dutt was very fond of my father, who called her Sergeant-Major, because she was tough and a strict disciplinarian. She called him Engineer Sahib.

My mother was with my father in the Railway Hospital in Calcutta when he died. The news of his death must have come through to Darjeeling late at night. Aunty Dutt called me into her bedroom early in the morning. I thought that she was going to scold me for some wrongdoing, otherwise I would not have been summoned so early, even before going to school. When I went into her room, she was still lying in bed. She quietly asked me to sit down beside her. I thought that what I had done must be serious and she was going to slap me, but she held my hands very tenderly and told me that my father had died the night before and I had to be very brave and look after my mother. The news came as a complete shock, as I knew my father had been ill for a long time, but I had not expected him to die. I didn't know what I was supposed to do and how I could help my mother.

Aunty added that if I didn't want to go to school that day, I could stay at home. But Sanjoy was going to St. Joseph's School as usual and, not knowing what to do with myself at home the whole day, I also decided to go. The nuns were very sympathetic; they commiserated with me at the untimely death of my father—'He was such a young man,' they said. But to me at eleven, forty-seven seemed a very long way off, and I retorted, 'No, no, he was not young, he was an old man, he was forty-seven.' Now, of course, at seventy-three, I think I am young and feel that old age is at least ten years away. If I live to be eighty-three, I wonder what I will think then.

My father died on the night of 27 September 1942 and I became twelve about three weeks later on 20 October. It was a very special birthday as I was reaching the age of reason, and my mother had earlier written to me that she would come to Darjeeling and we would celebrate it in a big way. I was quietly excited about this and had been making many plans. But, of course, when my father died she didn't come to Darjeeling for a while. Her father managed to come to Calcutta with great difficulty; almost all the train services were disrupted owing to the Quit India agitation started against the British on 9 August 1942.

Babujee took Ma to Lucknow, and everyone thought that we would all live with him there. I didn't know what was happening and had not seen Ma or spoken to her since Daddy's death. I felt very cut off as the post was late in coming, owing to the dislocation of the trains. Making a trunk call was a big thing in those days and very rarely done. I missed Ma bitterly. Aunty Dutt was especially good to me and had a green woollen dress made for my birthday. She also prepared some of my favourite dishes, but told me that I couldn't ask friends over, as it was a time of mourning and not of celebration. So it was a very quiet and lonely birthday; truly the age of reason had arrived and it was a clear and cold dawn. There were no friends, no gifts, no warmth. But Aunty was wise; she presented me with Louisa May Alcott's *Little Women*, and I became totally absorbed in it.

My mother came to Darjeeling at the end of November to take us to Lucknow for the winter holidays and to decide on the future course of our lives. I got a real shock when I saw her. It was only then that the true import of my father's death hit me. She was dressed all in white—the widows' colour. The large maroonish-red powder bindi that used to adorn and light up her face was gone. Her beautiful coloured glass bangles had been broken; one gold bangle was all she wore on each wrist. No jewellery, no bright clothes, no smile—what remained was just a strained and courageous visage tense with grief and with worrying about how she would look after and properly educate the four of us. My heart went out to her but I didn't know what to say or do. Eight-year-old Tuttu, however, pushed some money into her hands, telling her that she would need it now that Daddy was not there to provide for us. Ever since Daddy's death he had been saving up his pocket money and it was all of two rupees.

★

We stayed with the Dutts, but were acutely aware that we were dependent on their goodness and generosity. This was galling, but there was no choice. They were more than grandparents to us and were strict, disciplined and caring. But as children we didn't really understand their goodness, and we resented their discipline. As for the full extent of their generosity, we learnt about that only by chance.

One day a messenger brought an envelope from St. Paul's School. As I was the only person in the house at the time apart from the domestic staff, he handed it to me. The envelope was addressed to Mr S.K. Dutt, but since it was from my brothers' school, curiosity got the better of me and I carefully opened it. Inside, I found a receipt for money received by the school from Mr Dutt. That seemed rather odd. I told Ma about it and she learnt, for the first time after many years, that a major portion of the scholarship being given to the two boys, ostensibly from the school, was in fact being given by the Dutts. This ruse had been adopted in order to ensure that we were not embarrassed by their generosity. They were a retired couple and not flush with money.

I often wondered about Daddy's illness and death but was afraid to ask Ma for fear of upsetting her. So I didn't know the details till fifty years later.

Recently, I found a letter written by Daddy to his brother Shanti when he was working in the Army Dental Corps of the British Army Medical Service and was posted at different places in Africa, the Middle East and Italy during the Second World War. Daddy and Shanti Uncle were particularly close as Daddy had been responsible for bringing him up. The letter was written about six months before Daddy's death and sent from Calcutta by air mail. The eight-anna stamp bore a profile of King George V and the words, 'India Postage'. At the top of the envelope my father had written and underlined 'On active Service' and addressed it to 119952 Capt. S.B. SETH, A.D. Corps, 14 C.G.H. M.E.F. It was posted on 4 April 1942 and received at Base Air Post Depot on 9 April 1942.

3, Belvedere Park
Alipore
4th April '42.

My dear Shanti,

Received your loving letter after a great expectation. I am glad to know that you are keeping good health. Yours must be an arduous job. It is good that it still keeps cool in the night at your end. Please write to me your welfare every week. We are very anxious as we did not receive your letter so long.

I have not been too well, it is my old heart trouble. I caught flue in the beginning of February and since then I have been in a bad way. If I could get a fortnight or so off I can probably get over it. But the authorities either insist on my going on long leave say eight months or no leave at all. I cannot afford eight months leave. However, if I am not better soon I shall put in for four months leave and get a refusal in writing. My trouble is I do not know where to spend the leave. If one is ill one does not want to go to new places and wants a certain amount of comfort. Brahma and Achal's houses are out of question, though I like Biswan it is dirty and Brahma cannot make better arrangements, in fact I have not heard from him since last four months or so. He is too busy with his own affairs and so is Achal. Had you been here I would have had a brother who could have been of some more help.

Michi is at Lucknow and is working hard for his exams. Tuttu and Shashi are doing well at Darjeeling but poor Leila has not been too well. She had an attack of a malady called Korea or is it Corea? She is better but we are rather anxious about her. Rest is O.K. We all feel that Japan will sooner or later get it in the neck but at present she is doing too well. We do hope the barbarians get a good beating.

With lots of love

Yours affly,
Raj Behari

At the time I had no idea that my father, ill as he was, had so much difficulty in getting leave from the Railway authorities. Since he was not given short leave and continued to work as hard as ever, he eventually developed a serious heart condition and was hospitalized for months in the Railway Hospital in Calcutta, where he died. My mother had nursed him tirelessly and could not believe that he would not recover. She was hysterical once she actually realized that he was dead. She clung to him and in her anguish argued with the doctor, 'But you told me he would get well and I believed you.'

Michi bhai, who was there at the time with my mother, described Daddy's death in a letter fifty years later.

> A-8 Ashoka,
> 3 Naylor Road,
> Poona 411001
> 23rd September 1992

Dearest Leila,

As you know I write to the three of you about this time and previously to Ma. This year it will be 50 years since Daddy's death and I will probably not write again. Chapters have to be closed but the memories will linger. I have never told any of you of the actual details. We had no reason to believe that his condition had deteriorated very badly. It was a Sunday like it is this year.

The Quit India movement was on, but was generally fizzling out except in parts of Bihar. Stalingrad was besieged but there was talk that this was a trap into which the Germans ultimately fell. We were staying at the B.R. Singh Hospital and one of Daddy's colleagues had asked me out to lunch with his family. When I got back later in the afternoon, there also did not seem to be any particular deterioration but he had been ill and struggling for several months. I remember it was just getting dark when the doctor took me aside and told me that if you want to say a few last words to your father you better go in now. I was completely baffled and stunned that I said, what is wrong. He said—'Well, he is already started turning blue at his feet and it is just a matter of a little while'. I do not think Ma had been told. I have never asked her and she has never told me, but when I went into his room, the nurses were fussing around and Ma seemed to have some strange foreknowledge because she was hyperactive and busying herself with things. You have to remember that he was lying in bed for so long that he had bed sores, continuous drip, so very frail and obviously breathing was not easy but we had been through crises like this before. However this time when I went up to him he had a strange look in his eyes, part beseeching, part affectionate, part expectant and maybe a little frightened. He could not speak. He just lifted his hand and put it on my head. Sounds a bit like a movie script but it is not quite that bad. It took him another hour and I do remember that when he did speak he asked for the time and strangely enough it seemed to be his main concern. What is the time? I think that as he died he probably soiled himself (sordid, but this is the way we go) and Ma had no idea that she was cleaning a dead body. Luckily by that time Kewal Uncle and a few others maybe Miradi, Sir L.P. and Lady Mishra (Chachi) had arrived. They took her away. It was about 8.15. We had been given a small room in the hospital and I think we lay awake most of the night. I was too young to understand the finality. I do not think I was scared but I was apprehensive of the future. I did not realize then that Ma was only 36 and I was only 16½. It would be nice and dramatic to say that I swore that I would look after the family but I did not even know that I had to do it. The pleading beseeching look has stayed with me. It was only last year for the first time I told Shanti Uncle about it and now all of you.

I do not think that Ma or I or together took any

vows and I still remember that when I was to get married, Uncle Dutt who had done more than anybody else to keep the family going, objected. Aunty Dutt who is not sufficiently appreciated by us said what nonsense, after all he is now providing a home for Chanda and the children. Of course I became very anglicized but that was the flavour of the period and I think because of it were all able to get a start in life . . .

Perhaps only I knew him as a father and a human being. Leila got a lot of fatherly affection in 1941 when she stayed back in Calcutta. For Sashi perhaps some memories, but he was too young to know him as a person but only as a father. For Tuttu he was a myth. At eight he could only have been in awe and in affection. I still remember the letter he wrote when he got the news in school, 'Pa told me that Daddy had died, I did not know what to do so I cried.' Well shall we leave it there as I think that beseeching pleading last look has been answered and we now approach the winter of our years.

With as much love as always.

Yours truly,
Michi Bhai

★

Ma and I lived with the Dutts in their house, Sanjoy Bhawan. My brothers came over from school on the weekends. Uncle Dutt had bought a narrow triangular plot of land on the beautiful hillside just above the Capital Cinema and wanted to build a house there. It was to be a home for their old age and would eventually be left to their grandson, Sanjoy—so it was named Sanjoy Bhawan. As Sanjoy wasn't in Darjeeling at the time of the laying of the foundation stone, I was asked to perform the ceremony. I felt honoured but also nervous and, since I was just ten years old, my hand shook while spreading the cement. I was upset and had a sense of foreboding, but everybody laughed and made light of it.

A fine two-storied house with a wonderful view of the snow-clad Himalayas was built, partly on stilts in order to give it extra strength and space. We lived with the Dutts on the first floor. In order to augment their income, the Dutts let out the ground floor to an English couple called the Parkers. They had a delightful baby called Michael, whom I admired from afar but was not allowed to touch. The Dutts were of the view that the house should only be let out to foreigners, preferably the English, as they would look after and maintain it properly.

Uncle Dutt, being an engineer, had supervised the construction of the house whereas Aunty was responsible for the interior decoration. She did it up exquisitely and with loving care. The house contained beautiful objects collected over the years, including a large white Burmese Buddha seated on a lotus, carved in stone. She had lovely linen, all specially hand-embroidered, silver cutlery and elegant imported bone-china crockery. I was particularly fascinated by her brick-orange-coloured Chinese cups and saucers with black dragons on them, which were taken out only on very special occasions, and which we children were rarely allowed to touch.

There were three bedrooms, one for Uncle, one for Aunty and one that was used by my mother and me. Uncle's and our bedrooms were adjacent and each had an attached bathroom. They were on the right-hand side of the house whereas Aunty's bedroom was on the other side. Adjacent to Uncle's bedroom there was a large living room, rounded on the front with five large glass bow-windows facing the garden and gate. A gorgeous panorama of the snow-covered mountains spread out before us here, and we spent many hours watching their beauty in the changing seasons and light. There was a dining room and a kitchen behind the living room, and also a little room where Aunty, sitting on the floor Bengali-style, cut vegetables on a boti, a scythe-shaped knife set on a wooden base. (This was very different from her formal, westernized, outgoing, English-speaking image, though even when she went out she did keep her head covered with the sari, pinned down with clips on either side and a gold brooch holding it in place on her shoulder.) There was also a formal drawing room which had a little library tucked away in an alcove in the far corner. It had many interesting books, mainly in English, both fiction and non-fiction, as well as poetry and a ten-volume set of Books of Knowledge. I spent a great deal of time in that corner browsing and reading quietly, as the formal drawing room was rarely used.

All along the panelled walls of the wooden staircase, brass motifs of animals and plants had been embedded, and I loved looking at them when walking up the stairs. The only eyesore was a public toilet just across the road from the gate at the far end of the garden. But Aunty had a wooden, latticed fence put up as a screen and planted a passion-flower creeper to cover it up. I used to spend a lot of my time in the tiny glass hothouse in the garden which was full of cyclamens, geraniums, clivias, freesias, fuchsias, begonias, shepherd's purses and lady's slippers, all painstakingly and lovingly cultivated by Aunty. My favourites were the white fuchsias hanging on a thread which looked like headless ballet dancers with their red capes. I also spent time tending and admiring the flowers, reading in the elongated, triangular garden or trying to find four-leafed clovers, which were considered lucky, on the grassy banks alongside the structural stilts.

Sanjoy Bhawan was my home for seven years and I felt a

sense of security there, even though I was, strictly speaking, a guest. The Dutts were very careful not to let us feel the weight of their generosity. I had a little study desk under the stairs to the attic, which Uncle Dutt had got specially made for me. I did my homework there and kept my books inside it. It was the only space that was really mine, as every other place was shared, including a double bed with my mother. But the desk was my own little world and my secrets were locked securely in it, particularly in my diary which was tucked away inside. I loved the place, it was a part of me. But not having a home of our own made me feel that I had to be beholden to those who gave me space. I secretly envied them. Vikram very sensitively expressed this feeling in one of his earlier poems, 'Homeless':

> I envy those
> Who have a house of their own,
> Who can say their feet
> Rest on what is theirs alone,
> Who do not live on sufferance
> In strangers' shells,
> As my family has all our life,
> And as I probably will.
>
> A place on the earth, untenured,
> Soil, grass, brick, air;
> To know that I will never have to move;
> To review the seasons from one lair.
> When night comes, to lie down in peace;
> To know that I may die as I have slept;
> That things will not revert to a stranger's hand;
> That those I love may keep what I have kept.

When I left Darjeeling in December 1946, after completing school, little did I realize that this beautiful, sunny house which had been my surrogate home for seven years would disappear less than four years later, leaving its owners homeless.

In 1950, Sashi bhai had typhoid. He was not recouping well in the sultry heat of Calcutta and Ma was worried. The Dutts invited him to come and stay with them in Darjeeling. So Sashi bhai and Tuttu decided to go, despite the fact that the journey was now long and arduous as a result of the partition of India. Earlier, one took an overnight train to Siliguri on the broad gauge line and then either a car three hours up the hill to Darjeeling, or the small train, huffing and puffing up the hill for some seven or eight hours. The overnight journey now took a day and a night, with a steamer trip thrown in from Sakrigali ghat to Manihari ghat, as the Assam Rail Link Project had not yet been completed. However, the choice between the car and the train from Siliguri onwards remained the same.

As schoolchildren we had of course preferred the journey up by train along the Darjeeling Himalayan Railway, which was built to a two-foot gauge. We called it the toy train. It was opened in 1881, and was a marvellous feat of engineering, with the narrow line zig-zagging its way up and looping around, sometimes even doing a double loop around the crest of a hill to reach the top, and then meandering down again. Naturally, while it was chugging uphill, the speed of the train as it approached the top was slow. Once, travelling in a school party, a bunch of us got down from the crawling train on one side of the loop and rushed across to the other side to clamber onto the train again, much to the consternation of our teachers.

Sashi bhai and Tuttu opted for seats in a taxi as they had had enough of a hot and steamy train journey in early June. After a couple of weeks of eating well and being fussed over by the Dutts, relaxing and roaming around Darjeeling, they were suddenly housebound. The monsoon had arrived in a big way and it was raining hard and incessantly. There were stories of landslides all along the road from Kurseong to Darjeeling. After ten days of continuous rain, it was even rumoured that some temporary shops and shanties had slid down the hillside.

On the fateful day, it had been raining unceasingly from ten in the morning. Sometime in the late afternoon, the hillside alongside the road running above Sanjoy Bhawan had slid onto the right side of the house, where the two bathrooms stood. The ground floor tenant at the time, an English colonel, decided to remove some of his precious carpets and belongings and shift to the Planter's Club nearby. After dinner, the old Nepalese retainer, who had been working with the Dutts for years, and was no longer youthful but was still called 'Boy', retired for the night to his little lodging about a hundred yards away from the house. A little after 10 p.m., the two bathrooms collapsed. Uncle and Aunty had been fearing this might happen because of the weight of the landmass that had collapsed earlier on to the road. But they were still hoping against hope that there would be no further damage. Having built the house, Uncle knew its strength.

Nevertheless, they pressed my brothers to leave. But Sashi bhai and Tuttu refused to budge without the Dutts. A little later the whole house shook and shuddered, but still remained intact. My brothers were very frightened. Uncle Dutt sensed that matters were serious and once again tried to persuade them to leave and take shelter in the house of a Mr Chatterji, who lived near the Capital Cinema. As for themselves, they would stay in their home, and if fate so decreed, go down with it. But my brothers were adamant that they would not leave without Uncle and Aunty. The Dutts reasoned with them but to no avail and were now in a dilemma. They were torn between their responsibility to the boys and their own desire not to leave their home, which contained much or all of what they loved.

Naturally, once they realized that these young lives were in their hands, they had no option but to leave themselves. But the only way out of the house now was from the kitchen door at the back. Lighting a torch, they got to the door. But when they tried to open it, they discovered that it had been locked from the outside by 'Boy'. This was something he always did before leaving at night, so that he could let himself in early to give his master and mistress their bed tea. Uncle, Aunty, Sashi bhai and Tuttu were trapped and in great danger. It was pitch dark and past midnight. Now that they had decided to leave, they were desperate to do so. The four of them started shouting, 'Boy, Boy!' at the top of their voices through the open window with the rain pouring in. There seemed little hope of being heard, as 'Boy' would be tucked in bed inside his closed room. But as if by telepathy he heard the voice of his master who had brought him up and whom he had served faithfully for many years. It was almost as if he had sensed the danger and fear in his dreams. But when he woke up and came out, he saw what had happened and took stock of the situation. There was a sheer drop of about eight feet from the projection near the kitchen door to the land below, much of which had slid down the hillside. Boy managed to clamber up the wall of the building and somehow open the lock and jump down. Sashi bhai and Tuttu insisted on Uncle and Aunty going down first, because they were fearful that if they themselves left first, the old couple might change their mind. Somehow Aunty in her sari and Uncle, all of sixty-four years old, managed to jump; Boy stood below, ready to break their fall. Then very slowly they proceeded down the bank of the slippery hill, watching every step, as one wrong move might send them hurtling down the slushy khud-side. It took some time for them to reach the flat road below, and they heaved a sigh of relief when they did.

It was 2 a.m. when they arrived at Mr Chatterji's,

thoroughly drenched. They banged the front door, crying out 'Shibu, Shibu'. But there was no answer. They continued to shout and scream and thump the door for a good fifteen minutes, which seemed like an hour, before they were heard. The Chatterjis gave them dry clothes to change into and put my brothers to sleep in their son's room. But Uncle and Aunty could not sleep and sat huddled in the drawing room.

As soon as the first rays of morning light appeared, at about 5.30 a.m., Uncle rushed out to the open area, near the entrance door and looked up. Lo and behold, the house was still standing, straight as a sentinel, its outline etched in the magical light of the dawn. A flicker of hope lit Uncle's heart, and he thought, did I misjudge the signs and panic unnecessarily? He went inside to share the news with Aunty. But at 7.30 they heard an enormous, ear-bursting, crumbling sound and rushed out. Before their very eyes, the whole building, with all their loved possessions inside, had caved in like a house of cards. Uncle sobbed loudly and unashamedly and kept repeating, 'It's gone, Indu, it's gone.' Aunty, stoically, without a tear, held him and comforted him as one would a child.

A Suitable Boy

Darjeeling was bitterly cold in December 1946 when we sat for our University of Cambridge School Certificate Examination, and the heating in the hall was totally inadequate. Our fingers were frozen and our feet numb. But we marched on, repeating: 'Onward, Christian soldiers, onward as to war,' and praying to 'Our Lady of Quick Help' for inspiration. At the end of the examinations, the woman invigilator who had come from England wrote in my autograph book: 'God gave us memories so that we might have roses in December'. Why memories of roses, I wondered, for in Calcutta, Banaras and Lucknow, where we would be going for our winter holidays later in the month, roses would be in full bloom. The Englishwoman was obviously speaking from her own perspective, perhaps remembering the last rose of summer. Were perceptions really so different, I thought.

We would spend the three winter months travelling, while living out of suitcases—a few days in Calcutta with good friends of my parents, a few weeks in Banaras with Achal Uncle, and the rest with Babujee and Bhabhijee in Lucknow. We loved Achal Uncle's small home in Banaras, which we called 'the rubber house', because it expanded with affection and hospitality to somehow accommodate huge numbers of visitors, making everyone feel welcome. He had a large family, and it was fun for all of us cousins to be together. Achal Uncle, who was a doctor, would come home from work late at night, bringing special delicacies from the city. We would be woken up when he returned and fed aloo ki tikki and chaat and barfi.

Babujee's house, on the other hand, was spacious and comfortable, with only Babujee, Bhabhijee and their daughter Sheila living there. There was a beautiful garden with many varieties of roses and bougainvilleas. But we had to be well-behaved and quiet and eat whatever was put in front of us— quite often vegetables that we didn't particularly relish. Babujee, though he was affectionate, had a terrible temper. The moment we heard the horn of his car, everyone would get very nervous. Even Ma and Bhabhijee would hurriedly put away their sewing, especially if they hadn't spread a white sheet on the floor, which Babujee insisted on as a precautionary measure whenever they used a needle.

There was a long gap between our final examinations and our results. The papers were shipped out to England, corrected, the results were announced, and then the certificates given. All this took about six months, as it was just a year after the Second World War. I was naturally anxious about how I had fared, having been out of school, studying in Khulna, for so many months during that final year.

I often thought of my father, whom I had adored. He had promised to send me to the University of Cambridge to study if I did well in school. In fact, my whole attitude towards my studies, which had earlier been very casual, changed because of him when I was eight. I had failed in class and come second from the bottom. But that shame was not all. Gulu Kola had come last and I was now clubbed with her, as we were the only two failures. Everybody knew she was stupid, and now I was stupid too. I was also apprehensive about how my parents would react, especially my father, who had such a fiery temper. But my father didn't scold me. All he said was, 'I am confident you can do better; after all, it's been said often enough that genius is 99 per cent perspiration and 1 per cent inspiration. Work hard and all will be well and I will send you to college in England to study and shine there.'

Now that my father was no more, I knew that no matter how well I had done, this was not to be. But I was anxious to learn something that would enable me to quickly get a job and earn money. I joined St. Helen's Convent, Kurseong, in early 1947 and did a six-month secretarial course—shorthand, typing, bookkeeping and accounts. Kurseong was close enough to Darjeeling to make an occasional visit. The only real friend I made in Kurseong was Shirley Freese, an Anglo-Indian girl from Hapur, who was an orphan. She was teaching in the nursery classes because she didn't have the money to go to college. She taught for two years and earned and saved money so that she could study for two. She was very focussed and courageous and was also a marvellous raconteur; she was to become a lifelong friend.

We were both in Kurseong on 15 August 1947, when India became independent. There was an air of tremendous excitement and celebration everywhere. At last we were saluting our own flag. We heard Pandit Nehru's 'tryst with destiny' speech on the radio. It was the first time I had heard the word 'tryst' and tried to ascertain its meaning. Ma had sent me a simple white sari with a green and orange border—matching the colours of our flag—and I felt very proud wearing it.

Living in Darjeeling and Kurseong, both hill stations, where there were hardly any Muslims, we were in a sense isolated from the communal tensions of the times and the Great Calcutta Killings. In Punjab, the partition of the country had been bloody and devastating, with many of the Muslims moving to Pakistan and almost all the Hindus and Sikhs to India. I remember, a number of years before this, hearing the voice of Muhammad Ali Jinnah thundering out his demand for a separate country for the Muslims. I had also heard small children in Muslim areas of Calcutta shouting—in Hindi rather than in Bengali—'Hindustan, O Hindustan! Larke lenge Pakistan.': 'India, O India! We will fight and get Pakistan.'

A new name had been coined, a new nation came into existence, and I had to learn to redraw the map of my country. On the western side, 'Mother India' had lost part of her head, shoulder, arm and elbow, and on the eastern side a curious piece resembling that of a jigsaw puzzle. Even now, fifty-six years later, I find it hard to look at the map without a twinge.

I had completed my school studies at the age of sixteen from Loreto Convent, Darjeeling. But now I had to plan my future. I wanted to work, but my mother felt I should continue my studies as I had done so well in my exams. In those days, as there was no good college in Darjeeling, the question arose as to where I should pursue my future studies. The choice was between Lucknow, where Babujee lived, and Calcutta, where Michi bhai, aged twenty-one, had just joined Andrew Yule and Company, a British managing agency, as an apprentice. He was living in a chummery with five others. Since Calcutta was likely to be our future home, my mother decided it was better that I study as a boarder in Loreto College, Calcutta, where I was readily admitted to do the Intermediate examination in Arts from the University of Calcutta. It was only after this had been completed in March 1948 that I could even think of studying for the Bachelor of Arts degree.

Loreto College, Calcutta, was not like a real college, such

as Presidency, where students more or less had the freedom to come and go as they liked. Being run by the nuns, strict discipline was observed; it was more like an extension of school, so we referred to Loreto as 'scollege'. Mainly a day college, it had only a very few hostellers. Where we went, whom we met, and when we returned all had to be noted down in the going-out register, so that the facts could be checked later if the need arose. Meeting and going out with young men was a particular taboo.

Most of the teachers were Irish nuns, but we were taught English by a young Indian Christian woman, Romola Lahiry. She used to dress very simply, in a sari and without any make-up. She had no brothers and one of her two younger sisters was in college with us. We learnt that Miss Lahiry was supporting the entire family on her salary, as her father was ailing. She was a very good teacher, always smiling, sympathetic to our needs and patient in dealing with our problems. We idolized Romola Lahiry as we could relate to her more than to the nuns.

The nuns were also trying to change, now that India was independent of the British yoke. They decided to put on an Indian play instead of the usual Shakespearean dramas or those about the Annunciation and Nativity. They settled for the story of Rama with music and the minimum use of language. But they could not find anyone to act as Hanuman. All the college girls wanted to look beautiful in saris and jewellery, or be powerful and strong as Rama and Lakshmana, but nobody wanted to be a monkey with a long tail hanging behind. After all, the play would be seen by everybody, including the young men from St. Xavier's College. The nuns were distraught: how could we have the Ramayana without Hanuman? So, eventually, I opted for the role and thoroughly enjoyed myself.

Moyna Ganti, who came from Dehra Dun and was

fatherless like me, was also a boarder. We became good friends and very soon she and Michi bhai, who used to visit me, fell in love. It all happened under the very noses of the nuns, but they were totally unaware of it. We had learnt how to beat the system. She was allowed to go out with me, since I was a female; I was allowed to go out with a male, as he was my brother; and he was very anxious to take me out, which he might otherwise not have been, because of Moyna; the three of us had a good time together. We were only allowed to go out on weekends. So my brother used to write letters to Moyna during the week. Unfortunately, he had the most horrendous and illegible writing, and poor Moyna had to get her love letters read out by me!

Moyna was very attractive and had a lot of oomph and style and daring. Led by Moyna, four of us hostellers once went out together wanting to do something naughty. In the going-out book we filled in the entry, 'Out and About'. All the wickedness we could manage was to go to Firpos in Chowringhee and order one crême de menthe and share it between us, imagining that we were getting thoroughly drunk. Our normal outing was to walk down Middleton Row, turn left on Park Street and go to 'Mags' (Magnolia Restaurant). Moyna and I would then order one chilli con carne and one Magnolia ice cream between us. The first was a Mexican dish with red beans, minced meat and chillies and we got two slices of bread with it. So it was quite filling—and in any case that was all we could afford.

Michi bhai was tall, fair and very good-looking and could do no wrong in my mother's eyes. He was her prince, her Raj Kumar. She obviously thought that in good time he would marry a fair, traditionally beautiful girl. In fact, offers of marriage to such girls from Khatri families started coming in in 1948. Since he was only twenty-two, my mother discouraged these overtures though they were from the right caste, saying that Michi was too young and had not yet settled down in his profession. Ma was then utterly shocked when he declared that he wanted to marry Moyna and would like to bring her over so that they could meet.

Moyna's mother was Bengali and her late father came from a village near Guntur in Andhra Pradesh. Since her surname was Ganti, in college we used to affectionately call her, 'Ghanti, the Bell'. When she went out, she dressed in chiffon saris, which accentuated her rather voluptuous figure; her carriage was confident and she spoke softly and intelligently on a variety of subjects. All in all, she was extremely alluring, with large, expressive eyes and a sensuous mouth. She had a beautifully glowing, dark, smooth complexion, with none of the anguish of teenage pimples or blackheads.

Michi bhai was enraptured by her and could not imagine that my mother would not be. But Ma was very upset when she learnt of Moyna. Apart from her sensuous features, Ma just could not bear the idea of Moyna's duskiness. She tried to dissuade Michi, but without success. She even went so far as to say that she would not fondle his 'black' children. Since I had introduced them, I became the villain of the piece. When my mother realized that Michi was all set to marry Moyna, she tried to persuade me to get Moyna to use some very special cream and mud packs that she had procured, to make her complexion fair. I was completely flabbergasted at the suggestion and angry with Ma for behaving in such a colour-conscious manner. I could perhaps have forgiven her if she had had some doubts because of a difference in upbringing, but to have reservations because of the colour of Moyna's skin was appalling. Anyway, they did get married and my mother came around and loved not only Moyna dearly, but her three beautiful children as well.

In Loreto College, our movements were monitored and so were our studies. We were given regular homework. I still remember the evening of 30 January 1948. About fifteen of us boarders were doing our homework in the first-floor classroom, when one of the nuns came in and announced in a calm but anguished voice that Gandhiji had died. We were all shocked and wanted to know how this had happened. She said that he had been shot. We were totally stunned. 'Who did it, who did it?' many of us asked agitatedly. She replied, 'We don't know yet, but it was at a prayer meeting.' She added that we were now free to go to our rooms, if we so liked, but we should not leave the building, as there might be trouble. After she left, we all huddled together in the room, talking in whispers, because we were full of grief. For all of us, in Nehru's memorable phrase, the light had gone out of our lives, and we felt the cold chill of fear and darkness enveloping us. We started speculating as to who the murderer might be. One of my classmates, a Maharashtrian, said with great anger, 'It must have been a damn Muslim who did it. They can't be trusted.' Ironically, it turned out to be a Maharashtrian Hindu, Nathuram Godse.

★

I was nineteen when I met Premo in Kanpur in February 1950. I was married to him thirteen months later. It all seems so long ago. Sashi bhai, while studying at Banaras Hindu University, thought that I would never get married because our family had no money. So, when I was seventeen, quietly and unbeknownst to the rest of the family, he responded to a matrimonial advertisement which appeared in a newspaper and which specifically stated 'no dowry'. He carried on a steady correspondence with the people concerned. It was only when things started coming to a head and they finally stated that they wanted the would-be groom's passage to the United Kingdom to be paid for, that he realized that the matter was not so simple. When he told my mother about all this, she was terribly shocked.

My mother was very anxious that I get married, as all Indian mothers are (or at least used to be), once their daughters turn seventeen or eighteen. The legal age of marriage for a girl, in those days, was sixteen. Michi bhai had already got married to Moyna, my best friend from college, in March 1949. Thereafter, Ma kept telling Michi bhai that he was not taking his responsibilities seriously and not introducing me to the right type of boys. But what could he do? He was working in Andrew Yule and Company and his friends were covenanted assistants working in British firms, who wanted to marry smart and stylish girls, which I was not. So nothing seemed to be moving and my marriage was a constant topic of anxious discussion.

At nineteen, I already felt that I was being left on the shelf and marginalized, as there appeared to be no life for a girl without marriage. However, among Michi bhai's friends there was a young Christian man who worked in another managing agency, and who appeared to like me. He was intelligent and sensitive. One night, when we were all going to a party, he bought some fragrant bela flower garlands for the five women in the group. Two of them just dropped the garlands, the other two wound them rather casually around their wrists, and I was the only one who received the gift with genuine delight and immediately wrapped it around my chignon, its rightful place. This was the start of his liking for me. He had a sonorous voice and when asked to sing at a party, came up with songs like 'I'll walk beside you through the world today'. No words of affection were ever exchanged, but a pleasant tension developed between us. Moyna and Michi bhai started teasing me, and my mother grew alarmed. She was apprehensive that love might develop between this dark Christian boy and me. This was not the sort of marriage she envisaged. For her he was a most unsuitable choice. But because of this, my marriage became a source of even more intense worry for her. She opened her heart and discussed the subject ad nauseam with anyone who was willing to listen.

When Ma went to Delhi in the winter of 1949 to spend time with Mr Pershad (the same good friend of my late father who had looked after us when we had the car accident) and his family, my marriage was very much on her mind. His daughter Chiri was older than me and had many friends who were boys. She was not married, but since her mother had died many years earlier, there was not much pressure on her. Ma told her that she should find a suitable boy for me.

Premo had just returned from England. He had studied with Chiri at St. Stephen's College in Delhi and they had done English Honours together. They were a class of five and were taught by the erudite Dr Samuel Mathai. Thereafter, Premo had gone in 1947 to Northampton in England to do a course in Boot and Shoe Manufacture. It was just after the Second World War, food and clothes were rationed, and life was quite difficult. Premo didn't have too much money, so he worked during the night and studied during the day. He had sold his mother's jewellery to go to England and was determined to make good. At the end of his studies, he stood first in the final examinations.

On his return to India, he came to see Chiri. Ma happened to be present when he told Chiri his news and showed her his certificates and medals. Ma liked the young man's manners and looks, though he was rather short. He reminded her of her husband, who had also struggled to make good. When he left, she mentioned to Chiri that he seemed the right type of boy for me, provided he didn't expect a dowry. Chiri told Ma that when Premo was in Delhi before going to England he had had a Sikh girlfriend but that she had no idea how things stood between them now. Premo had started working in Kanpur in Cawnpore Tannery; she would write to him, if Ma wanted, and ascertain the position.

In early 1950 I went to Delhi, taking an extended New Year holiday, as my mother, who was still there, insisted that it would be good for me to do some sight-seeing. She knew I loved travelling and seeing new places and so I fell into the trap—not knowing what was actually planned for me. So instead of my seeing Delhi, I was seeing and being seen by young men with a view to marriage.

Once I arrived in Delhi, Chiri invited her friends over, both young men and young women, so that there could be some relaxed and lively interaction. Since it was around New Year, flush and rummy were played almost every evening. The Punjabis love fun and consider it auspicious to play cards and gamble during this period. They believe that if you win at Diwali or the New Year, you will make money all the year through. I didn't want to play, as I didn't have too much money to gamble away. But one of Chiri's young friends, who took a fancy to me, saw me hesitating, and insisted that he would place the money on my behalf.

He was a polite, polished and pleasant-looking man and came from a very good and respected family. I quite liked the little I saw of him, but my mother immediately rejected him as being too rich and from a business family. My mother at forty-four was young but wise. She had seen life the hard way and realized that marriage into such a family, even if they had no demands, would make me very unhappy. I would always be compared with the other daughters-in-law. For Ma it was not possible to fulfil even the very minor expectations of a good marriage feast with simple festivities for a large family and group of friends. Besides, she had somehow taken a fancy to Premo and pressed Chiri once again to write to him. Though Chiri was a little hesitant, she wrote the letter.

Chiri was apprehensive about the reception her letter

would get and asked to be forgiven if Premo felt that she ought not to have written. But she was straightforward in what she wrote and requested him to be equally frank and not to feel any sense of obligation about making a commitment. She explained to him that it was at the behest of her good-looking aunt, whom he had met, that she was writing. Her aunt was impressed with him and thought that he would be a suitable match for her daughter, Leila. Her aunt also felt that Leila's late father would be happy if such a marriage came about, as he appeared to be like him, honest, steady and sincere. Chiri described me as being five feet tall, not very fair, and attractive 'in an Indian sort of way'. She said that I had got eight A's in my Senior Cambridge examination and was working as private secretary to the General Manager of the Assam Rail Link Project. She further added that Michi bhai, aged twenty-four, was in Andrew Yule, Sashi bhai, aged twenty-one, was with Bird and Company, and Tuttu, aged seventeen, was studying at St. Xavier's College in Calcutta. She told Premo that if he had no commitments and was interested in getting married, he should come to Delhi, where we could meet and decide for ourselves. She said that I was like her little sister and that she felt responsible for my marriage.

Premo responded within a few days, frankly explaining the position, and said he would very much like to meet me and see where it went from there. But unfortunately he could not come to Delhi as he did not have any leave, having taken on his new assignment only recently. Chiri wrote back to say that she would be very happy if we met and liked each other adding: 'Papa is also very much in favour of this, as Uncle Seth and he were like real brothers.'

So after a few weeks, my mother and I returned to Calcutta via Kanpur, which was where her sister, Tara Masi, lived with her family. Premo, who had been informed of our arrival, came over to her house at a specified time. It was then that we met. He was wearing brown and white co-respondent shoes, fawn-coloured gabardine trousers and a cream-coloured silk shirt. He was chewing paan, which made his lips look red and messy. He seemed pleasant enough, but this 'England-returned' man spoke English with a rather Indian accent and seemed to be showing off about his work and achievements. I was frankly put off.

But it appeared that he liked me and told my mother so at the end of the next day. He found me, so he said, unassuming and intelligent. Ma was delighted and wanted to know my reaction. I made it clear that I was not bowled over by Premo, and that, having met him only twice, it was a bit unfair to expect a balanced reaction from me. Unless I got to know him better, I could not take a decision. Ma was nonplussed and disappointed. But she knew that I was stubborn and that there was no point in pressing the matter further. When Premo asked for permission to write to me, Ma readily agreed. This started our correspondence, which was good because through our letters we got to know each other and to understand each other's lives.

I learnt that Premo was an orphan, and that his Maama, Radha Krishan Khanna, had persuaded his wife to look after him. In early 1924, he acceded to his wife's anxious wishes and decided not to go abroad on the condition that she breastfed the infant Premo, whose mother had just died, together with their own six-month-old child, Taro. Such were the bonds and generosity of the extended family system. So Premo and Taro were suckled at the same time and became very close. Premo was eight before he knew that his uncle and aunt (whom he called Baoji and Bibiji) were not his real parents. Till then he was known as Premo Khanna. Even after he was given his own surname he lived with his Maama and Maami till he left home.

In September 1941, Premo's blood-brother, Kedaro, who was six years older than him, died of an obstruction in the intestine, leaving behind a two-year-old daughter and an eighteen-year-old widow, who was pregnant. Baoji thought that it would be a good idea for Premo to get married to his widowed sister-in-law, Bimla. But Premo was totally opposed to the proposition for various reasons. When, despite his protests, Baoji pressed him to comply, Premo left home.

He did not disclose his whereabouts and had to fend for himself. As he had no money, he realized he needed to take on the first job that came his way. One day he just walked into a Bata shop in Ambala and asked the manager if he could work there. Looking at the way Premo was dressed and talked, the manager said he did not have any job to offer him. He mentioned in passing, however, that he was looking for a shop-boy, and asked Premo if he knew someone suitable. Premo offered himself. The manager was embarrassed and said that the job was not proper for him, as it meant cleaning the shop, carrying and bringing out shoes, and stacking them again. Premo assured him that he would be happy doing all this and would be satisfied with the meagre salary that was being offered. He soon made himself quite indispensable to the manager, who became a friend and in due course recommended Premo as an assistant in a Bata shop in Mussourie, where there happened to be a vacancy.

Premo took on the assignment there but could not afford to rent lodgings; with the permission of the shop manager, he used a partly open space at the top of the shop to sleep. Since it was very cold and he did not have enough money to buy blankets, he slept with all his clothes on, covering himself with just a khes or cotton blanket. In the morning he would brush his clothes, polish his shoes and be as smart as ever.

One day, some friends of Baoji, who had come to Mussourie for a holiday, entered the shop to buy some shoes.

They recognized Premo, but he pretended not to know them. They asked him his name, and he prevaricated. They were suspicious but not certain that it was him. They reported the incident to Baoji. Taro was immediately sent off to try and locate Premo and to persuade him to come back home, on the clear understanding that the question of his marriage to Bimla would not be brought up again. He returned home to a greatly relieved family; there was a reconciliation and a fond reunion. But shoes were to become a passion of Premo's and to play an important part in his life.

In 1939, Premo had gone to study in Government College, Ajmer. There he participated in the individual civil disobedience set in motion by Nehru against British rule and later in the Quit India agitation instigated by Gandhi. Premo surreptitiously hoisted the Congress flag on the college flag-post as part of this civil disobedience movement. As a marathon runner he was swift on his feet and could run to the building, climb up to the flag-post, take down the Union Jack and hoist the Congress flag, all in a jiffy. The Principal of the college, Mr Seshadree, who had been conferred an MBE, was very upset to see the Congress flag fluttering on top of the college building and wanted to take action against the person or persons involved. But first he had to find out who they were.

Premo was always smartly dressed in white drill trousers, a cream-coloured silk shirt and well-polished shoes. He was never seen in a khadi kurta-pajama and Gandhi cap. He seemed a most unlikely person to have had any part in the hoisting of the flag. So Mr Seshadree sought his help in finding the culprit. Premo was also given a small amount of money to entertain other students over tea in order to investigate the matter. But of course the seditious flag-hoister couldn't be found. Premo was egged on by the spirit of nationalism and by his friends' admiration, and practice made him swifter and smarter on the job.

After some time the elusive flag-hoister struck yet again. He took off his shoes some distance away, sprinted to the spot to hoist the flag, and returned quietly later to collect his shoes. But a chowkidar doing his rounds had spotted a pair of shiny brown shoes lying under a tree. He picked them up and brought them to the college office. No one came forward to claim them. Premo was short and had small feet. The shoes were ultimately traced to him and when the Congress flag was found waving atop the flag-post, he was put in the dock. Mr Seshadree was livid and rusticated Premo from college immediately and without a hearing. Premo had no recourse as the Principal refused to see him and would not even give him any kind of transfer certificate that would enable him to gain admission to another college.

There the matter stood for several years. Finally, Sir Maurice Gywer, who was the Vice-Chancellor of Delhi University, heard Premo's tale and admitted him to St. Stephen's College, where he did his degree in English Honours.

The course at St. Stephen's was virtually like a constant tutorial, with a class of only five students: one young woman, Chiri Pershad, and four young men, three of whom were Muslims.

The ace sportsman of the College, Shuja-ul-Islam, was also a Muslim. His family was in the leather and footwear business. He was a friend of Premo's and was going to Northampton to study Boot and Shoe Manufacture. Premo too was tempted to go. One of his reasons for studying abroad was that he wanted to better himself for his Sikh girlfriend.

But when Premo's grandmother, Maji, who was barely literate, learnt that he was planning to go to England by air, she was very unhappy. She protested, 'I know you will not listen to me and will fly, but do tell the driver to keep close to the ground!' Such was her love and concern. But when she learnt that he was going to study Boot and Shoe Manufacture she was even more unhappy. Why did he want to become a cobbler? It was a low and polluting occupation. No high-caste Hindu had anything to do with the leather trade. It was left to the low castes and Muslims to deal with dead animals and the skinning of cattle. She added, 'You are an orphan boy and I love you very much, but you are very stubborn. In any case, if you are going to England to study, you should become a barrister, a doctor or an engineer. If all you want to become is a mochi, then I just cannot understand why you must go to England for that.' None of this, needless to say, had any effect on Premo since, like all young people, he would only be influenced by the opinion of his peers.

My mother's views were very different to those of Premo's grandmother; at that very time, in a different town, she was teaching us that all work was worship and that it was no disgrace to be a shoemaker, but only for a shoemaker to make bad shoes.

When Premo returned from England after having worked and studied hard under difficult circumstances, he was confident and happy. He had seen a bit of the outside world, learnt a trade and earned medals from the City & Guilds of London Institute for standing first in their technological examinations for Boot and Shoe Manufacture and excellent certificates from his teachers at Northampton and his principal, Mr Thornton. He was ready to start work and marry his young Sikh girlfriend. But that was not to be.

Premo's girlfriend used to live in a house adjoining his. She had a beautiful voice and used to sing songs from her window. Premo, who couldn't sing, would get her brother, who was a friend of his, to sing a suitable song in reply. Their love affair was from afar, just glances and words and maybe a quick, hesitant touch; but it deepened when he went abroad and corresponded regularly, sending her letters to a friend's address. On his return, once he had a job, they wanted to get married and so she broached the subject with her mother. Her mother, who apparently liked Premo, believing him to be her son's friend, was horrified. She was an orthodox Sikh woman and could not even contemplate that her daughter should want to marry a non-Sikh. When she saw that her daughter was serious about the matter, she threatened to commit suicide.

Premo and his girlfriend hoped that she would come around, especially as the girl's married sister, who lived in Lucknow, liked Premo and was supportive of them and even agreed to Premo and his girlfriend meeting there occasionally. But it soon became clear that the mother was adamant. Slowly, they realized that there was no future in their relationship, as she was very close to her mother and was not willing to take the risk of running away and facing the consequences, whatever they might have been. Reluctantly, they decided to make the break and the letters between Kanpur and Jullunder became fewer and fewer. But it was hard, and they had not fully succeeded in coming to terms with it. Premo was forthright enough to tell me all this, and it deepened our understanding and love.

When we met in Kanpur, Premo was working in Cawnpore Tannery. Soon thereafter, he was offered a very much better job in Cooper Allen, an English company. Unfortunately, his employers would not release him because he was doing a good job for them, and consequently Cooper Allen did not take him. It was a real dog-in-the-manger attitude. Premo was so upset that he resigned immediately, without waiting to find another job. He then applied to various concerns, including the Bata Shoe Company. There he was interviewed by Mr Khaitan, the Chairman of the company, and offered a job as a group foreman in the factory. It was not exactly what Premo wanted—it was not, for a start, a managerial job—but he decided to accept it: it was in Batanagar, only thirteen miles from Calcutta, which is where I was. This gave us an opportunity to get to know each other better. Premo used to come over on the weekends and we spent a good deal of time together, chaperoned by my younger brother, Tuttu. Premo was kind, considerate and caring. He was also confident and optimistic. He was colour-blind, but that did not stop him from appreciating the colour of my sari and praising it as a 'beautiful sea-green', when it was actually magenta.

Some time after Premo and I got to know each other well, he wrote to Baoji, his Maama, that he planned to marry me. Strangely, his Maama knew my father briefly when they were both at the Thomason College of Civil Engineering in Roorkee. Thereafter, their paths didn't cross very often, as my father joined the railways and Baoji became an engineer on the canals. But he must have seen my mother in her youth at some function with my father because, when Premo sought his blessings and mentioned in his letter who my parents were, Baoji wrote back, 'If she is as intelligent as her father and as good-looking as her mother, she is fine.' Though I was neither, Baoji became very fond of me. Unfortunately, I could not talk to him freely in Panipat, as it was just not done in the context of the joint family. When he came to stay with us much later in Patna, it was different.

We were engaged on 23 July 1950. Premo placed a ring on my finger: it had two diamonds of equal size and sparkle, side by side, and to me represented the closeness and equality of our partnership. He also gave me a gramophone record of Malka Pukhraj singing 'Abhi to main jawaan hoon' and a large bottle of Quelques Fleurs. I was thrilled—I had never had a bottle of perfume before.

On the morning of 13 March 1951, I woke up with a queer feeling in the pit of my stomach . . . I was to be married that day. I was twenty years old, very nervous, and unsure of myself and the future. But the past had not been easy, so I did look forward, if hesitantly, to what was to come. Premo was to arrive at seven in the evening, but he didn't turn up. He was always very punctual and we had sent a car bedecked with flowers to fetch him. As the moments ticked past, I wondered what would happen if the auspicious time for the wedding passed us by. We were not the sort of traditional family that would have tried to find anyone who was available so that I didn't remain unmarried.

Premo and his party eventually arrived just a few moments before the specified time for the jaimala or exchange of garlands. They had arrived somewhat early from Batanagar, and had therefore decided to go for a drive on Red Road, not far from the Ganga. There they had a flat tyre, only to discover that the spare tyre in the boot was also almost airless; hence the delay.

I was sitting inside the house, all dressed up in my red tissue patola sari, which my mother had bought for two hundred and fifty rupees, which seemed an exorbitant price to me. I started wondering if it was an unlucky sari. It certainly was very expensive by our standards, as Ma had hardly any money. She had bought me only two new saris, one for the wedding, and the other, a white silk Banarasi katan with a beautiful ambi pallav and small red and green and gold butis all over, for the reception. Premo came from a traditional family, and so Ma had bought six new Banarasi silk and gold brocade saris for them, one for Maji, one for my mother-in-law and four for my sisters-in-law: one nanad and three bhabhis. Altogether, she spent fifteen hundred rupees on the saris, a big chunk of the six thousand rupees that were to cover all the wedding expenses.

Ma repeatedly asked me if there was anything special I wanted for my wedding. I knew her financial constraints and so refrained from asking for anything. But I did very much want some photographs to be taken of the wedding, and ultimately I very hesitantly told her that it would give me great pleasure to have a few photographs which I could look at later. We made inquiries and found that the photographer would charge a minimum of a thousand rupees for seven photographs. So that's what we got.

Ma also got made a champakali gold necklace with a pair of little earrings to match, which cost one thousand rupees, and a set of pearl and gold kurta buttons for Premo, which cost three hundred rupees. The remaining two thousand two hundred rupees were spent on the wedding expenses proper, such as the pundit, the vedi and soft drinks and Magnolia's vanilla ice cream for the more than two hundred relations and friends who were invited. It was a very simple affair and this became especially apparent because a colleague of Premo's was also married on the same day in Calcutta. There an elaborate dinner, with many varieties of fish and sweets, was served, and a great deal was spent on lighting and decoration.

I knew how difficult it was for Ma to have made this celebration possible. But she wept and said to me, 'If your father had been alive, it would have been so different.' I tried to console her and tell her how much I valued all she had done. I also reminded her how lucky we were that there were no dowry demands from Premo or his family and that the baraat from Delhi and Panipat consisted only of four men: his sister's husband, his two cousins Gopi and Taro, and the old family retainer, Ganga Datt.

We spent our wedding night in Meera and Aloke's large air-conditioned bedroom with attached bathroom in their posh first-floor flat in Ballygunge Park Road. Uncle and Aunty Dutt were now living with their daughter and new son-in-law after the collapse of Sanjoy Bhawan. As a wedding gift, Aunty Dutt gave me a beautiful pearl and ruby necklace, one of the few pieces of jewellery that she still had, and Meera presented me with exquisitely embroidered table linen. She also decorated her bed and bedroom with fragrant flowers so that we would be surrounded with beauty and scent while we made love. Premo had a tough time removing all the safety-pins which Moyna had used to keep my wedding sari in place, before we could go to bed.

Batanagar

After we were married Premo and I lived in Batanagar, near Calcutta. Batanagar was a small town built by the Bata Shoe Company for their workers and officers, in Nungi village, 24 Parganas. It was where their factory was located. Premo was just a group foreman, and not entitled to live inside the manager's colony, known as Colony Number 1. But he wasn't going to let that pass. He had agreed to accept the position of a group foreman, provided he was given accommodation inside Colony Number 1, as he knew it would be very difficult for me to adjust to living in the other very Bengali, bhadralok colonies of Batanagar. The reason he had accepted a foreman's position, though very reluctantly, was because he had been told repeatedly that an Indian could not and had not ever been taken directly as a manager. One had normally to start as a worker and climb up the ladder. Giving him the position of a group foreman directly was itself very unusual.

Housing in Batanagar depended on the job one was holding and so giving Premo accommodation in the manager's colony meant bending the rules. When he argued that even while on probation for six months he had been living inside Colony Number 1 with Sandip Sen, another apprentice, and using the managers' club and swimming pool, he was reminded that that was at a time when his status was not clear, and that no rules as such had been involved.

Anyway, after much discussion, he got house number 36 on Second Street in Colony Number 1. Second Street consisted of identical semi-detached, double-storied houses. Each house had a front verandah and a long room on the ground floor, which was the drawing-cum-dining-room, and a small store, kitchen and servants' quarter. At the top of the stairs there was a toilet and a separate bathroom. The rest of the accommodation (also upstairs) consisted of one single and one double bedroom, both small, and a verandah. Premo and I took the double bedroom. As Michi bhai was going with Moyna on furlough to London, their baby son Rajiv and Ma moved in with us almost immediately. Since there was not enough space in the other bedroom for a baby cot, Rajiv's cot was placed in our room. This set tongues a-wagging: Mr Seth had not only married a lowly typist, who couldn't even give a dinner feast for the marriage, but he had been forced to do so because a baby had been born. The rumour ricocheted between the Bengali bhadralok and the Czech community until it became the entire truth. That then was our entry into Batanagar.

That we were different from the other Indians was quite apparent. We mixed freely and on equal terms with the Czech management. The Bengalis looked upon us as those up-country people, there being hardly anyone else from North India in the colony. One day, one of the factory drivers, Shukla, came over to see Premo in connection with his son's education. Premo was sympathetic, asked him to take a seat in the front verandah, offered him a cup of tea and, after discussing the matter in detail, helped him to chart out a good course of study for his son. It was evening and the nosey neighbours who passed by were astounded to see a driver was being entertained as a guest and an equal. They wondered what on earth would transpire next. Ironically, some years later, Shukla's son became a union leader and sat opposite the Managing Director of the company, bargaining on equal terms for the workers.

Most of the Czechs held no passports and had only a 'white paper' indicating their identity. During the Second World War, Bata Shoe Co. Ltd. was declared enemy property and the Czechs had to report regularly to the police. M.L. Khaitan, the young and astute lawyer of the company, who had became its Chairman, managed to ensure that the company's assets were not confiscated by using his good offices with a Mr Sen, who was the Custodian of Enemy Property.

Much later, it was this Mr Sen's young son, Sandip, who was appointed a management trainee straight after graduation, and who shared bachelor accommodation with Premo. He started his probation period four months after Premo and it was to continue for a year, when his designation was to be decided. On completion of his probation he was put into the managerial grade without any fuss.

Premo was pleased for him, as they had become friends, even though Sandip was seven years younger. At the same time, Premo was very resentful of the fact that he had been denied the manager's grade on what now appeared to be spurious grounds. Premo had come first in the City & Guilds of London Institute examination for Boot and Shoe Manufacture, whereas Sandip was just an ordinary graduate with no special qualifications for the job. Premo naturally protested at the injustice of it all. And though he did not want Sandip to be dragged down, he insisted that he should also be made a manager immediately, with retrospective effect so that he had the proper seniority and would not suffer later on. He had no patron or mentor in the Bata management to fight for him; but, after a great deal of persuasion and brow-beating, justice was eventually done.

★

After I got married, Premo's mother, Bibiji, told Ganga Datt, who had attended our wedding, that he should stay on and help me set up home.

Ganga Datt had worked with Baoji and Bibiji for many years and had been one of the smartest servants employed by them. He was a pahari from Ranikhet. But he was tall and wore a turban. This was not because it was a family tradition, but because he served a master, Baoji, who was a superior being, having been part of the ruling hierarchy, a government servant of the British Raj. Ganga Datt looked very stately and impressive. He prepared meat and chicken dishes in the outside kitchen, which Bibiji never entered, and where the utensils for cooking them were kept separately. He was also the one who served drinks and food if any European or official guests were invited. Bibiji didn't speak English and rarely came out on these occasions. But she was at the heart of the household and ran the house from inside it. Ganga Datt had seen Premo growing up and had developed a special affection and sympathy for this cheeky and brave little boy. He had carried him on his shoulders and saved him from many a beating for his naughtiness.

So Ganga Datt was to be my surrogate mother-in-law, teaching me the ways of the Panipat household, telling me about Premo's special tastes in food and helping to set up my housekeeping regime. He was efficient and experienced, but a law unto himself. He brooked no interference in his domain and I, who was just a young and inexperienced bride, was overawed by him. Except for handing over money whenever and as soon as it was demanded, I appeared to have no function in the running of the house. I was left to concentrate on arranging the two sticks of furniture that we had and buying and putting up the curtains.

Ganga Datt cooked what he wanted and served it the way he liked. If and when I tentatively made a suggestion, he rejected it, telling me that Premo liked it differently and that he was cooking his favourite dishes. I was cowed down completely: a second-class citizen in my own home. After a few weeks, we decided to ask a friend and his wife over for dinner. I decided that we should serve some western food as Ganga Datt had reportedly told me that he was adept at cooking a good roast chicken and an excellent caramel custard. I was confident the food would be good, but apprehensive about the service.

Ganga Datt always served Premo first and me afterwards, and that too a bit grudgingly. So, not wishing to provoke a direct confrontation with him, I told Premo to tell him that, though I didn't mind him serving Premo first in general, that particular evening, since we had guests, he should offer the food first to the ladies. When Premo told him, he replied curtly that he knew the etiquette to be observed while serving guests; not only would he serve the ladies first, but the lady guest before me. Ganga Datt insisted that I should be told that he didn't need to be taught these niceties. As for me, I should consider myself lucky that he had made a concession and I was being given food at the same time as Premo, whereas correctly, my husband should eat first and I should then eat off the same plate after him.

After this tirade, and despite my lack of confidence in running a home on my own, I decided to request Premo to pack off my surrogate mother-in-law back to Panipat. Of course, this was easier said than done. Apart from his salary, we had to provide Ganga Datt with a set of clothing including a pair of shoes, plus sweets and laddoos to take home and a piece of jewellery to show off in Panipat—just like a true baraati—before he consented to depart.

★

After I was married, for a short while I continued my job as a stenographer at the Assam Rail Link Project, where I earned a monthly salary of two hundred and fifty rupees. The shorthand, typing and bookkeeping that I had learnt at St. Helen's Convent, Kurseong, had been very useful.

I was also studying privately for my B.A. English Honours. The examinations were due in May 1951 and I would normally have got married after they were over. But Premo and I had decided to get married in March as Michi bhai and Moyna were leaving for the UK in April and we needed to provide a home for their baby Rajiv and Ma.

Soon after Ganga Datt's departure for Panipat, I went to stay in the hostel in Loreto House College, for about three weeks, as it was not possible to study and sit exams conveniently from Batanagar.

I was a private student but the nuns accommodated me and made a special concession because married women were not ordinarily allowed to stay in the hostel. Premo used to try and visit me on odd days, and had to plead with Pancratious, the burly and vigilant gatekeeper, to let him in. After the exams were over, I returned to Batanagar but was very apprehensive about the results, especially as my Hindi was so poor. Sometimes I got quite depressed and despondent about how I would fare. Mother Joseph Loreto heard about this and she very generously wrote to cheer me up, telling me not to worry about the results. She said: 'The success of failure is often greater than the success of success. It teaches you to rise and get on.'

In June, about three months after the wedding, we went to Panipat to meet Baoji and Bibiji and all the relatives. Premo's brother's widow Bimla and her two daughters, Poochi and Rajni, aged eleven and nine, came from Delhi to spend time with us. The two young girls, enamoured of a new bride, hung around me. Premo's elder sister Kailasho—a very affectionate and selfless soul—also came from Delhi. Later on she expected me to take part in many of the functions of the wider family—but forgave me when I couldn't because I was a working person.

It was beastly hot and there was no electricity. I had to keep my head covered, something I was not used to, and dress in my wedding finery to be viewed by all and sundry. Some distant relatives wanted to know what I had brought by way of dowry; some looked me up and down and made remarks such as, 'She is not fair and only has a wheatish complexion.' This made me especially hot! We used to sit all day under a large neem tree in the garden to keep cool.

Before I arrived at Krishnapura House, my in-laws' home in Panipat, Bibiji was very worried about how she would speak with me, as Premo had, unknown to me, informed her that I spoke no Hindi and knew only English and Bengali. Isa, a grown up niece of hers, had lived in Bengal and was visiting her for a few days. Bibiji requested her to stay on longer, so that she could interpret my Bengali. Bibiji was pleasantly surprised to find I could speak Hindi. When Bibiji asked Premo why he had spread this false story, he said, 'So that you would not expect too much from her and would be pleased when you found out.' Of course, they could have asked Ganga Datt, who had been with us in Batanagar, but it never struck Bibiji to check what Premo had told her.

Ganga Datt was the only one who knew me when I arrived in Panipat. In fact, he was pleased to see me. He decided that since I was a bit of a memsahib, not like Maji and Bibiji and the other two daughters-in-law, he should impress me by making special 'langra' mango ice cream.

Because there was no electricity, the ice cream was made bucket fashion, which meant a lot of work, as it had to be constantly churned by hand. The ingredients were placed inside a steel container, which was placed in a large wooden bucket. The space between the two was filled with ice, as well as some salt and sawdust, to prevent the ice from melting too soon. There was a churner in the steel container connected to a handle outside. Rotating it continuously for hours was a tough job and a real labour of love, but the result was delicious.

Late one night Premo suggested that we go for a swim in a nearby tank-like pool. I asked him if it was in order to do such a thing. He said it was fine; his sisters-in-law did the same. I was surprised and said, 'Do they swim in swimming costumes?' 'Oh, no, they swim with their saris on,' he replied. 'I don't think I can manage that,' I said. 'No, no,' said Premo, 'you wear your swimming costume under your sari and when we get there you take your sari off in the dark and swim and cool down. Then put on your sari and we'll come home.' So I agreed to go with him. There was no one there and we had a pleasant swim in the dark night with just the stars watching us. Or so we thought.

Next morning we left very early to catch a bus to Delhi to meet some of Premo's friends there and to see a play. When we returned the day after, we were received with sullen looks and wondered what was wrong. There was a well in the large courtyard of the Krishnapura House. The village women were permitted to come through the back door, fill their pitchers with water, and leave. But before they left, they were offered 'chanch' to drink. In many homes in the Punjab, butter was made from curd rather than cream. Chanch was the residue after butter had been churned out of dahi, and was light and refreshing. It appeared that some village women had seen us that night and complained that I was swimming in the nude. 'So shameful, so shameful, the young bride brings a bad name to Krishnapura village,' they complained to Premo's paternal step-grandmother, Maji, who was a domineering lady with very strong opinions. They thought she would be pleased with the gossip and would tick me off severely. But she shouted at them and said, 'Alright, alright, I don't believe what you've told me, but even if it is correct, she was with her husband and even if she *dances* in the nude with him, it's no business of yours!'

Uma bhabi, Taro's wife, upbraided Premo for making me swim in the nude. Premo explained to her that I was in my swimming costume and the village women must have presumed I was in the nude. Uma bhabi said, 'Anyway, you should have known better than suggesting this swimming business to Leila, as you know how the people around this area react. It was unfair of you to have misguided her. Maji was very angry, but she defended her own.'

Nobody said anything to me and Uma advised Premo not to bring up the subject, even as an explanation. I toed the family line, though I did want to have my say. The coolness from Maji and Bibiji wore off in a day or two and they were once again very welcoming. Gopi's wife Rama, Taro's wife Uma, and Premo's wife Leila were back to eating lunch out of one large thali.

I remained in the inside courtyard of the house with the women, whereas Premo sat on the round cemented chabutra outside the house near the garden and talked with Baoji and the other menfolk in the evening. I didn't really get to talk to Baoji, but he was anxious to send his youngest son Munna to Batanagar with me, as he knew I was interested in academics, and could discipline him into studying—and losing weight. Munna, a very affectionate and jovial young lad, who was enormously obese, came to stay with us in Batanagar. I had the unpleasant job of reducing his intake of rotis from twenty to five in slow stages, and instilling in him some interest in reading rather than only watching films, which he classified as good, very good and fantastic. There was no such thing as a bad movie for Munna.

I resigned my job in the Assam Rail Link Project at the behest of Premo's father. He did not fancy my working as a stenographer and promised to send us two hundred rupees a month if I gave it up. He had arrived at this figure after calculating that I would have spent at least fifty rupees of my salary on bus fares.

Life in Batanagar was routine with swimming and tennis, and movies at the Club House in the evenings. I also started teaching some of the Bengali ladies living in Colony Number 1 how to play bridge. This made me very popular and they in turn taught me how to cook fish, Bengali style.

Kalyani Banerjee, or Koly, with whom I became very friendly, was a very good cook and she loved feeding people. She was an enormously cheerful person and we had a lot of fun together. She tried to teach me Bengali as well, which I learnt to speak, but did not learn to read and write. So she read out to me some of Tagore's stories in Bengali, in particular her favourite novella, *Shesher Kobita*, literally, the Last Poem. It tells the romantic story of barrister Amit Rai, who loved two women, Ketaki and Labanya and couldn't make a choice. He said, 'The love that freely pervades the sky is the mate of our souls; the love that blends with each little daily act is the help-mate of our homes. I want both of them.'

However, Labanya eventually makes the choice with her poem, 'Farewell My Friend'.

Talking about choices, Premo told me soon after we were married that he had a small amount of money and that we could either go to Switzerland or some other similar place for our honeymoon or buy a small second-hand car. I was more practical than romantic and it did not take me long to decide that I wanted the car. We bought a small Standard convertible car, ironically, from a Swiss gentleman in Calcutta for four thousand five hundred rupees, spending everything we had. We then realized that we didn't have enough money to buy the petrol to drive it back to Batanagar, and borrowed a few rupees from him to do so. The car gave us many hours of pleasure and even a little pain.

One day we were going out for lunch to a friend in Calcutta. Premo wore his favourite cream silk shirt and cream Irish linen trousers. He wanted his beige socks to wear with his brown shoes, but discovered the socks were dirty. He took me to task for this. I tried to persuade him to wear some other socks, but he would have none of it. He said he would go to the party without socks, and if anybody noticed, he would simply tell them about the sorry state of affairs in his household, that his wife had slipped up and failed to wash his socks. I was alarmed and immediately rushed off to wash his socks; I then dried them by holding them out of the car window all the way to Calcutta, so that my arms were aching by the time we arrived. Luckily, the socks had dried and Premo agreed to wear them before entering his friend's house. It was a great relief. I wonder what I would do today if such a situation arose. I'd probably say, 'Go right ahead and put your bare feet into your shoes if you can't wear socks of another colour.'

Money was always tight, given Premo's modest salary. But the great advantage of the Bata system was the weekly rather than monthly payment of salary, so that one did not feel deprived for long. The weekly payment used to be given in cash in an envelope that indicated all the deductions for housing, furniture, electricity, income tax and so on. A paltry sum would be left inside the packet for food and other necessities. Every week, we would have to decide whether to buy one bottle of beer, which Premo liked, or two tickets for the cinema, which was my choice. I was, therefore, very alarmed when I became pregnant. How could we afford a child, I thought.

I had become pregnant despite having thoroughly and carefully read Van de Veldt's *Ideal Marriage*. This was a book which Premo presented to me after marriage as my theoretical introduction to sex. He also advised me to have a heart-to-heart talk with Dr Kovarik about birth control. She was a Parsi lady doctor married to a Czech working in Batanagar. Obviously, I hadn't practised correctly what I had been taught.

I was not yet twenty-one and not yet six months married when Vikram was conceived. When I realized I was pregnant, I was upset. I thought about having an abortion but, given my convent upbringing, promptly rejected it. Ma told me that each child comes with his own food and fate, and that I should not worry unnecessarily. I therefore lulled myself into relaxing and enjoying the experience of potential motherhood and the process of becoming a parent.

Premo and I rejoiced in the first stomach kicks and the knowledge that the baby growing inside me was healthy. I am short and as I grew large, carrying all before me, I turned into a ball. The Batanagar doctor, Dr Rizvi, began to suspect that I might be carrying twins. Double financial worries lurked, and an x-ray was done. Fortunately, there was only one foetus.

Dr Rizvi was married to an Englishwoman and they planned to go to England on 20 June, the day the baby was due. He had asked me to consult some other doctor as well, in case the baby did not arrive before that date. I had therefore consulted Dr Fischer in Calcutta, who was the choice of all the more westernized young women who were

Ma's father.

Ma's stepmother.

My parents—when young.

Uncle and Aunty Dutt
in Darjeeling.

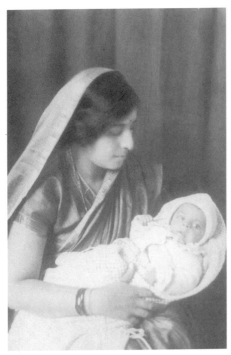

Ma and me.

Sheila Masi, Michi bhai, Sashi bhai
and me (in the chair) at 14 Jopling
Road, Lucknow.

Sashi bhai' (at the top), me and Tuttu at the gate of Craig Mont in Darjeeling.

Mother Joseph Loreto.

Our Lady of Quick Help.

Premo's family—Baoji, Bibiji, Taro, Gopi and Premo (extreme right).

Daddy at forty-five.

Ma at seventy-five.

willing to be examined by a male gynaecologist. He had a tremendous reputation and also charged a tremendous delivery fee.

I hoped that I would not need to call Dr Fischer and willed the baby to be born on or before the 20th. When the birth-pains began that morning, I was very relieved. We drove to Calcutta and I was admitted into the Elgin Nursing Home. After a few hours, when the nurses took me into the labour room, they tried to get in touch with the doctor. They discovered that Dr Rizvi was not contactable, as he was on his way to the station by a circuitous route, and Dr Fischer, who was contactable, was busy playing golf. He told the nurses to tell me to 'hold on'. I, of course, had other plans. So I pushed and pushed (while I screamed that I would never have another baby and was told by the nurses that they all said that and were back the next year) and Vikram came into this world with the help of the wonderful, well-trained Anglo-Indian nurses and no doctor at all. Once I knew he was hale and healthy, I was relieved that I would not have to pay Dr Fischer's fees. Premo, who was airily unconcerned with such matters, was delighted with his first-born.

Meanwhile, there were tussles on the home front. Premo was a workaholic and a fighter. He was ready to take on any sort of challenge. He was, among other things, looking after department number 454 which made Goodyear welted shoes. It was not doing too well and he had taken on the challenge of turning it around and ensuring that it made 600 pairs of shoes a day. He left the house at about six in the morning and returned in the evening very late, sometimes after midnight.

His late homecoming really irked me, and one day, in desperation, I sent his bed-roll to the factory with the message that he should stay there. It had the desired effect; he came home immediately. But his daily report to me dwelt on the number of pairs made. He was so obsessed by this that even I was infected, and would rock my baby, chanting, 'Six hundred, six hundred,' thus willing Premo to reach the magical figure.

The Czechs in Batanagar were all in permanent managerial positions, even though not all of them had the necessary qualifications. They were very hardworking, and in their quaint English insisted that they worked 'very hardly', and that this was why they deserved to be 'permament'. Some of them drank quite a lot. One of them, fuelled by alcohol, pranced off the roof of his house, singing: 'If birds can fly, why can't I?'

Looking back, I realize that it must have been a tough life for them. They had fled their country because of the Nazis, had not returned because of the Communists, and were now stateless. Far away from their homes and their larger families and all their childhood associations and friends, with no passports and no prospects of returning home, they must have been very insecure. Batanagar must have seemed to them like an oasis. Here existed a group of people who shared the same language, the same culture, the same jokes. They were dependent on each other and the job that Bata provided, since they were not properly qualified for any other. Most of them had joined the Bata factory in Zlin as young student trainees and worked their way up. When they came to India to start work in the Bata factory, they knew no Indian language; they spoke even Pidgin English with difficulty and diffidence. So naturally Batanagar was their whole world, the straw they clung to and were reluctant to let go of. It was only natural that Thomas Bata, who had succeeded in saving the company and them, was to them a god—a distant god, since he ran things from Canada. They were always grateful to him, watched every step and movement of his, and wanted to fulfill all his demands and desires.

We too, having joined the Bata family began to partake, though somewhat more sceptically, in its ethos and rituals. Premo was to remain with Bata for almost twenty-five years.

part two

&

From Bar to Bench

Mother in Law

In May 1954, Premo was given an opportunity to work in the Bata Development Office in Old Bond Street, London. We were naturally very pleased as it was the first time two Indians were being posted there. M.K. Sengupta would advise the Board on marketing, and Premo on technical development to improve productivity and quality. Premo felt that Vikram should stay back in India until we found proper accommodation. At first we would have to live in a hotel or boarding house where it would be much more difficult with a child. Since Premo had been to England before, I accepted his superior knowledge about the situation. Though we were excited about going, it was a big wrench for us to leave Vikram, who was not yet two. Of course, he was very attached to Ma, who had been living with us; she and Vikram would now go and stay with Sashi bhai and his wife Usha. Vikram began to think of them as his parents, but Ma showed him a picture of us every day to keep him informed of our existence. She also insisted on talking to him only in Hindi; she felt that if the seeds of the language were properly embedded in him, he would not forget it when he went to live in England.

We travelled from Calcutta to Bombay by a first-class, air-conditioned carriage, very posh and elegant, quite different from today's air-conditioned train coaches. Going to England was something I had always dreamed of, for it was the land of Shakespeare and Wordsworth, of Oxford and Cambridge, of the silvery Thames and the gardens at Kew. As a child I had heard so many stories about the country from my parents that my favourite dessert was 'strawberries and cream, like Mummy and Daddy used to have in England'. To celebrate our departure, we opened a bottle of chilled champagne at the Calcutta railway station and shared it with Ma, my three brothers and two sisters-in-law, Moyna and Usha, who had come to see us off. The liveried attendant who served us reminisced about the last of the Englishmen who had left India.

At Bombay we transferred to a large passenger ship belonging to the P&O Company, which ran a fleet of luxury liners. Though we travelled first class, the cabin we were allotted was tiny, with bunk beds and a single porthole at the height of five feet. It did, however, have an attached bathroom. We were told that the sea voyage from Bombay to London had been reduced to a little over two weeks, that we would be going through the Suez Canal and not around the Cape of Good Hope, and that our first stop would be Aden. As the Arabian Sea was very rough and the ship was rolling, for a couple of days I was very seasick. I could hardly get out of bed, and the thought of food was nauseating; this was the fate of most of the passengers. Premo, however, was among the few who didn't succumb, he found the experience exhilarating. He would go and sit on the deck and gaze out at the rough sea and then enjoy his meals in the almost empty dining room. He also managed to get to the washing and ironing room below, where a few non-seasick women joined him. The journey was otherwise uneventful, except for an incident involving one of my favourite saris. It was torn but, despite Premo's grumbling, I still insisted on wearing it. One day, when I emerged from my bath, I couldn't find it on my bunk, where I had laid it. When I asked Premo where it was, he gleefully lifted me up to the level of the porthole and let me have a last glimpse of the cloth through the glass, bobbing up and down in the ocean before it finally sank. At the time I was very upset. I was reminded of when my favourite squeaking rubber doll had slipped out of my hands into the sea near the Sunderbans, where my father had taken all of us for a steamer holiday. I remembered how he had consoled me at the loss and tried to teach me detachment.

There were bridge and fancy-dress parties and much socializing on the deck. We won a prize of five pounds (a large sum of money in those days) in the bridge competition, and immediately spent it in the ship's shop on a teddy bear for Vikram, whom we missed a great deal. We got off at Aden, where the ship docked for a few hours, and spent them roaming in the bazaar; I was delighted to be on firm ground again. For days all we had seen was 'water, water everywhere'. Then, as we passed through the still waters of the narrow Suez Canal towards Port Said, it was a joy to see people on land waving out.

The meals on board, though served in some style, were repetitive, but their names were changed from Bombay curry to Malabar curry to Egyptian curry and the like. By the end of the voyage I was fed up and longed for home food, just some plain rice and dal with a squeeze of lemon. I also yearned for a home of my own. The grey overcast English sky that greeted us at Tilbury docks was depressing.

Finding a place to live in London proved more difficult than I had thought. My head was full of magazine pictures from *Beautiful Homes and Gardens* and I imagined that all of England was like that. The Bata officials who received us at

Tilbury drove us to a poky little hotel, where the dining room was in the basement and the smell of frying clung to the curtains. My cosy image was shattered. I realized that the place was gloomy, grey and bleak, and the food was dull and bland. My spirits didn't rise when I went out in the evening to buy a newspaper and was greeted with 'Latest Murrrders in the Standard'. When I inquired about a particular shop, I was told, 'Its cloused to die'. One thing that did give me a rather ignoble pleasure was to see Englishmen and Englishwomen cleaning the toilets and the floors. It was something that I could not have imagined before leaving India. It gave me a kick to see the whites who had lorded it over us in our own country now serving us in theirs.

Every morning after Premo left for work, I went house-hunting. The idea was that I would shortlist a few places and that then we could make a joint decision. We started off by looking in the newspaper for places that were 'to let' in the central part of London, near Premo's place of work. However, we very soon discovered that any place there was entirely beyond our budget. We had to decide where to look next. We finally opted to look in North London, as Shanti Uncle, my father's youngest brother, lived in Hendon.

Most of our weekends were spent looking for a place to rent. Often, even after I had spoken to the landlord or landlady on the telephone and they had agreed to show us the premises, they would back out when we got there and they realized we were Indian. The excuse they gave was that the premises had already been let out. I found this galling, and on one occasion I put it openly to them that they were refusing us on racial grounds: when I'd called only a few minutes earlier, they had given me directions to the house. The attitude of the people depressed me, as did some of the very dingy digs that were available. In one place I found a kitchen and a bathroom created by partitioning the same room, and in another there was a lavatory but no baths or shower. When I asked how and where we would bathe, I was told that there were public baths nearby! All this was totally unacceptable to us, as Indians bathed every day and kept the toilet and kitchen as far apart as possible.

After much searching and disappointment, we eventually found an airy, two-bedroom, first-floor flat with a large and spacious kitchen on Finchley Road in Golders Green. The house belonged to a German lady who was married to an Englishman, Mr Philips. The only snag was that access to our floor was through their ground floor rooms, and Mrs Philips could note all our comings and goings. We noticed that she spent all her time cleaning and keeping the place spotless, but nobody ever seemed to visit; it was just for her husband and herself.

★

Shanti Uncle, who lived in Hendon, was a dentist. He was married to Helga (or Henny, as she was always known), a German Jew, whose family had been exterminated during the Holocaust. Shanti Uncle and Aunty Henny invited us for tea and bridge, but not to stay.

Uncle had been supported by Daddy while he was studying dentistry in Germany. He had then come back to India in 1937 but could not get a job, as the British didn't place much value on his degree. Shanti Uncle knew that the German degree was quite advanced and that with a little effort and a few months' study he could get a British degree. He decided to go to Edinburgh to requalify. He was in London when the Second World War broke out. A few months later, he joined the Royal Medical Corps of the British Army. After my father died in 1942, Uncle started sending my mother some money to help her with household expenses. He was on active service in Italy when a shell blew off his right forearm.

The British army tried to rehabilitate him and he eventually got a research job with a dental products firm. Uncle found the job boring and felt his talents were being wasted, but he didn't seem to have a choice. Henry, a German friend of his from their student days in Edinburgh, was practising in London and doing reasonably well. It was he who spurred him to start practising again and offered him the use of his own surgery for any patients Uncle might have. He even feigned an unbearable toothache in the middle of a weekend in order to force Uncle to operate on him and to get over his fear of not being able to take up dentistry again.

I was very apprehensive about Uncle's skills as a dentist. I hoped that I would have no dental problems while I was in England as I would be faced with a dilemma. I would be afraid to go to Uncle, but realized that he would be hurt if I didn't. Anyway, the decision was ultimately made for me. I developed an acute toothache on a Saturday night and could hardly bear the pain by Sunday morning. No dentist would see me before Monday morning, if then, so I was forced to turn to Shanti Uncle, who told me to come over immediately. He was gentle and kind while he examined me. He was keen to save the tooth rather than pull it out. As the nurse who assisted him did not come on Sundays, Aunty Henny came into the surgery to help. They were a wonderful team.

Uncle had a large surgery facing Hendon Park with a big window projecting into the front garden and giving plenty of light. It was a cheerful room and it made me feel relaxed. Uncle and Aunty's concern for me was also very reassuring. I knew that Uncle had painstakingly learnt how to work with his left hand and gloved artificial right forearm. Aunty helped Uncle silently and efficiently. She put the bib onto me and helped adjust the dental chair to the correct position. She passed him the instruments he needed without being asked. Uncle was very short and she was very tall and she persisted in wearing high heel shoes, which made her even taller—but she bent and held the mouth mirror in a manner that made it convenient for him to see. She put rolls of cotton in my mouth to isolate the tooth. He x-rayed my tooth and she operated the x-ray machine. She changed the drills on the hand piece, wiped my chin when I drooled, and filled the glass with water so that I could cleanse my mouth. She talked about other matters to try and keep my mind off the tension of the dental treatment, and she succeeded. Meanwhile, Uncle had completed his work on my tooth. It was a well co-ordinated operation.

We got to know them slowly. Uncle was very affectionate and, despite having lived away from home for so many years, retained the Indian trait of constantly persuading a visitor to eat more. He treated me like a little girl and wanted me to sit on his lap and spoil me with chocolates and gifts as a father would. He called me his little 'pinni'. Aunty Henny, on the other hand, found it difficult to suddenly start loving these grown-up nephews and nieces whom she didn't know.

She was very German, in that she made no allowances for people who were unpunctual and prided herself on being very frank. Unpunctual people were immediately struck off her future guest list. Since we were Uncle's close relations, it was difficult for her to strike us off, but we were tense when we were invited to 18 Queens Road, knowing that a regular ticking off was in store if we were late.

A few months after we arrived in London we were invited to a party at their house. Both Premo and I, as we left, thanked them profusely for the wonderful evening. After a few days I telephoned them about some other matter. Uncle was rather cold and asked me somewhat sarcastically whether I was very hard up. I was intrigued and asked him what he meant. He said, 'Do you need some pennies?' and I said, 'Why?' He answered, 'Because I thought that you were saving them up and that that was why you didn't ring Aunty and thank her for all the trouble she took over the party. Everyone else did.' I was dumbfounded, as it had never even struck me that I should call again the next day to repeat my profuse thanks, as apparently all their European friends had.

One evening we went to their house and parked our car on the opposite side of the road, next to Hendon Park. Uncle was upstairs, and Aunty Henny shouted out to him, 'Shanti, Shanti, your relations are here.' I said to her, 'Aren't we your relations too?' and she smiled. But just then we heard a loud bang outside and the nurse, who was in the surgery, called out to Aunty Henny that she thought that someone had banged into our car. Premo rushed out to see what had happened and, since he didn't return immediately, I went out too. I found him struggling with a fat, drunken Englishman, who had damaged our new Hillman Minx, and was trying to escape without giving his name. People were passing by; I called out to them to help hold him, but they just looked and went on. In the meantime Aunty Henny, who had been watching from the door, swung into action. She called for a taxi, helped push the drunk into it and, accompanied by Premo, rushed to the police station. It all got reported in the *Hendon Times*, and was the subject of much discussion between Aunty and her friends. When the court case eventually came up for hearing, the drunk couldn't deny his inebriated state, but said that he had no money to pay damages and complained that Mr Seth had done 'jujitsu' on him, otherwise he would have got away.

After we settled into the Golders Green flat, we invited Shanti Uncle and Aunty Henny to dinner, and I made Indian food for them. My cooking was very basic but they were very appreciative. The fragrance of the spices must have wafted down to Mrs Philips and she was not pleased. Nor was this the only thing that displeased her. In the master bedroom there was a large, old-fashioned double-bed with sensitive springs with a spring mattress on top of it. This was more comfort than we were used to; in fact, we found the bed most uncomfortable to sleep on or turn in. We hankered for our hard Indian bed with its cotton mattress. Premo then thought of buying some planks of wood and had them cut to size. Bringing them to the flat, he placed them on the wooden frame of the springs and then screwed them down lightly. On top of that he placed the mattress, thus eliminating one set of springs. Mrs Philips was aghast. She was also terribly upset when, excited about the White Christmas that I had so often dreamt about, and elated by the silently falling snow, I forgot myself and came into the house with wet shoes.

Mrs Philips' rules and regulations about the house were jarring, not to mention her repeated threats to raise the rent on one pretext or another. On a previous occasion she had grumbled that we had too many visitors and that the wear and tear on the carpets was excessive. In fact, we had very few friends in London at that time. And Mrs Philips was very disturbable. If the door-bell rang, she was disturbed; if we laughed loudly, she was disturbed; if we listened to Indian music, she was disturbed; if the steps creaked when we came home late at night, she was disturbed. We realized that it was time to move. In any case, we were expecting Michi bhai and Moyna to arrive with Vikram and we did not want to bring him up in such a restricted atmosphere. We wondered what Mrs Philips would do when she heard the pitter-patter of small feet above her.

We soon set about house-hunting again and this time we found a very small, semi-detached, two-storied house with a little garden at the back which was dominated by a large apple tree. This was 133 Willifield Way, Hampstead Garden Suburb. It had a really tiny kitchen and if there were two people in it at the same time, one at the gas stove and the other at the sink, their bottoms touched. The front door opened onto a very small lobby with a coat cupboard, a staircase leading upstairs, and three doors: one leading to a narrow larder, another to a toilet, and the third to a longish room, which was the drawing-cum-dining room. Upstairs was a bathroom without a toilet, a drying cupboard, two small bedrooms and a loft. The house was very sparsely furnished with just two sofa chairs for the drawing room and a worn-out carpet. We made a divan out of our old packing-cases to sit on or for our guests to sleep on, if necessary. There was no refrigerator or television. But despite all that, we were very happy in our little home and spent a few relaxed years there. We had friends and family come and stay, we had parties and freedom and laughter. The landlady, Mrs Marks, lived far away and never came to inspect. Her only regular communication with us was a card, usually illustrated with a Marc Chagall painting, which arrived at Christmas—with good cheer and good wishes.

★

When I first arrived in London, I had decided to do a six-month Montessori diploma course, hoping to start a small nursery school when I returned to India. But, encouraged by Premo, and prodded by my own desire to study something more challenging, I bought a book called *Careers Encyclopaedia*. This described different courses of study, their duration, their admission requirements, costs, future prospects and other information. Most important of all, it set out preferred aptitudes for any particular course. It said, 'Of the many qualities that go to make a successful Barrister, the most important appear to be a sound constitution, quickness of thought and a certain nimbleness of wit.' It added, 'Patience and thoroughness are also important attributes.'

Of the five essential qualities mentioned I could claim only the last two. I was influenced to apply for admission to the Bar not because of any love of or aptitude for Law, but because I would need to look after three-year-old Vikram, who was soon to arrive from India, and therefore needed a course where the attendance requirements were not too strict. At the Bar in those days, for attendance one had to 'keep Terms'. At the time, there were four terms, each of twenty-three days' duration. A person kept terms 'by dining in the Hall of one's Inn of Court on any six days in each term'. One had to keep a total of twelve terms, but could be exempt two. Most overseas students kept ten terms, as they were anxious to return home, for either personal or financial reasons. But attendance in Hall meant that one had to be present 'at the grace before dinner, during the whole of dinner, and until the concluding grace' had been said.

To be called to the Bar, it was not enough to eat dinners, as had been the case in earlier times, when you mingled with judges and senior lawyers who decided if you were a person fit to join the Bar. In 1954-57, when I was in England, one had to pass various written examinations; Part I consisted of five subjects, which a candidate could pass one at a time, if he or she so wished, and then there was a difficult Part II or Final Examination, also consisting of five papers, which one had to sit during the same week. Three examinations for Call to the Bar were held each year under the supervision and direction of the Council of Legal Education.

I was a member of Lincoln's Inn and had chosen it instead of the other three i.e. Middle Temple, Inner Temple and Gray's Inn, because it was the only one whose library was still intact as it had not been bombed. Further, it was located next to the Council of Legal Education in 7 Stone Buildings where most of the lectures were held. My reasons for joining the Bar were entirely practical; there was no emotion involved, as I had no relatives who had been engaged in law. But I enjoyed my law studies thoroughly, as the teaching was excellent and fun. We had stalwarts such as C.H.S. Fifoot, a born actor, who regaled us with stories that sent us into peals of laughter while he instilled in us the fundamentals of contract and tort, and R.E. Megarry, who explained with great lucidity the dull details of property law. I had heard from Lily, an Indian classmate, that Dimitry Tolstoy's lectures on Divorce Law were extremely illuminating and I thought I would listen in before deciding whether to take up the subject. This class was held between 5 p.m. to 6 p.m. and I stayed on and was enthralled. But when I came home, Premo was already there and in a foul mood, sullen and sarcastic, because he had had to actually switch on the lights himself after entering a dark and unwelcoming house. I promptly decided to drop my intention of studying divorce as a subject, out of fear of its occurrence at home.

★

Vikram was a little fellow, just three years old when he arrived in London with Michi bhai and Moyna. They had also travelled on a P&O steamer from Bombay together. Vikram was afraid of my brother, who was rather large and autocratic, and looked to Moyna Maami to help him face his fears, including those of Michi Maama's shouting if he wet his bed at night. When he arrived in London, Vikram was not too sure of us, and it took some time for us to bond together. A few weeks after he arrived, we took him on a holiday along with our friends, George and Elsie Little. George later taught me to drive. I was so slow and cautious when learning that I used to wave the cyclists past me. But eventually I passed my driving test from Hendon, which was known to have strict examiners.

The five of us travelled all over England in our Hillman Minx with a caravan attached to it. We not only visited Stratford-upon-Avon, where we saw a wonderful performance of *Othello*, but also drove right up to Edinburgh, as Elsie was a Scot. It was a wonderful holiday and 'good and cheap', a very important consideration in those days. Another bonus of the caravan holiday was that Vikram had to sleep in a hammock above our bed; he realized that it would be a disaster if he wet his bed, and simply stopped doing so.

Vikram soon felt quite at home in the house on Willifield Way. If I was working downstairs, I would often make him run up and fetch me things which I had forgotten. He soon started saying, 'Have I to do everything? Have I to do all the work in this house?' and if he didn't want to do something, his excuse was 'It's too heavy for me'.

We put Vikram in a small nursery school called Welgarth Nursery and K.G. School, which was reasonably close but meant changing buses at Golders Green bus terminal. I took him to school by bus and, when he was reluctant to leave me, told him in English that I would return soon. Since Vikram didn't know any English at the time, he assumed that there was a Mr Soon who would come to fetch him, and kept querying me in Hindi as to who Mr Soon was and when he would arrive. Since we wanted him to learn English quickly so that he would not feel so isolated and lost in school, we insisted on talking to him only in that language. However, we told his teacher that if he wanted to go to the toilet he would say 'shu-shu' and they should take him. There was a young Kenyan girl who worked as a helper in the school. She knew a few words of Hindi and was a source of solace and comprehension for Vikram.

He started to pick up English words very soon and use them freely without embarrassment. Pointing to a flower, he would say, 'Look, see, phool.' Shanti Uncle bought him a toy excavator and tried to teach him the word, but Vikram kept asking me, 'X ka Beta kaun hai?'—wondering who was the son of X. It took him some time to realize that the machine was the 'X ka Beta'.

Since all my female English friends were introduced to him as Aunty Elsie, Aunty Rosie, and so on, when a little English girl in Kenwood Park wanted to be friendly with Vikram, he asked me which Aunty she was. But the poor little soul was too bewildered by all this Englishness suddenly and quickly thrust upon him, and when an elderly European gentleman, probably missing his own grandchild, tried to be friendly, Vikram refused to respond, despite our prodding, and kept repeating to me in Hindi, 'Woh hamara nahin hai, woh hamara nahin hai.' ('He is not ours, he is not ours.')

I had two very good friends in London and both were Indian.

Neera Sen was a friend from Loreto College, Calcutta, and was in England studying art. Her father had died when she was young and she was as poor as a church-mouse. She had tremendous grit, lived on bananas and milk, and spent what little money she had on buying paper and paint! Lily, on the other hand, whose full name was Urmibala Ray, was the daughter of the Chief Justice of Orissa and was studying for the Bar and that was how we met. She had a tremendous sense of humour and her happy voice and laughter preceded her and announced her affectionate presence. The two of them often came and spent the weekend in our home and we formed a close-knit foursome.

On New Year's Eve in 1954-55, after saving some money for the purpose, we took Neera and Lily to see *My Fair Lady* and enjoyed ourselves thoroughly. The next New Year we saw *The King and I*.

★

Early one morning, our front door bell rang and to our utter amazement, we found my mother standing on the doorstep. She had arrived from India by air on a cheap chartered-flight ticket offered to mothers; she had been missing Vikram and could not do without him. I marvelled at her spirit in coming unannounced and wondered what she would have done if we had not been at home. Perhaps she would have gone to Shanti Uncle, whom she also loved dearly. She had brought his favourite vegetable, 'arvi', packed inside her shoes in her suitcase. We scolded her for not letting us know about her arrival but Vikram was delighted to see his beloved Amma.

Shanti Uncle was also delighted to see his Bhabhi. Ma cooked the arvi for him. Some of it she boiled, flattened, and (after adding turmeric, salt and ajwain) deep-fried. The remainder she cooked in a sweet-sour gravy. Uncle relished it but Aunty Henny made a face at the gooey stuff.

Cooking is not one of my favourite activities. I learnt to cook in England with the help of *The Dalda Cook Book* which I brought from India because I had no choice: I had to feed my family. I also wanted to be able to prepare Indian desserts like gulab jamuns and kheer. After I had improved my skills, Premo invited one of his more enterprising English colleagues and his wife to dinner. I made an elaborate Indian meal, with chicken curry but without chillies. But I was not overjoyed when they merely pecked at the food and went into raptures about the virtues of 'nicely boiled potatoes'.

I was squeamish about buying and cleaning meat, never having done it before. The lamb in England was full of fat and smelt very different from the Indian goat meat that we called mutton. I would go into the shop, look at a leg of lamb and come back without buying it. But when a few of Premo's friends arrived from Pakistan, and he invited them for dinner, I had no choice. I bought the meat, painstakingly removed all the fat and cooked a meat curry. I also made some vegetable dishes. They were very appreciative and thanked us for the wonderful vegetarian meal!

If I was at home alone, I didn't bother to cook. My friends Neera and Lily had nicknamed me 'Sausage over the Sink'. This was because I would grill a sausage, pick it up with my fingers, turn around from the stove and eat it while holding it over the sink—thus saving myself from washing and cleaning pans, crockery, cutlery and linen.

★

In the summer of 1956, Premo and I went by car to Europe. We planned our holiday so that we could meet my school friend Yolande Paul in Paris. We hadn't met for ten years and wondered whether we would even recognize each other. She was welcoming and practical. We did the sights of Paris together, including 'under the bridges' and my favourite, the Sacre Coeur at Montmartre. Premo and I went to the Moulin Rouge on our own and later, as if in a dream, walked together hand in hand through the streets of Paris till the early hours.

Shanti Uncle loved Switzerland and was very keen that we visit it. We loved its snow-capped beauty despite its commercial attitude to tourists. But one night, as we were driving along, we heard a mysterious bell-like sound in the distance and, just seconds after we had driven over an unmanned railway crossing, we felt the vibrations of a train whizzing past behind us with its bell clanging loudly. We were so shaken at what might have been our fate that we had to stop and recover our composure. We wondered whether it would even have been possible to identify us and whether Vikram and Ma would ever know why we hadn't returned.

Italy, with its love of family and religion, fashion and art captivated our hearts. Whether it was Michelangelo's *Pieta* in Rome or the *Last Supper* in Milan, the humanity and intensity of the Renaissance artists deeply moved me, and because of my background I was also affected by the religious stories behind the works.

Driving from Italy to Spain along the Mediterranean coast of France, we stopped in Monaco. There, with hardly any money in our pockets, we visited one of the most expensive casinos in Monte Carlo—an experience that was both exciting and enchanting. We both dressed up well, parked our Hillman Minx next to the Bentleys and Rolls Royces and walked in boldly, wondering what they would do to us if they discovered how poor we really were. Would they grab us and ask us to leave because we were only there out of curiosity? Or would they publicly denounce us?

But it was only when we reached Spain that I felt the warmth and easy ways that reminded me of home. I had left India in 1954 and I was increasingly homesick. Our long afternoon siestas in rooms darkened by slatted, wood-shuttered windows in the Esplendido Hotel in Barcelona resulted in due course in our younger son, Shantum.

As we travelled by car, Premo driving and me map-reading without knowing the language, we often found it difficult to find a loo. It was not quite like India where, when desperate, you could go into the open countryside. Here towns and habitations and private farms merged one into the other. I remember that we stopped at a wayside shop and bought a black and white ceramic Madonna, which I still have, in order to use their facilities. The toilet at the back of the shop was antiquated, slippery and dark, but a great relief!

As Premo drove, I sometimes read aloud to him. The book I was reading from was a memoir by John Gunther called *Death Be Not Proud*, which recounts the struggle with a brain tumour of his seventeen-year-old son, Johnny, who eventually died. There is a short chapter at the end by Frances Gunther, Johnny's mother. She says she wished they had loved Johnny more when he was alive. Of course they loved him very much—but what did loving more mean now? She writes: 'To me, it means loving life more, being more aware of life, of one's fellow human beings, of the earth.' She adds that it means obliterating the ideas of evil and hate and 'the enemy' and caring more and more about other people at home and abroad. When we returned to London, we embraced our four-year-old son Vikram with 'a little added rapture and a keener awareness of joy'.

Vikram was very stubborn and found it almost impossible to say sorry. Once, when he had been rude to Lily, I made him stand in a corner facing the wall till he apologized. But the little fellow stood for three hours till my patience was exhausted and Lily was pleading with me not to be so harsh. When, at the end of this battle of wills I asked him sternly, 'Sorry bolne ka dil hai?' he replied, in a tiny voice, 'Dil hai,' but even then wouldn't utter the word 'sorry'. He was only willing to admit that he was minded to do so.

He was also very obsessive. Once, when he decided that he wanted a small gramophone, he thought and talked of nothing else. He also used devious means to remind us of it. He would raise his arm or foot at an angle and ask us what it resembled; and he never failed to point out a portable winding gramophone when he saw one. In order to preserve our sanity, we quickly bought him one. He loved music, and could identify the 78 r.p.m. records even before he learnt to read properly. He must have assessed that I was tone deaf; when I tried to lullaby him to sleep he begged me not to sing. He stated that he only wanted my friend Koly, who was visiting us from Batanagar, to sing to him.

Vikram became very friendly with one of the two unmarried sisters living next door and would crawl through a hole in the garden hedge to their home, returning laden with goodies and bonhomie. When I tried to teach him some

English manners, he often contradicted me as he felt the lady next door knew better.

Living in England, he soon assumed an English identity and became Kevin White. Kevin talked constantly about germs in the drinking water, the cleanliness of the cutlery, and the weather. However, he did find it a strange country, where it was dark in the day and light at night; the dreary winter dusk at even 3 p.m. upset him whereas the summer light that stretched till 10 p.m. kept him from sleeping. But he loved the gardens, the gorgeous flowers, and the wildness of the Heath and the countryside. Kenwood was a place he particularly loved. He also became very interested in the bus routes and the Underground and tried to work out the cheapest and quickest route to get to our house. Whenever a friend arrived, he or she was cross-examined at length as to the route taken and informed triumphantly how a halfpenny could have been saved.

Vikram was very keen to see the Tower of London, and we set aside a whole day for the trip. But that morning, he suddenly started hiccuping and couldn't stop. We tried various remedies, such as making him drink water from the other side of the glass, holding his breath, and so on, but to no avail. We were worried, and thought we should take him to a doctor. Vikram was very unhappy that the Tower of London trip would have to be indefinitely postponed, but there appeared to be no way out. Premo went to the telephone; he returned and told Vikram that he had just heard that the Tower of London had fallen down. Vikram, aged four, was so upset that he would *never* see it that his hiccups immediately stopped, and instead of going to the doctor we went to the Tower of London.

Vikram had a tadpole in a bowl, which he would watch and feed regularly and look after. He became very attached to the tadpole and when it suddenly died, he was distraught. We had to go through the whole ritual of a proper burial in our back garden for him to come to terms with the impermanence of life and reality of death.

At the end of a year and half in London, Vikram spoke the Queen's English, read rapidly and was totally immersed in the beautiful *Splendour* series books we bought him. Even when he went back to India, he would say, 'What a lovely sunny day!' which was an odd remark in a heat-wave. He was also brazen enough to pass judgment on his peers with the remark that their English was atrocious.

Towards the end of 1956 there was tension over the Suez Canal and threats of it being closed indefinitely. We were worried about the situation and decided that it would be best for Ma and Vikram to fly back immediately to India. So when his little brother Shantum arrived, Vikram was not there.

Shantum was born on 15 April 1957. We had been in London for almost three years. The Bar Final exams were due in a few months. I had already passed Part I. First, I did the Roman Law paper, then Constitutional Law, Criminal Law, Contract and Tort and finally Hindu and Mohammedan Law. I had secured a first class in the Hindu and Mohammedan Law paper and Professor Alan Gledhill, who taught us, had been very pleased.

In the late evening of the 15th I was not feeling too good. Premo drove me to Queen Mary's Hospital at the top of Hampstead Heath. After the formalities of admission were over, he was told to go home: when the baby arrived, he would be duly informed. This seemed rather heartless and clinical. We Indians are used to having our families around us when we are in pain; I felt quite tearful to be left alone. It was so different from the Elgin Nursing Home in Calcutta, when my mother stayed with me and walked me about, rubbing my back and speaking soothingly, till I was actually taken into the labour room.

After a cursory examination, I was put into a room for four despite my having requested a single room. I was told single rooms were only given if a patient's condition turned serious and the doctor required her to be alone. After a while I was taken into the labour room, where a young Frenchwoman—hidden behind a blue screen—was screaming that she could not bear the pain. It was apparently her first baby.

My pains were coming fast too. But I was determined not to scream or make a fuss, as I didn't want to be seen as an emotional wimp of an Indian in front of the British. I clenched my fists tightly till my knuckles were white and bit my lips, but didn't let any sound escape them. I pushed and pushed and almost willed the baby out.

The nurses declared it was a boy. I was disappointed, as we had so much wanted a girl, for then our family would be complete. I knew that Premo would be waiting anxiously, so I requested the nurses to give him the news. He asked if he could come and see me. The nurses were astounded. They told him that it was the middle of the night and that he should come during visiting hours. I so longed for him to be near and to hold my hand while I rested and relaxed after the great exertion of delivering the baby. Instead, the nurses handed me my comb and told me to sit up and comb my hair. It was a great effort, especially as my long hair took some combing, but I could not let these English nurses see my discomfiture and welling tears.

By the next day the Frenchwoman and I had become friends. Premo arrived during visiting hours with a bottle of stuffed olives—as he knew I would prefer that to the usual chocolates. He also told me he would go shopping with Aunty Henny on Saturday and buy clothes and other things for the baby, as well as groceries for the home. I had not bought anything for the baby, as I was superstitious about buying things in advance. (In India new-born babies were normally dressed in old clothes, either because it was considered 'ashubh' or inauspicious to make clothes in advance of the birth or because old cloth was soft from use and washing and would not chafe the tender skin of the baby.) Vikram's things, which could have been handed down, had all been given away in India many years earlier.

Despite my best efforts and that of the hospital staff, I didn't have enough milk for the 'baby with the black hair', as he soon came to be known. English babies have hardly any hair on their heads at birth, and even if they do have some, it is hardly visible because of its light color. His black mop earned our baby boy a great deal of popularity.

I was, however, chided by the hospital staff for my bad planning, 'Don't you see the hospital is almost empty?' they asked. They told me that a large number of babies were born before 1st April, as parents could then avail themselves of the tax benefit for the whole year. Some women even had a Caesarean done in order to gain this benefit. I was stunned, as this was something I had never even thought about. In fact, our baby was not planned at all—he was just the result of our European holiday, an Esplendido Hotel creation.

Premo took a half-day off and brought me and the baby home. Shanti Uncle and Aunty Henny, who had no children of their own, were extremely pleased with the little boy's arrival and wanted to adopt him, especially as they knew that we had wanted a girl. It was difficult to explain to them that we didn't want to part with the child, particularly because Aunty Henny was so highly strung, having suffered so much after losing her family in Germany. So we did the next best thing and named the baby Shanti after my Uncle, who was very pleased. At home in India, however, this created a great rumpus. My mother sent me a rather blunt letter in which she said that she was upset that I hadn't kept Indian sentiments in mind. She wrote, 'You know that you cannot name a child after an older relative. Every time you scold him or slap him you will be using your Chacha's name and that is just not done. This western idea of naming a child after an older relative, as a tribute to that person, is not acceptable.' So I was torn between the two traditions and did not want to annoy either Ma or hurt my Uncle. I decided to coin a name, retaining a part of my Uncle's name and changing a bit to make it different. I named the baby Shantum, to chime with Vikram.

Since Shantum was born in London, he was entitled to be registered as a British citizen, and the hospital authorities asked me if that was what I wanted. I discussed it with Premo who, being practical, thought it was a good idea. But my patriotic feelings prevailed and we decided against it, knowing that Shantum would have the chance to make his own decision when he turned eighteen.

The Czechs, being stateless, were very keen to get British nationality. The Bata management in London asked Premo if he was interested in acquiring British citizenship; if so, they would continue his assignment in London, so that he would have a good chance of getting it after five years of residence. Premo asked me what I thought; I was clear that I didn't want it. I had strong feelings about keeping my Indian citizenship, which we had got after years of struggle with the British only ten years earlier. I was homesick for the country to which I belonged—a country I could criticize without fear of being told, 'If you don't like it here, go home.'

Shantum was a wonderful baby. We referred to him as Gugluram and he grew plump on Cow & Gate milk. (Vikram had been called Guthlipum as he was lean and strong.) I used to feed him with the bottle and as soon as he could hold it, he would help himself, flinging the bottle away immediately it was empty or when he had had enough. After a few glass bottles had been successfully flung and broken by him, I decided to change over to plastic bottles.

As Premo was at work, Shantum and I were alone in the house most of the time, and I used to get very depressed. Maybe it was the effect of lactation. It had been so different when Vikram was a baby. Then I had been surrounded by family and friends, whereas now in England it was just Shantum and me. I would wheel him to the market and leave him outside the shop in his pram, while I did my shopping, keeping one eye on him and an ear alert for his cry; whether it was the fishmonger, the grocer or the delicatessen, in those days the shops were too small for prams. We bonded with each other, but the hustle and bustle and loving care of a whole family was missing. Maybe that's why he started talking much later than most Indian children do. When I later took him to Panipat, Bibiji was very worried that he hadn't started talking even though he was a year old. He was a good baby, and on his return to India in December enjoyed the belated camaraderie of a whole family and of friends.

★

Shantum was born in mid-April and my Bar Final examinations were due about mid-September. With no domestic or family help, I was house-bound or at least baby-bound. Whatever preparation I had to do for the final examinations had to be done at home, without attending lectures or getting any guidance. I was naturally anxious and nervous.

We were frantically looking around for a baby-sitter, so that I could have at least a fortnight's respite before the final examinations. But as the days passed, it seemed that the only choice would be for Premo to take time off for the crucial few days of my actual examinations. The closeness of the exams, my lack of preparation and our not finding anyone to take care of Shantum were driving me to despair. Premo finally applied for a week's leave.

That very afternoon, the bell rang and a well-dressed, healthy-looking young woman with ruddy cheeks walked in. She had seen our notice seeking a baby-sitter in the neighbourhood shop and wondered whether we would be interested in a baby-minder instead. I didn't know what this meant, but quickly said yes, though a little apprehensively. When I discovered it meant leaving the baby in her house rather than her coming to ours, I was a bit wary. I took her address and Premo and I walked there that evening, taking Shantum along in the pram. It was only a short distance away, and she had two small children of her own. She told me that she had seen our bright-eyed, black-haired baby in the pram near the shop and had been charmed. We could see that she was a kindly and gentle spirit who dearly loved children, and we decided to take her on.

Every morning, Premo would take Shantum in his pram to Mrs Shirley's house and bring him back in the evening on his way back from work. It worked out very well and the Shirley family became so fond of Shantum in that short time, that they used to visit him later and bring him clothes and gifts. The Shirleys' seven-year-old son and five-year-old daughter doted on 'the little Indian baby'. Mrs Shirley even knitted him a blue and white striped suit. So eventually, I took my exams feeling comparatively relaxed, though I was not as well-prepared as I would have liked. But is one ever?

Premo pampered me and kept a hot meal ready for me when I returned home each day after doing the exams. The first evening he made grilled trout garnished with olives. He then served me strawberries and cream to cheer me up.

The Bar Final results were due to be published at midnight on 27 October 1957. That morning Premo and I drove to

Northampton (with Shantum in a carry-cot in the back seat) to say goodbye to some of Premo's old college friends and teachers as we were due to go back to India in a few days. I didn't know what would happen if I didn't get through the exams, as Premo's assignment in England was over. His successor, a Frenchman, André Salaun had already arrived with his wife. We had been so happy in 133 Willifield Way that we recommended it to him. In fact, we had even vacated the house as a friendly gesture, especially because his wife was pregnant, and were now living in digs.

Anyway, that evening we drove straight from Northampton to the *Times* building, arriving there just after midnight. Though I had been tense the whole day, Premo, the perpetual optimist, told me I had nothing to fear. On the way, with a view to celebration, he bought a large bottle of whisky and a small bottle of sherry from a pub, as the shops had closed. But there were no glasses to drink from, and Premo had to persuade the landlord to sell him two sherry and two liqueur glasses, treating this not as a sale but as if they had been broken by him.

As we neared the *Times* office, a young man suddenly jumped onto the bonnet of our car. I recognized him as a student named I.I.I. Qazi, who had failed his Bar Final exams numerous times. We didn't know what he was trying to do. Commit suicide? He was gesticulating and shouting—'Top! top!' We thought he wanted us to stop our car, which we did. Qazi, generous soul, was deliriously happy that I had come first, despite the fact that he had failed his exams once again. I wouldn't believe him and so we slowly drove on to the *Times* office, where I saw the newspaper and my own name printed in black and white at the top of the list: Seth, Mrs Leila . . . Lincoln's Inn.

I was amazed—and suddenly very hungry. Premo said he had often thought that I might come first, though I myself had not been all that sure even of getting through. He wanted to celebrate immediately. This was difficult, as it was long past midnight and we had baby Shantum in the car with us. But Qazi, who lived nearby, said he would look after the baby while we went to a restaurant and ate. On the way to the restaurant we woke up Lily. At the time she lived in a hostel for overseas women students, and it was quite a job to get her down at that hour. We sat in the car and had a few drinks together and then went to eat. She too was so genuinely delighted that she swigged some whisky without realizing what it was, being a teetotaler.

When we went to Qazi's place to collect our baby boy, we were told that he had got up once and cried a bit—which had alerted the landlady, who came to Qazi's room to find out what a baby was doing there. Though she didn't believe Qazi's story, she helped him soothe the baby back to sleep.

On Saturday, 2 November 1957, the following editorial appeared in the *Evening Standard*:

Love by degrees

'Time was when the phrase "a fair young English girl" meant the ideal of womanhood. It meant a girl who could be trusted alone, if need be, because of the innate purity and dignity of her nature; but who was neither bold in bearing nor masculine in mind; a girl who when she married would be her husband's friend and companion, but never his rival.'

So ran the lament of Mrs Lynn Linton in Saturday Review for 1868. But worse was to come. In one more decade they were founding women's colleges at Oxford. And in the Final Honours Schools for 1957, Lady Margaret Hall took, it just appears, the highest percentage (86) of first and second classes. St. Hilda's had the second highest (82); Somerville the third highest (79); and St. Anne's the fifth highest (74). Only Queen's, among the men's colleges, was in the first five places.

Help! Help!

The announcement was on Monday. The masculine world of learning was taking a ruminative pull on its pipe preparatory to advancing a complete explanation for this little lot when, on Thursday, a chasm opened from which nothing has since been heard save faint little gasps for help. This was the publication of the Michaelmas Bar examination results.

Five hundred and eight students, the vast majority of them male, sat the final examination. Of these, only 152 passed in full. Of these 152, only 10 obtained distinction. Of these 10, three were women, and one of them—a married woman—came first.

At a gallop

Were it not for one more piece of recent information, it might almost appear that man's place in society is undergoing a certain process of deflation. But Mrs Judith Hubback has been conducting a survey among 2000 married women graduates. It appears that only two in every 100 of wives who went to college contrive to combine motherhood with the full-time practice of a profession, and that most of them have no other occupation than domesticity. One marked characteristic of the graduate group, however, is that it has a perceptibly higher fertility than the female population at large.

It remains, in fact, much the same as when the poet contrasted sportswoman with blue-stocking:

See Diana clear fences
Ah!—who can resist her?
But then see how papers are cleared by her sister!
Their chances seem equal
For love, as one sees,
Comes sometimes at a gallop, and sometimes by degrees.

A few days later, on 6 November 1957 to be precise, I went with Premo to Simpsons of Piccadilly to collect some trousers he had ordered. An elderly gentleman, who was serving him, kept looking at me in a strange way. His English reserve kept him from asking what was on his mind. Ultimately, curiosity got the better of him and out popped the question. Was I the lady whose picture had appeared in the *Star* the previous day, holding a baby under the caption, 'Mother in Law'? When I said yes, he insisted on shaking my hand and added that he would tell his daughter that he had met me, to encourage her to do well in her studies. This is what the paper said:

Here's a mother who knows all about the law—28-years-old Lucknow-born Mrs Leila Seth. She has come top over all men candidates in the latest Bar Finals examinations.

Yet while she studied she had to look after her husband, five-years-old son and six-months-old baby.

Mrs Seth decided to go in for law when her husband, a technical advisor for a shoe company, was posted to this country three years ago.

Until her second son Shantum—the name means Peace—arrived in April she found it comparatively simple to combine studies with house-keeping in Finchley for husband Prem, 33, and elder son Vikram—Victor.

After that she decided to skip the lectures at Lincoln's Inn, and until a friend took over a fortnight before the exams continued to look after the family.

There were a couple of minor inaccuracies—Vikram means courageous or heroic, not Victor—but Premo and I enjoyed my little burst of publicity. The Indian newspapers picked up the information from the English papers, and my mother proudly showed the news item to all her friends and acquaintances.

Shortly after the results, I received a letter from a Mr Harwatt, who was the Secretary to the Council of Legal Education, informing me that because of my results in Hindu and Mohammedan Law and the Bar Final, I had qualified for the Langdon Medal. This medal, when engraved, would be sent to my address at 133 Willifield Way, London. N.W.11. I wrote back to say that I was on my way back to India and had moved from the said address. As a special case, Mr Harwatt had the medal engraved quickly and handed it over to me with his warm congratulations on my 'very fine result and good wishes for the future'.

I was called to the Bar 'on the twentysixth day of November One thousand nine hundred and fiftyseven' but in absentia, as I had left for India by then. (Coincidentally, twenty-sixth November was later declared Law Day in India, because that was the day in 1949 that we the people of India had given to ourselves a Constitution.) The Certificate of Standing sent to me states that I 'was called to the Degree of an Utter Barrister' (whatever that might mean) and that I had signed the Roll of Barristers of the High Court of Justice, Queen's Bench Division. There was a red seal on the certificate and it looked as grand as it sounded. There was also a footnote which said: 'The above form of Certificate is for the use of Barristers who are going to any Colony by the Ordinances of which they may be required to produce a

Certificate that they have signed the Roll of Barristers, but it is not necessary that Barristers intending to practise in England should sign the Roll of Barristers or obtain such certificate.'

But I was less proud of the grandiloquent language of this document than of the few simple lines written by one of my teachers, Professor Alan Gledhill: 'Mrs Leila Seth is probably the best law student I have known in twelve years' experience as a teacher at the University of London and the Council of Legal Education. When she received her gold medal for outstanding brilliance at the Bar Final Examination—a rare distinction—it was not only my opinion but the opinion of all my co-examiners that it was richly deserved.'

Alas, unknown to Alan Gledhill, inflation had debased gold to silver. But the medal shone nonetheless, and when I returned to Calcutta, I was told that Jyoti Basu (the Marxist politician who was to become legendary as the longest-serving chief minister of West Bengal and who was a barrister himself) was keen to meet me and congratulate me.

★

I had been quietly saving twenty pounds a month so that I could buy some household goods to take back to India. I wanted to buy a fine dinner set, and after many trips to various shops we had chosen one. We had finally agreed on a gold and red-bordered design on a creamy white background made by Royal Aynsley and available in the China Craft shop in Golders Green. We had also decided to buy a Bush radio with an automatic record-changer in a walnut-wood cabinet, some lamps, kitchen gadgets and two Vono folding bridge tables. Premo wanted to buy some clothes for himself. I told him that I had saved about six hundred pounds for making these purchases. He told me that he would be able to trade in our little car for about four hundred pounds, so that altogether we would have a thousand pounds available.

I was waiting for him to sell the car before actually ordering the goods to be exported with us to India. Premo told me that a car dealer was coming in the evening to finalize the deal. But he didn't show up till late and so I went upstairs to bed. I must have fallen asleep when I heard Premo's voice gently asking me, 'What colour do you want for the Daimler Century?' I was wide awake in a moment and jumped up, asking, 'Daimler Century? Daimler Century? Where is that car coming from?' 'It's a bargain I'm getting,' said Premo, 'in exchange for our Hillman Minx.' He then quietly added, 'And six hundred pounds.'

I had immediate visions of all the things lovingly chosen by us being thrown away and replaced by just a car. I said loudly in my most autocratic voice, 'No colour, no Daimler Century. You are *not* buying that car.' I then added in a more reasonable tone that cars were available in India, whereas these special household goods were not, and that we had spent so much time and energy looking for each item we wanted to take back. And, in any case, could he imagine the repercussions, if he, an erstwhile group foreman with his future designation in India still undecided, would be driving around Batanagar in a Daimler, while the Managing Director and the Chairman both drove mere Austins. 'Your habit of showing off will cause us no end of problems and I can't *allow* it.' So that was that.

★

Before returning to India, Premo and I had planned a holiday in Italy, ending in Genoa, where we would board the Llyod Triestino steamer back to India. At the last minute, Premo had to pull out as he was assigned some work by Mr Bata, which had to be done before he left. He insisted, however, that I go to Italy myself, especially to the Isle of Capri and the beautiful deep-blue lagoon, since one never knew whether we would have another chance to come to Europe. I went, and though I was a little afraid, did enjoy myself. I was particularly scared of travelling alone and being accosted by young Italian men, and also nervous about how Premo would cope with Shantum in the plane from London to Italy. But I managed to skillfully avert the overtures of the Italian charmers and I need not have worried about Premo either. He told the air-hostesses that his wife had left him and the baby for another man, and that he now had to look after Shantum on his own. The air-hostesses deluged him and Shantum with sympathy, fussed over them with anxious care, and wondered how heartless a mother would have to be to leave so beautiful a baby.

The trip back to Bombay was pleasantly uneventful; we found the air-conditioned Llyod Triestino line and its smaller ships more comfortable than those of the P&O by which we had come to England. On board, I thought of the three years we had spent in England with some nostalgia. They had been fruitful years. I was now a mother twice over. I had done a Montessori diploma and was a Barrister-at-Law. I had travelled in England, Scotland and Europe and enjoyed theatres, gardens, museums and shops. I had learnt to cook and run a household without any servants and to look after a baby without any help from my mother. I was more confident and less dependent on Premo. But I longed to go home and be with my family again and rejoin the familiar circle of my friends in India, with whom punctuality was not a fetish and thanking people was not just a polite habit. I also did not want to do boring household chores for a while and dreamt of putting my feet up and saying to the staff, 'Pani lao.'

★

I returned home to India in style, carrying my baby in my arms and my academic halo around my slightly swollen head. But I soon came face to face with the nitty-gritty of life and the tough world of practice at the Bar. My dream of starting a small nursery school had been totally dashed by the brilliance of my Bar Final results! Now everybody expected me to practise and perform. But this was not easy.

On our return, Premo immediately started work in the Bata factory at Batanagar, while I had to set up home. Vikram, who had come back earlier with my mother, was already in a Nursery and Kindergarten school in Ballygunge in Calcutta. This meant transporting him daily from Batanagar to Calcutta. We had to buy a car and I had to find the courage to drive in the city. I also had to find some good domestic help to look after Shantum and our home. Apart from this, I had to find a senior barrister in whose chambers I could 'devil' as a pupil for twelve months.

We soon sorted out our settling-down problems in Batanagar. But finding a senior who would take me in his chambers as a pupil for twelve months took some doing. 'Pupillage' is an apprenticeship to a senior, enabling one to acquire a proper knowledge of the technique of the profession. It means following the senior around like his shadow and seeing and hearing the manner in which he addresses and handles the court. It entails learning professional usage—to get a 'Passover', for example, without mistaking it for a Jewish festival. If one makes good use of this training period, one can be invited to continue in the chambers. This means assisting a senior in routine and less-important work and giving opinions or appearing in court when he is unable to do so, thus providing the experience for one's own future practice.

I now set about looking for a good senior to get 'attached to'. I went to see Mr Ahmed, the Registrar of the Calcutta High Court on the 'Original' side, who maintained a list of about thirty names of those barristers who were entitled and willing to take pupils. I asked his advice as to whom I should join. In reply he asked me whom I knew. I told him I didn't know any of the gentlemen mentioned in the list, nor anyone else in the legal profession. He was astonished and asked me, 'Why then are you joining the profession?' I retorted that he should tell me who was the best and leave the rest to me. He hemmed and hawed, not wanting to express a final opinion, but when I insisted, he gave me two names, Sachin Chaudhuri and Elis Myers. I remembered a piece of advice which had been given to me as a child: if you want to taste the best fruit, you must climb the highest branches. The name Elis Myers sounded too English, so I decided that I should join the chambers of Sachin Chaudhuri. But that was easier said than done.

I thought that I would telephone Mr Chaudhuri and seek an appointment. But it was impossible to get him on the line. His calls were all filtered and he obviously didn't talk to strange women. I realized that I had to find someone who would speak to him about me before I could get an appointment. In India, tracing friends and relatives of a well-known man is not such a difficult job, but it is tedious and embarrassing to ask for a favour. Anyway, after a seemingly never-ending month filled with bouts of despondency, I was granted an interview with the great legal luminary.

I was full of fear and trepidation when I went to meet him but put on a brave and smiling expression. Despite the fact that he had some idea why I had come, he wanted to be clear about the matter and asked me, 'Why?' in his grave and gruff manner. After I told him, he said, 'Instead of joining the legal profession, young woman, go and get married.' I replied, 'But Sir, I am already married.' 'Then go and have a child,' he advised. I responded, 'I have a child.' 'It is not fair to the child to be alone, so, young lady, you should have a second child.' I replied: 'Mr Chaudhuri, I already have two children.' Taken aback for a third time, he said, 'Then come and join my chambers, you are a persistent young woman and will do well at the Bar.'

Though Mr Chaudhuri had been so reluctant to take me on, once he had agreed, he encouraged me and helped me in numerous ways, extending a sincere hand of friendship.

It was a very quiet and sombre set of chambers. Apart from me, the only other lawyer was Pesi Ginwalla, who had plenty of work but hardly spoke a word to me or anyone else. He would pace about, thinking things out and communing with himself. The work in the chambers was mainly company law, income-tax law, complicated contract cases and some constitutional matters—hardly the sort of thing that would immediately warm the cockles of the heart. The one great advantage of the chambers was their location, in 2 Old Post Office Street, just across the road from the Calcutta High Court. One could work during the day in the chambers if there was no matter on hand in court. Again, because the court was so close, conferences were usually fixed immediately after court hours, and one could pack up and go home in the evening. This was not the case in most other chambers, where one tended to waste time during court hours, as the offices were located in the senior's house, and conferences were held late in the evening, sometimes spilling over till midnight. Other juniors often referred disparagingly to our chambers as the English-style chambers and to my senior as the dry and dreary Lord Chow! But these chambers suited me fine, even though there was not much fun and laughter in them.

After chambers were closed in the evening, I drove to Sashi bhai's house in Ballygunge, picked up Vikram, who spent the hours after school at their place, and drove to Batanagar. We had bought a second-hand light-blue Plymouth. It was a large car for me to drive, and some young Bengali men found it a subject for comment: 'Bogal kata blouse porechhe, abaar gari chalachhe!', they said disparagingly— 'Not only is she wearing a sleeveless blouse, but she's also driving a car!' I ignored these remarks as Vikram and I drove back home together. I caught up with all his school activities and tried to be a good mother, reciting poetry or telling stories or teaching him his arithmetic tables on the way home, as I had done on the way to school in the morning. As soon as we got home, I transferred my attention to Shantum, who had been looked after by his ayah, with a lunchtime visit from Premo. The late evenings, dinner and the night belonged to Premo. Since school started early and the chambers only opened at about 10 o'clock, I spent the time in between at the American Library, a source of relaxation after the early morning rush. But this state of affairs was not to last long.

In mid-1958, Premo was transferred from Batanagar to the Bata factory at Digha, near Patna. I didn't go with him immediately. For one thing, I had to complete my one year of pupillage before I would be entitled to practice, and for another, we were not sure how long he would remain in Patna. It was rumoured that he had gone there to help close down the factory.

When it became apparent that he was going to stay on, I joined him with the two children. Though he had in fact been sent to close down the factory, which was running at a loss and suffering from numerous labour problems, Premo drew up a scheme to get things going again. He told the Board that he was confident that he could turn the factory around. They were not at all sure it could be done. But they made him Factory Manager, and gave him two years to show results or else face the music. Premo is a born fighter and loves a challenge, and in a short time he made the factory into a profitable unit; indeed, he greatly enlarged its scope of activity. The work force also increased from 515 workers to 1,500, thus creating much needed employment in economically poor Bihar.

We were to spend ten very happy and fulfilling years in Patna.

Afraid of Bats

I moved from Calcutta to Patna in 1958, a few months after Premo was transferred there, but I actually started practising law at the end of 1959. I was one of only two women advocates in the Patna High Court at that time. The other, Dharamshila Lal, was a veteran and a very successful criminal lawyer. She was from Bihar and her father, Professor K.P. Jaiswal, was a well-known historian. Both her personal and her matrimonial life had been difficult, and this had hardened her. She was unafraid. Everyone in Patna had heard of her, and the courts were used to her bold and forceful manner. Yet she did not hesitate to jangle her bangles if the judges appeared not to be listening. She was the sole female star.

Suddenly, I had arrived in the Patna High Court and Dharamshila wasn't particularly friendly or helpful. I suppose I had expected some automatic female solidarity. It was not as if I particularly wanted to join her chambers. In fact I wanted to do mainstream civil and constitutional work.

I would have liked to join the chambers of P.R. Das, who had been referred to by the famous D.N. Pritt as 'the best lawyer east of Suez.' He was brilliant, lucid and eloquent. He had a silvery voice and presented the most difficult propositions of law in a manner that could be understood even by a simpleton. I had occasion to appear with him in a couple of cases and observed that when he was not making headway with the judges, he would repeat the proposition but in a different manner. He once told me, 'Repeat, repeat, and again repeat, but do it in such a way that the judge does not feel stupid, for then it will be a disaster.' He continued, 'Remember, judges don't always take things in the first time.' And he should have known, for he had been appointed a judge at a very young age. However, he didn't last on the bench for more than two years, and resigned. He realized that he liked playing the game much more than being the umpire. When faced with one of his own judgments, cited by the other side against him in a case, he told the court, 'That was the opinion of a foolish young judge but I am now expressing the view of a mature and experienced lawyer.'

I had, however, been warned in advance about the 'glad eye' he reportedly gave the girls. In the event, I joined the chambers of K.D. Chatterji, a well-respected senior lawyer who did civil, constitutional and company work.

When I joined the Patna High Court, I was the subject of much curiosity and discussion. There used to be a Barristers' Association and an Advocates' Association. The library of the former had few members and there was comfort and space and quiet to work in, while that of the latter was crowded, noisy and chaotic. I was a member of the Barristers' Association, while my senior, K.D. Chatterji, was a member of the Advocates' Association. As a result, I flitted between the two libraries. The advocates, in particular, were fascinated. They watched every move of mine, and one of them even asked me why I wore a particular type of blouse. This interest extended to the clerks. An advocate, Lalit Mohan Sharma, later to become the Chief Justice of India, had been away for many months in England for medical treatment. On his return, the first thing his clerk told him was that a young woman had started practising in the Patna High Court.

As my husband was the manager of the Bata Shoe factory, we lived in a beautiful old house that had once belonged to the Maharaja of Chainpur. People could not therefore understand why I was roaming around the hot and dusty corridors and courtrooms (there was no air-conditioning in the Patna High Court in those days) and spending my time with uncouth clients, arrogant company executives and inquisitive lawyers. The lawyers were unsure how to treat me, especially as I appeared confident and smart in my crisp white, black-bordered cotton tangail saris (starched with mica flecks) and Chinese-collared, three-quarter-sleeved white poplin blouses, spoke English well, and arrived at the High Court in a chauffeur-driven black Plymouth Belvedere, allocated to the Factory Manager.

The few members of the Barristers' Association were getting on in years. Apart from me, who was in my late twenties, there were just two other young members, who were in their late thirties. It was a dying breed as very few Indians were now studying for the Bar in England. Yet the older members resisted changing the rules and admitting anyone other than a barrister. Some years later, however—and very selectively—some senior advocates were admitted. There was a strong sense of camaraderie as we all sat around the dining-table during the lunch break, eating what we had brought, whether diet biscuits or paranthas and kebabs—and sharing the court gossip of the day.

There was, unfortunately, no proper women's toilet. A musty storeroom, a good distance away, had been allotted for this purpose. It was kept locked and the key was with Dharamshila Lal. After my arrival, it was decided that the key should be kept with the librarian, Khadim, a gentle and quiet man. However, Dharamshila, who was not used to this arrangement, sometimes forgot to return the key to him, and there was quite a crisis when she had to be sought out in court and the key retrieved from her handbag. The most awful part of it all was that this room was infested with bats. I was just terrified to go inside. Having heard stories that bats clung to your hair, I used to cover my head with the end of my sari, clinging to it while using the toilet. The room was dark and full of old, discarded files and every time the door squeaked open, the bats started flying about in great agitation. I wondered how Dharamshila coped and if there was some magical way in which I could stop the bats from flitting about.

At first, I was too afraid to say anything to anybody, but as my terror increased, I complained to Dharamshila. She looked surprised and said shortly, 'How do you intend to practise and do well in Bihar if you are afraid of bats?' That certainly put me in my place. In due course, as my confidence increased, I somehow managed to tell the President and Secretary of the Bar Association about the matter and get all the files and bats removed.

When I joined the Patna High Court late in 1959, the Advocate-General of Bihar was Mahabir Prasad, a kindly old barrister. He was allowed to appear in private cases, provided the State of Bihar was not involved. A little later, when he was briefed in a private matter, in order to encourage me, he told his junior that I should be briefed too. A sum of fifty-one rupees was given to me as a token payment. It was my first fee. I was naturally very pleased and wanted to do my bit. But when I asked for the papers pertaining to the case, they were not handed over. Apparently, there was just one set of papers among the three of us. The local junior was reluctant to part with them, and intended handing the full brief over to Mahabir Prasad the day before the matter was due to be taken up. I finally got a few minutes to see the papers, but couldn't make much sense of them. I hoped to learn more when the case was argued, and made polite enquiries as to when and in which courtroom that would happen—to be met with stony silence, as apparently both were a matter of chance. This was my first experience of a brief. I found it all very frustrating and felt quite bewildered.

In due course, one of the two younger barristers, Akbar Imam, helped me find my feet—and learn the ropes. Akbar, the son of a Supreme Court judge, had a flourishing criminal law practice. He told me that there was a belief among litigants that barristers knew no law but were good on facts and therefore made good criminal lawyers. There was another popular notion that Muslims were good at arguing cases whereas Hindus knew the intricacies of the law better. So when a litigant who had a civil case asked a very senior lawyer before engaging him whether he was a Muslim or a Hindu, the lawyer replied, 'I am a Hindu Musalman.' Another story still doing the rounds was that when a Bihari villager's appeal came up before one of the last English judges of the Patna High Court, the appellant asked his lawyer who belonged to the same caste as him, 'What is the caste of the judge?' The shrewd lawyer promptly replied, 'The same as ours.' This satisfied the litigant as he felt that he was now assured of justice.

Akbar advised me to argue criminal cases free, amicus curiae, as a friend of the court, so that I should be seen and heard. I took his advice. In those days there was no provision for legal aid except in murder and very serious cases. So from the daily list of the court which was hearing criminal appeals I sought out those cases where the accused was going undefended and took the permission of the court to assist in some of them.

The very first case I argued was a dacoity appeal. ('Dacoity' is the joint commission of a robbery by five or more people, and is a serious offence, punishable with imprisonment for life.) The accused had been sentenced to ten years' rigorous imprisonment. I read through the papers from cover to cover, but had no idea what to look for and how to proceed in the matter. I turned to Akbar. He asked me, 'What caste are the accused and what caste are the witnesses?' I was totally bewildered by the question and wondered what relevance it could possibly have to the case. He said there was often caste enmity in the villages and that this was often the basis for false accusations. I was badly shaken and couldn't believe that this kind of thing happened in free and independent India. Akbar smiled at my naiveté. Anyway, I soon discovered that the witnesses and the accused belonged to the same caste; I was relieved, because this was an argument I did not want to make.

But I wondered what else I could argue. Akbar read the brief cursorily and could not see much hope in the case. When I read the brief a second time, I decided to consult the almanac. It transpired that the crime had been committed on a dark night and that the witnesses could only have identified the accused by the light of their lantern. The lantern in question was a material exhibit in the case. However, on further detailed examination of the record, I found that there had been no oil in the lantern. I was thus able to establish that the witnesses could not have seen the accused and that the identification was therefore false. The judge, Mr Justice Ujjal Narain Sinha, accepted my contention and acquitted the accused. I was really pleased.

It appears that when the accused were released from jail, they were pleasantly surprised. When they learnt that a young woman had argued their case, my fame spread among the robbers and thieves! A few weeks later, a litigant came to Patna High Court looking for a young woman lawyer and, since I was the only one, he easily managed to trace and brief me. When he learnt my name, he immediately started addressing me as Leila Babu, as if I was a man.

It made me unhappy when I realized that however hard I worked, the younger male lawyers kept spreading the rumour that I was not serious, and that, being a woman, I could not run around like them and get things done. Further, I was a fashionable and frivolous woman who, because she had no need for money, would quit a case without notice. None of this was true but it is difficult to counteract a canard. Luckily, the older lawyers, to whom I was no threat, and who saw how hard I was willing to work, were very helpful. S.N. Datta, when invited to become the Senior Standing Counsel for the Income-tax Department in the Patna High Court, insisted that I be made the Junior Standing Counsel to assist him. I hardly knew any income-tax law, so he, in fact, taught me the rudiments.

After a few years of practice, I was put on the panel of junior lawyers for the State of Bihar. This meant that when asked to appear for the prosecution, I would earn thirty-two rupees a day, irrespective of the number of cases I handled. The amount was paltry, and sometimes I had to do two or three cases a day, mostly criminal appeals or revisions, but the great advantage was that I got an opportunity to argue the cases myself and be seen and heard. I was often pitted against well-known senior lawyers appearing for the accused. This naturally made me work very hard and tested my mettle.

I once found that among the criminal appeals allotted to me by the State of Bihar, there was a case of rape. At first I thought I should return the brief and inform the State that I would not handle it and that it should be given to some other lawyer. However, on advice from Akbar, whom I constantly consulted, I decided to argue the case. I soon discovered that Dharamshila Lal was appearing for the appellant. Since the only two women lawyers in the Patna High Court were arguing on opposite sides in a case involving rape, the courtroom was full of curious and prurient men. There was not an inch of standing room and the crowd overflowed into the corridor.

I was a bit embarrassed and didn't quite know how I should deal with the matter, though I had prepared the case thoroughly and studied the law carefully. As it was an appeal filed by the accused after conviction, Dharamshila had to start the arguments. I found she was most matter-of-fact and went into great detail on the question of the extent of penetration as the matter pertained to a young girl of fifteen. This gave me the confidence to be explicit and meet all her contentions without any awkwardness. I eventually succeeded in the case, despite Dharamshila's astute arguments, and the conviction was upheld.

This might have been a triumph, but there were also moments of deep dejection. When a death sentence is passed by a sessions judge, it does not become effective according to Indian law, unless it is confirmed by the High Court, even if the accused does not appeal. The accused is also entitled to a lawyer at the expense of the State. Such a case was allocated to me. I was perturbed. I read the brief over and over again and could not find anything to say in favour of the accused. Once again I spoke to Akbar; he too was not hopeful but suggested a possible line of argument.

I argued the case with the utmost vehemence but without success. I also pleaded for the sentence to be reduced to life imprisonment. The death sentence was confirmed. For days thereafter I couldn't sleep properly. I kept thinking of this man whom I had neither seen nor met, who was going to be hanged. The principle of the death sentence being given only in the 'rarest of rare' cases had not yet been enunciated by the Supreme Court of India. I wondered whether the death sentence was really necessary and what effect it had. Did it stop others from committing crimes or was it merely a case of an eye for an eye and a death for a death?

The new Advocate-General of Bihar, Lal Narayan Sinha (who later became the Attorney-General of India), had heard me arguing some small matters. He requested the State of Bihar to allocate me as a junior to assist him in some of their complicated cases. He also suggested my name as a junior to the Advocate-General of Uttar Pradesh for the case pending in the Patna High Court regarding the Bihar-UP boundary dispute. Apart from praising me, Lal Narayan also told him that I was originally from Uttar Pradesh.

Lal Narayan was a man of few words and his arguments were always brief and to the point. His knowledge of English was basic but his exposition brilliant. It was a real pleasure to appear with him and watch his strategy in the case and his handling of the judges' queries. He had a certain equanimity of demeanour. He attributed this to the fact that as a young junior he travelled to court every morning in a carriage with his father-in-law, who wasn't particularly punctual. Lal Narayan would mentally will the horse to move faster so that he could be in time for court. This morning ritual made him very tense, until one day he realized that it was a matter beyond his control, and he learnt to relax.

Of course, I went regularly to the chambers of my own senior, K.D. Chatterji, and worked on all his cases and followed them in court, whether I was formally briefed or not. He appeared regularly for large companies like Imperial Tobacco, Tata Steel and Bata. Tata and Bata were household names, and Biharis often said that the three best things in Bihar were a job in Tata, a pair of shoes from Bata and a young girl from Mithila (the area from which Sita hailed).

I was once briefed for the respondent in a case to assist Lal Narayan Sinha and discovered that K.D. Chatterji was appearing for the appellant. I told KD about it, but naturally I never discussed anything about the case. KD also made sure that the papers and notes pertaining to that case were not left lying around. I went to Lal Narayan's office, which was almost across the road, and planned our strategy. KD had obviously prepared well and I overheard his clerk telling the client before going into court, that the chances of his succeeding were good.

However, as soon as the case was called out, Lal Narayan got up and took a preliminary objection to the appeal. KD was taken aback. He had come fully prepared to argue the case on merits but had not anticipated any preliminary objection. He had to pray for an adjournment to examine the aspect raised, and was somewhat embarrassed. He was a bit surprised that there had been no inkling from me, but understood. His clerk on the other hand was extremely upset. He repeatedly said to me, 'You should have warned Sahib, you should have warned Sahib, even if you did not tell him what the preliminary objection was about, at least you should have told him that you were planning to make one.' He didn't appreciate that when a lawyer is appearing for a particular party, his loyalty is to his client and that in this case I had known that the element of surprise would be in my client's favour, at least temporarily.

I soon started getting a lot of work as a junior in important matters. I also started getting other cases, both civil and criminal, to argue myself. On one occasion, I was briefed to do a case in North Bihar, on the other side of the Ganga, and had to take a steamer across to Chhapra. When I went there to argue, I found a huge crowd had collected at the Magistrate's court. Apparently, they had all come there to see and hear me, because they had never seen a woman lawyer before and were astounded that such a creature existed.

Since I lived in a house inside the Bata factory precincts,

it was not possible for me to have my office there. After I started getting some work of my own, I took a room on rent, quite close to the High Court in a house called 'Ashirbad', which meant 'Blessings'. I used to sit there in the evenings, after court hours, and employed a clerk of my own.

A good clerk, as anyone associated with the law knows, is very important for the success of a lawyer. I thought that I had landed the right one after a great deal of searching and interviewing. The man was honest and active. Though he lacked experience, he was very loyal. I was pleased with him and expressed my appreciation.

Since I continued to go to K.D. Chatterji's chambers in Kadam Kuan in the mornings before court I often used his clerk to do some of my work. I was astonished to hear from him that my clerk had been boasting that he was in love with me and that I reciprocated his affection. I was in a dilemma as to what to do, but after some thought I decided to put it to him squarely. He did not deny the fact that he had been talking about his feelings for me and was surprised that I was angry. He had taken my appreciation for his work and my polite manner of talking to him as an indication of my affection. At times he was over-confident, puffed up with pride and love, and at others he begged forgiveness for his behaviour and wept. I didn't know what to make of all this and how to deal with him. When I threatened to dismiss him, he was distraught, as he had no other source of income. On Premo's advice I sent him to see a doctor, who diagnosed him as schizophrenic. We had him treated and he seemed to have recovered. Quite soon thereafter, however, he had a relapse and we found ourselves unable to handle the situation. I got his brother from the village to come and take care of him. Of course, I had to start the hunt for a clerk all over again, and I made sure that this time he was not young.

There were no solicitors in Patna and so junior barristers

could deal with clients directly, like other junior advocates. One day, a man walked into my chambers. He said he was an engine-driver and had been convicted of criminal negligence and sentenced to two years' rigorous imprisonment. He wanted me to appear for him.

The story he told me was bizarre and tragic. In Bihar, during festival time, hundreds of poor people travel without railway tickets on every train. On one such occasion, it was decided by the ticket-checkers to take strict action and offload all ticketless travellers. This they managed to do, despite a great deal of agitation and slogan-shouting. The guard then gave the green signal for the train to proceed. The engine-driver started the train. Unknown to him, a few of these ticketless travellers, including women and children, had climbed on to the roof of the railway compartment and were sitting on top. The train gained speed and passed under a low bridge. The passengers who were sitting bolt upright on the roof had their heads smashed and severed, while those lying flat and some infants were saved. It was only when the train arrived at the next station, and a huge hue and cry was raised, that the enormity of the tragedy became apparent. Somebody had to be blamed immediately in order to calm people down, and the conductor, guard and engine-driver were taken into custody. The surviving roof passengers alleged that when they saw the low bridge in front, they shouted for the train to stop, but their cries went unheard.

The trial took many years. Now, with his conviction, this experienced engine-driver was likely not only to go to jail but also to permanently lose his job and thus his only means of sustaining his family. He appealed to me. At first I was appalled. The fact that so many men, women and children had died clouded my mind. But when I thought about it carefully, I realized that he was not to blame. The guard, who should have noticed the passengers on the roof, should never have given the green signal till every one of them had been brought down.

I took on the case. As my father had been in the Railways, I felt a special bond with the engine-driver and his family. I worked very hard on the matter and studied a great deal about steam-engines, their mechanical systems (including the brakes), and their method of functioning. I wanted to find out whether sound from the roof could have reached the engine-driver.

The case dragged on for many days since it was also linked with the cases of the guard and the conductor. I had been paid for only one day, but my belief in the driver's innocence drove me on, and we won the appeal. His relief—not so much at avoiding jail as at retaining his job and thus being able to look after his family—was evident. Not having the means to show his appreciation in a material way, he brought his entire family to meet me, and they all insisted on touching my feet. For me it was the ultimate recognition.

White Pillars

Life in Patna opened new horizons on the home front as well. After living in modest houses with small rooms in Batanagar and London, we moved into a palatial old bungalow. It was a single-storey house with high ceilings and massive circular pillars supporting the front verandah. The very thick mud and plaster walls kept the interiors of the house very cool, and later on, once we had installed a number of air-conditioners, it became a real oasis from the burning summer heat of Bihar. When we first arrived, the house was in poor shape and needed major repairs. Inside, it was dark, and the flooring was of dismal gray cement. The electricity and plumbing were dreadful. The roof leaked, and buckets had to be placed strategically to prevent the floor from getting wet. Premo and his colleague Louis Weisz had been living there in true bachelor fashion with steel almirahs in the sitting room.

Mohammed Matin, the bearer, who had been there for many years and had served various factory managers and their families, like the Czech Vytopils and the Canadian MacKenzies, was not too happy to have an Indian replacement. He had been virtually running the show. When I gave any

instructions, he constantly told me how things had been done
in the past. He would never tell us in Hindi that dinner was
ready, but insisted on saying in English, 'Master, soup on
table,' even if we were only having dal and rice. When I asked
him to serve ice cream at a tea party, he turned around and
said, 'Madam, the English don't have ice cream with tea.' For
a moment, I was taken aback and my American friend Lilly
Banwell, who was standing nearby, stepped in and said, 'But
the Americans do.'

Matin knew everything about the house, where the
crockery and cutlery was, which linen had to be dry-cleaned
and which hand-washed and which could be sent to the
dhobi. He knew where the plumbing was bad and the wires
broken and how they could temporarily be fixed. He was
small and polite and walked about silently in his white
uniform and white tennis shoes. He had a handy remedy for
most of the ills of the house and was irreplaceable until it was
properly renovated.

When Premo approached Mr Vyoral, the Managing
Director, for funds to repair and renovate the house, he was
a bit reluctant to oblige. For one thing, the company was not
prepared to spend money until they were confident that the
factory would not be closing down and would make a profit.
For another, Mr Vyoral felt that the old house was a 'money
guzzler' and that it would be better to run a bulldozer over it
and build a set of modern flats for the Factory Manager and
other officers and guests. I too felt that I would be quite
overburdened with the upkeep and maintenance of this old
white elephant and was inclined to agree with him. But
Premo resisted Mr Vyoral as he could see the beauty of the
old house and how fabulous it would be if properly restored.
I was persuaded to agree with him. I am so glad that Premo
stood his ground. It would have been a real shame if the old
beauty had been pulled down. He pleaded for a fraction of

the money that would have to be spent in making new flats, and he obtained it.

An English engineer who worked with the company in Batanagar was sent to examine the house and to give his advice. He too was clearly in favour of the big house. With his technical and engineering skills and my aesthetic input the house was transfigured. The banging and crashing and the smell of paint was with us for many months. But the result was well worth the inconvenience. A beautiful home emerged—comfortable air-conditioned bedrooms, large bathrooms with glazed tiles and modern fittings, and a private air-conditioned drawing-cum-dining room. The public rooms, such as the front verandah, the lobby and the immense formal drawing-and-dining room had an airiness about them. The long dining-table, which could seat twenty people, was placed closer to the large, now modernized, kitchen, which could cope with parties for upto two hundred people—an astonishing number, considering my previous experience of housekeeping. (The very large sprung wooden dance floor at the back, however, was not repaired, as it would have cost a fortune to do so.)

The pigeons that messed up the front verandah could not be shot, as that was considered inauspicious, but we got rid of them by firing an airgun nearby. The geckos I got used to with time. Though there were snakes in the grounds, they now rarely entered the house.

The house was painted white on the outside. It became a large, lovely and comfortable home. Many people came to see it and the changes that had been wrought. We wanted to give it a name. Somebody suggested 'White House', but I thought that would be too pretentious and decided on 'White Pillars'.

When we first arrived, the spacious garden all around the house had a 'CPWD look'—as if it had been cared for by the bureaucratic and unimaginative Central Public Works

Department. The flowerbeds were demarcated with bricks, the corners of which stuck out like triangles, limed white. Round flowerbeds full of floppy cannas were arranged all over the front lawn. There were more weeds than grass. I removed the canna beds to make an uninterrupted lawn and had dhoob grass planted. The flowerbeds were shifted to the edges. I planted McGredy's Sunset roses four-deep in a bed in front of the house, close to where a small Cycad was slowly inching upwards. Super Star roses were planted near the huge side lawn, where an old sandalwood tree stood. I placed a stone bench under the tree, and had a small pool, with a fountain in the middle, constructed nearby, which I filled with white water-lilies. The murmur of the water drizzling on the lily leaves, the cool breeze rising from the pool and the fragrance of the sandalwood were enchanting.

Premo had no love of gardening and could not recognize any flower except a rose, but he loved the refreshing, rich green of the expansive lawn. As for the children, there was a large neem tree on the other side of the garden, and we built a rabbit hutch around it for them. A swing, see-saw and slide were also installed nearby.

From my childhood days in Darjeeling, where Aunty Dutt had let me help out in the garden, I had always loved flowers. Now I had a wonderfully large canvas on which to indulge my imagination. I planted a number of creepers, including the splendid, bignonia venusta, with its orange blossoms that came out in January and February. I also planted a number of annuals, such as dahlias, chrysanthemums, larkspurs, sweet williams, Californian poppies, pansies and sweet alyssums. A stringed trellis was set up for old-fashioned sweet-peas. In the shady areas I planted red salvias and white, mauve and purple cinerarias. I proudly planted the gladioli, rare in the plains in those days, which had been brought from Sikkim, and daily watched their growth. One morning, when

I went into the garden, I found that a gladiolus that had just started flowering had been cut. When I scolded Sarju, the peon, who had been deputed to work for us as a gardener, he was astonished and said to me, 'What was so special about it? After all, it was only a baby canna.' I decided it was time I sent him to the nursery in town to get proper lessons in gardening; in due course, he became quite an expert. We then experimented with growing celery and asparagus and artichokes in the back garden.

Our family lived in the major portion of White Pillars. Near the rear, there was a side entrance leading to living accommodation carved out for Shanti Jain, the Personnel Manager. His wife Asha and he had two small children, Priya and Pantu, and they were friendly with our children. We were the only two families living within the factory premises. Vikram was entranced by Asha, who sang melodiously and, apart from North Indian classical music in the khyal style, was also fond of bhajans and thumris. We were like one big family.

Our other close friends were Sarla and Amar Mishra. Sarla is a Sindhi and Amar a Maithal Brahmin. When they decided to get married, his family was not pleased, though eventually they came around. Amar worked with ITC (the Imperial Tobacco Company in those days). He too was fond of Hindustani classical music and organized musical soirées. Sarla and I were very close, and her daughters Ameeta and Vinati were good friends of our children. We spent many pleasant hours in each other's company, chatting, swimming, picnicking and exchanging notes on how to bring up our children—and handle our husbands. We became even closer after the Sino-Indian war of 1962, as we were holidaying together in Darjeeling when it broke out and we had great difficulty in returning to Patna. We imagined we could see the Chinese coming over the mountains.

Amar believed in playing Holi with great gusto. He would gently spread coloured powder on friends' faces, and while they were protesting mildly, he would quietly lead these unsuspecting people to a tub of coloured water. Before they knew what was happening, he would give them such a ducking that they were drenched through and through. After that thandai, laced with bhang would be offered. Everyone who drank it became high, and many burst into song.

Usually, the evening function on Holi was in our house; all our friends gathered, bathed and freshly dressed, the men in crisp white kurtas with specially crinkled sleeves and white pajamas, and the women in colourful starched cotton saris. As they entered to the sound of sweet music playing in the background, we sprinkled them with rose water, welcomed them with a gulal tika applied gently on the forehead, and offered them drinks and food.

During our Patna years, Eid fell during the summer, and we celebrated it with our Muslim friends like Aziza Imam and Begum Riyasat Hussain; they always offered us the most delicious sevian and kebab and raan. We also heard the great Begum Akhtar sing at a private baithak in one of their homes. Margaret and Sanjar Sarwar Ali also served excellent meat dishes made by their cook from Rampur.

Diwali was another festival to celebrate, and it fell around the time of my birthday. Gifts and Diwali sweets like malpua, new clothes, and glittering diya lights and fireworks were magical when shared with friends. Then came Christmas, with children's fancy-dress parties at the Bankipore Club or at the homes of friends like Margaret and Brian Elliot of Burmah Shell or Jean and Edge Semmens of the British Council, whose little daughter Judy insisted on calling us the Sex family. There was also a large New Year Ball at the Bankipore Club, which was attended by the so-called elite of Patna. The young companywallas danced to the Moosa Band,

and the government servants and their spouses watched and made comments, so a good time was had by all.

Apart from this, we entertained officially in quite a lavish style at White Pillars, when VIPs like Tom and Sonja Bata or Moti and Raja Khaitan deigned to visit Patna. Senior bureaucrats, lawyers and company executives and their spouses were invited and lights twinkled in the garden while Bengalee Ram, our cook, who looked like a wrestler, provided us with hot, freshly cooked, mouth-watering hors d'oeuvres.

Dr Zakir Husain, the then Governor of Bihar, a very cultured man and a great educationist, once visited the Bata factory. After he had been shown around, Premo brought him home for lunch. We had arranged a small sit-down meal for him and I took out my personal—bought in England— Royal Aynsley crockery, crystal glasses, silver-tipped cutlery and damask linen for the occasion. We served European food: vichyssoise, followed by Chicken Kiev (luckily the butter didn't squirt out when cut, but seeped out gently), served with asparagus and mint potatoes. The dessert was a very light apricot soufflé. It was a simple three-course meal, and Bengalee Ram excelled himself. Dr Zakir Husain thanked him personally. He had a discerning eye and spotted our blue-and-white coffee cups as being Spode china.

One of my closest friends was Ira, the wife of my senior, K.D. Chatterji. I often had breakfast in their home when I went to his chambers, before going to court along with him. He was short and dark and had butterfly ears and she was tall and fair and queenly—a generous spirit, who dressed in fine muslin Bengali saris and made excellent Bengali food. Their only child Kali Das (or Bubul as he was known) was a few years older than Shantum. When he was eleven he went to Doon School and Ira found the separation extremely difficult.

We also got to know their good friends Popul Bhattacharya and his wife Shuma, and their two girls, Chumki and Bubli.

Popul was a lawyer but more involved with public relations than with law. Shuma loved food and talked and dreamt about it. They did things in style. They lived in a grand old house called The Retreat with Italianate marble statues in the garden. Bearers wearing white gloves and tennis shoes served dinner in their house. The crockery was English bone china and the cutlery heavy Georgian silver. Western food was served. Almond soup and smoked hilsa fish, cooked in the smoke of jaggery and puffed rice, were special delicacies, as was mulberry ice cream. It was said as a compliment that Popul was an Englishman on the outside, while KD was an Englishman on the inside, and Akbar was an Englishman both inside and out.

In the Bar Association we were a small, compact group and Akbar was a special friend. He was unrestrained in his manner and when he saw me from afar, he would shout 'Leila Bella' in the High Court corridors, much to my embarrassment. His tubby little daughter, Tehmina, was a favourite in our family and stayed with us quite often, whenever Akbar went out of town to do a case in the mofussil or the Supreme Court. She lived with Akbar as he and his wife, Zeenat, were estranged. When Akbar first started practising law, he used to sit in his chambers, reading poetry and eating chocolate, hoping for a client to appear. His astute clerk, who solicited work and was an expert at obsequious 'pairvi', was not amused. He would give potential clients glowing accounts of how good and serious a lawyer his master was. But when the client would see round-faced Akbar, sitting and eating a bar of chocolate, he would think he was a child and run away. When Akbar became well-known, some people told the old clerk that 'pairvi' was no longer necessary, to which he replied, 'Aadat se lachaar hun'—'I can't help it, it's become a habit.'

Akbar was a brilliant criminal lawyer and argued his cases

with great conviction. He would almost invariably appear for the accused, and would tell me something like, 'The man gave a gentle tap on the head of the deceased with a stick and he died; what wrong did the poor man commit?' One day, quite unlike him, he started telling me, 'This was a really gruesome murder—really, quite horrible.' I was a bit surprised but soon realized he was appearing for the prosecution.

Akbar was a great favourite of the whole family; Vikram even forced him to play Monopoly with him. I was really sad when he became seriously ill, had to be rushed to London for dialysis, and died some months later. He was too vibrant, too young to die.

Although I was at first wary of Dharamshila, I appeared with her in a couple of cases and greatly appreciated her competence. She was redoing her house in Exhibition Road and visited me a couple of times to see what I had done with White Pillars to get some ideas and check out our local contractor. One day in court she felt unwell and had to go home. Luckily, I went with her, as she had only male servants and there was no one to help her change or take care of her. We called the doctor and it turned out that she had had a heart attack. Her sister, who was a doctor in Ranchi, came immediately to take over, while her economist son, Sanjay, arrived later from Europe. I developed a growing respect and affection for her.

★

Most company executives were posted in Patna for about three years. Since we stayed there for about ten, the faces kept changing. Fewer and fewer Europeans and Americans and more and more Indians held such posts. Kanwaljit Singh (or Tony as he was known) came to look after the affairs of Burmah Shell. He and his wife Kumkum were a charming

Premo arriving late for the wedding accompanied by his brother-in-law and Ganga
Datt and ushered in by Michi bhai.

Pushed by Moyna and Chiri
towards Premo for the jaimala.

Premo and me in Batanagar.

Vikram, Shantum and Aradhana, each four years old, taken five years apart.

Mother in Law with baby Shantum.

Aradhana with me.

Vikram—with his determined look.

White Pillars, Patna, with the 'CPWD look' garden.

Inside White Pillars: Dr. Zakir Husain (centre), Mr. Vyoral (extreme left), Ma, me and Premo.

and interesting couple and were to become close friends. He had visited America on an exchange programme called the Experiment in International Living. He now wanted to organize such a programme in Patna for young Americans. It meant lodging a young man or woman in your house for about three weeks and letting him or her experience life in an Indian home. He asked us if we would put up the leader, Dick Levy, and we readily agreed. It was comparatively easy to place the girls in homes where there were other young women or young married couples. But most Indian homes in a provincial town like Patna were reluctant to take in young men, as they were concerned about their daughters or their wives. It was hardest finding a placement for a young black man, John Philips.

Sujit and Meenakshi Mukherjee, recently returned from graduate school in the USA, heard about our difficulties, and, being sensitive and generous, immediately offered to take him in. Sujit was teaching English at Patna University and Meenakshi was doing odd teaching jobs and writing. It worked out very well. The whole experience of the Experiment in International Living was fun: there were about twenty young people in all. There was a wonderful mixture of lightheartedness and seriousness. One day they visited the cremation ghats on the banks of the Ganga—and also some astrologers, to whom they put searching questions. They jointly gave a barbecue party for their host families; since we had a large house and garden, we offered to let them host it there. It was an enriching experience: we learnt a great deal about each other's cultures, and it even made us think more deeply about our own culture and country.

In Patna, life was not just parties. Inside the factory gate we were protected from the poverty and lethargy just outside. Every morning, as I was driven to the High Court by our company chauffeur, Vishvanath Singh, I used to see people in dirty rags and uncombed hair sitting on string beds, some with one wooden leg broken, on the roadside outside their shanty dwellings. They seemed not to have the energy or the desire to improve their lot or perhaps didn't know how to. Or perhaps they were even too poor and exhausted to think. I wanted to help them and rouse them to get on with their lives and do something to change their situation. I told Premo that it seemed sinful to have these lavish parties while people were so poor outside. I said that I should go and work in the villages around the factory area. Premo responded that it was difficult to do things in this manner, and that I should make up my mind whether or not I wanted to devote my life to them. He said that he had known what it was to be hungry and cold and he felt for people, but also knew that his strength lay in working in the factory and trying to increase production and improve quality so that more people had a better deal and ultimately more could be employed. He had also set up a new canteen, thus providing wholesome meals for the workers. As for me, he felt I should try and help people by giving free legal advice to the needy, as the law was my profession and strength. I saw sense in what he said and did just that.

Premo himself had a problem that caused us much anxiety. This was the flare-up of his psoriasis. We had first noticed large white patches on his head in the ship on our way to London just three years after we got married. It looked like dandruff and we did not take it too seriously. After some time in England, it spread a little, and we went to a specialist, who diagnosed it as psoriasis. When the doctor told Premo it would take months to heal, he was angry and upset. We didn't know that in fact it would be years and years—and that it would spread in a pernicious form all over his body and even on his face and hands, so that he would be embarrassed to meet people or to shake hands. It was a real heartbreak. What about our children? Was the skin disease contagious? We were plagued by doubts. Premo had to get a certificate from the London hospital, stating the non-contagious nature of the disease before the hairdresser agreed to cut his hair. We tried all sorts of treatment from arsenic to cortisone to coal tar baths. It became so bad that his body was covered with big, ugly lumps of dry white skin which had to be soaked and rubbed off in a hot bath and the exposed tender red skin had to be softened with ointment. He had to be hospitalized in Guilford for treatment. Sometimes the skin would crack and bleed. I felt really sorry for Premo and for myself. But I remembered what Ma used to quote to me: 'I felt sorry for myself that I had no shoes, until I met a man who had no feet.' At times like these I was grateful that it was not infectious or contagious. What would we have done if it had been? When we returned to India, much to our relief, the psoriasis subsided. We had been told that it was basically a disease of the temperate regions.

After a year or so in Patna, the psoriasis reared its ugly head again. Premo was told that sulphur baths in the hot springs at Rajgir might help. Rajgir is one of the oldest continually-inhabited cities; it was the capital of the ancient kingdom of Magadha at the time of the Buddha. It is not too far from Patna; we started going there on weekends, but to no avail. Someone else suggested a no-salt diet and Premo tried that. Another person suggested oil massages and Premo found a masseur to come and massage him on the weekends. This gave him some relief but was not a cure. We wondered why a disease, supposedly of the temperate zones, was showing up in a tropical region. Some said that it was triggered by stress, others hazarded that it arose through contact with leather. Some rumour-mongers even suggested that Premo had some deadly, infectious disease and that no one should go near him. They claimed that in fact that was why we had sent our children away to boarding school. Needless to say, this was not true but the insinuation hurt.

★

The reason why we sent Vikram away to boarding school had to do with the way he was turning out. We tried not to spoil him, but in the factory compound all the security staff and durwans would salute us when we strolled around, and as a result Vikram got puffed up with a sense of self-importance. He also became quite rude and sulky.

Once, when he was six, we visited one of the young officers working under Premo in Patna. His wife had taken a lot of trouble to make some special coconut sweets, which other children loved. When Vikram was offered the narkul naru he turned up his nose, made a great fuss and wouldn't even taste a bit of it, despite her very endearing coaxing. We tried to prod him into good manners, but it had the opposite effect. He became sullen and silent and would not even say namaste or smile when leaving. We were thoroughly embarrassed and cross and decided not to speak to him till he wrote a letter of apology and promised to correct his misbehaviour. This is the letter which, under duress, he produced to appease us.

My dear Mama,
I shall always obey you and my elders.
I shall never pinch the servants and everyone.
I shall always say salam or namastay.
When I go out to anyone's house, when the people of that house offer me anything I shall not fuss.

Lots of love and kisses.

Vikram

But this contrition did not last. His studies too were suffering. When we moved to Patna we had put Vikram in St. Xavier's, which at that time was an English-medium school, even though St. Michael's was much closer to us. Now we realized that he did not have any friends nearby and that this made him especially lonely—and consequently difficult. We decided to send him to boarding school in Dehra Dun. Since Welham Boys' School was preparatory to the well-known Doon School (which only took boys in at eleven), that's where he went at the age of six.

At the beginning of the first term I took Vikram to Dehra Dun myself. We travelled by train, a long journey of two nights and a day. The Doon School and Welham School parties were on the same train. Despite the fact that some teachers were accompanying them, the boys got down at all the stations, shouting and laughing and eating all manner of food, and sometimes jumping on to the train after it had started moving. My heart was in my mouth. However, I tried to push these fears out of my mind and stop my imagination from roaming. All through the journey I kept preparing Vikram for our painful parting with tales of how wonderful and exciting boarding school life would be.

When we reached the school, I went to meet the Principal, Miss Hersilia Oliphant. I told her about Vikram's little problems, health- and diet-wise. She was a large-built woman and had an aristocratic and autocratic air about her. She bent down and talked tenderly to Vikram but dismissed me rather summarily with, 'He will be fine here. I love the children but have no patience with the parents.' After I had been shown around the school, I was told to leave and not hang around Vikram, as it would make his parting from his mother even more difficult. I can still remember the lonely little boy standing by himself, waving good-bye with held back tears slowly rolling down his cheeks, while I waved to him and kept smiling at him till the taxi turned the corner. Then my own tears came in a torrent. I had the rest of the day to spend in Dehra Dun before catching the train back at night—I was debarred from going back to the school and visiting Vikram again. I spent the afternoon in a movie hall and began the lonely return journey back to Patna with a heavy heart.

Thereafter, Vikram started travelling with the school party to and from Patna. At the end of each vacation, after a day of tension and trauma at parting, usually sought to be alleviated by his favourite dessert, a flaming baked Alaska, he would catch the train late at night, often being asleep when we took him to the station. This little sleeping boy being sent so far away by his hard-hearted family became the object of pity and the topic of gossip for other parents.

During his summer and winter holidays in Patna, Vikram read voraciously and soon started appropriating my books and making a library of his own. I had instilled in him a love of poetry and one of the first books which he took over was the *Albatross Book of Verse*.

Once, when a friend of mine, Dr Kovarik (who, some years earlier in Batanagar, had advised me about contraception), came to stay with us and I was not at home but in court, she chatted with Vikram. She said to him, 'It must be wonderful to have such an intelligent mother.' Vikram replied, 'I do not care how intelligent she is, she is never here when I want her.'

When my friend repeated the conversation to me, I felt it was time for introspection. I wondered how to find more time. I had prided myself on giving as much concentrated and attentive time to him as I could, and especially on inculcating in him my love of English language and literature. But obviously that wasn't enough, something was lacking. How was I to create that fine balance between my work, my obligations as a wife and my duties as a mother, so that none suffered? Should I give up my legal work? Was I failing my children? The answer to my doubts appeared soon after. One day when Vikram and I were having a serious conversation about poverty and its problems in and around Patna, he turned to me and said, 'Mama, I am so glad that you work and use your mind and don't talk to me only about the price of onions and the stupidity of servants.'

I tried very hard to balance my work and home life, but sometimes it was difficult. On one occasion I had a long-standing promise to take Vikram to a film, when I was suddenly called upon to draft an appeal and a stay application for a man who was being evicted from his house. I spoke to Vikram and explained the urgency of the matter and asked him to decide what I should do. Even though he was a small boy and had been looking forward to going, as English movies were only shown on Sunday mornings in Patna cinema halls, he made the correct decision, and the appeal and application were filed on the Monday.

Vikram was always full of queries and addressed them to whoever came within his ambit. My lawyer friends were asked questions such as, 'Which is the crime that, if committed, is not punished, though the attempt is punishable?' They were often flummoxed, till he came up with the answer: 'Suicide.' My friend Ira Chatterji refused to be cross-examined by him; she gave him affection but no answers. Vikram was also a great tease. He apparently told Shantum that reading the headlines of the newspaper would improve his English. Shantum followed his advice conscientiously and on reading a particular headline asked his elder brother what a budget was. Vikram told him that it was a baby budgerigar!

When Vikram was nine, Premo and I, who were going to Europe for a holiday—a perquisite provided by the Bata Shoe Company—took Vikram with us. The trip would largely coincide with his summer holidays, but he needed to take a couple of weeks' leave from school as well. Miss Oliphant, who was usually a real stickler about not granting leave, willingly agreed on this occasion, as she felt that it was a great educational opportunity. She knew that I would take him to museums and monuments, churches and cathedrals, musicals and plays.

In England we once again stayed at 133 Willifield Way, as André Salaun and his wife were away in France and very generously offered us our old home. We had great fun at Stratford-upon-Avon and visited all the sights connected with Shakespeare, including Ann Hathaway's cottage. In London, I particularly remember how enthralled Vikram was by the musical *Oliver* and wanted to be taken again. He learnt the names of the capitals of most countries and identified their flags. He then took a devilish delight in testing our knowledge and that of our friends. He was also a great source of logistical support, as he would quickly translate what something cost from pounds, francs, Deutsch marks or lire directly into rupees.

In Norway we stayed in Brandbu with a friend of Premo's from his college days in Northampton, and witnessed the almost-midnight sun. Later, we went to Copenhagen and saw the little mermaid—she is surprisingly tiny—and enjoyed the beauty and the music of the Tivoli Gardens, as well as the excitement of the roller-coaster rides. Vikram was particularly gleeful to see how frightened a friend and I were! In Holland we went to Madurodam, the tiny little replica city, where ships docked and trains went round and even the miniature tulips were perfumed. Vikram's excitement was complete when he saw a very, very small Bata shop in the market area.

American friends of ours from Patna, Bob and Jerri Grausom, were now posted in Frankfurt. When Vikram met Jerri, he immediately touched her fur coat. He was fascinated by the texture of objects, especially fabrics. He would go forward and touch a person's clothes, sometimes even those of a stranger, just to feel and experience the differences between velvet, satin, silk and other materials.

He hated eating eggs at that time and would get sick if he discovered he had eaten one. I thought this was a matter of the mind and wanted him to get over it. Jerri had just acquired a waffle-maker and was very keen to make pancakes for us and serve them with golden syrup. I told her not to disclose, even if asked, that eggs were an ingredient. Sure enough, as the pancakes were brought in, Vikram wanted to know what went into them. He happily ate and enjoyed them, oblivious of the fact that they contained eggs. Such are the devious ways employed by parents to train children. Of course, the more direct way to submission was also used.

We went on to Rome and then to Paris, where we spent time with my schoolfriend Yolande, who was now married to Cang, a Vietnamese, and had two small boys. Vikram enjoyed himself thoroughly and loved seeing the stained glass at Notre Dame lit up by brilliant sunlight.

★

In September 1962, after founding and running Welham School for twenty-five years before retiring, Miss Oliphant died. She had been full of energy even though she was over eighty. Vikram wrote to me from school: 'Miss Oliphant died in England. She had a heart attack but became slowly better, then had another heart attack and died. We felt very sad when the news came yesterday and are still. Mr Marshall proclaimed today as a holiday. We are not to make a noise. We have to read books or colour pictures.' Vikram was particularly upset, as he very much liked her. After his first term in school, she had referred to him as 'very intelligent but inclined to feel he is a law unto himself.' Later she thought he was 'a well-mannered boy with a brain teeming with ideas'.

Another teacher Vikram was very fond of was Miss Meisenheimer, who taught English elocution and singing. She instilled in him a love of the sound of words. The new Principal, Mr Marshall, while acknowledging Vikram's lively interest and initiative in dramatics, felt that he was too determined to 'acquire encyclopaedic facts and figures, to have time to relax and be a boy'.

Good at studies, Vikram won a number of school prizes, particularly in English and Mathematics. When he left Welham at the end of 1962, however, he received only certificates as the prize money was donated to the National Defence Fund in the name of the student. He was disappointed but knew it was right, as the money was going for our jawans who had fought the Chinese under very difficult conditions, without proper and adequate clothing in the freezing Himalayas.

In 1963, Vikram joined the Doon School. It was considered one of the best boys' schools in India at the time. You usually had to register your child at birth if you wanted him to get in. Michi bhai had registered both his sons and upon his advice I followed suit shortly after Vikram was born. There was also an entrance test; a boy was normally admitted at about the age of eleven.

The Doon School was founded in 1935 and hoped to incorporate all that was best in both Indian culture and the English public school traditions. It is situated in Dehra Dun, in a valley in the foothills of the Himalayas. Because the Forest Research Institute had been located here earlier, trees, shrubs and creepers of many varieties cover the area. The classroom windows open onto the gardens with the foothills of the Himalayas as a backdrop.

Within the general framework of discipline and the curriculum there was freedom for a boy to choose what he wished to do—in art, music, science, carpentry, motor mechanics and so on, or in games; or in his leisure activities— such as rock climbing, fishing, browsing in the school library or serving as a volunteer in the local Cheshire Home for the handicapped. Boys were encouraged to ask questions in the classrooms and to discuss problems with the masters. Vikram pointed out the difference in approach between the missionary school that he had attended in Patna and the Doon School.

He said that at St. Xavier's they put a cup in front of you and asked you to draw it, whereas at Doon they gave you a sheet of paper and asked you to draw what you liked.

Premo and I believed that a good education was the best gift we could give our children and we sent the two boys to Welham School and then the Doon School, despite the high fees and our own limited resources: school fees took up more than half of Premo's salary. But I was faced with a great dilemma when Michi bhai, who was living in Delhi, withdrew both his sons from Doon on the grounds that scholarship was being ignored there at the expense of extra-curricular activities. I was naturally anxious and made a special trip from Patna to meet the Headmaster, Mr Martyn. He explained that right from the start the school had been keen to impart a broad-based education but had not underestimated the importance of the academic side. He said that the examination results were regularly analysed and were not very different from the teachers' expectations of different boys.

I also learnt that apart from his administrative duties, Mr Martyn had made it a practice to teach English himself to the lowest form in the school, so that he got to know each boy individually, and could afterwards watch his progress right through school. He assured me that the school's methods of teaching and character-building would be of great help to Vikram, who was basically a loner and self-contained. Vikram had not been overawed by Mr Martyn; when the Headmaster had bent down to talk to this short little fellow and tweaked his nose, Vikram had tweaked his nose right back. This had created quite a stir and had provided gossip for the news column of the Doon School Weekly.

Vikram had seemed to do well in school, right from the start. He got good marks in the end-of-term examinations, took part in painting, carpentry, debating and chess, and earned the bronze badge for swimming. He appeared happy and well-adjusted. The climate in Dehra Dun was good and the surroundings of the school beautiful. We decided to leave him there.

There is no doubt that the biggest influence on him in school was his housemaster, Mr Gurdial Singh (referred to as Guru by the boys), a bachelor and an avid lover of the mountains. He had been a part of various Everest expeditions. His very first report about Vikram at the end of 1963 was as follows:

> Masters teaching Vikram have sent in the most glowing reports about him. He has a keen and incisive mind, and is very quick in getting to the heart of any matter. He has an accurate ear for music, and is a delightful companion in every way.
>
> He has been working on a monumental quiz book in partnership with a friend of his.

Guru taught geography and guided Vikram in many ways. He encouraged him to appreciate Western classical music and allowed him to listen to his prized collection of records. He also instilled in him a love of adventure and daring. He watched Vikram's progress with great interest and referred to his immense industry and ability. Once he wrote, 'Always cheerful and confident, he is very good value indeed.' Guru said that Vikram had developed a keen sense of right and wrong and had independent views. 'Fortunate is the school which has a boy like him on its rolls, and fortunate the housemaster who has a boy like him under his care.'

Guru called him 'an absolute gem in every way', especially as Vikram who was short and small turned out to be a good trekker. Guru also referred to the unselfish energy he put into the School Weekly. At the end of the 1968 term Guru said:

> Vikram is an indefatigable worker, and he maintains without difficulty his distinguished level in studies. Congratulations on winning the Maths Prize! As usual he has put in an enormous amount of energy in

other spheres of school life, in dramatics, in debating, in first aid, in music and in editing the Doon School Weekly. Indeed, he has been a pillar of strength in many of them . . .

The pillar, however, was soon struck by disaster. The first information of this came from Shantum, who had just joined the Doon School a few months earlier. This is what he wrote.

My dear Mama and Papa,
    How are you? I'm fine.
    Yesterday I heard from Bhaiya that he was being no more a prefect. I am very sad because of this because the boys will start teasing me. I have got 3 bad chits and 1 good chit. I got the bad chits in Sanskrit, Algebra and Arithmetic and I got the good chit in Sanskrit. It is quite surprising to get a good chit and a bad chit in the same subject. I have finished my work in the class so I am writing to you now.
    Please can you send me some peanuts. They are peeled and are in packets.
    Please send me a few packets.
    The boys in Foot House are real bullies. I have got a very good friend here he is Bhaiyas friends cousin his name is Sandeep Hosali. I have not yet gone to get my clothes from Welham School. I don't get any spare time.

Your loving son
Shantum

Premo was away in England when this letter arrived and I was naturally very distressed to receive it; I realized something serious must have happened for Vikram to have been removed from prefectship. I hoped that Shantum had got his facts wrong. I wondered whether to write to Guru or Vikram or the Headmaster. I knew that if it were true, Vikram would be very unhappy, being an extremely sensitive child. I was also concerned about what would happen with regard to a scholarship to a public school in England that the Headmaster wished to recommend Vikram for, and that Vikram had set his heart on. Since I was alone and had no one to discuss the matter with, I was sad and anxious and bewildered. But Vikram's letter arrived two days later and clarified matters.

Jaipur House, Ye Olde Doon School,
D. Dun, U.P.
One very gloomy Holi (Mar. 15) evening.

My dear Mama and Papa,

Something rather tragic has happened. We regret to inform you that your son is no longer a prefect "for breaking school rules". The series of events leading to this are as follows:

1) One very hungry Friday afternoon, AB, XY and Vikram Seth came back from the English book-depot half-starved and desperate. Jumping towards the pantry, they were horrorstruck to find it shut, locked and barricaded, and so a hastry plan was made.

2) Three furtive criminals crawled up the stairs.

 towards Mr (or rather Messrs.) Browne's and Nugent's room (these are two English teachers fresh from school) . . . What are these furtive criminals going to do?

3) This is the room of Messrs. N. & B., no-one is inside. The door is not locked. Some remnants of tea lie on the table in the middle of the room.

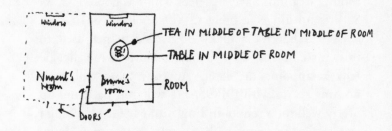

4) In sneaks XY, one nasty, wicked boy, with eyes on tea in middle of room. In front of doors stand V. Seth & AB, two nasty, wicked boys, to give the alarm.

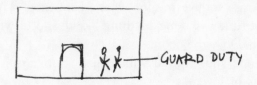

5) Up the stairs, four at a time runs Nugent!

Manages to catch glimpse of one fleeing figure and 2 guilty looking guards.

Well, after that, we denied having been in the plot, but owned up afterwards.

Christopher John Miller MA (Cantab.) sentenced us to 1 Y.C. each for lying (!) rather than for entering room. "I cannot have a prefect who has got a Y.C. V. Seth is no longer a prefect." (Date: 14-3-'68)

I still haven't actually been able to get used to this. It's come as rather a shock. He tells me that he *may* re-appoint me later. Anyhow, this will have nothing to do with OPOS. He will still back me up pretty well for a school in England. Mr Gurdial Singh was at first v. angry with us, but he's calmed down now. We've apologised to Nugent and Browne.

Occasionally, however, I get fits of depression. I do realise I've been a silly fool. I've explained everything to Shantum, and now I've explained everything to you. Please forgive me for what's happened. This is the first time I've done anything like this, & it will be the last. <u>Do write soon</u>.

I hope you enjoyed your trip to Bombay,
Lots of love,

Yours affectionately,
Vikram

A few days later I received a letter dated 18 March 1968 from Mr C.J. Miller, the Headmaster of Doon School, addressed to Mr P. Seth, regarding 250 J. (Vikram's school number was 250 and J stood for Jaipur House.) The Y.C. that Vikram had referred to in his letter was a yellow card, which was given for bad behaviour or bad results. OPOS (or Office for Placing Overseas Schoolboys and Schoolgirls in British Schools) was an organization established by various governmental and quasi-governmental bodies in the UK on the recommendation of the Headmaster's Conference.

250J

Dear Mr Seth,

At the beginning of this term Vikram was made a Prefect, but a few days ago I was compelled to announce that he was no longer a Prefect and I would like to explain what has happened.

About a week ago a young master returning to his room in Jaipur House saw Vikram and another boy outside the room and discovered a third boy inside, in circumstances which suggested that they might have been trying to take away something from the room. Vikram denied that any boy was in the room and persisted in the denial for some days until he eventually told the truth.

I am sure you will appreciate that it is impossible for me to have a boy as Prefect who has lied to his housemaster and to me about a matter of some importance. Vikram is feeling remorse for what has happened and I am sure that this is an isolated incident which in no way reflects his usual conduct. I have told him that after what has happened he cannot be a Prefect, but that this would in no way prevent me from recommending him as strongly as I can for an OPOS Scholarship to England next year.

I expect that Vikram will have told you something about this but I thought I ought to write to you myself to make the position clear.

With best wishes,

Yours sincerely,
C.J. Miller

As Premo was away, I replied to the letter on 21 March as follows:

250J

Dear Mr Miller,

As my husband left suddenly for the United Kingdom on 15th March and will not be returning till the 1st of April, I am acknowledging your letter of 18th March addressed to him.

I do appreciate your writing and explaining the circumstances under which you felt compelled to announce that Vikram is no longer a Prefect. I fully understand your attitude and stand in the matter.

Vikram has written to his Father and me and explained everything and for him it is a tragedy, as he writes, 'Occasionally, however, I get fits of depression. I do realise I have been a silly fool. I've explained everything to Shantum and now I've explained everything to you. Please forgive me for what happened. This is the first time I've done anything like this, and it will be the last.'

He does not say so, but knowing him, I presume he felt a false sense of loyalty regarding the boy who was in the room and as such denied it. I do also appreciate what you have told him about the OPOS scholarship, because I also feel it is an isolated incident, as he has a very strong sense of honour and what is right and wrong. One learns only by one's own experience and the hard way with disappointments, and I am sure this entire incident with its attendant punishment will help to further mature him.

My husband has as from the 1st of March 1968 been transferred to Calcutta. I propose to stay on here till the end of May, when I will join him in Calcutta with the children, provided we have found suitable accommodation by then.

Thank you once again for writing, and hoping this finds you in the best of health.

Yours sincerely,
Leila Seth

★

Vikram was very fond of Shantum. There was, however, a gap of five years between them, and despite this love, the baby brother who suddenly arrived from London in December 1957 occasionally appeared to get in his way. The usual childhood sibling jealousies developed and became more marked when we went to Patna in 1958. On one occasion, we were motoring back from Nalanda, which is famous for the ruins of an ancient Buddhist university. Premo and I were in the front; in the back, Vikram, aged seven, was teasing Shantum, aged two. He kept pinching him and making him cry. He was warned a number of times, both by Premo and by me, to desist, but he persisted. Then Premo stopped the car and dragged Vikram out and stood him on the side of the road and drove off. My heart was in my mouth, as we were on a highway, and I kept looking back. Vikram was so shocked at being left behind, that he stood still for a moment, looked right and left, and then dashed across the road to the railway line opposite and stood on the track. He obviously knew that this would terrify us and that we would return immediately to pick him up, which of course we did.

Shantum adored his elder brother and wanted to do everything like him—including having a photograph taken at the age of four in a similar pose and in the very same pullover, as in a photograph of Vikram's taken by Bennett's in London, just before he left for India. But the difference in personality was apparent from the results. Vikram was a moody, thoughtful child, while Shantum was a smiling charmer.

The first school Shantum went to was run by an Anglo-Indian lady, Mrs Marks, in her house in Patna. There were three children in the school: Shantum, Bubul, and a beautiful little girl, whom neither knew. Her affections and preference became a bone of contention between the two boys and, naturally, Shantum managed to charm her. Thereafter, Shantum went to the Notre Dame Academy run by American nuns in Pataliputra Colony. Our friends Sarla and Amar Mishra's two daughters also studied there. Shantum used to go and have lunch with them every school day as they lived near the school. Their grandmother used to tell them stories of her village, and Shantum was enthralled.

Near the Bankipore Club there were sand islands in the central portion of the Ganga. A whole group of us went across in country boats, with children, servants, food and drinks, for a picnic. The children were all playing together at the edge of the sand. Suddenly we heard Vikram shrieking. Matin, who was closest, rushed across to him and found him lying flat on the ground, holding on to Shantum's hair. Shantum was in the water and could not be seen. Matin managed to pull him out. We all pounced on Vikram, because we thought he was pushing him into the water. But we soon realized that we had misjudged the situation. In fact, Shantum had gone paddling; an underwater sand-ledge had suddenly collapsed, and he was being pulled under. Realizing this, Vikram had lain flat on the sand and grabbed hold of Shantum's hair, so that he could try to pull him out, but he found that he too was being drawn in, until Matin rescued both of them. Shantum was totally wet and had no change of clothes, so we made him wear a little girl's spare frock, much to his disgust. We were deeply shaken by the disaster that had been averted.

When he was six years old, like Vikram, Shantum went to boarding school at Welham's in Dehra Dun. His first report indicated that he was a good boy with good table manners and that though 'he takes a little time with his meals he eats well and sleeps well'. The story goes that he was so slow at eating that one day at lunch he didn't realize that all the other children had eaten and left. When this little six-year-old finished his meal and tried to get out, he found the dining-room door bolted from the outside. He tried to raise the alarm, but there was no one to hear him. So when the staff opened the door at teatime, they found a small, tear-stained boy fast asleep on the floor.

That Shantum loved his food was not in doubt—though, strangely, he never grew fat. All his requests to us in the letters he wrote home were about tuck. Could we send him 43 ice creams and 43 Coca-Colas for his birthday? He even aspired to become President of India so that he and his friends could have ice creams and orange squash without limit. He demanded homemade cookies, mango pickle made by Premo's sister, and toffees from Kwality in Dehra Dun. He was discriminating and specific in his requests. He was not averse to making deals with friends, such as obtaining extra toast and jam in lieu of milk. He obviously considered these little gains an achievement, as he proudly wrote to us about them. His letters from Welham School were at first short and formal: we were addressed as Mother and Father, which he probably copied off the blackboard. In the course of time we became Mummy and Daddy, then the informal Mumps and Pups, and finally our true selves as Mama and Papa.

Like Vikram, Shantum was admitted to Doon School and also went to Jaipur House. He preferred interaction with people to burying himself in books. He was good at debating and first aid and Captain of both. He was a house prefect in his final year, and encouraged and helped others. His favourite activities appeared to be to play bridge and to watch films, which were always referred to as 'fantastic', to go for picnics and to follow intently the internal politics of school and staff as well as the goings-on between students. He was very affectionate and caring and bowled you over with a sudden comment like, 'Mama, your smile is my bread—keep smiling.' But procrastination was a habit with him and punctuality virtually unknown. However, he was innately intelligent, and got a first division in his Indian School Certificate examination in 1973.

Mr Gurdial Singh, the housemaster who had earlier been a mentor for Vikram, wrote about him,

> Shantum is a bit of an enigma; at times he reaches first division standard without difficulty, at other times he is at the bottom half of his form in performance . . . He obviously has plenty of natural ability but his industry is spasmodic; hence the quality of his academic achievement, though generally good, is not uniformly high . . .

Guru referred to Shantum as a likable person, highly companionable, a live wire and an asset to the school community.

★

Vikram was born in 1952 and Shantum in 1957. They were wonderful boys—but we longed for a girl. Premo and I decided in 1961 that we should have one last try. There was no amniocentesis in those days, or if there was we were unaware of it; we put our faith in prayer and luck instead.

When I was nine months pregnant, my friend Ira decided to have a shaad for me. The idea behind the ritual was that there should be no hankering, no shaad. Ira did it in the traditional Bengali way and invited some women friends for lunch. She cooked all my favourite dishes, which she served me on a silver thali. It was an elaborate meal, starting off with fried tender neem leaves and aubergine, five types of fried vegetables, dal with coconut and other delicacies, and ending with fish cooked in mustard, chicken curry and mutton korma. A kheer to sweeten the mouth was the last dish. Ira was a fantastic cook and put affection in with the other ingredients.

Clearly, the shaad worked, for I was relaxed and happy and the childbirth was an easy one. On 10 April 1962, I had gone to see a movie in the evening, had returned home at 9 p.m. and had had dinner. Just after dinner I felt a little uncomfortable and decided to go to the Holy Family Hospital, which was reasonably close to our house. The baby was born soon after. Dr Neidfield, an American nun, informed me that I had a daughter, I was delighted. So was the rest of the family. The little girl was given gold chains, rings, bangles and karas as gifts. The choice of her name was hotly debated; Anandita, Sadhana or Aradhana were all mooted. Was she to be named 'the giver of happiness', or 'devotion', or what she really was—the answer to a prayer? We settled on Aradhana which variously means worship, adoration, prayer.

Aradhana was a little princess who was thoroughly pampered by her Papa. I tried to keep the balance but at the same time give her the freedom that the boys had enjoyed. She was full of life and vitality and verve, which she still has in abundance. She had a beautiful smile and a loud scream. We called her Holy Terror, because though she was a delightful baby, the strength of her lungs dominated our hours of supposed rest. When she was good, we called her by the more mellifluous name of Babaloo.

Vikram and Shantum loved her dearly but didn't see too

much of her as they were in boarding school. When they were home on holiday, they read to her. She was especially fond of hearing them read from *Winnie the Pooh*—so they started calling her Pooh Bear.

In 1967, when Aradhana was five years old, there was a drought in the state. Her school, Notre Dame Academy, was collecting money from students and staff to donate to the Bihar Famine Relief Fund. Students and staff were expected to give five and ten rupees respectively. Aradhana had heard heart-rending stories of the hardship caused by the drought, and wanted to give a large amount. She kept pressing me to give a hundred rupees, as if she were Lady Bountiful. I felt that she should share not only in the joy of giving but also in the cost. I wanted to test her sincerity. Her birthday was a few weeks away, and she was looking forward to a party with her friends. I put it to her that she had a choice: to do without the party and donate the cost of it, or to have the party and give only what other children were expected to. She was in a quandary. Premo thought it was unfair to put the burden of such a choice on a child of five. But I was clear in my mind that she had to decide for herself. She came back to me a day later. She was quiet and thoughtful and must have cogitated the matter for some time. She told me she wanted to give the money. She had taken a hard decision and we were deeply proud of her.

The workers, staff and management at the Bata factory also collected money for the drought, and it was handed over to Jayaprakash Narayan, the well-known and respected Gandhian and socialist leader. Normally, because such an important person was coming to receive the money, an elaborate tea party would have been arranged. But I insisted that only a cup of tea be served, and that all the funds that the company had been willing to spend on the tea party should be added to the amount already collected and handed over for digging wells in Bihar.

Aradhana was taken to school (where, at this age, she only went for half the day) and picked up by Vishvanath, our chauffeur. One day he forgot to pick her up. It was May. The temperature in Patna was over 40 degrees Celsius. After waiting for over an hour at the school gate in the noonday sun, our six-year-old had the sense to get someone to telephone us. Premo's secretary received a garbled call at about 1 p.m. that no one had come to pick her up from school. Luckily, it was the summer vacation and the courts were closed, so I was home. The car was immediately rushed to the school. Owing to confused directions and some other work he had to do, Vishvanath had forgotten to pick her up and nobody had realized it. We were all very repentant, especially as she had been waiting alone near the school gate in the blazing sun. Only after waiting for more than an hour had she gone back to the school building to make a call.

When she came home, burning red and hot as a ball of fire in her bright red school uniform, she didn't show any emotion. But obviously, she had felt abandoned. I immediately clasped her to myself and took her to the bathroom and poured cold water all over her to cool her down, and her ayah rushed to get a glass of cold drinking water from the refrigerator. The ayah poured out a glass from a bottle in the fridge and gave it to her to drink. Aradhana complained that there was something strange in the glass, but we put it down to the fact that she was hot and dehydrated and confused. Despite our cajoling, she just refused to drink it down. I was puzzled, and tasted the water. It was pure gin! For some strange reason, someone had put a bottle of gin in the fridge, and the ayah had unwittingly given Aradhana a whole glass of it. I thanked my lucky stars that she was so stubborn. Our little Pooh Bear was a brave and born survivor.

★

One sad memory of our years in Patna was Michi bhai and Moyna's divorce. Divorce in those days, despite the liberalized laws, was an unusual and even shocking matter—moreover, my brother and sister-in-law had three children. I advised Michi bhai and Moyna not to wash their dirty linen in public but to go for a divorce by mutual consent. I also advised Moyna to press for a lump sum settlement rather than a monthly payment, for the latter, if not paid, was messy and difficult to enforce. Michi bhai thought at first that I was favouring her, though he came to see that that was not so. Only a fair dispensation could have minimized bitterness. I appeared for Michi bhai and a very good friend of mine appeared for Moyna. Eventually, the whole affair was conducted in such a civilized manner that they remained friends. After they both remarried, Michi bhai and his wife, Mohini, spent a holiday with Moyna and her husband, Harald, in Germany.

Our own marriage was a happy one. There were, however, difficult times when there was a clash between my duties as a lawyer and as a wife. I remember one particular day after a lot of tension I told Premo, who was very disgruntled, that I had decided to stop working, since my work seemed to make him unhappy. He replied, 'I know that your work is one of your hands and that the family is the other. How can I ask you to cut off one hand? No, no, you must work and we will adjust.'

In 1968, when Bata transferred Premo to Calcutta as the Management Development Advisor, I was loath to leave Patna. We had a lovely and comfortable home and a really interesting garden, which I tended with care. Premo, as Factory Manager, was king of all he surveyed and I was getting on with my law practice.

We were both respected in our own professional spheres. For entertainment, there was the Bankipore Club: the library, the swimming-pool, open-air English movies on the banks of the Ganga, excellent 'goli' kebabs made by Nathun, the Club's cook, picnics with friends, fairs, fêtes and the garden competitions with their annual 'war of the roses'. We had made some really good friends, as is only possible in a provincial town, where there are hardly any grand cultural and social distractions and one is so dependent on one another. We had spent some very happy years in Patna and our daughter Aradhana had been born there.

So had my fourth child, Ira, about whom I will now write.

Ira

My brother Sashi and his wife Usha had lost three children. It was heartbreak without end. Their son Deepak was a few months old when he died. He was their first child and the light of their eyes; they didn't know what had happened and were totally unnerved. After some time they decided to have another child. Another son was born and they named him Gautam, after the Buddha. They watched him closely and carefully and heaved a sigh of relief on his first birthday. They thought all was well—but it was not to be. He became paler and paler and soon passed away. A post-mortem was done but nothing was established. Time passed but the acute pain and emptiness remained. Family and friends didn't know what to say or do. Doctors advised them to try for another child, as there didn't appear to be anything wrong that they could diagnose.

After some time, a baby girl was born. She was beautiful, and they named her 'the new one'—Naveena. They thought their luck had turned, especially as she was of a different sex. She was a happy and lovely child, much loved by all the family, including her cousins. There was a sense of relief when she turned two. But as she grew, her head seemed to be too heavy for her neck and she tended to tilt it slightly to one side. Sashi bhai and Usha were naturally very anxious and consulted the doctors, who once again were not sure what was wrong. My brother even contemplated giving up his lucrative job in Calcutta with a British managing agency and taking up a teaching assignment in Darjeeling if the doctors thought the mountain air would help revive her. But Naveena too developed a little paleness, which the doctors ultimately diagnosed as leukaemia. Shortly afterwards she too died.

Sashi bhai and Usha were devastated. What they must have gone through is difficult to imagine, let alone describe. The family was the fulcrum of Usha's existence. She had a lot of love to give. She and Sashi bhai longed for a child but were afraid to have another. This time the doctors also did not persuade them. It was like the end for them. They gave away all Naveena's clothes and toys to the orphan children at Mother Teresa's Shishu Bhavan. Mother Teresa insisted that Usha distribute them to the children herself and see the smiles on their faces.

By then we had three children, Vikram, Shantum and Aradhana. With two boys and a girl, our family seemed complete. Premo and I could sense Sashi bhai and Usha's pain. I tried to persuade them to adopt a child, but my brother was reluctant. He was conservative and worried about the family a child might have come from. Premo and I discussed the matter further and decided to have a child and give it to them. Usha and Sashi bhai were overjoyed.

All the while I carried her inside me (of course I did not know the sex of the baby at the time) I agonized over what I would do if the child was born with some birth defect. My own family was complete. I did not want another child—but I could not have gifted her if she had been less than perfect. I also tried not to get too mentally attached to the little one inside, kicking away. Vikram, when he saw me at home looming large in front, a few days before the baby's birth, made my day when he said, 'Mama, you look doubly lovely.' It reminded me of the old Chinese expression of describing a pregnant woman as 'the woman with happiness inside her'.

I was active and arguing in court till a few days before the baby's birth. As I intended to go back to work soon afterwards, I didn't tell anyone there that I was expecting: my sari and my loose black barrister's gown covered all. The judges and lawyers were taken aback when an adjournment was sought owing to the baby's birth. Of course, my family and close friends knew all about it, and my children were especially excited about the baby that would go to Usha Maami.

Usha had come to Patna a few weeks before the expected date of delivery, which was at the beginning of January 1967, so that she could take over from day one. My labour pains started soon after lunch on the 6th, and I went into the Holy Family Hospital. It was my fourth delivery and I was thirty-six, so I told the children that the baby was likely to arrive in a few hours. At six in the evening, all dressed up and led by Vikram, they arrived in the hospital with gifts to see the baby. No baby had arrived till then, so they returned home disappointed.

It was a long and painful labour and the little girl arrived only in the early hours of the 7th. Dr Neidfield was the same gynaecologist who had been present at Aradhana's birth, almost five years earlier.

Since I had told the doctors and nurses that the baby was for my sister-in-law Usha, who was present in Patna, they thought it best that I not start feeding the baby; Usha held her and fed her with the bottle. She was a cute little baby, but very different looking from the first three children. Sashi bhai, who was in Calcutta, was elated and wrote to me on 8 January 1967:

I was delighted to get the news of the birth of a little baby girl yesterday.

I am sorry to learn, my sweet sister, that you had a long and difficult labour. It is not possible for me to express in words my feelings of affection, pride and gratitude to both of you for all that you have so willingly done, and sacrificed, to give Ushi and myself the happiness which we have so much sought.

After I came home from the hospital, there was much joy and laughter all around and Usha was, as she said, 'bursting with happiness' while handling the baby.

My brother took a few days off from work around 26 January, the Republic Day holiday, and came to Patna to take the beautiful baby back home. I did not realize, despite my earnest efforts at trying not to get too attached, how difficult the days immediately following would be—but I tried to fill them quickly with work at the High Court and activity at home.

Those few days we were all together were really wonderful, full of love and hope for the future, and I cherished the memory for long afterwards. Premo and the three children were so caring of me, Usha, Sashi bhai and the little one, conscious of the special bond that linked us all. Love overbrimmed all around and I tried to remain as detached as possible so that I should not be too possessive of the darling fifteen-day, six-pound girl when she left.

When Usha and Sashi bhai wrote to me from Calcutta about their joy and happiness, I knew that that joy more than compensated for the pain of separation. A friend wrote to me when she heard the news: 'She is doubly parented and quadruply loved, a source of great pride and love.'

She was named Ira, since both Usha and I had a special friend with that name. My friend was compassionate, gracious and regal. Usha's friend was understanding, sensitive and beautiful. Ira also means earth and nourishment and is another name for the goddess of learning, Saraswati. On Ira's first birthday, Usha wrote to us: 'It is not easy to put into words the feeling of being given a new lease of life, that is exactly what it feels like to have little Ira with us. The happiness you have given us along with her is not possible to describe but it is there for you to see.'

Little Ira grew up to be a lovely girl, compassionate and kind. She went on to study at Loreto House, Calcutta, and was the pride and joy of her parents. Love and laughter permeated her being and her brown eyes twinkled with delight.

When Ira was about two, after Premo was transferred from Patna and our family moved back to Calcutta, we saw a great deal of her. Then, three years later, I moved to Delhi for various reasons, but Premo stayed on in Calcutta. Since he was alone, he shifted to Usha and Sashi bhai's house. At that time Ira and he got to spend a lot of time together; they had great fun and became particularly close.

When she was very young, before she could hear tales from others, particularly distorted ones from the servants, Ira had been told that she had come out of my stomach and had jumped into the arms of her mother Usha. She thought this very funny and stored the information away. She treated us four in the most natural way, knowing that Usha and Sashi bhai were her parents and that we were her Uncle and Aunt, her Phupha and Bua.

When Ira was eight years old, it was discovered that she had a hole in her heart and that she needed an operation. Her parents were afraid, almost desolate. They brought her to Delhi, as Usha's parents were there, as well as us. Ira was operated on by Dr Venugopal, one of the best heart surgeons in the country. Luckily—or by the grace of God, as the surgeon said—her operation was successful and her parents were reassured. Each person's courage strengthened the spirit of others in the family, and the understanding between us helped us get through this painful crisis.

When Ira returned to Calcutta, she was eager to show off her scar and all her presents to her school friends, but unfortunately they could not visit her, as there was a chicken-pox epidemic in school and Usha and Sashi bhai wanted to protect her from even the slightest chance of an infection. She was looking forward to a hero's welcome and was very disappointed. Ira had many friends in Calcutta; she loved her school as well as her home in Belvedere Estates, Alipur.

In 1983, Sashi bhai had to move to Bombay on promotion. From friendly and culturally-active Calcutta to unfamiliar and business-like Bombay was a big leap for a sensitive teenager. The culture and value systems of the two cities were very different. Though there was a lovely view of the sea from Flat No. 5, Hill Park, Malabar Hill, a luxurious accommodation provided with the job that Sashi bhai was holding, Ira had no friends with whom she could enjoy it.

In fact, the sea looked as grey as the skies because of the heavy monsoons. The Bombaywallahs assured them that later in the year the sea would turn a beautiful blue-green and the sunsets would be enthralling. While Sashi bhai had his work to occupy him, Ira and Usha had time on their hands and missed Calcutta and their friends terribly. However, they hoped that gradually they would learn to like Bombay.

With some effort and with the help of contacts, Ira got admission into the prestigious Cathedral School. She made a few acquaintances and appeared happy. But appearances are deceptive: the change was difficult for her. She was a sixteen-year-old and in Calcutta had been studying in a convent school that was exclusively for girls. Cathedral was a co-educational school; most children had been there for many years, and had their own friends, affiliations and groups. It was difficult for a sensitive child to break in. They found this young, unsure, family-protected, Calcutta-style girl, without a boyfriend or the experience of having had one, rather strange and, basically, had no time for her.

At the age of sixteen, your peers are more important than your parents, and Ira longed for their admiration and affection. She was a pretty child, although small and very short, and when she discovered that boys were a necessary part of any discussion, she started making up stories about them, mostly imaginary, to impress the girls. But children can be unwittingly cruel and the girls refused to include Ira in their set. She felt rebuffed and lonely and unhinged. She was always repeating the phrase, 'Remember, love makes the world go around.' And who should know this better than her, who was a product of love and a gift of love and surrounded by the love of her parents and family?

Usha and Sashi bhai brought Ira to Delhi for a holiday. Though Aradhana knew that she was her blood sister, we had taught her to look upon Ira as a cousin so that there would be no confusion in the relationship. Vikram and Shantum were also there, and Ira saw the three of them teasing each other and having a lot of fun. Maybe she felt isolated, being an only child.

We do not know what went on in her head, but she slowly became depressed and difficult. At first, her parents thought it was just that she was missing her school and friends in Calcutta and was going through the usual teen tantrums. But when it appeared to be more serious than that, they took her to see one of the best specialists in Bombay. He started treating her and she responded well. Her parents, as always, surrounded her with sunshine and love.

One morning early in November 1984, my brother went for his usual walk, while Ira and my sister-in-law were still sleeping in their fourth-floor flat. When he returned, he went to wake up Ira. She was nowhere to be found. She normally never left the flat without telling them, so he woke Usha up and they searched the entire flat but without success. They wondered what could have happened and where she could have gone. On the balcony they noticed a stool that was usually not kept there. They thought that something in the garden might have attracted her, as she loved nature and flowers. They rushed down to the common garden below and looked everywhere, desperately calling out, 'Ira, Ira'. They did not find her, and were about to return to their flat, despondent, when they heard a faint voice calling out, 'Mama, Mama', and recognized it. They found her lying in a bush, bruised and with broken bones, but her beautiful face didn't have a scratch. They picked her up gently and tenderly. She said, 'Mama, I don't want to die,' and then closed her eyes.

After Ira's death, when Usha was very depressed, she used to say, 'I should never have taken her, my stars are not good for children.' When people ask Usha now whether she has any children, she smiles sadly and says, 'I am not one of the lucky ones.' Such is the heartbreak of a mother.

Equal Plus

Our move to Calcutta in 1968 was professionally very important for Premo. I was less enthusiastic about shifting from Patna, where I was doing well and had spent ten happy years.

After having lived in that large and magnificent old house, it was hard to find accommodation that we liked in Calcutta. But being roofless was not an option. The shift coincided with Vikram's final year in school and his Indian School Certificate examinations were looming large. We therefore decided to take a house on rent in Darjeeling for the summer months, when the boys were home from school; Premo, meanwhile, stayed with Sashi bhai in Calcutta.

Vikram did very well in his Indian School Certificate examinations, despite the fact that, owing to a grave leakage of papers from a school in Mussourie, fresh examinations had to be held a few months later, during the winter holidays. Students living far away from school were allowed to take them at centres nearer home. It was a stressful time for Vikram, he was suffering from a migraine throughout his mathematics paper and had to tilt his head in order to avoid the blind zone in the middle of his vision and piece together the questions bit by bit. His aggregate result (in his best five subjects, a score of one point being the highest score in a subject) was five; he was the first so-called 'five-pointer' in his school.

Shantum in the meanwhile had been more seriously unwell. He complained of sudden giddiness. One day at school, while working on a wooden bowl at the lathe machine, he fainted. We were alarmed and decided to bring him home to Calcutta for check-ups and treatment. He joined a private school known as Miss Higgins' School for a term. I never met Miss Higgins, if indeed there still was one, but Champak Basu, a childhood friend of Moyna, was Shantum's class teacher. She gave him more or less individual attention, as there were very few students in the school.

Aradhana was six and went to school at Loreto House in Calcutta, with the Irish nuns. This was a change in style from the more easygoing American nuns of Notre Dame Academy, but she took it in her stride. I was keen that she learn Indian dance and opted for Bharatnatyam. I had been taught Kathak for a short while, as Ma was very keen that I do something which involved music. Ma had decided on dance, as the singing teacher she had engaged to teach me had resigned in despair. I knew that Aradhana, like me, was unlikely to be able to sing well, so dance was the next best thing. But her dance teacher didn't last too long either. This time it was the student who revolted. Maybe Aradhana resented the very strict discipline; she didn't like doing things she was told to do.

One evening, Sachin Chaudhuri, in whose chambers I had devilled many years earlier, invited us to dinner. He and Sita Mashi kept a beautiful home. While walking upstairs, both Premo and I, who were obsessed with the thought of finding suitable accommodation, simultaneously and silently expressed a wish to live in a place like this. We were utterly surprised when we learnt from them that they were planning to move elsewhere. Their daughter, who was at the time living downstairs, was going to move upstairs, to their place, and the ground floor with its beautiful garden would be available for us to rent. They agreed to the rent which the company had budgeted for us on the condition that we undertook all the necessary repairs and renovation. We were excited and happy at the prospect of soon having a beautiful home of our own. As it turned out, the whole process took much longer than the two months we had envisaged, with the house needing major repairs. During this waiting period, we stayed in my younger brother Tuttu's tiny flat, practically taking it over. Once the house was ready, I was very relieved. I had a home once more; I could start working properly again.

★

At the end of April 1969, Premo received a letter from Michael McCrum, the Headmaster of Tonbridge School in Kent, informing him that Vikram had been given an OPOS scholarship and that the school would be very pleased to have him there from September. Mr McCrum also felt that Vikram's obvious choice of three A level subjects should be Pure Mathematics, Applied Mathematics and Physics.

Vikram was delighted. But meanwhile, I had been hearing harrowing stories about schoolboys indulging in drugs and sex in the UK. I was very apprehensive, as I knew that teenagers were especially susceptible to peer pressure. I began having second thoughts and discussed them privately with Premo. He told me, 'Vikram will never forgive you if you do not let him go after he has won the scholarship.' Reluctantly, I accepted the fact that he should go. My father's youngest brother, Shanti, who lived in London and was a dentist, and his German wife, Henny, had agreed to take care of Vikram during the holidays, and to act *in loco parentis* to him. This somewhat eased my mind.

Influenced by my friend Koly, I took Vikram to the great Kali temple at Kalighat for a blessing before he left. But it was a distasteful experience for him as we were hustled and jostled about. I calmed him down and, by way of contrast, gave him a beautifully-carved stone image of Saraswati to guide and inspire him in his studies.

We saw Vikram off with mixed feelings. I was worried for him. How would he manage to travel in foreign lands? He was so forgetful. What would he do if he lost his passport? He was a very sensitive child. How would he face racial discrimination and 'Paki-bashing' from the skinheads. He was a short, shy and serious boy, with just a few good friends made slowly over the years. How would he cope with the big, tall, confident white boys? Would he be able to make friends quickly, who could give him solace in the loneliness of being away from home? Or would he, under peer pressure, fall into the pit of soft, or even hard drugs, that appeared from all reports, to be pervasive in the English public schools in those days?

We knew from Welham and Doon School that he was a loner and not a team player; he liked swimming, chess, crosswords, music and poetry. But like most intelligent and exceptional children, he had a complex character and valued silence and space to think. Financial worries too might weigh heavily on him. Though his tuition, board and lodging were entirely covered by his OPOS scholarship, he would be dependent for his holidays on Shanti Uncle and Aunty Henny in London, as we could not afford to bring him back to India. The stringent foreign exchange regulations in effect in India did not permit us to send him money, so he would also be dependent on Shanti Uncle for his pocket money.

How would he manage? Perhaps we would not see him for many years. But I knew that Premo was right: I had to let Vikram go. I had to let him cross the seven seas and find new ways for himself, to take his own decisions and make his own mistakes.

I need not have worried. His first letter informed us that he had managed to get asparagus at every meal in the plane, had arrived safely, and was roaming the streets of London, but had decided not to visit the wax-works of Madame Tussaud as the entrance fee was too high. Thereafter, it took a few weeks of settling down in school and at the end of September, he wrote: 'Altogether, I'm quite happy here. The masters and boys are decent types—there doesn't seem to be any anti-coloured feeling in school at all. Besides myself, there are four other foreign boys here—an American, two Africans and a Pakistani.'

★

After Vikram left, I started going to the Calcutta High Court every day, even though I had no work. I would go conscientiously at ten in the morning and leave only after four. I didn't like sitting in the Bar Library when there was no work, as was the custom, gossiping about judges and lawyers and discussing the politics of the day. Instead, I sat in different courts and listened to various senior lawyers arguing. As I had been junior standing counsel (income-tax) in Patna, I eventually got some work to assist seniors in that area. This was very hard for me, as I had been used to arguing cases in Patna and had a standing of my own. But I had no choice.

I also thought of attending the chambers, after court hours, of Siddhartha Shankar Ray, a barrister known to his juniors and younger friends as 'Manu da', who had interesting work of all types. I went for a few days to see what it would be like. I discovered that Manu da kept unusual hours. When he returned home after court, he would sleep for a couple of hours, then have a massage and bath, and only sit down to work sometime after seven, going on till late at night. I realized that if I joined his chambers, I would never meet my husband and hardly see my children. Instead, I decided I would try to attend the chambers of Dr Devi Pal, an advocate who was dealing exclusively with tax law and who had the largest income-tax practice in the High Court at the time. When I asked him whether I could attend his chambers, he said he was more than willing, but wondered how we would function during court hours as we belonged to two different libraries in the High Court, he to the Advocates' Library and I to the very exclusive and elitist Barristers' Library. I assured him that I would manage well enough, as I would mostly stay in the courtroom.

Dr Devi Pal had none of the suavity of the barristers, but he knew his income-tax law inside out. He spoke loudly in court and had a tendency to shout, but was very successful in winning cases as he was well-versed and well-prepared, whereas the tax department, normally represented by his brother-in-law, another Pal, didn't quite match his legal acuteness.

Listening to Devi Pal I certainly learnt the law, but it was Manu da who was a master of court-craft. He believed that in order to succeed it was important not only to know the law but also to know the proclivities of particular judges and how they reacted to certain arguments. He also liked citing decisions from the different series of law reports, thereby giving the impression of wide reading and a vast and varied library. I once asked him why he had quoted a judgment from the Sales Tax Reports when I had found the same decision in the All India Reporter. He replied that it was much better to place a navratan—a necklace composed of nine different jewels—before the court than a string of pearls. 'It will dazzle them,' said Manu da.

At that time in the Calcutta High Court, Justice P.B. Mukharji was the presiding judge hearing tax matters. He was very intelligent and erudite and had a trenchant and sarcastic sense of humour so that even a dull subject like tax could be quite lively, especially if the barb was directed at someone else. As Devi Pal was a very busy lawyer and appeared not only in the High Court but in tribunals as well, I sometimes got a chance to start the argument if he was not there in time. Unfortunately, he never discussed either his general strategy or his specific arguments with his juniors, so one was left to one's own devices. I learnt that Justice P.B. Mukharji was impressed by references to English case law and texts, and therefore referred to one such book in my arguments. As I could not procure another copy of the book for the judge, I handed up my own copy to him. In it was a beautiful picture-postcard of a woman and child, which I generally used as a bookmark, and which I had forgotten to take out. The oversight could have proved dear. I learnt later that I had been in danger of being hauled up for contempt, for trying to influence a judge who was much impressed by beauty. In the event, because of my total and expressed innocence in the matter, I was let off with a sarcastic comment and a smile.

★

In 1970, Premo went on a management course to America and returned by way of Japan. I decided to join him there as I had always longed to travel further east. I arrived in Tokyo and stayed at the airport hotel, as arranged. Premo was to arrive from Seattle within a few hours and I sat and waited for him in the airport lounge. I watched all the Japanese businessmen coming home and bowing to their children and their wives, who bowed back. It was all so restrained: no embraces, no hugs, no kisses—very different from the emotional scenes at home.

When Premo's plane did not arrive at the scheduled time I made an inquiry and learnt that Northwest Airlines had gone on indefinite strike. I was deeply anxious. I wondered what I would do if he didn't arrive as I did not know a soul and had no money other than the $20 we were allowed in those days under our foreign exchange regulations. After many inquiries from different counters and persons and after a number of hours, I was informed that the airline was trying to put its passengers onto other airlines, but we would not know on which flight, if any, Premo, would arrive. I didn't know what to do in a strange country where I did not know the language; most of the Japanese in 1970 could not speak English. But instead of moping, I decided to spend a little money on a train ticket and go into town on the monorail to cheer myself up, just looking around. I knew that you did not have to pay anything to enter a shop or the large multi-storied departmental stores.

I was so relieved when Premo arrived a day later that I fell into his arms and cried. We had a wonderful time and visited the different Buddhist and other sites. The tourist guide, a young woman, kept repeating to us that the Japanese were economic 'animals', and that work and remuneration were all that mattered to them. When I asked her how old a certain temple was, she replied, 'Very, very old. Two hundred years! I mean, the old wooden temple, which was here earlier was that old; but it burnt down and this present one is eighty years old.' Coming from India, I was amused at this, but said nothing.

But the Expo exhibition in Osaka was an eye-opener. It was the first time I had seen fountains dancing to music, or moving pathways or three-dimensional audio-visuals. I can't forget the one I saw and heard whose subject was water—the basis of life, white and thunderous while rushing down and then gurgling gleefully along as a blue stream. I couldn't see and experience enough of everything there, but before I left—and almost compulsively—I had to visit the Indian complex although everything I saw there was already familiar to me.

Premo's foster-brother Taro's son Vinod was living in Japan at the time, in a small town called Ishi on the island of Shikoku. We flew there from the main island, saw where he worked, and met the teacher to whom he was apprenticed. The teacher and his wife, who had been to the USA, invited us to stay a night with them. This was quite unusual because one is not normally invited into a Japanese home. As we passed the streets, we saw very small, very beautiful gardens, but no birds. Vinod's teacher's house was furnished a little differently from the others: it had a sofa-bed, which had been brought from America; we slept on that rather than on the usual futon on the floor. But the bathroom had a big tin tub, in which you sat and bathed, and this took some working out on our part. A fabulous Japanese meal had been prepared, including fried, crispy seaweed, which was very thin and got stuck to my palate, and raw fish, which I didn't want to eat!

The science or art that Vinod was studying under his master was an unusual one—chicken-sexing. Apparently, it required a great deal of skill. It was also an unusual sight to watch. Hundreds of day-old chicks were brought in a basket and each was turned over and felt to determine its sex. The males were immediately thrown into a cauldron of boiling water and the females were preserved. (This is quite the opposite of what happens after ultra-sound tests on pregnant mothers in India, where 999 female foeticides take place out of a thousand.) I was told that the idea behind chicken-sexing was that it was not profitable to spend money feeding and rearing the male chicks, as they could not reproduce. I found the process of throwing these chicks into boiling water quite horrifying, and it was not much relief that they were male and not female.

★

In the meanwhile, Vikram, who was at Tonbridge, was working very hard, but his subjects had changed. He was now studying English Literature, Pure Mathematics—and German, because he had discovered that Oxford University required a European language as an entrance requirement. He had also—because it required no special preparation—taken the SAT examinations and obtained a full scholarship to Harvard, though I was not too keen for him to do undergraduate studies in America, where I believed the classes were huge. He worked very hard, but it was not as if he wasn't having any fun. He competed in crossword competitions, compiled crosswords, took part in lectures and debates, readings and dramatics, and edited the school newsletter, *Grapevine*. He even tried to learn driving, though he seemed to think that the car would follow the road by itself. (After a while he gave that up and took up riding instead.) He spent time with Shanti Uncle and Aunty Henny in London and with our friends, the Semmenses, in Devon—and, armed with his six months' worth of German, went off for six weeks to hitch-hike in Europe by himself.

He wrote to us about his adventures and difficulties, but had to make his decisions himself. We were too far away and ignorant of the actual situation to be a part of the tension and trauma or to help him with anything but general advice.

One such decision related to his academic future. Not having lived in the UK for three years, he was ineligible for a government grant to go to university, only entitled to the £60 per annum which was the traditional stipend if he won a scholarship. But Mr McCrum was very keen that Vikram should study in England and, on the strength of his Harvard scholarship, convinced Corpus Christi College, Oxford, to cover his expenses and fees if he passed their selection process. In December 1970, having taken his university examinations, he went up to the college for his interview. He was enormously happy and relieved when one of the tutors said, 'Well, Mr Seth, we look forward to seeing you next year.'

There was a nine-month gap between admission to Oxford and entrance, so Vikram came home at the end of December. We were delighted to see him—and for a few months at that. He taught at the Doon School for a term and out of his first month's earning of 250 rupees he gave his grandmother 100 rupees and me a similar amount. So that we would always have something special to remember a gift as precious as this, my mother bought a very fine gold chain and I, a pair of gold and black earrings.

★

B.P. Khaitan and his son Pradeep Khaitan (or Pintu to his friends and colleagues) lived at 52/3 Ballygunge Circular Road; we lived at 52/5. They were partners of a very successful family firm of solicitors. I had been briefed by them in Patna when I was practising there. When I moved to Calcutta, they started sending me the odd junior brief. Pintu once asked me to give an opinion in a slightly complicated company income-tax matter. In order to preserve confidentiality, it was often the practice not to disclose who had sought the opinion, so the brief came marked 'XYZ Co. Ltd.—Querist'. I had little work and was very anxious to prove myself, so I worked very hard on the brief and gave my opinion. I did not receive the small fee marked on the brief in gold mohurs for quite a while, but did not raise the matter. I knew that the collection of fees by solicitors, and their proper distribution was always a slow process. I also hoped to be briefed by the same solicitors again sometime soon.

Many months later, Pintu came up to me at a party and said: 'I don't know whether I should tell you this, but when I sent the opinion you gave in the matter to the querist company, they were not at all happy and wanted a proper male opinion! They asked me why I had taken the opinion of a woman lawyer. I replied bluntly that I had taken the opinion of a good young barrister and was not concerned about her sex.' I smiled when I heard this, but was also a bit apprehensive and wondered whether I had given a correct opinion. Pintu continued: 'I then sent the brief to one of the best senior lawyers for his opinion, but I also sent your opinion along with the brief. It has just come back after a great deal of time. The senior barrister has only written a short note at the end of your opinion: "After due deliberation, the best I can do is to endorse the opinion given".'

I was relieved and very pleased. I also realized, however, how difficult it was for a solicitor to brief us young female lawyers coming up in the profession. (I was reminded of an incident when a client was taken to consult a woman lawyer, and protested, 'I wanted to go to a lawyer, not a woman.') Incidentally, my fee for giving the opinion was three gold mohurs, i.e., Rs 51, whereas the fee of the senior lawyer who endorsed it was thirty gold mohurs, Rs 510. But the client was happy that he had an authoritative male opinion.

At the time, in the Calcutta High Court, and possibly all over the country, there were not too many competent women lawyers. Very few of us had put in more than ten years in the profession, so we were not a force to be reckoned with. There were no women judges in any of the High Courts, nor had there been any in the past, except for Anna Chandy, who had been appointed many years earlier, in 1959 to be exact, to the Kerala High Court.

Michi bhai, who by then had become a senior executive in Andrew Yule & Co., sought my opinion informally on one of their legal matters. When I asked him why I was not being briefed formally, he told me that the company would rather brief a male lawyer. I thought this was extremely unfair. He agreed with me, but said: 'All things being equal—fees, standing, ability and expertise—almost every company or man, for that matter, would do what we have done.' He added, 'It is only if you are Equal-Plus that you can hope to make some headway.' I realized then what I had to do.

I worked very hard, but did not make too much headway. Though I was often despondent, I never stopped trying and kept on going regularly to the High Court and attending chambers. I knew it was like having your own shop: the day you didn't open would be the one when the lone customer or client would turn up.

But little by little I realized that we were not likely to settle in Calcutta, much as I loved it, and despite the fact that my friends and family were there. I knew that I, as also my work (whatever little there was), would be uprooted again.

This was because Premo felt that he was reaching a sort of dead end with Bata's. He had been very successful as a young factory manager in turning around a losing concern and making it a very vibrant and prosperous unit. Premo had suggested that the company needed to do a major recruitment drive for young executives, as there was a tremendous dearth of good talent. Thomas Bata and the Board accepted all his ideas as to how this should be done, and he received a lot of kudos. He was posted to Calcutta as Management Development Advisor to carry out these ideas. He had then been considered for a post on the Board of the company. Yet when it came to actually appointing a new director, they chose a Bengali with a pedestrian administrative record. The 'sons-of-the-soil' sentiment was gaining strength in Calcutta. Premo soon realized that, not being Bengali, his chances of making it right to the top in a Calcutta-based company were remote, given the public mood at that time. He was quite disillusioned, and felt we should move.

There was also a strong Naxalite terrorist movement

which combined with this antipathy for non-Bengalis. An acquaintance of ours was the secretary of the Tollygunge Club. This club also kept horses, and horse-racing was one of its activities. A young man who was employed to look after the horses slashed one of them with a knife. The secretary took strict action and had the police take him into custody. A case was started and he was jailed for a short while. On coming out of jail, he came to the club and shot the secretary dead in his office. The secretary was a North Indian and the young man a Bengali. The sympathy of the staff and servants was with the young Bengali as they felt he had been treated too harshly—after all he had only slashed a horse! This incident unnerved us all and was a further reason for pushing us to the conclusion that we must move.

I was very sad at the thought of leaving Calcutta. Despite its grinding poverty, the city was exceptionally vibrant and full of character; I loved the cultural atmosphere and way of life. I could speak Bengali and most of my good friends were from Bengal. I had been to school in Darjeeling and to college in Calcutta and knew its ins and outs well, as students do. Our first married home had been in Batanagar. Premo and I had often toyed with the idea of buying 52/5 Ballygunge Circular Road and making Calcutta our permanent home as my three brothers were also there. I loved the slow-moving, understated movies of Satyajit Ray and the Indian People's Theatre. Jamdani saris, mustard oil and fish cuisine, and Durga Puja celebrations were dear to me. I enjoyed the affection of the people, especially when I spoke to them in Bengali. I dressed and felt almost like a Bengali and Premo teasingly says that when he first saw me he mistook me for one.

The three years spent in Calcutta strengthened our family bonds. My brother Tuttu and I would often go off to see a movie after dinner. Since we lived on the ground floor and had a lovely garden, all three of my brothers with their families and Ma would come over for Sunday lunch, and we would spend many pleasant hours together. Each of us was doing reasonably well in our own sphere. Michi bhai was a senior executive with a British managing agency, Sashi bhai was reasonably high up in the hierarchy of the National Insurance Company of India and Tuttu was working with the Bengal Chamber of Commerce. Premo was the Management Development Advisor of Bata Shoe Company, and I was slowly making my presence felt in the Calcutta High Court. We each had friends from our respective professional spheres and, as I had been in college in Calcutta, I had other friends as well. As such, we had a large circle of friends and acquaintances and a lively social life.

One of the few new friendships I made during this period was with Ruma Ghose, a young woman lawyer of great integrity and intelligence. When I was introduced to her by Lily, I felt an immediate sense of friendship. Ruma was a Bachelor of Comparative Law from Oxford. Like me, she had lost her father early in life and she and her siblings had struggled to make good. We both hated wasting our time sitting in the Barristers' Library and gossiping. At first we didn't have much work and decided that we should write a law book together. We started working on a book on Indian tax law and made many visits to the National Library in Alipur. Nothing came of the research we began, as we both soon started picking up work. But the friendship has lasted all these years and now, to my great delight, Ruma, now Ruma Pal after her marriage, is in Delhi as a Supreme Court judge.

It was in Calcutta that we found our gardener Sona, who had been an art teacher in a village in Orissa. He stayed with us for thirty-five years, and practically became a member of our family. We helped his sons get settled in life. He and I moulded each of the gardens that we had thereafter. I, with my knowledge gleaned from gardening books, and he, with his practical experience and green fingers lovingly transfigured garden after garden as we moved from house to house. He was against entering the gardens for competitions as he felt that all our energies and those of the plants would then be directed to produce something beautiful for a particular day and not for our enjoyment and delight over a long period. I fully agreed with him, and we spent many happy hours together. Premo often joked about my love of Sona's work and the time I spent with him. All three of my children learnt to love flowers and trees and the peace of a quiet, fragrant garden.

Since we had decided to leave Calcutta, the question was where we should go, and there was only one viable permanent answer: Delhi. Both of us came from North Indian families and spoke Hindi.

Premo had studied at St. Stephen's College in Delhi and he had friends and family there. Some of our very good friends from our days in Patna, such as the Jains and the Mishras, had also shifted there. Then, of course, there was the Delhi High Court and, to cap it all, the Supreme Court of India. (I felt it was necessary for me, as a lawyer, to stabilize my practice in a single place.) There were good colleges and schools in Delhi, and Dehra Dun, where Shantum was studying, was close by. So was Panipat, where Premo's extended family lived. So we took a calculated decision that we would settle in Delhi, though I was totally unfamiliar with the city. For me the move was hard.

On 3 December 1971, we had a large farewell luncheon party in the garden. That night the Bangladesh War of Liberation broke out. It was, from the Indian point of view, a swift and successful war and ended even before the trucks bearing our luggage rolled out of Calcutta about three weeks later.

Emergency

I moved to Delhi first, to test the water. Premo followed more than a year later, when he was finally able to find work in the area. When I first arrived, in October 1971, I stayed with friends. Sarla Mishra had inherited a portion of her father's house at 9 Kautilya Marg in Chanakyapuri and agreed to rent it to me.

Curiously enough, several years earlier, I had had something to do with Sarla gaining possession of this flat. She and her sisters had been having problems with their two brothers, who had not wanted to give them their share in the house that belonged to their deceased father. Sarla and her sisters had filed a case and wanted to know if they were in a strong position. I gave a written opinion setting out the facts and the law and indicating that they had equal rights in the self-acquired property of their father. I also opined that the brothers' claim that it was a 'dwelling house' and thus could not be partitioned at the sisters' behest, was spurious, since the father had let out a part of it in his lifetime. Since her brothers knew that I was a good friend of Sarla's, I asked Lily Ray, now Mookherjee, provided she agreed with my opinion, to sign it so that it would have greater force. Fortunately, the case was amicably settled.

The flat was on the ground floor. It was large-roomed and had a small front garden. I moved there in early 1972 with Aradhana, aged nine, a lot of luggage and furniture, an old Ambassador car and one servant, but no husband. It was a difficult time; I used to go to Calcutta in the chair-car of the Rajdhani Express to visit Premo for one weekend every alternate month, and he used to come to Delhi the other month to visit us.

I had never lived on my own, and it was a new experience for me to be the head of a household for rations, rent and the renewal of licences. I realized how much of the responsibility of running a home was shared between husband and wife, and what a relief and joy that was. I really appreciated all that Premo had been doing, and sorely missed his cheerful presence. Luckily, he stayed with Sashi bhai, Usha and their daughter Ira in Calcutta, and so was not as lonely as he would have been if he had had to stay in a guesthouse or hotel. But the separation—which was to last a year and a half—was tough for both of us.

Aradhana was particularly unhappy at the move and felt that I was solely responsible for this separation from her loving and indulgent father. Life was not particularly easy for us, as we had to fend for ourselves, with depleted staff and accommodation compared to Patna and Calcutta. There was no company car or driver. I drove the old Ambassador myself, and Aradhana went to school on the bus. Being in a new school—Loreto Convent in Delhi Cantonment—she had to adjust and make new friends. I refused to buy a TV because I thought she was much more interested in other activities than studies, and feared that if I got a TV, even the little time she spent reading and doing homework would disappear. All this added to her frustration. Life improved somewhat when

Aradhana discovered that one of her school friends, Rachna Chopra, lived in the neighbourhood. She had company in the evenings.

The original idea was that we would live in Kautilya Marg, which we had done up at some expense and effort, for at least three years. Suddenly, however, when her husband Amar was unanticipatedly transferred out of Delhi, Sarla found that she needed the place for herself. There was no way that I would not accommodate her, and as soon as I possibly could. This was very unsettling for Aradhana. I started looking for a suitable place to shift to anywhere in Delhi, but Aradhana wanted to stay close to Rachna. While I was desperately looking around, she and Rachna started making their own enquiries. These two ten-year-olds would cycle around the area and check out if there were any flats 'to let'. Determined as they were, they succeeding in finding one, and thus we moved to 122 Malcha Marg, which was even closer to Rachna. My resourceful daughter had done what I couldn't have done myself.

It was very difficult for me to get the lease, though, as I was a lone woman—and a lawyer to boot. Most landlords thought that I would either run a house of ill-repute, or never vacate or, once having got in, would file a case before the rent controller and get the rent reduced. It was difficult to establish my credentials and persuade a landlord that I would not do any of these things. I was in fact quite desperate.

I asked Premo to come to Delhi to meet the landlord, who would perhaps then be satisfied that I was a decently married woman. When Mr Kumar, the elderly owner of 122 Malcha Marg, who lived quietly with his wife on the ground floor, eventually agreed to give us the flat on rent, he told Premo, 'Your wife has an honest face and I am confident by looking at her that she will not be rowdy and difficult, even though she is a lawyer.'

The first-floor flat on Malcha Marg was tiny and had small rooms. It was so small, in fact, that most of our large furniture would not fit in and had to be stored. The stairs to our flat were narrow and our bed and almirahs had to be hauled up through the verandah. We could only fit in a small dining-table for four, and when the whole family was together, we had our breakfast in batches. The only saving grace was the largish barsati room on the second floor, which I turned into my office, and a terrace, where I made a roof garden with numerous potted plants. Luckily, we were in a crescent and faced a park, so the flaming red tops of the gulmohur trees gave us great pleasure as the summer began; and later, with the first monsoon rains, we would get the wondrous scent of moist earth.

The relationship between a mother and a daughter is a very complex one. Aradhana and I had been close to each other, but when Premo came for short periods, we both wanted his attention and time. Aradhana, our Pooh, couldn't understand my desire for some privacy and our wish to have the bedroom to ourselves. She was resentful and banged doors to attract attention and often said hurtful things in front of friends and relatives. I thought that it was a terrible rift, that it had happened all because of our decision to move to Delhi and that the damage was permanent. All this made me very sad. But after talking to some friends, I discovered that this was the normal teenage tension between mother and daughter. Thank God, it disappeared as the teen years passed, and we had a proper home life again.

Aradhana's earlier school reports always found her to have 'a very pleasing personality', but added, 'though intelligent, she needs someone to push her to work.' At Loreto Convent, however, her teachers found her distracting the class and talking too much. They made it a point to tell me that I really needed to do something about it. I spoke to her; she told me that the school discipline was galling. If she so much as ran up the stairs, it was considered unladylike, and she was punished. She insisted that she didn't like studying there and wanted to move, because the teachers didn't understand her. We toyed with the idea of sending her to boarding school, preferably Welham Girls High School, since Shantum was at the Doon School in Dehra Dun. But she didn't want to go to a boarding school and insisted that she needed a change of school in Delhi. I gave her an ultimatum: either she could go to boarding school or she would have to improve and adjust in Loreto, as it was very difficult to gain admission to an acceptable alternative in Delhi.

Some time afterwards, she told me that she was going to sit for an exam to try and enter Modern School, Vasant Vihar, which had opened recently. I was stunned. I didn't even know of the existence of the school. I found she had done her own research and was all set to go. I went along with her wish to sit the exam, and she was admitted. It was a co-educational school, and its style of functioning was very different from that of Loreto Convent. It clearly suited her, and she flowered. She became a little leader and, in due course, House Captain. She always disliked, and still does, being told what to do. She wants to make her own decisions and follow them. Though I had always thought that the Convent was good for her, I was obviously wrong: her change of school did wonders for her. She knew what she wanted, and she went for it.

Our friends Shanti and Asha Jain, who had also moved to Delhi, were very protective of us. When I was suffering from a terrible stomach pain, they rushed me to a doctor. In fact, it was Shanti's doctor brother, Shama, and his wife Mavis, who looked after me, while Asha looked after Aradhana. We turned to them with many of our problems.

★

It had been over a year since Aradhana and I had moved to Delhi, and Premo was still in Calcutta, where he was now the Sales Manager of Bata. The strain of the separation was telling on us. After some time, Premo asked for a transfer as Factory Manager of the Bata unit at Faridabad, about twenty-five miles from Delhi. Though this was a bit of a comedown for him, it brought us physically closer and we were more of a family again.

When we decided to move to Delhi, Premo had said, 'You have made two moves for me; one from Calcutta to Patna, the other from Patna to Calcutta. I'll now make one move for you.' But I was not quite sure how much the move was to my advantage in my profession. However, the benefit of having practised in two High Courts, i.e. Patna and Calcutta, was apparent when I came to Delhi. As lawyers in both places knew me, I got some work from each of them in the Supreme Court of India.

At about this time, Ujjal Narain Sinha, who was now the Chief Justice of the Patna High Court, sent me a message enquiring whether I would be interested in becoming a judge of that Court. I was just forty-two years old and naturally very pleased at the honour that his offer represented; but I declined, as I knew that, unlike in Delhi, there was nothing that Premo could do in Patna.

From 1972 to 1978, I practised in Delhi both in the High Court and in the Supreme Court, first as an advocate and then briefly as a designated senior advocate. Khaitan & Co., for whom I had done some work in Calcutta, had an office in Delhi and started briefing me occasionally. When I came to Delhi, the High Court was located in Patiala House, with courtrooms and chambers that were neither suitable nor comfortable. It was only later that it shifted to its own modern, air-conditioned building, with murals representing the scales of justice, the symbol of balance. The

Supreme Court of India, however, was housed in its majestic building designed in its very architecture to look like a balance from above. Both these superior courts and their judges appeared independent and inspired calm and confidence. However, very soon the winds of change were to blow through them.

★

In order to explain the background to what was to disrupt and divide the courts and the legal profession, I will now have to don my lawyer's bands, and present a compressed account of a particular case.

In 1970, His Holiness Swami Kesavananda Bharati, the head of a muth or religious establishments in Kerala, challenged two state acts (dealing with land reform, including the management of religiously owned property) in the Supreme Court. It was likely that he would succeed in his challenge. This was because the Supreme Court had, in an earlier case— that of Golak Nath—already decided, albeit by the narrow majority of 6 to 5, that there were constitutional limits on legislation (indeed, even on constitutional amendments themselves) that contravened Fundamental Rights, including the right to property, mentioned in Part III of the Constitution.

Litigation is a slow process. While the matter was pending, certain constitutional amendments were passed by Parliament. One of these expressly empowered Parliament to amend any provision of the Constitution, including those relating to Fundamental Rights. This was passed in order to get over the decision in Golak Nath's case, but this amendment was itself challengeable.

When the decision in Golak Nath was to be reconsidered in Kesavananda, a bench of thirteen judges was constituted by

Chief Justice Sikri. It was a case of enormous import, not only for the momentous matters in the case itself, but for the entire balance between the executive and legislature on the one hand, and the judiciary on the other. The hearings continued for about seventy full days. Most other work in the Supreme Court was at a standstill. I had been in Delhi for under a year, and it was a wonderful opportunity for me to listen to the best brains of the Bar.

The hearings concluded in March 1973, and the judgment was delivered a month later, almost immediately before the retirement of the Chief Justice.

The thirteen judges delivered eleven separate judgments. Justice Shelat and Justice Grover gave a joint judgment; so did Justice Hegde and Justice Mukherjea. These were among the judgments that were not particularly favourable to the government's position. All the judgments were long and decided different aspects in various ways. A brief statement signed by nine of the judges giving the essence of the decision was also handed down. (It is believed that the others did not sign this because there was disagreement as to whether it reflected the exact decision.) It was all very confusing. I think that the very brief summary given by Granville Austin, an independent historian, in his book *Working a Democratic Constitution* represents the position as well as possible: I reproduce it here.

> The majority judgment—by seven judges of the thirteen-judge bench—overturned the anti-Parliament, anti-amendment rigidity of the Golak Nath decision; upheld the constitutionality of the Twenty-fourth and Twenty-fifth Amendments (except for the 'escape clause' in the latter); but it also ruled that an amendment could not alter the basic structure of the Constitution.

Despite the two amendments having been upheld, the Government felt defeated because the 'basic structure' doctrine, which became the bedrock of subsequent constitutional interpretation, limited its freedom.

Two days after the judgment, the three seniormost judges of the Supreme Court of India were unprecedentedly superseded, and the fourth in line, Justice A.N. Ray, was sworn in as Chief Justice of India. Mrs Gandhi believed him to be a 'reliable radical'. In the normal course, the seniormost judge, Justice Shelat, who was due to retire in two months, would have been appointed and thereafter, in succession, Justice Hegde and Justice Grover. All three immediately resigned.

Lawyers and judges alike were very agitated about this grievous blow to the independence of the judiciary. We were all in a state of high tension and the Supreme Court Bar Association passed a resolution condemning the action as 'a blatant and outrageous attempt at undermining the independence and impartiality of the judiciary'. M.C. Chagla, a very well-respected former Chief Justice of the Bombay High Court, who moved the resolution, called it a 'black day'. He stated that what was left of democracy and the rule of law was fast disappearing. A few lawyers who attempted to move counter-resolutions were prevented from doing so.

The anger of the Bar was directed in particular against two lawyers (not present at the meeting) who, it was believed, had advised the Prime Minister. One of these, Mr Kumaramangalam, continued to defend the supersession and said it was vital to take into account the philosophy and outlook of a judge. It was well known that Mohan Kumaramangalam, a Marxist, advocated a 'committed' judiciary. The other, Law Minister Gokhale, tried to explain that the supersession was not meant to affect the independence of the judiciary, and that anyway, the question of the relevance of the social philosophy of judges was nothing new.

About a week after the supersession of the judges, the Supreme Court Bar Association called a meeting to expel both these members. Mr Gokhale's daughter and son-in-law, Sunanda and Murli Bhandare, both practising lawyers in Delhi, were good friends of mine. Just before the meeting, Sunanda took me aside on the verandah outside the Supreme Court Bar Association Library, and told me confidentially and with great anguish that when things settled down and the facts came out, it would be clear that her father had not supported the supersession but, being the Law Minister, he was not at present in a position to speak out.

The meeting was stormy: tempers were high and loud voices were raised to expel both these traitors immediately. Their supporters were shouted down and not allowed to speak. Though I was a member of only one year's standing, I quietly and firmly raised a voice of caution and asked: 'Is it legal to expel members without giving them an opportunity of being heard. I do not know the rules; what do they say? In any case, an immediate expulsion violates all principles of natural justice, and as lawyers it hardly behoves us to do this.' At this point, some others supported me and said that such an expulsion would be open to challenge and might defeat its own purpose. It was then decided to first issue show-cause notices to Messrs. Gokhale and Kumaramangalam as to why they should not be expelled.

A number of meetings and discussions took place all over India and lawyers boycotted courts for a day to show their resentment at the government's action. Sitting judges, of course, didn't speak out openly, but retired judges and the three superseded judges who resigned did. Justice Shelat stated that the supersession would make judges suspicious of each other even in the High Courts, as they became aware that their opinions might affect their advancement. Both the

Bar and the judiciary felt it was a time for introspection and for finding ways and means to initiate a new appointment process for judges.

Most of the legal fraternity felt that the supersession of the judges was a sort of punishment for their not toeing the government line, and that Indira Gandhi wanted to browbeat the judiciary into submission. She was attempting to unbalance 'the power equation among the three branches of government and distorting the seamless web'. Granville Austin, from whose book this phrase is drawn, has referred to it as 'an act of extreme centralization of power. The government's vigorously proclaimed motive for the supersession was furtherance of the social revolution, for which an accommodating Supreme Court was needed. No doubt, several members of the cabinet were so moved, but the Prime Minister's motive was personal.'

This last comment refers to Mrs Gandhi's animosity in particular towards Justice Hegde, who had given a decision unfavourable to her with regard to the admissibility of evidence in a case pending in the courts which challenged her election as an MP, and therefore her very position as Prime Minister.

★

We hoped that matters would improve, but they deteriorated. As the months passed, power increasingly shifted from a complaisant Parliament through the Cabinet to the Prime Minister and her coterie and later to her second son Sanjay, who had no constitutional authority whatsoever, and to his caucus.

In September 1974, the government expanded the provisions of the Maintenance of Internal Security Act 1971 (popularly known as MISA) by ordinance. It allowed preventive detention for upto one year before review by an Advisory

Board. The total permitted detention was increased to two years.

In early 1975, Jayaprakash Narayan led a People's March on Parliament. He charged Mrs Gandhi's Congress Party with corruption and her with becoming a dictator. He made common cause with Moraji Desai of Gujarat, the leader of the Congress (O). There was President's rule in Gujarat and Mrs Gandhi had used this device to twice postpone fresh elections. Finally, Mr Desai announced an indefinite fast unless elections were held. Mrs Gandhi gave in and fixed them for 10 June 1975.

On 12 June, in the evening, Mrs Gandhi got news that her party had lost in Gujarat and that the Opposition would form the Government. On the same day, in the morning, she had learnt that she had been found guilty of corrupt election practice. (The corrupt practice of which she had been convicted was using the services of state and central government officers in her campaign.) This decision meant that her election to Parliament was void and that she was debarred from holding elective office for six years. However, the single judge of the High Court who had decided her case had stayed the judgment for twenty days to give her an opportunity to appeal to the Supreme Court. Politicians, press and the public at large hotly debated whether she should step down while she appealed to the Supreme Court. But she decided not to. It is rumoured that her son Sanjay convinced her that if she handed over power to any stand-in prime minister, he would not vacate his position for her later, even if the court exonerated her.

Sanjay and his crony Bansi Lal, the Chief Minister of the neighbouring state of Haryana, commandeered buses and organized regular demonstrations of Mrs Gandhi's supporters at her residence and elsewhere in order to create an atmosphere that she was indispensable to the nation.

The Supreme Court was on long summer vacation. The vacation judge, Justice Krishna Iyer, heard Mrs Gandhi's matter on 23 June 1975. N.A. Palkhivala, the noted senior lawyer, appeared for her and prayed for an unconditional stay till the disposal of the appeal on the grounds of grave hardship and irreparable loss to the appellant and the country.

From this point on, events were to move very fast. On 24 June 1975 Justice Iyer granted a conditional stay of her conviction. He allowed Mrs Gandhi to address Parliament but denied her the right to remuneration as a member or to vote or participate in the Lok Sabha debates, pending a decision by a larger bench.

In the meantime Sanjay Gandhi was hard at work in the Prime Minister's house. With the help of a few trusted persons, including Bansi Lal, he was secretly preparing lists of Opposition leaders who should be arrested. On 22 June, the home secretary, who believed in going by the rules, was transferred. He was replaced by a more pliant officer who would be willing to do as he was bidden.

Rumours were rife about such goings-on and the Opposition was pressing for Mrs Gandhi's resignation. On the evening of 25 June in the Ramlila Grounds at Delhi a massive meeting was addressed by Jayaprakash Narayan in which he asked for a nation-wide satyagraha protest to force Indira Gandhi to resign. He also exhorted people not to obey illegal and immoral orders. Shantum went to hear him and came back inspired and enthused.

Earlier in the day, Mrs Gandhi had summoned Siddhartha Shankar Ray, who had become Chief Minister of West Bengal, to her house; she apparently told him that the country needed shock treatment as it was moving towards chaos and anarchy and sought his help and advice. That night, she wrote to President Fakhruddin Ali Ahmed recommending that a proclamation of Emergency 'be issued tonight', and he obliged by signing the attached proclamation. A cabinet meeting was called for 6 a.m. the next morning not to consult its members but rather to inform them of the action taken.

Democracy was snuffed out in the small hours of 26 June. Sleeping politicians and Opposition leaders, including Jayaprakash Narayan and Morarji Desai, were taken from their beds into detention, even before the proclamation of emergency had been published in the Gazette of India. Mrs Gandhi claimed that democracy had given too much liberty to the people of India and that they were trying to misuse it and weaken the nation's confidence.

The freedom of the Press was extinguished the same night. Electricity to the presses of the newspapers was cut off at 2 a.m. on the 26th morning. This was to ensure that the detentions could not be reported. The next day, orders were issued by the Home Ministry prohibiting any reports relating to detentions without prior authorized scrutiny. Thereafter, the Censor Board took over, and the reporting even of certain Parliamentary and Supreme Court proceedings was stopped. Rumours were afloat that Sanjay Gandhi had even ordered the courts be shut down, but that Siddhartha Shankar Ray managed to have his order countermanded.

On 27 June 1975 the right to move the courts for enforcement of some of the fundamental rights guaranteed by the Constitution was suspended by a presidential order. Later, public gatherings were banned and the provisions of preventive detention made more stringent. Later still, the government suspended the right of citizens to move the court for the preservation of certain freedoms such as the freedom of speech. There was a pervasive atmosphere of fear. People were afraid to talk even to their friends, as they were not sure who might betray them. As news was censored, rumours circulated without check. People were arrested at bus stops for making some small critical remark about the Emergency.

Jail conditions were poor even before the Emergency. They became worse as thousands were detained. The arbitrary exercise of power continued apace. Without giving any proper notice to its inhabitants, the shanty-town near Turkman Gate in Delhi was demolished with bulldozers and bullets. Forcible sterilization programmes, allegedly at the behest of Sanjay Gandhi, brought fear and bitter anger to a huge number of citizens.

With the unlimited powers of the Emergency and with most of the effective Opposition in jail, it was not difficult to have protective amendments to the Constitution passed in Parliament. The thirty-eighth constitutional amendment was passed to debar judicial review of the proclamation of Emergency. Mrs Gandhi was panicky about her appeal in the election case in the Supreme Court. The thirty-ninth amendment was therefore also quickly passed removing the Supreme Court's authority to adjudicate election petitions pertaining to the elections of the Prime Minister, the Speaker, the President and the Vice-President. Such petitions could only be decided by an authority established by Parliament. This was indeed a very personalized amendment, and clearly the President, Vice-President and Speaker had been tagged on so that the motivation behind it should not look too obvious. The amendment also stated that election laws passed prior to the amendment were not valid and that judicial decisions holding elections to be void were also invalid. The newly-passed Election Law (Amendment) Act, the Representation of the People Act 1951 and the Representation of the People (Amendment) Act 1974 were perniciously placed in the Ninth Schedule (a device originally intended for land reforms), thus debarring them from judicial review.

Senior advocate Asoke Sen argued Mrs Gandhi's election appeal, as Mr Palkhivala had opted out when the Emergency was declared. Fali Nariman, Additional Solicitor General, the only law officer in town on the day of the proclamation of Emergency, had not been consulted about it, and had quietly resigned thereafter. Senior advocate Shanti Bhushan, appearing for Raj Narain, the rival candidate to Mrs Gandhi, challenged the retrospective character of the constitutional amendment and the Election Law (Amendment) Act as being violative of the basic structure doctrine established in the Kesavananda case. Asoke Sen however submitted that in view of the revised laws there was nothing to argue at all. A nine-member bench heard the matter. Though some judges expressed their views in open court that retroactive legislation was repressive, and felt that retrospective laws about corrupt practices in election matters were particularly unfair, they nevertheless decided that it would not be legally valid to strike them down.

But by a five to four majority, the Court, while holding Mrs Gandhi's 1971 election to be valid, struck down a part of the thirty-ninth amendment. They did this for different reasons. But Justice Khanna clearly said that placing certain elections beyond judicial challenge violated the principles of free and fair elections, which were essential in a democracy and were part of the basic structure of the Constitution.

Mrs Gandhi found this basic structure doctrine, which placed constraints on the Government's ability to pass laws, to be anathema. An abortive attempt was made to get the Kesavananda decision reviewed and the basic structure doctrine set aside.

She wanted to curb the independence of the judiciary and in December 1975, about a month after the judgment, a Paper entitled *A Fresh Look at Our Constitution—Some Suggestions* started circulating. It proposed drastic changes for the High Courts and the Supreme Court. A 'Superior Council of the Judiciary' chaired by the President with the Chief Justice of India and the Law Minister as Vice-Chairmen would decide all administrative matters in the judicial field. The members 'would include two judges from the Supreme Court and two from the high courts elected by secret ballot plus four members elected by Parliament and four nominated by the President'. This Council would have the authority to interpret laws and the Constitution as well as to determine the validity of any legislation. This Paper also advocated that all judges should be appointed by the President in consultation with the council of ministers of the central or the state governments. This would mean that the courts would become 'mere appendages of the administration' and in Mr Palkhivala's picturesque words 'mice squeaking under the Home Minister's chair'.

★

Numerous detentions had taken place in the early hours of 26 June 1975 and were still taking place all over India under the Maintenance of Internal Security Act. As a result, habeas corpus petitions were being filed in various High Courts. Despite censorship, information about these cases and their decisions was trickling out.

The government had raised a preliminary objection in all these cases. It contended that in asking for release by the issuance of a writ of habeas corpus, the detenus were in substance claiming that they had been deprived of their personal liberty in violation of the procedure established by law. This plea was available to them only under Article 21 of the Constitution. But since the right to move for enforcement of that right had been suspended by the Presidential Order dated 27 June 1975, the petitions were liable to be dismissed at the threshold.

This preliminary objection, despite the proclamations of Emergency and the various presidential orders and ordinances that were being passed to keep ahead of the courts, was rejected by the High Courts of Madhya Pradesh, Allahabad, Bombay, Delhi, Karnataka, Punjab and Rajasthan for various reasons. The State Governments and the Government of India promptly filed appeals in the Supreme Court. (The High Courts of Andhra Pradesh, Kerala and Madras upheld the preliminary objection of the government.)

On 1 September 1975, the Madhya Pradesh High Court had ruled in Shivkant Shukla versus Additional District Magistrate, Jabalpur, that habeas corpus as an instrument to protect persons against illegal imprisonment was written into the Constitution. Therefore, Parliament or the Executive could not abridge its use by the courts except by constitutional amendment. Some of the other reasons given by the High Courts for not accepting the government's preliminary objection were: that a detenu could challenge an order as ultra vires, that is, if, on the face of it, it had been passed by an authority not empowered to do so; or if it had been passed mala fide or for extraneous reasons or if the detaining authority had not applied its mind to the relevant reasons. They also held that the court's jurisdiction included knowing the grounds of detention, although the Government, by two ordinances—retrospective at that—had sought to deny detenus (or the courts) any information regarding the grounds of their detention, and had sought to exclude recourse to the concepts of natural justice and common law in detention cases. In some cases the High Courts granted certificates of appeal to the Supreme Court as they felt that the cases involved substantial questions of law, which the Supreme Court should decide.

All the Government's appeals against the habeas corpus rulings were clubbed together with Shivkant Shukla's case and came to be known as ADM Jabalpur. The Supreme Court Bar Association was full of rumours that Chief Justice

Ray would constitute a 'suitable' bench. Telegrams were sent to him from all over the country requesting or demanding that the bench be constituted according to seniority. Members of the Bar were extremely agitated and in a most unusual gesture, C.K. Daphtary, a former Attorney General, called on the Chief Justice and suggested he follow the seniority criteria. Chief Justice Ray was rather annoyed at this intrusion, but did constitute the bench accordingly, leaving out Justice K.K. Mathew who was due to retire in January 1976.

The hearing started on 15 December 1975. The case went on for thirty-seven days and the hearing concluded on 25 February 1976. On 28 April 1976 the judges held by a four to one majority that a detention order could not be challenged on any ground during the Emergency. In coming to this conclusion they obviously overruled all those High Courts which had decided in favour of the detenus. The bench of five included some of the brightest judges. They held that no citizen had standing to move a High Court for a writ of habeas corpus in view of the presidential order dated 27 June 1975. They also held that detenus could not challenge a detention order as either factually illegal or mala fide in law and that the provision for not revealing the grounds of detention was valid. Further, they held that Article 21 was the sole repository of the right to life and personal liberty against the State, and this article had been explicity suspended. However, Justice Chandrachud expressed 'a diamond-bright diamond-hard hope' that reported misdeeds of whipping, stripping, starving or even shooting detenus would not tarnish the record of Free India. And Justice Beg astoundingly pronounced that 'the care and concern bestowed by the State authorities upon the welfare of detenus who are well-housed, well-fed and well-treated, is almost maternal. Even parents have to take appropriate preventive action against those children who may threaten to burn down the house they live in'. As senior advocate and jurist H.M. Seervai said, while the High Courts 'rose' to the occasion, the Supreme Court 'sank'.

It was left to a single good and courageous judge, Mr Justice H.R. Khanna, to dissent and to uphold the right to life and liberty. This certainly was not easy to do in the fear-filled atmosphere that prevailed at the time. While doing so he reiterated the observations of Chief Justice Hughes: 'A dissent in a court of last resort is an appeal to the brooding spirit of the law, to the intelligence of a future day, when a later decision may possibly correct the error into which the dissenting judge believes the court to have been betrayed.'

Attorney General Niren De had argued that the rule of law existed only within the four corners of the Constitution and that natural rights did not exist outside it. Justice Khanna, referring to Article 21, which deals not only with liberty but also with life, asked him, if a policeman killed a person for reasons of enmity and not of state, was there to be no remedy? Niren De replied that, consistent with his argument, as long as the Emergency lasted, there would be no remedy, and added, 'It shocks my conscience and may shock yours.'

However, Justice Khanna held that Article 21 could not be held to be the sole repository of the right to life and personal liberty. In fact, it was an essential postulate and basic assumption of the rule of law in every civilized society. He added that Article 226 which empowered the High Courts to issue writs, was an integral part of the Constitution and could not be bypassed by the presidential order; and that rights created by statutes which were not fundamental rights could also be enforced during the period of Emergency. Further, there was no contradiction between the power of the government to detain a person under preventive detention and the power of the court to examine the legality of such a detention.

Needless to say, Justice Khanna paid for his views; he was

superseded by Justice Beg and not made Chief Justice of India when he should have, by virtue of his seniority, at the end of January 1977. But he was applauded by many in India and abroad, and his picture was later installed in the Supreme Court after the fearful shadow of the Emergency had ceased to cover the land.

★

I was immediately and personally affected by the decision of the Supreme Court in ADM Jabalpur as I was myself assisting in a detention case in the Delhi High Court at the time. Bansi Lal, who was the Chief Minister of Haryana and a crony of Sanjay Gandhi, had a mala fide detention order passed against Murlidhar Dalmia. The Haryana police tried to arrest him but somehow Mr Dalmia eluded them and hid in his house in Delhi. He then moved the Delhi High Court to quash the illegal order of detention and prayed that, pending the disposal of the critical case of ADM Jabalpur now pending before the Supreme Court, the execution of the detention order in his own case be stayed.

There was great drama involved in getting him to the court of Justice Rangarajan and Justice Aggarwal, who were hearing the matter, without his being arrested—especially since the police had the full backing of both Bansi Lal and the all-powerful Sanjay Gandhi. Luckily, their courtroom was on the ground floor of Patiala House, in a corner to the front of the building. After a great deal of argument by retired judge V.M. Tarkunde and senior advocate Soli Sorabjee, Mr Dalmia's arrest was kept in abeyance pending the disposal of the case. This was perhaps the only case of its kind where the execution of a detention order was stayed during the Emergency.

Mr Dalmia was an old and sick man, though arrogant

and difficult, and he attended the legal conferences and the hearings regularly after the stay order was passed. But the Haryana and Delhi police were always hovering around, as they feared he might escape. Over time, despite his arrogance and his dictatorial nature, I developed a strong sympathy for him. The case dragged on endlessly and even the members of the bench changed. On 28 April 1976, when the case was still pending, we heard of the Supreme Court's shocking decision in ADM Jabalpur. All the senior lawyers were in the Supreme Court at the time and it was left to me, in view of this judgment, to withdraw Mr Dalmia's case in the High Court. The Haryana and Delhi police, who kept a constant watch on Mr Dalmia, immediately pounced to take him away. Many of us had hoped, indeed expected, that the Supreme Court would have decided otherwise. We had thought that Justice Chandrachud and Justice Bhagwati would have upheld liberty as Justice Khanna did. But now, no challenge was permissible in any detention case as the preliminary objection of the government had succeeded. I was devastated at the judgment and felt like a pallbearer of liberty. All I could do was request the police to treat Mr Dalmia gently and take good care of him. With tears in my eyes, I said goodbye to him. I went home and wept at the loss of freedom and justice.

★

At the time it was not possible to contemplate that things would change again. The Supreme Court had shamed itself. The press had been censored more by themselves than by the censors; they were required to stoop, but they chose to crawl. Most of the bureaucracy bent over backwards to please Indira Gandhi and that extra-constitutional authority, her son Sanjay. Some people felt that Mrs Gandhi had virtually abdicated in Sanjay's favour and wondered what sort of influence he had over his mother. Even some of her supporters were worried that the Emergency was turning into his personal idiosyncratic dictatorship. Those rare souls who spoke out even restrainedly were either transferred to innocuous posts or else kicked up and out of the country. Our good friend Dr Ajit Mazoomdar, who was a Secretary in the Finance Ministry and had had the temerity to mildly query one of Mrs Gandhi's dubious fiats to her face, was suddenly sent off to Manila. But there was no dearth of people who were willing to comply and sing songs of Indira's greatness; the Congress Party President, Dev Kanta Borooah, went so far as to proclaim: 'Indira is India and India is Indira.'

After the proclamation of Emergency on the basis of 'internal disturbance' and the clampdown on the press, I decided to keep the newspaper of 25 June 1975 in order to be able to show my grandchildren, if I ever had any, that we once had a free press. I thought that the Emergency might never end. I started reading *Gulag Archipelago* to try to understand all that could possibly happen to us.

At first, the Censor Board did not censor cartoons, and cartoonists like R.K. Laxman in the *Times of India* subtly gave us some news, but soon even cartoons were censored. But some devious messages got through despite the censorship. On the morning of 26 June 1975, the Bombay edition of the *Times of India* printed an obituary: O'Cracy—D.E.M., beloved husband of T.Ruth, loving father of L.I. Bertie, brother of Faith, Hope, Justice, expired on 26th June.

Apart from the Censor Board, the government used every means to stop some judgments from being reported, even in the law journals like the All India Reporter. They even tried to prevent certain judgments from being pronounced. A very respected and elderly politician and contemporary of Jawaharlal Nehru, Bhimsen Sachar, had been arrested because he had written an open letter to Indira Gandhi less than a month after the Emergency was declared, in which he had reprimanded her for muzzling the press. He said that if her father had been alive he would have created the slogan: 'Democracy is in peril, defend it with all your might.' Mr Sachar's daughter, Bharati was married to the well-known and well-respected journalist Kuldip Nayar, who had also been arrested for his direct and fearless writings. She challenged both these arrests by a writ petition and, after hearings extending over many days, Justice Rangarajan wrote a very detailed and erudite judgement releasing Mr Nayar. (The government had meanwhile released Mr Sachar as he was unwell.) The judgment was based on the ground that the right to personal liberty pre-dated the Constitution. The government got wind of the judgment and in order to prevent it from seeing the light of day, sought to withdraw the order of arrest. It did so on Saturday, knowing that the judgment was due to be pronounced in court on Monday. But the judges—Justice Rangarajan and his brother judge on the bench, Justice Aggarwal—went ahead and gave their decision, refusing to be fobbed off by this ploy.

Both the judges had to pay dearly for this. Justice Rangarajan, who was a permanent and senior judge, was transferred to the Gauhati High Court in distant Assam. Justice Aggarwal, who was an Additional Judge, was not made permanent. Since he had been elevated to the High Court from the Delhi Judicial Service, he was sent back to the district courts a few months after this judgment despite the recommendation of the Chief Justice of the Delhi High Court that he be retained.

Although Article 222 of the Constitution provided for the transfer of judges, this was rarely done. From 1950 to 1975 there had been only about twenty-five transfers, in each case with the concurrence of the Chief Justice of India and the personal consent of the judge concerned. This had developed into a convention and in 1963 the Law Minister had given an assurance to Parliament that this convention would be continued. In the 1974 annual joint conference of the Chief Justices of the High Courts and the Judges of the Supreme Court it had been resolved to recommend the preservation of this convention. But suddenly, in May and June 1976 sixteen High Court judges were transferred and Mrs Gandhi announced national integration as the reason. As a result of these arbitrary transfers, some judges became reluctant to hear certain cases, recusing themselves for fear of reprisals.

Justice Sankalchand Sheth of the Gujarat High Court courageously challenged his transfer notification. The Censor Board had specifically banned the reporting of transfers, but information circulated in the legal community. His lawyer was the famous and fearless jurist H.M. Seervai, who informed the press that another lot of transfers was in the offing. It was believed that the government wanted to transfer many more than the sixteen judges already transferred. The figure was said to be anywhere from fifty-six to seventy. Apparently, lists had been prepared by Mrs Gandhi and her son Sanjay, circulated to the Home and Law Ministries for discussion, and sent on to the Chief Justice to sign or resign.

Justice Sheth had urged in his petition that transfers could be made only in the public interest and not to punish or injure or intimidate a judge. Further transfers without consent violated judicial independence and the basic structure of the Constitution. The Gujarat High Court heard the matter, upheld Sheth's contention and issued a writ ordering the government not to implement the transfer. The government immediately filed an appeal in the Supreme Court.

It seemed as if the Emergency would never end and that things would never be normal again. I was deeply depressed. Some lawyers told me, 'Wait and see, freedom will be ours and we will have all our rights back.' At the time it looked like a pipe dream. Indeed, the Lok Sabha term had been extended yet again till March 1978. But suddenly, on 18 January 1977, Indira Gandhi announced elections and released the members of the Opposition who were in jail. Why she did so is a mystery and a matter of speculation. Of course, she believed she would win; she did not know the extent of the alienation, bitterness and anger in the country. It was her own censorship that defeated her; she was not really aware of what was happening around her.

★

Vikram was away in Stanford at the time of the Emergency. But Shantum was not with us either. He left soon after the proclamation and was living quite a difficult life in England.

Shantum's last year at Doon had been a successful one. He had been Captain of Debating, which was appropriate, since he enjoyed arguing, and also a prefect in Jaipur House— a good but unpunctual one, according to his housemaster. He got a first division in the Indian School Certificate examinations, and was happy at the result.

In July 1974, he joined St Stephen's College in Delhi. He wanted to do Economics Honours, as he felt it would be good for a career option, but failed to get admission, so he opted for Mathematics Honours. He felt it was important to be in St. Stephen's College because Premo had studied there earlier. He needed transport to go there and come back and wanted us to buy him a motorbike. We thought this dangerous and got him a moped, a sort of motorized cycle. According to Shantum, it blew about in the wind and couldn't climb an incline easily. It was too slow for him; he could neither give a lift to the girls nor impress them. It wasn't cool.

Not happy with the situation, he was forever trying to persuade me to lend him my old Ambassador car. He had just turned seventeen and I told him he was not entitled to drive. He said, 'It is awful having a lawyer as a mother, because you only tell me the rules and what I can't do; whereas all my friends of the same age are merrily driving their parents' cars.'

After a year or so, he decided that mathematics was not for him and that he should study Boot and Shoe technology in England, just like Premo had done many years earlier. My Shanti Uncle in London, who had wanted to adopt Shantum at birth, was now only too happy to sponsor him. So off he went to Leicester in August 1975, and it changed his life. For one thing, he came face to face with racial discrimination for the first time.

Shantum was a good-looking young lad, who loved wearing smart western clothes. He was very fond of the good life and even went without lunch for about a month in order to buy a diamond stud for one ear. He felt that clothes and manners maketh the man and believed that he could charm the girls he fancied, which he did. But he had no idea about so-called Paki-bashing and was totally perplexed at the way the white lads reacted to the browns, spurred on by the National Front. One evening, when he was going out with a white girl, a group of skinheads assaulted him and spat on him. The police were worse than unhelpful. He was traumatized. From an easygoing charmer he became an angry young man. He joined the International Solidarity Campaign. After Steve Biko's death at the hands of the South African police, he involved himself in the anti-apartheid movement. Later he participated in the anti-nuclear movement and the feminist movement and was involved with trying an alternative style of living. He gave up eating meat and fish and gradually changed his mode of dress from shirt and trousers to kurta-pajama with a gamcha tied around his head. He became what he called a Cultural Activist.

We did not want him to come back to India during the Emergency. We missed him greatly and he us. For our twenty-fifth wedding anniversary he sent us a very large card, about 18 inches by 24 inches, with a picture of a cheerful little boy and girl, wearing a top hat and a white wedding veil respectively, with champagne glasses in their hands. He wrote a very long and warm message inside and post-dated it for our anniversary.

13th March, 1976

Dearest Mama and Papa,

Just sitting down here and saying to yourself that you are going to write a note is very difficult. So many little detached thoughts come into your mind but you don't know what to write. You want to say so much and yet nothing seems to flow from the pen.

Today is one day when I really wish the whole family was together. Bhaiyya I am sure is feeling as homesick as me today. I remember so many of the beautiful small little things you have done for me, for which I can't thank you enough, and just thinking of them moistens my eyes with tears of joy and happiness, at realizing what lovely and valuable parents I have and also little droplets of sorrow for not being able to be with you on this milestone. But then we will be travelling on and I am sure that I will be able to catch up and be with you at the next marking post. 25 years is a long time in a life, to imagine for someone like me who can only remember 1/3rd of my years vividly and yet you have done it, lived together beautifully and happily to achieve something you can be proud of. In a country like this where there are so many broken families and unhappy children, I feel I am exceptionally lucky to have a fantastic family where everyone smiles and where my thoughts can drift to whenever I feel lonely and down. You are parents I am so proud of, and show off about to friends, some of whom keep quiet, because they are ashamed to talk about theirs.

Today is one day when you will be looking back and thinking of what has happened over the past 25 years, but I can't remember most of those years and so am looking forward to the next twenty-five.

I have spent very little of my life at home with you except for the first five or six years of my life which I do not remember at all. But I think it was a very good thing you sent me to boarding, it helped me not to get too dependent on you and yet respect you and love you very much. Actually I think I only respect you for your achievements and not as parents. As parents I adore and love you.

I am very tired and sleepy as it is past 2 o'clock and thoughts are coming very slowly but I know I must send this wish and congratulations by tomorrow morning if it has to reach you near in time.

Well I seem to have dropped off to sleep last night and so am continuing now, the next day. I received your lovely invitation card this morning but then alas!

I can go on writing forever it seems but I must control myself and end off soon as this card will never get posted otherwise.

Please send me the photographs if you take them of the laughter and happy faces on the 13th.

I don't think I need to say it again but it always seems to flow through my thoughts into the pen that I miss you very very much. We have not seen each other for so long but then on the 13th I am sure we will be very close again as our thoughts are sure to meet and cross.

I better rush to the post office and hope that this monster reaches you safely and in one shape (flat).

Lots of love and as we used to write in Welham

x x x x x x x x x x x x x

Shantum

Shantum had saved some money from a holiday in Goa. He had left this in Delhi with his friend Aman Nath, whom he now requested to buy a silver bowl for us. Aman presented this to us on the right day after having it engraved 'TO MUM AND DAD, FROM SHANTUM OF LEICESTER. Either Aman did not know that we were not Mum and Dad, but Mama and Papa, or else he was giving Shantum an English identity. Aman also designed our invitation card for the occasion.

During the Emergency one could not serve a meal for more than twenty-five people. So we decided to have a lunch at 1 p.m., and also—for close relatives and friends—a dinner at 8 p.m. The next day Premo and I left to spend three days in Khajuraho. The erotic sculptures on the facades of the temples are exquisite; we spent a slow and unhurried time together, our mode of conveyance there being the humble cycle-rickshaw.

Shantum did exceedingly well at the Boot and Shoe course; he stood first and got a medal from the City & Guilds of London Institute in 1976, similar to the one his father had got in 1948. After completing his course, he worked for a couple of years with Eatoughs, a shoe factory, in Coalville, Leicestershire, and continued to stay in the poorer part of Leicester, the inner city area.

★

When I came to Delhi at first I was briefed mainly on the tax side in the Supreme Court. But gradually Umesh Khaitan started briefing me in other matters as well. I began to appear quite often as a junior with the senior lawyers B. Sen and C.K. Daphtary who both had their offices in their houses in Maharani Bagh.

One evening, as I was driving back home to Chanakyapuri from Maharani Bagh, I had a flat tyre. It was late, and quite dark. I did not know how to use the jack on my Ambassador and was wondering anxiously what to do. Finally, I hailed an empty taxi and asked the driver if he could help me. The old Sikh driver not only helped me change the tyre but categorically refused to take a tip for his services and time. He said, 'You are like my sister.' It reminded me of the young English bobby who had once walked me home to Finchley because I had missed the last connecting bus late at night and was afraid of a drunk hovering nearby. When I thanked the young constable, he said, 'It's nothing. It's my duty. I have to take care of you, sister.'

B. Sen is one of the few lawyers still practising who appeared in the Federal Court of India. But he was and is very young looking. The first time I went to his house and saw a young man playing ball with a little girl in the front garden, I could not, would not, believe that he was B. Sen. When he took me into his library, I insisted that I wanted to see Senior Advocate Sen.

Mr Daphtary, on the other hand, was a portly gentleman who looked his age and had a wonderful sense of humour. He was quick-witted and his style of argument was incisive yet informal.

I also appeared with the remarkable and versatile Asoke Sen. He had a razor-sharp mind and could switch effortlessly from tax law to criminal law to constitutional law to civil law. I especially liked appearing with him; he discussed his strategy and line of argument with his juniors in the conference, so one knew how his mind worked. He was very busy and often would not turn up in court, and I would be forced to take his place. Though arguing a case at short notice—or none at all—made me nervous, it gave me many opportunities to be seen and heard in Delhi, especially in the Supreme Court, which I otherwise might not have had. Since the Supreme Court is the court of final resort, clients, even if poor, want to get the finest lawyer that money can buy and do not want to entrust their case to juniors.

I soon started arguing small cases independently as well as assisting in large cases. During the Emergency, the senior advocate S.V. Gupte introduced me to the Rajmata of Gwalior and her daughter Vasundhara Raje so that I could deal with her matrimonial problems. He had watched me arguing in court and also felt certain of my integrity. He was confident that I would not get bought up by the other side as some lawyers in similar cases had been.

One important case in which I appeared was Bennett Coleman, pertaining to government control of the availability and price of newsprint and its relationship to the issue of freedom of expression. The senior advocate S.N. Kakkar had come from Allahabad to argue for one of the parties. When he saw me in the corridor outside, he asked me if I was Chanda's daughter. When I said I was, he told me that he was my Maama. I had known that my mother had a cousin who was a well-known lawyer in Allahabad. I was delighted to meet him so unexpectedly and to know that I looked recognizably like my mother.

In January 1977, I myself was designated a senior advocate. I was looking forward to doing some interesting cases, but unfortunately, soon thereafter, I was laid up in bed with acute backache, which was diagnosed as spondylitis and a slipped disc. So when the elections were called that month by Mrs Gandhi and all the excitement bubbled over after the long reign of public repression, I could not go to any of the rallies or public meetings. Friends and family would sit around my bed and tell me everything that was going on. It seemed as if we might have freedom again. We all hoped against hope that there would be a new government; that there would be no arbitrariness, discrimination or violation of human rights; and that the rule of law would be restored.

Disgraced

Premo turned fifty at the end of 1973 and decided that it was time he shifted to a job which offered him a wider scope even though the remuneration would not be as good as before. But this job had to be in Delhi, where Aradhana and I were. The State Trading Corporation of India, popularly known as STC, needed a director to look after and build up its leather and shoe division. Premo went for an interview and was selected. They wanted him to join soon; he therefore resigned from Batas, effectively burning his boats. But then, to our dismay, and despite their commitment, STC did not issue a letter of appointment, apparently because Premo had psoriasis. What this had to do with the job, no one knew. It was an unpleasant skin condition but certainly not life-threatening and did not hinder his work in any manner.

We were in a state of turmoil. We had no real savings except the Provident Fund with Batas; we lived on our monthly salary and earnings. How were we going to manage with children in school and college, and me still trying to get a proper foothold in legal work in Delhi, and the bread-winner without a means of livelihood? Anyway, after much cajoling and persuasion, STC saw the stupidity of it all and the appointment letter was issued. Premo took on his assignment with great zeal and zest and, in his usual manner, thought and talked and dreamt of nothing else. Little did he know what a rude shock he was in for.

I had just fought a case that had brought me my first five-figure cheque. I immediately went out and bought Premo a fine, large pashmina shawl. I remembered the time long ago in Patna when I got my first fee of fifty-one rupees. I had kept it in an envelope as a memento, occasionally looking at it and putting it back. I had thought then that if one day I earned one thousand rupees a month, it would be wonderful and, together with Premo's earnings, more than I ever wanted!

On Premo's joining STC we shifted to 17 Golf Links, our third Delhi home. We had the first-floor flat and the barsati room on the roof. There were three large bedrooms and a big drawing room with a large separate dining room. Our furniture, kept in storage for so long, was brought out and fitted in comfortably. On the roof we made a beautiful potted garden with bougainvilleas of many hues and a sitting area under a large, colourful garden umbrella. It was pleasant to sit out there in the winter, and entertain our friends. My office was in the barsati room and completely separate from the rest of the flat. The rent was 2,100 rupees per month, out of which I paid 700 rupees and Premo paid 1,400 rupees, recoverable from STC.

Premo had no experience of working in government or the public sector, and didn't realize that hard work and excessive interest were not appreciated, indeed, misunderstood. He was extremely outspoken and didn't suffer fools gladly. He often used the word 'Nonsense!', which led some people to believe he was arrogant. He pushed his staff to perform, as he wanted results fast. He was in a hurry to get things done. He had many ideas about how, instead of selling unfinished leather abroad for almost no profit, finished leather could be exported instead. Even stitched uppers, if not yet complete shoes, could be manufactured for export. Thus, the 'value added' in India would increase, and India could gain in wealth, foreign exchange and employment opportunities.

Premo arrived in the office earlier than the appointed time and stayed till late. This meant that his staff had to do the same. They resented this change, used as they were to the lackadaisical government style of working—coming to office late and then spending most of the day chit-chatting. One of the officers, who had apparently been suffering from depression, jumped from the fifth floor of the office building, and died instantaneously. It was shocking and sad. But the staff union immediately tried to put all the blame on Premo and started shouting slogans such as, 'Done to Death'. They claimed that it was the pressure of work that had led to his death and that Premo was responsible. We were aghast, and didn't know what to make of all this hostility.

Premo pressed on with his work regardless, and tried to get his staff too to take pleasure in the work itself and their sense of achievement. But another crisis soon developed. The confidential reports of his staff had to be written and Premo brought them home, spending the best part of a weekend and taking a great deal of trouble over them. He set out the good and bad characteristics of each member of staff, thus giving them an idea of the area in which improvement was needed. This was totally misunderstood; there was almost a strike. Premo was finally persuaded to change the reports: it was explained to him that even the slightest adverse remark could affect people's promotions and their whole careers; all the good words said of them would be of no avail. So a wishy-washy, un-thought-out, meaningless report which simply said 'Good' was better than one which said 'Excellent' but pointed out a minor flaw. No wonder nothing ever changed in the behaviour and working habits of government servants and public sector employees.

One of Premo's duties was to select and approve reliable suppliers for export of quality goods. One such supplier suddenly turned up, unannounced, early one morning at our home. After a few pleasantries were exchanged, he pulled out some packets of money and tried to hand them over to Premo, saying, 'You have just joined work. You must have a lot of expenses in setting up home; here's a little help.' Premo was taken aback. He bluntly told him, 'This is not on.' Late that evening the same gentleman turned up at the house again, this time with a much larger and fatter packet. He said, 'I should have realized that what I brought you this morning was too little and therefore insulting for you to accept. I apologize for my mistake.' Premo was horrified and told him, 'You are much older than me and out of respect for your age I am not reporting you to the police, but surely you know that what you are doing is totally wrong and unacceptable. Your products are good and they stand on their own merit.' The old gentleman replied, 'I am doing what I have always done and no one has taken umbrage the way you have. It is I who am surprised.'

Premo worked madly, like a man with a mission—that's how he had always worked. He didn't realize that in government or the public sector, people thought he must have a personal reason for doing so, such as making money on the side. I told him to slow down, but he pushed on regardless. The leather industry in the South was comparatively more sophisticated than in the rest of India; that of the North, concentrated around Agra, was still very backward. Premo tried to inspire the Agra entrepreneurs to improve, so that they could compete with the others and also export goods with confidence. He helped them with tools and machines manufactured in the country; he also felt that certain machines needed to be imported for effective improvement.

Enquiries were made and the machines ordered. Before the selection process and the placing of orders, Premo informed the other directors and the chairman, in writing, that the agent of two of the machine manufacturers, Kanwaljit Singh, was a very good friend of his. Some of the machines eventually found to be appropriate .were those of Torielli, an Italian manufacturer, whose agent was this friend.

Work went on apace, and the export of finished leather and shoe uppers grew by leaps and bounds. Ministries and ministers tried to bring pressure to ensure that their favourites were given orders. Premo would have none of it, and in his usual blunt fashion told them off. He was only interested in getting the job done well. Even the Prime Minister's Office tried to persuade him to give some orders to charming operator, Mr Grandi of Roma! Well, in June 1975 the Emergency was declared. There was a lot of pressure and many people toed the Government line, but we were not among them. Premo was not willing to do anything that was not based on merit, and he made no bones about it. He enjoyed the sheer pleasure of getting on with the job, and we valued our reputation above all else.

The Emergency was a trying period for some, and—as I have described before—a terrible period for others. Our freedoms were robbed from us, and our world was full of fear. When elections were declared in early 1977, we were relieved, though apprehensive; but when the Cow and Calf—the symbol of the Congress Party, run by Mrs Gandhi and her son Sanjay, who lorded it over the country with extra-constitutional authority—lost, we were jubilant.

We celebrated the victory of the Janata Party in March 1977 and were impatient that they could not quickly settle on a prime minister and form a government. It was a relief when they eventually did so, even though it was the acerbic and dour Morarji Desai who was elected to office. Imagine our surprise when we heard stories circulating soon thereafter that we were Congress cronies and that I was a regular visitor at Indira Gandhi's house during the Emergency. I had met her perhaps once in my life, at some large women's meeting. Being non-political, we had kept away from Mrs Gandhi and the people around her, nor were we close to those in power now. Some at STC, who had been extremely close to the Gandhi regime, fearing some kind of reprisal from the new government, tried to divert their animus onto Premo and got an enquiry started against him. He had heard some mumblings about what they planned, but did not take them seriously, as he knew he had done nothing wrong.

Imagine our consternation when Premo was suddenly asked to go on leave for three months on 1 June 1977 so that an independent internal enquiry could be conducted into the purchase of certain machinery, especially from Torielli. He was advised by friends and acquaintances to speak to the then political powers so that the enquiry could be halted. But, knowing that all his dealings were above-board, Premo was confident that nothing would come of the enquiry against him and that it would soon be over. He felt that it was completely unnecessary to speak to anyone and that the truth would prevail. I supported him in this view. But how wrong we were.

In this difficult time, both our great concern and our great comfort were our children. Vikram, after completing his schooling at Tonbridge and his graduation in Philosophy, Politics and Economics from Oxford, where he got a First, went in 1975 to Stanford University in California to do his Ph.D in Economics. He had a choice of colleges and scholarships in the US, but wanted to be on the West Coast, having suffered the English weather for so many years. He wrote his father a beautiful letter when he heard that he had been asked to go on three months' forced leave.

20th June, 1977

My dear Papa,

Thank you for your letter, I just got it. Needless to say it makes me very sad, both for the family and for the country, which seems eager to injure its most hardworking, capable and honest men. I was looking back at some of Mama's letters around the time of the election. She wrote—it sounds so strange now—"There was a great deal of enthusiasm and excitement here—after 20 months of a traumatic experience, when we were afraid to talk on the telephone, write letters or even discuss with acquaintances, our feelings and the injustices and excesses that were taking place, we are suddenly fearless and free. The night of the 20th—when the results started coming in and the trend was clear, people were dancing in the streets, in front of the Indian Express Office where the results were being put up and spotlight news was given. It was an exhilarating experience—just the same sort of feeling as when we won Independence . . . despite my back, I was there with the Jains, the Semmens and the Mazoomdars. Papa was delightfully happy and driving in a crazy fashion and so too was A Pooh perched on top of a tree with binoculars, reading out the latest news that was coming through." To read the letter and then to think what is happening now is to feel very bitter. "Suddenly fearless and free"—"just the same sort of experience as when we won independence"—"Papa was delightfully happy." When all we seem to have done is to have opened the doors to a witch-hunt, in which the powerful and the rich try to ruin the lives of the hard-working and the honest.

Papa—when I think of you working your guts out day after day from morning till night, not even taking weekends off, and with so much fairness that the thought of even accepting a meal from an STC supplier put you off—and then when I think of what people are doing to you now, it makes me almost ashamed to be an Indian.

You wrote, "For some unearthly reason I have been asked to proceed on forced leave with a threat of a possible CBI enquiry." The reason to me is not "unearthly". The forces are probably the very same whom you had to oppose in the course of working vigorously to improve the country's leather trade and production. These vested interests can cope with a quiescent and complacent bureaucrat. But once they find one who takes action instead of just letting things go on, there is no dirty trick they will not try to smirch his good name.

What can an honest man do against such dirty tricks? Just hope that justice is done and that the false accusations recoil against the accusers. Where money is involved, people are willing to become like animals— this phenomenon is hardly a new one. It is tragic that it should have manifested itself just as we were beginning to breathe freedom again.

It must be hard to face friends these days. Innocence is not enough, service to the country is not enough, sacrifice of a good job in Batas to do a more interesting and useful job in government is not enough. When there is an enquiry hanging over one's head— one might be pure as snow, but others will harbour suspicions and only among one's closest friends can one be truly at ease. When honour is gone, as you said, there is nothing to live for. But honour is based upon the truth. So long as you know that you have done nothing dishonourable, let the world say what it likes; the world says one thing one day, another thing the next. But honour is not thereby reduced.

I too have no doubt that the truth will come out and that this is "a temporary harassment". But I am sick to think what effect this must have on you, on Mama and on A Pooh. The clever stratagems of the dishonest have caused us all pain and grief—but when the enquiry is over, they will be shown to be the ones who have hurt the country.

On my front, there is little to say. It is my birthday today, but I feel a great sadness. Tomorrow there is a placement test for third year Intensive Chinese. Day after, the quarter begins; I will work hard, as you say, and not let such thoughts disturb me. By the end of the summer, I should be able to speak it fluently, read prose and poetry in it. Lately I haven't written any poems, but that is because my economics has been pestering me. I have just finished a 'comprehensive' qualifying exam in Economic History, for which I got an A, though I really think I deserved a B. In Chinese I got an A which I deserved (Modesty!) In terms of work, I'm looking forward to this quarter. By the way, I can now swim 75 metres of butterfly.

Here am I burbling on, when actually all I wish was that the family were together, so we could face this hard time together. It's strange that living apart for so many years should in a way have brought us closer together. In a way, I feel that the same is happening with Shantum and me. Maybe it's just that, quite apart from love, there is now mutual respect.

What's happening to you is terrible—but remember what Dr Johnson said: "A fly, Sir, may sting a stately horse and make him wince, but one is but an insect, and the other is a horse still."

Take care of your health. Exercise a little if you can. My lots of love to you and Mama and A Pooh. How is Mama's back? I will write to the whole family soon, but I thought I would write to you, because of what's being done to you.

Three months from now, the whole thing will be over.

Lots of love,

Yours,
Vikram

While we sat and waited for the truth to unfold, people who had vested interests in the corrupt system were hard at work. The allegation that I was very close to Indira Gandhi and on regular visiting terms with her was repeatedly reiterated, as also that Premo had made big money on machinery purchases. There were allegedly pots of gold buried by us in Italy and we had a beautiful Italian villa to boot!

On the morning of 27 July 1977—a date etched on my mind—I had bathed early and was about to go up to my home office in the barsati to prepare for a case. Suddenly I found myself surrounded by a group of men. They had orders to search our house and to seize whatever they felt was necessary, as a case was being investigated by the police. They were from the dreaded Central Bureau of Investigation, better known as the CBI. I was very upset as I had believed till then that the enquiry was just an internal matter relating to Premo's employers, the State Trading Corporation. I couldn't imagine that this was happening to us, who valued our honesty and reputation above all else. Premo was bathing, and they waited for him to come out. After showing us the permission to search and seize, the men fanned out into the various rooms of our home and took control of the telephones. They had posted plainclothes policemen downstairs so that no one could enter or leave. They then started looking through our cupboards and suitcases and examining all our papers. They asked me to hand over my keys and opened our Godrej steel cupboards, in which I kept my good clothes, some small pieces of jewellery, my household money and the bank locker key. They searched everything on the first floor. They also went to my office in the barsati room on the second floor and looked through my files. They read my love letters from Premo, my diaries and my children's letters.

I was devastated. I felt completely stripped and violated, my privacy destroyed. I felt ashamed and disgraced in front of my old and trusted servants, who always knew us as decent people and had looked up to us for guidance. I felt we were already being seen as criminals, without having been heard. What must our landlord, who lived on the ground floor, be thinking of us? We were not business people, who might be able to take this in their stride. We were honest professionals and proud of it. Why was this Janata government, which we had so joyously brought in, destroying us in this manner? Luckily, our impressionable fifteen-year-old daughter Aradhana had left for school in the morning, before the CBI team arrived. Thank God our two sensitive and straightforward sons were away in the UK and the USA.

The policemen took away Premo's passport, a few odd letters, income-tax files, bank statements, cheque book stumps, deposit slips and fixed-deposit receipts that they thought would be of use to them, made a list of those, and finally left. Fortunately, they did not leer and make rude remarks—as I learnt was often the case. I must give credit for this to the officer who was in charge, a S.N. Mukherji, Deputy Superintendent of Police/SPE/CBI. He was a sober man, who seemed to be a bit embarrassed at having to search our house.

After completing the search of the house, the police wanted to examine my locker in the Bank of India, Khan Market. I was very upset. I was at the time appearing as a lawyer for the Bank of India in a number of cases in the Delhi High Court and felt I could not bear the ignominy of having my locker searched. So I chickened out and did not accompany them to the bank. Poor Premo had to go with them and face the bank manager and the other officers. It must have been a horrendous experience for him: he neither knew the manager nor had ever operated the locker before, as it was used only by me for my jewellery.

Unknown to us, another CBI team was at the very same time searching the house of Kanwaljit Singh, and yet another team was going through the office of his firm. Apparently, the search at both their premises was much more unpleasant: while examining some of Mrs Singh's imported underwear and perfume, the police amused themselves by making lewd remarks.

We wondered what the case was all about. No one would tell us at first: it was all hush-hush. But we soon found out that on 25 July 1977 at 16.00 hours a regular case had been registered, RC2/77CIUC, for investigation 'under section 120B of the Indian Penal Code read with sections 5(2) and 5(1)d and 5(1)b of the Prevention of Corruption Act 1947 for criminal conspiracy against Shri P. Seth (Government Officer Class 1) and Shri Kanwal Jit Singh (Private Person).' The alleged criminal conspiracy pertained to 'Mr P. Seth, Executive Director of the State Trading Corporation getting a pecuniary advantage for himself and/or Mr Kanwaljit Singh from the purchase of certain machinery for the leather industry'. It was further alleged that these purchases were made 'in disregard of proper procedure'.

The investigation dragged on endlessly. The Central Bureau of Investigation gave priority to more pressing, politically pertinent matters. But to us each day's delay was an unbearable burden. We wanted it over with quickly so that we could get on with our lives and hold our heads high once again. I at least had my work to occupy me. It was particularly difficult for Premo, who continued to be on leave for over ten months and without pay for eight. He had no car and no occupation. He went for long walks and swam and played golf to expend his energy. Despite his anger and anguish, he took a very conscious decision not to drink any alcohol during this period as he felt that one could so easily drown in it. I am ashamed to say that I was of little help to him, as I suffered acute fits of depression. For the outside world, I went about my work with a brave face. When I met people at work I wondered what they were thinking about me and whether they knew about the case. Did they ask themselves, how can she defend me when she cannot even defend her husband? Has her husband made money? Is she honest?

On 19 July 1977 a Calcutta-based paper, *Business Standard*, brought out an article headed 'Rs. 30-million import scandal—STC Director suspended.' The facts stated in the article were not correct. We were outraged and wanted to sue the editor, publisher and owner. We consulted a senior criminal lawyer, who advised us against it. He said that this article had come out in a not very important newspaper, with hardly any circulation, and that if we filed a defamation case it would be reported in all the dailies and would generate a great deal of publicity and mud-slinging when the newspaper defended itself. Very reluctantly we took his sane advice and swallowed our sense of injustice. But what really hurt was when the wife of a very close friend asked Premo if these facts were true. If our friends could suspect us, what must others think, we wondered.

Premo was examined and re-examined by the CBI officials. He made endless trips to their offices for this purpose and to hand over the many letters and documents they required. They would not let him see their files or his own letters and notes, yet expected him to give complete answers to their questions from memory. Premo told them how his work and effort had made a great difference to the leather and shoe industry in India; how hard and unceasingly he had worked to further this endeavour; how even his worst enemies could not deny this. But one query, literally translated from Hindi, that kept coming up was, 'Why did you not fill the stomach of the file? Who in Government is interested in doing work? Work is not important, the important thing is to make sure that all the papers are in order. It doesn't matter if no work is done as long as the file looks complete. There is no punishment in Government for not doing work, problems only arise if you do.' What answer could he give, except to say that he had given up a much more lucrative job in the private sector so that he could do some good work for the leather and shoe industry and for his country?

We had believed that the enquiry would take a few weeks—at the most, three months. But the months passed, and it dragged on and on. We soon realized that our telephone was bugged and that our post was being opened. It was a real problem for us to keep our sanity and equanimity. Every morning when we got up from our fitful sleep, our first thoughts were, 'When, oh when, will this enquiry end!' Little did we know that the enquiry had spread beyond India. An alert had been sent to Interpol, based on certain speculations and rumours.

The rumours went something like this: Mrs Gandhi had huge monies tucked away somewhere. But where? And with whom? Vinod Parekh, the Chairman of STC, and his wife Lolly Parekh (daughter of the distinguished lawyer C.K.

Daphtary), were good friends of ours from the Calcutta days. Mr Parekh was close to the Congress Party, from whom he had sought a ticket to stand for the elections. He must therefore have helped Mrs Gandhi to park her money elsewhere. Mr Parekh, being a shrewd businessman, would not have kept the money in his own name, and must have given it to someone to keep. Could it be Mr Seth? We were appalled by these fantastical speculations. We, who had scrupulously kept away from politics (and from politicians) were being engulfed by it.

The worst was when we learnt that our twenty-year-old son, Shantum, who was struggling with his job at Eatoughs while trying to cope with the difficult racial situation in the area where he lived, was suddenly summoned to the police station in Leicester. He was quite bewildered as to why he had been called, and borrowed a friend's broken-down car to go there. The British police were amazed. Was this the young man whose father had made millions? If the stories circulated about his father were true, he should at the very least have had a proper car. The police also discovered that Shantum was living in very ordinary accommodation, which he shared with friends. They could not understand the situation. Where were the Gucci shoes, the Bentley car, the luxury flat and the flashy lifestyle?

The British police also contacted Shanti Uncle, who had lived in London for more than twenty-five years. He was like a godfather to Shantum. They wanted to check if he knew a Mr Kanwaljit Singh. He replied in the negative. The police, or someone on their behalf, had earlier tried to trick Uncle by telephoning his house and asking to speak to Mr Kanwaljit Singh, only to receive a surprised response that no one of that name resided there. The fact of the matter was that Shanti Uncle didn't know Mr Kanwaljit Singh. He had, however, heard of Tony Singh and met him a couple of times.

Fortunately, he didn't know that Tony was the pet name of Kanwaljit Singh. In fact, most people knew Tony only by his pet name. Only the CBI seemed to be unaware of the fact. Thank God for small mercies; had they known, they would have unnecessarily harassed my uncle further.

We presume that it was only after the British police drew a blank everywhere that they sent a clean report back to India. But the CBI was still not willing to close the case. As time passed, we came to realize why. One of the investigating officers, sensing Premo's sincerity and distress at the case dragging on for so long, told him: 'We are waiting for the "ishara", the indication, the political nod. If we don't find anything against you but are still told to proceed, we will have to book you under the provision of having assets disproportionate to your means. That case could go on for years, for it will then be for you to establish how you acquired each piece of furniture, cutlery, crockery, cut-glass, clothing, art, and so on, that you possess. If you can't account for everything, you could go to prison.'

I was terrified at the very thought of this eventuality and started preparing a list of our possessions and how we had acquired them, spending hours looking for receipts for our refrigerator, television, lamps and other items, and linking them up with old bank records. It was a very difficult and sad period of our lives. Even Premo, for all his sense of optimism, was losing heart, with nothing to do day after day, while not knowing when the agony would end. Despite that, he bought a 'Love is' poster to cheer me up. It read: 'There is nothing that we can't solve together.' And later, when things still looked gloomy, he added the words: 'When the chips were down.'

We are not superstitious or religious people, but during this period, out of desperation, we went to astrologers and paid regular visits to the temple in Khan Market and wore stones and iron rings and fasted as suggested—but all to no avail. We prevented Vikram from visiting Hywel Hughes, a very good friend of his who had tuberculosis and was in a sanitorium in Trieste, because it might be misunderstood. After all, Trieste was in Italy, and Italy was where we were supposed to have our villas and our pots of gold.

One or two of our old friends doubted us, most stood by us, some even fought openly for us. My friend Maya Mazoomdar, whose husband Ajit had returned from Manila where he had been banished for his quiet outspokenness by Mrs Gandhi, was very sympathetic and spoke to whomever she could in Government about the injustice of the situation.

Then suddenly one day, about ten months after the enquiry had begun, Premo was asked to take over as the Managing Director of the Handicrafts and Handlooms Exports Corporation of India, which was a subsidiary of the State Trading Corporation. This was obviously because the CBI had not found anything incriminating against him. But they still didn't close the case; they were waiting for the political 'ishara'. The irony was obvious a few weeks later, when Premo received an award from the President of India at a glittering ceremony in Vigyan Bhavan for good work done by his predecessor in the Handicrafts and Handlooms Exports Corporation of India—whereas for what he himself had achieved, the sword of Damocles still hung over his head. The CBI continued to summon him for unending interrogation.

As Premo's passport had been impounded, it was not possible for us to be with Shantum in Leicester for his 21st birthday on 15 April 1978, and this made us very sad. But his friend Bharat Kapoor went up from London to be with him, and he was happy. A month later, Vikram, who was coming to India from Stanford, met him in the UK. The brothers were meeting after almost three years. Shantum wrote to us:

I met Bhaiyya as he came off the train at Stafford as I had arrived earlier to spend the weekend with Hywel's parents. It was a most beautiful meeting and for the first half an hour or so it seemed as if we had nothing to say to each other and it was a real anti-climax, but once we got over the fact that we had not seen each other for nearly three years, it seems today there had been no great gap between our meetings and that our line of communication has grown to a lot of points of general common interest outside the family (which of course is an inexhaustible point of conversation). Intially he looked changed and very different to me but within the last 24 hours he has gradually grown back into what I knew. The one fact which is difficult to get used to is that he is nearly 26—five years elder to me. I think the gap was very obvious at our last meeting but not so now. For you, except Papa, the gap will have been 4 years. I guess you too will have an initial feeling of a change in him but very quickly realize that it is something you expect but is not there.

It's beautifully sunny here and I am lying on their lovely lawn with my shirt off. Bhaiyya is inside talking to Alun (Hywel's father) while he is playing the harpsichord. John (Hywel's brother) and a friend of his are here, too, for this weekend and so it is quite a full house. Hywel is still in Italy.

It was wonderful for Premo and me to know that there was such a close bond between the brothers and that our family ties were still tight despite the rifts of space and time.

Two months later, Premo wrote to the Director of the CBI regarding the inordinate delay of the enquiry proceedings and the return of his passport. He had wanted his passport earlier, but had been advised by the investigating officer not to ask for it, as a trip to Europe was bound to be misconstrued, even if it were for personal reasons and to help sort out some of Shantum's emotional problems.

What the enquiry did to us was horrendous. But what it—and events like it—did for the bureaucratic system was worse. It made people like us realize the futility of ideals and honest hard work. It made bad bureaucrats firmer in their belief that not working was the better option. It made them spend more time thinking about their transfers and promotions rather than the work that needed to be done, and made them into still more obsessive file-pushers. It made them realize that they could not be punished for shirking, but could be punished for doing solid work. The safest option was not to do anything worthwhile but to appear to be working and endlessly writing reports or attending committees.

It made a family like ours, which believed in working for the good of the country, think again. Premo was not willing to resign before he was reinstated. But once he was cleared, I insisted that he resign and look for private employment. I knew he could not function in the government system where the only consideration was keeping the files in order. Premo is a karmayogi and is happiest getting on with the job. Some people in government like Vinod Pande, the then Additional Secretary, Commerce, who knew the calibre of Premo's work and the difference it had made to the leather industry, tried to persuade him to stay on, but I was adamant. I did not wish our family to go through such an experience ever again. It had injured our reputation, which we valued beyond all else. It had kept our family apart, as we could not visit our sons or they us. It had hindered our young teenage daughter from enjoying life in the way she should have. The laughter in our house had for these many months been replaced by apprehension and fear. I would not wish my worst enemy to have to go through such a trauma.

My Lady or My Lord?

In early March 1978, when I was sitting in the Supreme Court Bar Association Library, I received a message that Mr Justice Chandrachud, who had become the Chief Justice of India a month earlier, wanted me to come to his chambers. I was surprised and—being somewhat anxious by nature—wondered if I had done anything wrong for which I was to be admonished. My sense of unease was quickly allayed; he welcomed me warmly. He said that for some time he had been thinking of recommending a woman to be appointed as a judge in the Delhi High Court and he could think of no one better. He asked me if Chief Justice Tatachari of the Delhi High Court knew me. I told him I had appeared in his court on a number of occasions and so I presumed that he did, though I had no personal contact with him. Justice Chandrachud asked me to send him a brief bio-data, which I did.

A few days later, Chief Justice Tatachari telephoned me. Speaking in a low and confidential tone, he requested me to come to his house that evening at about 5 p.m. He also added that I should come alone. I didn't quite know what that meant. Was it that I should not even take the driver? I decided to follow his advice literally and drove my Ambassador to his house at the appointed time.

I was ushered into his drawing room by a servant and asked to sit down. I sat at one end of a long four-seater sofa. After a short while, Chief Justice Tatachari entered, his ever-present large white U-shaped sandal-paste tika adorning his forehead. He was still in his court clothes, though without his bands and black coat. He sat down at the other end of the sofa, as if almost embarrassed to be alone with me in the room. Speaking in hushed tones from that distance he said that he was considering sending up my name for judgeship and wanted to know my reaction. I responded that we had been brought up never to refuse an honour when offered. Tatachari insisted that I should not mention the matter to anyone. I assured him I wouldn't, except to my husband. He agreed to that, but added that in case I became a judge I should not be influenced by my husband while deciding matters!

A few weeks later, Chief Justice Tatachari telephoned me and asked me whether I drank. I thought this was rather a strange query but put it down to his conservative views on women. I was a little peeved. Soon I learnt from him that it was not his query nor was it aimed specifically at me. It was based on a letter from the Law Minister, enquiring whether the persons recommended by him for judgeship took alcoholic drinks. If they did, they were required to give an undertaking to refrain. It was a Janata Party fad, or maybe a fad of the then Prime Minister Morarji Desai, who believed strictly in prohibition—though he drank his own urine as a form of therapy. He was certainly a killjoy! I knew that many of the sitting judges, both in the Supreme Court of India and in the various High Courts did drink and I wondered what would become of them. I also knew that Narinder Nath Goswamy, whose name was being considered for judgeship along with mine, used to drink. My husband certainly had a couple of drinks every evening and I thought nothing wrong of it. I hardly ever had a drink, not because it was taboo, but because I did not much care for it. I preferred nimbu pani in summer and soup in winter. On a rare social occasion I would have a glass of sherry or champagne. I had no intention of voluntarily giving this up, not because I could not do without it, but because I felt that if I could prejudice my own freedom in order to become a judge, I might be a poor protector of the freedom of other people later on. I did not want to give an undertaking and sign away my right. If I was not appointed a judge because of this, so be it. However, if a law required all judges to abstain from alcoholic drinks, I would abide by it. After much deliberation, I penned a brief letter to Chief Justice Tatachari to this effect. I wondered how Narinder Goswamy had got round it and what he had written. Many months later I asked him and he said quite casually, 'I wrote that I wouldn't drink in public.'

I did not hear anything from anyone for a long time after my conversation with Chief Justice Tatachari, nor did I mention the matter even to my mother or my children. But very little remains secret in Delhi. One evening at a large wedding party Justice Rajindar Sachar saw me, introduced me to his wife and started telling her that I would be joining him on the bench. I didn't know how to react and what to say and just smiled sheepishly.

The issue of women judges being appointed to the High Courts had been under discussion for a while. It became even more prominent in 1975, which was Women's International Year. In fact, till then, there had been only one woman High Court judge, Justice Anna Chandy. She had joined the Kerala Judicial Service as a munsif in 1938. In the course of time she had become a district judge, and later, at the age of fifty-four, had been appointed a judge of the Kerala High Court. This was as far back as 1959. Between then and a little before 1975, when the issue came alive, not much had happened. In the second half of 1974, a message was sent to me by Chief Justice Nand Lall Untwalia of the Patna High Court, sounding me out on whether I would be interested in an appointment there. As before, when Chief Justice Ujjal Narain Sinha had sent out a feeler in the summer of 1972, I again declined, and for the same reason: there was nothing that my husband could do in Patna, and we had decided to settle in Delhi.

Under the Constitution, in order to qualify for appointment as a judge of a High Court a person has to be a citizen of India and has to have completed ten years of judicial service or have practised for ten years in one or more High Court; a mixture of judicial service and practice for that period would also suffice. An academic or jurist of ten years' standing qualifies as well. Normally, however, a person is considered for judgeship only after fifteen years or so.

In 1975, there were quite a few young women of varying age and calibre practising law in Delhi. Among others, Urmila Kapur and I qualified under the criteria described above. Urmila had been practising in Delhi for many years. I had only practised there for four; the other thirteen years of my practice had been ten years in Patna and three in Calcutta. Mrs Kapur had a reasonable practice and was also the President of the very active Delhi branch of the Indian Federation of Women Lawyers. Urmila had helped to translate some documents from Hindi into English for Indira Gandhi's election case. She did this confidentially, at the request of Sunanda Bhandare, who was the daughter of the Law Minister. It is believed that Prime Minister Indira Gandhi and Law Minister Gokhale had set the ball rolling for her appointment in late 1976, but the elections intervened before the process could be completed and nothing came of it. The Law

Minister and the Chief Justice of India were different in early 1978 when the matter regarding the appointment of a woman judge was taken up again. Such is the path of fate and destiny.

★

On 25 July 1978 Chief Justice Tatachari swore me in as a judge. Narinder Nath Goswamy took the oath just after me on the same day. I was not aware of the high drama that had taken place around the sequence of our swearing in. It appears that my name was placed first and his second, since I was a designated senior advocate and he was not. But, being the son of a retired judge, Goswamy really understood the importance of seniority. I was oblivious to all these nuances, not having a soul from the family in the legal profession and not having discussed the matter with anybody, just as I had promised Chief Justice Tatachari. Goswamy got to know a few days earlier that he was to be sworn in second and immediately went to meet the Chief Justice of India. He told him that he was older than me and also of longer standing at the Bar and should be sworn in first or not at all. Chief Justice Chandrachud pacified him and said that since there was no likelihood of either of us becoming a High Court Chief Justice it didn't really matter and in any case it would now be difficult to change the order of appointment. He persuaded him to go ahead and take the oath.

When the Registrar of the Delhi High Court came to see me a few days before the actual swearing-in to get proof of my birth and my barrister's certificate, he asked me whether I wanted to take the oath in the name of God or make a solemn affirmation instead. I was perplexed, and asked him what others did. He said it was a matter of choice, but that as far as he was aware people invariably swore in the name of

God. I had been quite religiously inclined in my childhood but I was then going through a phase of questioning; I was not an atheist so much as an agnostic. I decided to make a solemn affirmation, while Narinder took his religious oath immediately afterwards. The oath is set out in the Third Schedule to the Constitution of India. The words are unambiguous, demanding and—in a strange way—intimate:

> I, (Leila Seth,) having been appointed a Judge of the High Court of Delhi do solemnly affirm that I will bear true faith and allegiance to the Constitution of India as by law established, that I will uphold the sovereignty and integrity of India, that I will duly and faithfully and to the best of my ability, knowledge and judgment perform the duties of my office without fear or favour, affection or ill-will and that I will uphold the Constitution and the laws.

When I repeated these words after Chief Justice Tatachari in a loud and clear voice, I experienced a tingling sensation, a mixture of excitement and fear. My conscience was alerted, especially by the expression 'without fear or favour, affection or ill-will'. I sensed the onerous responsibility of being a judge. It was an awesome power, almost like being God: a judge could take away a person's freedom, and indeed even his life.

Since the swearing-in was to take place in the Chief Justice's chamber and there were two of us being sworn in, I was asked not to bring more than five persons for it. Only my immediate family accompanied me: my mother (who shed a few tears at the thought of my father), Premo, Vikram, Aradhana, my sister-in-law Usha and ten-year-old Ira (whom I chose not to count in the quota). Shantum was away in England and was sorry that he could not be present, but he did his bit by sending me special stiff collars from there. I was at first very keen to have them, but I eventually gave them away to a male colleague as I found the double tension of wearing stiff collars and being a new judge too much for me.

The normal convention was that the new judge, after being sworn in, sat in court with the Chief Justice to benefit from his experience, and so I should have, as I was sworn in first. But there had been a great deal of discussion about this in the judges' lunch room a few days earlier. Chief Justice Tatachari, with his conservative ideas, was apprehensive about sitting with a woman, as it meant not only being together in open court, but also being alone in closed chambers thereafter for discussion and decision. His remark, passed on to me, was: 'Oh baba, no! I can't do it.' It was then decided that I would sit with the second senior-most puisne judge, Prakash Narain, who was westernized and suave and had impeccable manners. (Apparently, there had been a guessing game among the lawyers as to whom I would be sitting with and he was far and away the favourite.)

Justice Prakash Narain was charming and relaxed and put me at ease. He also subtly taught me how to change from being a player to being an umpire. I was used to arguing and doing the best for my client and case and then 'letting the damn judge decide'. I soon realized that I was now that damn judge; and that the tremendous responsibility stopped with me.

Another matter that had been hotly debated by the judges till the last moment was whether Narinder Goswamy and I were to be welcomed by the Bar when we sat in our respective courts, he with the Chief Justice and I with Justice Prakash Narain. This had been the normal convention. The President of the Bar Association felicitated a judge in open court on his elevation and bade farewell and eulogized him on his last day, and the judge responded on both occasions. But a few months earlier, when Justice P.S. Safeer retired, the Bar, which had been particularly unhappy at his behaviour with them in court, had in an unusual and very unexpected move decided not to bid him farewell in open court. They informed the Chief Justice about this. The judges felt that this was a slap in the face of the retiring judge and that it should not be left to lawyers to pick and choose in this manner. The Delhi High Court judges found a way out of the embarrassment by deciding that in future no judge would either accept a welcome or a farewell speech. Some of the judges were unhappy with this decision and felt that it should be reconsidered, especially since a woman was joining their ranks for the first time. But after a heated and long debate it was agreed that it was more in keeping with the judges' dignity not to allow a situation to arise where the Bar could decide to censure a judge in this manner. So there was no open court welcome for me or my colleague, Justice Goswamy.

A woman judge in the capital was certainly news, and after my appointment was announced, some reporters asked me to give them interviews. I desisted from doing so, as I had not yet been sworn in. But after I had taken the oath, I was inundated with requests, and acquiesced. I was the first woman to be appointed to the Delhi High Court, and my appointment received wide publicity. I was terrified that some reporter would ruin it all by writing about the enquiry still pending against Premo. But luckily the gossip columnists didn't seem to be aware of it.

One of the visitors who came to congratulate me was the wise and witty octogenarian, senior advocate C.K. Daphtary. After looking me up and down, he said, 'My dear, my dear, now that you have become a judge you are expected to broaden your mind and not your hips. Be careful!' He also gave me some sagacious advice: 'There are four types of judge—the timid judge, the dithering judge, the academic judge and the forthright judge. Be forthright.' And this is what I attempted to be.

The Delhi branch of the Indian Federation of Women Lawyers very generously threw a large party in my honour. Ironically, the president of this branch of the Federation was still Urmila Kapur. I was overawed with all this attention and didn't quite know how to cope. In fact, at this party, I was waiting for the Chief Justice of India to leave before departing, while he in turn was waiting for me to go first. I was unaware of this till someone pointed it out and I departed hastily.

I received letters of congratulation from colleagues all over India, and even some from as far away as Australia and Canada. But the ones that meant the most to me were the very affectionate letters I received from the Patna judges and lawyers, even though I had moved away from there as far back as 1968. While they wished me well, they expressed their sadness that I was not in the Patna High Court, where I could have gone some five years earlier.

I also received a loving and effusive letter from my low-key and quiet brother Sashi from Calcutta. I reproduce it because it expresses our family affection and clarifies the sentiments we felt towards our mother, who double-parented us from 1942. Sashi addressed me as Trillip whenever he felt especially affectionate; he had changed my name in stages from Leila to Lilly to Trilly and finally to Trillip.

My dear Trillip,

It was wonderful speaking to all of you last night and to learn that you will be sworn in as a Judge of the Delhi High Court this morning by the Chief Justice.

Throughout the night my mind has been flooded with old memories of our childhood and I know how proud and happy Daddy would have been at this achievement and recognition. Ma has with indomitable courage and fortitude brought us up in a difficult world and has given us a sense of values for us to cherish and to exercise in our daily life. For Ma, and for all of us in the family, it is a red letter day and we are proud of you and love you.

I know that if you had accepted you would have been a Judge of the Patna High Court five years ago—but this is different in that you are accepting a Judgeship after achieving an eminent position as a barrister as a Senior Counsel of the Supreme Court.

The last two years have been the most difficult ones for you and Premo and it is only because of the strength of purpose, courage and tenacity of both of you that your spirit has not been broken and you have passed these days without losing your balance. I hope and pray that this ordeal will soon be over and, in the years to come, it will be remembered only as a bad dream.

I wish I was with all of you today for your swearing in. It is really good that Vikram is there and that Usha and Ira are at Delhi at this time. I am confident that you will make a name on the bench and that you will in a few years be elevated to the Supreme Court.

I wish I could have met Vicky once again before he returns to the States but it may not be possible.

My lots of love to you and Premo, Ma, Vicky and Aradhana.

Affly,
Sashi

My family was delighted at my becoming a judge and I thought of how proud my father would have been. Despite coming from a very traditional family, he believed deeply in the equality of girls and boys. In the few years we had had together, he gave me all the freedom and opportunity to develop according to my abilities and wishes. Vikram wanted to ensure that this equality was maintained not only in substance but also in form and advised me to insist on being referred to as Ms Justice Leila Seth and not Mrs Justice Leila Seth. He argued that when a man used 'Mr', it did not indicate whether he was a bachelor or a married man. I was persuaded, though possibly as much by his argument, which appealed cunningly to my sense of order, that 'Mrs' would jut out in a neat columnar list of judges whereas 'Ms' would not. I instructed the High Court registry that since male judges were referred to as Mr Justice I should be referred to as Ms Justice. That was all right when written down, but people had to be taught how to pronounce the word 'Ms', unfamiliar at the time in India. It was regularly confused with 'Miss'.

In court the lawyers addressed me as 'My Lord', just as they did my brother judges. I was asked whether this was acceptable. I told them this was fine by me, as I knew they used the expression not out of any great respect, but only as a breather for their thoughts. At one time, when some lawyers had objected to the term on the grounds that it smacked of colonial and feudal times, the Supreme Court gave them permission to use the expression 'Your Honour'. But most lawyers continued to punctuate their arguments with the words, 'My Lord': it was just a matter of habit.

It was only when I sat with Justice T.P.S. Chawla, who was a barrister and a stickler for form, that he insisted that I be addressed correctly. Justice Denning in England had issued practice directions and said that the court should be addressed as 'My Lord' or 'My Lady' as the case may be. Since both of us were barristers and spoke the Queen's English with a good pronunciation and were particular about decorum and integrity, we were referred to behind our backs as the English bench. Once, when I asked a question of a lawyer in court and he started replying, 'My Lord . . .', Justice Chawla interrupted him and requested him to 'address the court correctly'. The lawyer was foxed: he had no idea what to do. When Justice Chawla repeated his refrain and later explained what was expected of him, the lawyer decided to turn his face towards Justice Chawla and answer the question as if it had emanated from him. He thought that that was the easier way out: address the Lord and forget the Lady. I think it was a very rare occasion when I was addressed as My Lady.

On the other hand, whenever I was being introduced to outsiders by most other judges, they would say, 'Meet our new lady judge.' I asked them, 'Why don't you introduce Justice Narinder Goswamy as our new gentleman judge. Surely my sex is apparent; I am not a new lady judge but a new judge.' But my colleagues, who were quite proud of having me among their number, couldn't understand what I was fussing about.

Not that their pride was untinged by chauvinism. In fact, at the very next celebration that was to be organized by the High Court, the judges jumped up and said with one accord, 'Now that we have a woman judge, we do not have to worry about the catering; she will make all the tea arrangements.' I put my foot down and said I certainly would not and that whoever was doing it earlier should continue to do so. It was quite enough that I took care of all this at home.

Interestingly, women lawyers too had expectations of me as a judge. They were rather surprised that I did not favour women litigants. In fact, Lily Thomas took umbrage at this when she argued a matter challenging a provision of the Indian Divorce Act 1898 pertaining to Christians, where the law had been changed in England to the benefit of women, but had not been changed here in India. She urged that since it was a colonial law, it should be treated as if it had automatically changed here as well. When I expressed the opinion in open court that there was not much substance in her argument, she was upset. Some time later, when she met me at a social function, she said, 'What kind of a woman judge are you that you don't give any special weightage to women? We had such high hopes of you.' I told her that though I could empathize with women, I was a judge and had to decide matters in accordance with the law. I held an even balance: I was not a judge for either women or men.

★

A few months after my appointment, I was introduced to Mrs Gandhi at a large party. She was out of power, had been ostracized by many, and had just started going out publicly again. I remember she was wearing a red silk sari and had a proud and aloof bearing. When my friend Sunanda Bhandare, whom she knew well, proudly introduced me as the first woman to be appointed a judge of the Delhi High Court, Mrs Gandhi looked at me and responded to my namaste with a cold glare and not even the semblance of a smile. I was chilled and struck dumb; we exchanged no words at all. I wondered whether it was insecurity, fear or contempt for the courts that made her react in this manner.

★

One day while sitting in court I was intently reading a judgment which had been cited by one of the lawyers appearing in a case. I heard some shuffling of feet and the soft murmur of many voices. I looked up and found the courtroom absolutely packed with dozens of people standing everywhere, staring at me. I asked my reader whether any specially newsworthy case had suddenly been assigned to me. He replied: 'Oh no, no. This crowd is a group of farmers whom Prime Minister Charan Singh has invited to Delhi to see the sights. They have just visited the zoo: and now they have come to see the woman judge in the Delhi High Court.'

★

Though I was a judge, we were still living on the first floor in 17 Golf Links, as we had not yet been allotted a government house. One evening we came home to find my old cream-coloured Ambassador missing from the road in front of the house where it had been parked. We were a bit surprised, but thought that Shantum, who was staying with us for a few days, might have taken it. But he was in the flat, and had no idea how it had disappeared.

Premo had a new cream-coloured Ambassador assigned to him by the Tata company, which he had joined after resigning from STC. He was always worried about it being stolen: it too was parked in front of the house. He used to tease me about my old car, saying that I would have to pay someone to take it away. But I loved it, as it made me independent and mobile, and I was very upset when it disappeared.

We immediately rushed to the nearest police station, which was on Tughlak Road, and reported the loss to the policeman present there. But he didn't seem to believe us. He said we had to tell him the exact time it was stolen, otherwise he could not record the matter. We told him that we didn't know, but that we had gone out at 3 p.m. and returned at 6 p.m. so it must have happened sometime between those hours. He said: 'No. You must tell me the exact time.' I said: 'I can't as I didn't see anybody actually driving it away.' He then said: 'Your son must have taken it.' I replied: 'If he had, why would I have come to the police?' The policeman hemmed and hawed, yawned and stretched, and turned to other business: he just would not record the first information report. Half an hour passed; I had visions of my car being driven out of Delhi into Haryana, Rajasthan or Uttar Pradesh and lost forever. Premo and I looked at each other in desperation.

At this stage, Premo said: 'The car belongs to my wife and she is a High Court judge.' These words had hardly been uttered than the policeman sprang out of his chair and rather angrily and aggresively demanded: 'Why did you not disclose this fact from the beginning?' We were made to feel that we had committed a crime by not doing so. The policeman soon recovered his composure and swung into action; he made phone calls, recorded the information in multiple copies, and was generally subservient. The car was recovered from near the Delhi border a few days later. But I wondered: if this was the fate of an educated couple who went to the police to make a genuine complaint, what must be the fate of others? How would they be treated if they were illiterate and poor?

★

A few months after my appointment, our house allocation came through. We moved to 7 Teen Murti Lane, a small house with a large garden. Aradhana immediately pressed her demand for a dog. Now that we had the grounds, we had no ground to resist. A friend offered Aradhana a puppy; I very reluctantly agreed we could take it after getting an assurance from her that she would not only house-train it but look after all its needs. The little black dog arrived; after much debate, Aradhana named him Oscar. He was an odd and attractive mixture of dachshund and a rare Himalayan breed.

Of course, what eventually happened was that I had to take care of Oscar when he cried at night, to house-train him, to see about his food and to take him to the vet when necessary. From not being a dog-lover at all, I became passionately fond of Oscar and he of me; his yelps of delight when I returned home from work always boosted my morale. So when he died suddenly, about two years later, both Aradhana and I wept copiously as if we had lost a family member. We buried him at the back of the vegetable garden, and we never got another dog.

★

I had been appointed as an additional judge for two years as there had been no permanent vacancy at the time. (The number of permanent positions depended on the 'sanctioned strength' of the particular court.) Invariably, additional judges had continued their tenure till a permanent vacancy arose, usually owing to retirement; they were then appointed as permanent judges of their particular High Court. But there had been two exceptions during the Emergency.

Now, once again, the Janata government having fallen, Mrs Gandhi and her son Sanjay were back in the saddle. The fate of the additional judges appointed during the Janata regime was the subject of a great deal of discussion and rumour. Many people felt that the new government might decide to drop them. I thought, on the whole, that since I was apolitical I would be continued. But even if I was not, the heavens would not fall. I could rejoin the legal profession and practise in the Delhi High Court again, as a bar against this applied only to permanent judges.

★

More than a year after I had been appointed a judge, the CBI felt that they had received their 'ishara' and closed their enquiry. By then, however, Premo, at my behest after our harrowing experience, had left government and rejoined the private sector. He joined Tata Exports and was based in

Delhi, though he went for a week every month to Dewas in Madhya Pradesh to take care of the leather and footwear unit they had set up there.

Shantum, too, was working with shoes; he was now with Clarks in Somerset. He came home to Delhi for a short while to familiarize himself with the Indian operations of the company. When he went to Agra to learn about hand-made shoes, he was horrified to find that one night's stay in a hotel cost more than a worker's weekly earnings. He decided to stay instead with a Jatav family and saw at first hand the very poor conditions in which they lived. Many Jatavs had rejected Hinduism, which treated them as untouchable, and become Buddhists. Shantum's stay in Agra helped convince him that it was more important to put 'people before profit' rather than follow the company's attitude of 'profit first and people afterwards'.

Shantum's boss, Lance Clark, however, was different, and cared a great deal about people. Shantum and he became friends and they had long discussions about what could be done to improve the world. But these discussions may have changed Shantum's life less than an incident involving Lance's car.

One night Shantum borrowed this brand new M.G. sports car to go out of town with his girlfriend, Lea. He was driving fast, very angry at the news of Margaret Thatcher's victory in the elections. It was dark. He didn't see a separator that suddenly appeared in the middle of the road, and he hit it at speed. The car flew into the air. It hit a strong red pillar box, hurtled over a hedge and landed in a garden. Since—in this case, luckily—he and Lea didn't have their seat-belts on, they were thrown out of the car through the windscreen. The two of them landed on the grass, injured but not dead. The sound of the accident woke up the residents and they rang the police. An ambulance arrived on the alert. But in the meantime, a middle-aged English woman, who lived in a flat facing the garden, rushed down and cradled Shantum's head in her lap and tried to soothe him through his shock and pain. He told her that his friend Lea must also be there somewhere and might need attention. They were both soon rushed off to the hospital. Luckily, Shantum had had a soft landing and his injuries were not as serious as they might have been. Lea had suffered concussion and other injuries, but slowly made a full recovery. When Premo later saw the car, he began to tremble. It was a total wreck—crushed and irreparable. No one who remained in it could have survived.

The experience totally changed Shantum. He felt he had been given a second lease of life—he could so suddenly have been dead. He lost his fear of death, and decided that he wanted to be of service to people, rather than worry about his own career.

★

In early 1980, Aradhana had successfully completed her studies at Modern School, Vasant Vihar, and was planning to enter college. She started learning how to type at home and went for pottery classes.

In my summer vacation that year, on the way to visiting Vikram in California (where Premo was to join us), Aradhana and I spent a holiday together by ourselves for the first time. First, we went to the UK to visit Shantum in Somerset and Shanti Uncle in London. We had a wonderful time seeing plays and sight-seeing together. I also visited Lincoln's Inn, where I had been invited by the Benchers to lunch with them at High Table. Justice Denning, who knew that he was much admired by Indian lawyers and judges, made a special effort to be present, much to my delight.

I was keen that Aradhana see Paris and so we made a brief

weekend visit. We stayed with my childhood friend, Yolande Paul, her Vietnamese husband, and their two adolescent sons. While Yolande and I chatted into the early hours, the boys showed Aradhana around the city, won her friendship with their Gallic charm, and made a big fuss over her. Aradhana, who had just turned eighteen, was enchanted by her first experience of Paris.

We next went to the East Coast of the USA. In Washington, DC, I visited the Supreme Court, which was in session. Each of the nine judges had chairs of their choice, unlike the standardized chairs of our Supreme Court. I had lunch with Chief Justice Warren Burger; afterwards, he gave me a booklet on Marbury v. Madison, a seminal case in American jurisprudence dealing with the right of the Supreme Court to review the actions of the Executive, which we had discussed.

In Philadelphia, we stayed with Dick Levy, the young man who had stayed with us in Patna as the leader of the Experiment in International Living. He was now a teacher and married, with two young boys. His wife, Dale, who was a lawyer, took me to the courts and introduced me to the judges; they asked me to sit with them for a hearing. It was quite an eye opener for me to see judges standing with their gowns on, just behind the courtroom door, waiting for the clock to strike the court hour so that they could enter on the dot. Punctuality gave confidence to the litigant about the earnestness of the court to do justice speedily.

As we were short of foreign exchange, we decided to take a train to Toronto to visit relatives and friends and to see the Niagara Falls. But Dick, who thought the train journey would take up too much of our time, insisted on buying plane tickets for us. We were very touched. But when we tried to thank him, he simply said: 'This is the least I can do for you. I learnt so much from India and all the love and care you lavished on me.'

This was my first trip to the USA and I did not want to miss out on New York. This was the only time during the whole trip that we stayed in a hotel—a comparatively small, inexpensive hotel. Though we normally always carried our passport and tickets with us, we decided to leave them in the hotel locker because we were worried about being mugged.

When we learnt that one of the largest Picasso exhibitions ever was on at the Museum of Modern Art, we decided to go and see it. After standing in a very long queue for half an hour, we discovered that it was not for tickets for that day but for advance booking; apparently, the show was booked for weeks. We decided to do the next best thing, and see the rest of the museum, but that too was impossible: we were told the exhibition had taken over the whole museum. But the lady at the reception, seeing my disappointment, offered to give us the very last two tickets out of a special visitors' quota for the day, provided we showed her our travel tickets and passports to establish our status. I cursed myself for not carrying these documents on this one day, but decided the opportunity was too good to miss. We jumped into a taxi, dashed back to the hotel, got our passports and airline tickets and rushed back to the museum. The receptionist smiled to see us; despite the demand for those tickets, she had kept them for us. I think the fact that I was wearing a sari and came from such a distant land helped. Both for Aradhana and me, the large and varied exhibition of Picasso's works was a real treat.

Premo, who had gone to the USA on work for Tata Exports, arrived within an hour of us at the San Francisco airport. Vikram was already there from Stanford to greet us. We spent our first day together cleaning out his room—especially his cupboard and kitchen. I enjoyed the university town and meeting all his friends and cooking for them. Vikram introduced me to some of the law professors at the Stanford Law School. I also went to the California Supreme

Court and met Chief Justice Rose Bird. Later, when we wanted to hire a car to travel around the state together, we realized that it was almost impossible to do so without a credit card, which neither Vikram nor we had. Eventually, we had to use a card belonging to one of Vikram's friends and reimburse him with cash. Premo did the driving and Vikram the map-reading and navigating, and it worked out well. As I was very keen to visit Disneyland, we spent Vikram's twenty-eighth birthday there, overriding his great reluctance. Altogether, we had a wonderful holiday; our only regret was Shantum's absence, as he could not get leave from his employers.

The four of us parted ways at Los Angeles airport from where Aradhana and I flew back to Delhi, Premo to Portland, Oregon on work, and Vikram back to Stanford.

We arrived in Delhi very late at night. Two young friends of Aradhana were at the airport to receive us. The very first thing they said to us—and in hushed tones—was that Sanjay Gandhi had died that morning in a crash while piloting a small plane. Coming back to India after visiting both my sons, my first reaction was, 'Oh my God, how terrible for his mother.' My second reaction was, 'Thank God it was not Rajiv, the sober, sensible one.' Sanjay had died living dangerously, leaving behind a young and courageous wife and a baby son. His death broke Mrs Gandhi's spirit.

★

After the courts reopened in June 1980, there were even more rumours floating around that those judges who had been appointed as additional judges during the Janata regime would not be made permanent by the Congress government. In the case of one such additional judge of the Allahabad High Court, whom the government was set against, they made their intentions clear. While enquiries were being made as to his political affiliations and likelihood of bias, his term was extended for just four months. He realized that the chances of his continuing were remote, and resigned in protest.

What would happen to me was an open question. Now that I was a judge, I did not meet Sunanda Bhandare very often, but at a function in the Indian Law Institute at the end of June, she took me aside and asked me if I was facing any problems about becoming a permanent judge. I told her I did not know, as I had no access to what was going on. She, too, did not know, since her father, who had been the Law Minister in Indira Gandhi's previous government, had died. But she said: 'I am sure Mrs Gandhi will not axe you, as it would be politically unwise for her to get rid of the only woman judge in the Delhi High Court—rather, the only woman judge in North India.' Sunanda was right. Seven days before my two-year term was due to expire, I was sworn in as a permanent judge of the Delhi High Court.

★

Soon after I became a permanent judge, a regular tax bench was constituted with Justice Ranganathan and me. It was unusual to have a bench of two judges who had almost the same seniority: he was puisne judge 12 and I was puisne judge 13. But this bench was probably constituted by the Chief Justice because Justice Ranganathan had come to the High Court straight from the Income-Tax Appellate Tribunal and I had done a great deal of income-tax work, first in Patna as junior standing counsel for the income-tax authorities, and then in Calcutta and Delhi, for the assessees. Justice Ranganathan was very knowledgeable and judicious and had a quiet and pleasant personality. I greatly benefited from the experience and we had no disagreements.

It is normal practice for judges sitting in Division Bench to take turns writing the judgments. One such income-tax judgment written by me (and later recorded in the law reports) pertained to the circumstances in which an assessee company could claim the benefit of a development rebate for the purchase of a plant. The matter hinged on the question of whether a building where saccharine was being manufactured was a 'plant'. After considering the law, what we basically decided was that the word 'plant' should be given a wide meaning, but that all buildings could not be considered to be 'plant'. The true test was whether the building was the means of carrying on the business or just the location for so doing. In order for a building or concrete structure to qualify for inclusion in the term 'plant', it had to be established that it was impossible for the equipment to function without that particular type of structure. In the facts of the case, we came to the conclusion that the building was the space or shelter where the business of manufacturing saccharine was carried on as opposed to the means.

Income-tax matters are normally dry, and relate to deductions, exemptions, allowances and development rebates. But they were Justice Ranganthan's forte. So when a matter came up which had a woman's angle, he requested me to write the judgment, even though it was his turn. The crux of the matter was to decide what the word 'jewellery' meant in tax parlance.

One Savitri Devi had some silver utensils and gold ornaments; she claimed they were not jewellery and therefore exempt from wealth tax. The Wealth Tax Officer treated both as 'jewellery' and included them in his valuation of her wealth. She appealed to the Appellate Assistant Commissioner, who held they were not jewellery as they were not studded with jewels and were therefore exempt. The Revenue appealed, but the Wealth Tax Appellate Tribunal affirmed the above decision. The matter was then referred to the High Court at the instance of the Commissioner of Wealth Tax. The Punjab and Haryana, Gujarat and Allahabad High Courts had taken one view, and the Orissa, Calcutta and Madhya Pradesh High Courts, the other. We finally decided that the word jewellery as understood in common parlance included gold ornaments and that the studding of precious stones was not a necessary ingredient for the ornaments to become jewellery, even in the context of our country. The word 'gehena' would certainly include a gold 'champakali' or 'hansali' or a wedding ring. Surely, when an Indian girl talks of her jewellery, she includes her gold bangles, chain, anklets and so on, even though they are not studded with precious or semi-precious stones. Consequently, we held that though the silver utensils were not jewellery, the gold ornaments intended for the personal use of the assessee certainly were.

Another interesting case, which I decided in early 1983, while sitting singly, related to inter-personal law. Vilayat Raj and Sunila, both Hindus, were married in June 1978. Their marriage was solemnized in accordance with Hindu rites and ceremonies. Two years later they had a child. Subsequently, they separated. In October 1981 Vilayat Raj (now Vilayat Khan, he having become a Muslim) filed a petition under section 13(1)(ia) of the Hindu Marriage Act 1955 for dissolution of the marriage on the grounds of cruelty. Even before the allegations of cruelty could be considered, Sunila took a preliminary objection that the petition was not maintainable. She submitted that since her husband converted to Islam, he had lost his right to move a petition under the Hindu Marriage Act. The District Judge accepted her submission and dismissed his petition. He appealed this judgment, and I allowed his appeal. I held that a Hindu marriage could only be dissolved under Hindu Law. The fact that the petitioner had since become a Muslim did not debar him from presenting a petition for dissolution if he was otherwise entitled to do so. It was clear from the provisions of the Act that it would apply even if one of the parties had ceased to be a Hindu. (In fact, under section 13 (1)(ii), Sunila could herself have obtained a divorce on the grounds that Vilayat Raj had changed his religion. But clearly she did not want to do so nor did she want him to be allowed to move a petition.) I rejected Sunila's preliminary objection and held that Vilayat Khan's petition could not be barred at the very threshold. I set aside the order of the District Judge and remitted the case to be dealt with expeditiously on the actual question of cruelty.

★

One case in which I was not directly but indirectly involved related to a so-called dowry death.

Sudha Goel lived with Laxman, her husband, and his family in a flat in Delhi. One night in December, hearing Sudha's screams, her neighbours rushed to her flat. They found they could not enter. Her brother-in-law, Subhash, was leaning against the door and holding the latch. The neighbours pushed the door open at last. Sudha's clothes were on fire. Her husband and her mother-in-law, Shakuntala, were sitting, unconcerned, in the next room.

Though, at the time, Sudha told her neighbours, 'These people have killed me, they have taken my gold and everything,' she was later forced by her husband's family to give a false statement saying that her clothes had caught fire while she was boiling milk, and that no one else was to blame. Since she had suffered extensive burns, she did not survive long.

It is almost always the case that out of apathy, or in the interest of 'good neighbourly relations' or because of the trauma of testifying in court, neighbours refuse to get involved in such matters. But in this instance, Sudha's neighbours were determined not to let her in-laws get away with it. They gave evidence in court about what they had seen and heard.

The District Judge sentenced the three accused—Sudha's husband Laxman, mother-in-law Shakuntala and brother-in-law Subhash—to death. It was among the first cases where a death sentence had been given in a dowry death case. The matter came to the Delhi High Court on appeal and also by way of reference for confirmation of the death sentence. Here the two-judge bench set aside the conviction and the sentence.

This led to a great deal of agitation. Many women's groups were very unhappy; they gave speeches and chanted slogans outside the High Court. They held up placards, and shouted that the High Court judges were murderers. As a result of this, a number of women, among them Brinda Karat of the All India Democratic Women's Association and Subhadra Butalia of Karmika, a legal aid and counselling centre for women victims of domestic violence, were summoned to show cause why action should not be taken against them for contempt of court.

The contempt matter was listed before Justice Sachar and me. We heard the women and their counsel patiently. Brinda Karat was particularly eloquent. We were faced with a dilemma. We both understood the motivation of the women's groups and realized that the greed and violence associated with dowries was destroying many young women's lives, but we had to protect the administration of justice from being ridiculed. People often don't realize that you can legally criticize a judgment but not the judge; nor can you impute motives to him. The placards and slogans were clearly contempt of court.

After analysing the law of contempt, and appreciating the motives of the contemners, we sentenced the accused to imprisonment, but only till the rising of the court. In a contempt matter the alleged contemners have to be present. We therefore had the matter listed for judgment in the afternoon, so that by the time we had finished reading the judgment, the rising of the court would be only a few moments away—thus striking, we hoped, a balance between law and justice.

It is worth mentioning what happened subsequently in the Sudha Goel case. An appeal was filed by the State against the acquittal of Laxman Kumar (her husband) and his mother and brother. The Indian Federation of Women Lawyers and others also filed an appeal. The two appeals were in due course—that is, after a number of years—heard together in the Supreme Court. But it appears that after Laxman had been acquitted by the Delhi High Court, he remarried; and when Laxman's mother Shakuntala was asked whether his second wife had brought any dowry, she quite openly said that she was satisfied with the dowry. (One would have thought that by now she would have known that dowries were illegal.) Laxman even had two children by the second wife before he was finally sent to jail by the Supreme Court to serve a life sentence for murder.

Two really disturbing aspects about many dowry death cases are the alacrity with which a man gets remarried after the unnatural death of his wife and the willingness of parents to give their daughter in marriage to such a man, even while he is out on bail.

In Indian society, the marriage of a girl appears mandatory. There is also a culture of silence that forces a girl to keep the marriage going at any cost. What one needs to ask is this: what sort of parents are they who marry their daughters off to men such as Laxman? What sort of parents are they who insist that their daughters go back to their husband's homes, when they know they have been ill-treated there? What kind of society do we live in that brings all these pressures to bear on the parents of girls?

I remember asking a good friend of mine, who rose to a very high judicial position, 'Will you give a dowry to your daughter?' He replied, 'I will, because it is a question of my daughter's happiness. Without a dowry, it would be nearly impossible to get her married in my state and community. But I will not take a dowry for my son.' It wasn't what I wanted to hear, but it was one small step forward.

The law can only act as a springboard. It is our mindset that has to change. Marriage must not be treated as the be-all and end-all of life for a girl. The education and the economic empowerment of a girl is necessary. Parents have to be strong in order to face and change society. People have to expose abuses and atrocities. We are the change we are seeking.

I am filled with admiration, for example, at Subhadra Butalia's courage and the efforts she has made in this direction. Her book, *The Gift of a Daughter—Encounters with Victims of Dowry*, was recently released; in this, she sets out the story of her endeavours. At 81, she continues with her social activist work. May her indomitable spirit strengthen our resolve.

Though in her book Subhadra has referred to Justice Sachar and me as 'two of the most enlightened judges', when she appeared before us in court, she had somewhat feistily dismissed us both as male chauvinists. Justice Sachar had mildly responded that though he wasn't a male chauvinist, he could still, without offense to logic, be called one, being male, but that surely she could not refer to his sister judge as a male chauvinist. Subhadra had responded that she perceived judges as male and that in any case I was referred to as 'My Lord'.

On a different note, when Justice Sachar and I were sitting together hearing criminal appeals, we had occasion to deal with a murder case where the young accused was sentenced to life imprisonment. After hearing the case, we were of the view that the evidence was not sufficient to convict him, and accordingly set aside his conviction and sentence. He came from a rural background and his mother was in court when we pronounced our judgment and ordered his release. She was so relieved and pleased that, not knowing better, she threw up her arms and loudly and openly blessed us, seated there together as a Division Bench, wishing that we remained ever united as a couple. We were astounded and wondered what our respective spouses would say to that!

★

Words and language—the tools of the lawyer or the writer— are crucial even from childhood as the vehicle of one's thoughts and ideas. This realization came to me very clearly from the example of two six-year-old boys: one, whose parents were separated and fighting for custody, and the other our chauffeur's son.

In the custody case, the boy came with his father to court. I took him into my chamber on his own to try and ascertain what was in his best interest. I asked him, 'Who do you want to live with?' He replied in English, 'With my father.' When I asked him why he wanted to live with his father, he said, 'Because he loves me.' I said, 'Doesn't your mother also love you?' He kept quiet. 'Do you like your father's house?' 'Yes, yes, I want to live with my father.' 'Are you sure?' 'Yes. I love my father and I want to live with him.' But he looked tense.

I suddenly switched to Hindi and said, 'Tell me honestly where you want to live?' Without thinking, he replied in Hindi, 'I want to live with my Nana and Nani, they love me very much and I love them very much and I will sometimes get to see my mother who comes to visit her parents off and on. I lived with them for many years when my mother was staying there. But my father took me away when she got a job out of town.' He started crying.

I realized then that he was expressing his true feelings and that what he had been saying earlier, in English, was a parrot-like repetition of what he had been taught to say. Obviously, aware that the language of the High Court was English and that he would be questioned in it, his father had coached him in English. But the truth had come out in Hindi, his mother tongue. He was then worried that his father would be angry with him for saying what he had. I put him at ease and asked him, 'Don't you want to stay with your mother?' He replied, 'No, with my Nana and Nani, for they are the ones who really love me and take good care of me and read to me and teach me.' So I made sure that he stayed with his maternal grandparents and was happy.

This brought home to me the importance of speaking in the language in which one thinks from childhood. But our driver, Sateh Singh, made me realize that things were more complicated. His young son Manjit was going to a good government school where the medium of instruction was Hindi. I found that Sateh Singh had managed to get him into a private school at considerable expense; here, especially as a proportion of his salary, the monthly fees were very high. I asked him why he was making the change. He replied: 'Because the medium of instruction is English. If he studies well, he can be a judge like you, whereas if he learns mainly Hindi, he will only be a driver like me.'

★

After our American holiday, Aradhana had joined Jesus and Mary College in Delhi. She decided to take up sociology and loved the fieldwork. On one occasion she went off to observe the life and customs of the Todas. She loved to work with people—and her friends, who were many, were all-important to her. Everything was judged by their standards. She is a doer, and after graduating decided to work in an advertising firm called Clarion. It was there that she got interested in film-making. She wanted to join the Master of Arts course in Mass Communication at Jamia Millia Islamia university. I was against her joining Jamia, as I had heard vague reports about its unruly and boisterous male students. But she slowly broke down my resistance by persuading me that the School of Mass Communication was different and separate and had a very good reputation.

Aradhana completed her course with honours and made many friends, one of whom was Bano Haralu, from Nagaland in the North-East. They made a few small documentaries together; the first of these was called 'Ballad of the Watermelon'. She also made some interesting documentaries— on juvenile justice, on art and artists based on an exhibition to raise money for CRY for child relief; and on the renowned artist and architect, Satish Gujral.

Soon afterwards, Aradhana began work as assistant director to Pradip Krishen on a film scripted by Arundhati Roy, who also acted in it—*In Which Annie Gives It 'Those Ones'*. Some of the shooting was done in our bedroom and our old carved mahogany bed is very much a presence in the film. Aradhana enjoyed working with them; the atmosphere was that of a large film family, very caring towards each other and enthusiastic about the project.

By now, Aradhana was eating, breathing and sleeping films. In fact, she was becoming so involved with work that I was worried she would never get married. She was over twenty-five; despite restraining myself, I must still have put a lot of pressure on her. My friends and colleagues told me continually that I seemed to have abdicated my responsibilities and that it was my duty to look around and find her a suitable match.

But it wasn't easy. When I suggested young men she

should meet, she was reluctant; and if I reminded her that friends of hers such as Pranita had had arranged marriages, she repeatedly responded, 'They were brought up thinking and knowing that their parents would find and decide for them. You didn't bring me up like that—so it's a little late in the day to ask me to comply.' I knew she was right. There was little I could do despite my fears and apprehensions that she might land up with someone unsuitable—or no one at all. I just had to wait and let her do it her way. That was the space I had given her, and to suddenly take it away because things were not happening as I had expected would be really unfair. Her brothers Vikram and Shantum were also very protective of her rights and sensed that there was much more pressure on her than on them because she was a girl.

I analysed myself and wondered why I was so keen that she got married. Premo and I had a happy marriage and I knew how great were the joys of companionship and loving care; also, what a wonderful joy children were. Naturally, the question of giving a dowry would never arise, naturally, she could come back to us if she were unhappy; but time was passing by and so were her child-bearing years.

There were many young men wooing Aradhana and one or two real faithfuls. Vikram teasingly referred to them as mushrooms since, in his words, whenever he came home on holiday, there was a new and varied crop; they appeared to spring up out of nowhere, sought to remain damply attached to the floor boards, and gave no clear indication, at first glance, of whether they were edible or not. Dhiren Bhagat, a brilliant and fearless young journalist, was a regular visitor in his new jeep. When, after seeing the lie of the land, he brought Vikram a bottle of malt whisky, even this exacting elder brother allowed that he might be fit company for his sister.

★

Vikram had gone from Stanford to Nanjing University in late 1980 to do field research on his thesis—'The Economic Demography of Seven Chinese Villages'. He had learnt Chinese at Stanford some years earlier. He was almost thirty and we had often talked to him about marriage and children. He was not averse to the idea but he wanted to be free to travel and do what he might want to do without the responsibility of a family. He returned to India for a holiday in September 1981 by what he described in an elliptical warning message to us as 'a more interesting route', partly legally and partly illegally—via Tibet. We were worried about his whereabouts when he did not arrive by the date he had indicated. When he finally did arrive at 7 Teen Murti Lane, the staff barred his entry. He was dark from trekking, thin from eating only raisins, unshaven, and—like a pedlar—carrying a jute sack on his back with all his belongings in it. On closer examination, our gardener Sona recognized him and let him in. He was happy to be home and be spoilt by me and by his darling Amma, my mother, who was soon going to be seventy-five.

Vikram had taken some wonderful photographs of his Tibetan journey and did a slide show for the family and close friends. We suggested to him that he write about his experiences: a long article, possibly even a book. And this is what he did. By the time Shantum and I visited him in China in the summer of 1982, the first draft was ready. Chatto & Windus accepted it and said it would be published the following summer.

One day Premo and I went to dinner with our friends Bitti and Akhilesh Mithal. A young friend of theirs, Shobita Punja, was also there. She told us that she had seen Vikram's book *From Heaven Lake*. I was quite surprised since I didn't even know it was out. Vikram had told us the publication date; it was still some weeks away. Trying to suppress my excitement, I asked her about the book. When she sensed my unspoken desire to see and handle it, she told me that she actually had a copy which had been lent to her by a friend who was likely to review it. Shobita very generously went home and brought the book for us. When I held it I felt really blessed. It was like holding one's first grandchild. It was a creature of mind and emotion, though its gestation period had been more than nine months.

Premo was due to go to London on some work and tried to plan the trip to coincide with the book's release. I had been to China in 1982, and could not afford to travel again so soon, but after seeing *From Heaven Lake* between hard covers I was very tempted to scrape together the money and join Premo. We went to London in August 1983. I wondered what happened at a book release. Well, the day before official publication, Vikram's publisher, Hugo Brunner, rang him up and said, 'Don't jump into the Thames if there is a bad review or no review at all. You, your parents and your brother are having lunch with me tomorrow, and we shall discuss it.' Vikram went out early the next morning and bought the *Guardian*. He opened it at the newsagents and saw that there was a review, but he didn't read it. He brought it back to the small hotel where we were staying, and we read it together. We were all very tense. To our immense relief, it was a very good review, and we were able to relax and enjoy our lunch.

To celebrate, I went with Shantum to the gardens at Kew. Premo went to work and Vikram decided to stay back in the Rainbow Hotel—as it turned out, to start work on his novel in verse, *The Golden Gate*.

★

The next day we left for the magistrates' court at Banbury, near Oxford. The hearing of the case against Shantum for obstructing the Queen's Highway was to take place that day. Shantum and a few others had protested in a non-violent manner by sitting down on the road just beyond the fence of a US air force base with first-strike nuclear capabilities in Upper Heyford. The trial was very interesting. There were elderly teachers and young punks with pink hair, peace marchers and students. There was even a young lad who insisted on calling himself Hastings 1066: his hair was shaved in such a manner that the figures 1066 appeared.

A special magistrate had come from London to hear the case, and we visitors waited in a queue to go into the courtroom. They only allowed as many people in as there were chairs. Premo, Vikram and I made it in a few cases before Shantum's. He was dressed in a brown-speckled khadi kurta with a white background, white pajamas, and a dark brown Jawahar waistcoat, with a red and white checked gamcha tied around his head. He was something of a contrast to the formally-dressed English magistrate. He argued his own case from the dock. When he was asked what he had to say in his defence, he told the magistrate that by sitting on the road he had been protecting his interests. The magistrate asked in a surprised manner, 'Mine?' Shantum said, 'Yes, yours and that of your children, born or unborn, because I don't want you and them to face a nuclear hazard.' Of course, the magistrate found him guilty, but before passing sentence he wanted to know if Shantum had a wife and children. Shantum said, 'Yes, all the world's children are my children.' The magistrate enquired, 'Mr Seth, apart from the world's children, do you have any you have begotten?' There was silence—in this case, we hoped, not implying an affirmative. The magistrate then sentenced Shantum to a fine of thirty pounds and a week's imprisonment if the fine was not paid. Shantum asked if he could pay the fine into some children's charity like the Save the Children's Fund. The magistrate said, 'No, into the Queen's coffers'.

Shantum refused to pay his fine and refused to let us pay it. A few days after his trial, Vikram, Premo and I had lunch with Lady Brunner, Hugo's mother, at Grey's Court, her home. She said to me, 'Being a judge, will you not be embarrassed if your son decides to go to jail instead of paying the fine quietly?' I replied, 'No, certainly not. In our country one feels proud if a person goes to jail for a just cause; we have the example of Mahatma Gandhi and Pandit Nehru and a host of others to emulate.'

Shantum never did pay the fine. He was after some months informed that he could pay it in three monthly instalments of ten pounds each. He still did not pay it. He was given a chance to pay it in even smaller amounts. But he still did not pay. He then got a final notice—after which the police were forced to take action. They telephoned Shantum on a Friday morning to tell him they were coming to arrest him. He asked them if they could possibly postpone the arrest till Monday, as he had a friend visiting from India. They generously agreed to do so. When they came on Monday morning, they found Shantum busy giving some instructions about work to his colleagues; he was at the time Vice-President of the Students' Union at the University of East Anglia at Norwich. The police waited patiently for him to finish. He then went willingly to jail; his friends threw rose petals and confetti on him as he accompanied the policeman. All this was reported in the local Norwich papers and local radio, and it helped to spread the message of peace. Shantum quoted Martin Luther King: 'We must either learn to live together as brothers or we are going to perish together as fools.'

Shantum was in jail from 21 to 25 January 1985 and wrote letters to us in India, to Vikram in the USA, and to his friends in the Campaign for Nuclear Disarmament. I treasured the letter he wrote to us and kept it very carefully, in fact so carefully that I can't find it now; but it was similar to the letter he wrote to his brother, which I reproduce:

Dear Bhayya,

Day 3 in prison, 6 p.m. and we have finished our tea/dinner—greasy chips, beans, an egg (which I refused), slices of bread with one pat of marg, and a bun. A jug of putrid tea. It's all reacting wildly in my insides. The food, though is generally of a decent standard (by what you might expect in prison). Mashed potatoes are a favourite, today was the first meal we did not get them. Food is in quantity—3 big meals a day. With exercise limited to half an hour to one hour a day and a waiting list to use the gym, you can imagine it's easy to put on weight here! It's quite a happy existence here, one which would suit you well for your writing. Tea in the morning and evening, no washing up, no cooking, regular hours to be let out of the cell for slop outs and food. There are of course lots of distractions, like the sound of keys and footsteps on metal stairs, voices, laughs, bangs, occasional screams and wails. I share my cell with two others. Till yesterday, it was Andy and Martin, but earlier today, Martin went to the Annexe and we were joined by John from the hospital.

Martin's very mild mannered, yet convicted of an armed burgalry at a Post Office, dead drunk and bread knife job, seems quite out of character with him. His 15 year old son (who he brought up on his own) visited him yesterday and that really made his day. Andy on the other hand claims to be a Hindu, is a mine of information about prison and its regulations and irregularities, and we have deep 'philosophical' conversations on subjects such as Karma, reincarnation and Samadhi. He's in for 3 months for dealing in speed. Have very much enjoyed their company.

John is a bit different in that he is not clean and tidy, difficult to talk to. I feel he is suffering mildly from some psychiatric disorder but he is most gentle and generous. I just feel what a waste of human energy in here, vegetating days, months, years, making no creative or constructive contribution to society. Instead locked up here for hours on end. For some of the longer term prisoners there is work, but it is so mundane and often futile, that most prisoners with intellect start making up little deals right under the noses of H.M.'s warders. We've just been let out for a slop out which means emptying our piss bucket, going to the toilet, shaving, bath etc. Think I will have a bath now—continue later.

A couple of hours later:

It's been quite an evening. First, one guy wore his pajamas (I guess a sign of defiance to the prison system) and then made a screaming and chanting act on the floor (the '3's as it is called) landing. It's known as 'cracking up' here. He made a lot of sense in the way he talked about how people are oppressed and locked up by shitty laws, made by the 'Supermarket World and its bosses'. His release from the aggression of the 'exploiters' was that each 'will meet his maker'. He was deadly serious and very tense. I've heard he's done it before. Well, this diversion/enlightenment caused me to miss my planned shave since we get regulated times for ablutional activities but did manage to brush my teeth.

Paul the guy who lost his cool last evening, did so again at lunchtime today. We got positively bad food (for the vegetarians) and he just threw the tray and all its contents out on the floor. He's been taken to the hospital now and I guess he won't be out till his release in March.

Dave, intelligent, but frustrated that he's unable to change the shitty world he finds himself in. His response is to go smash up a police car. Likewise there are many here who carry a healthy disrespect for authority and the State, but do not know the message of non-violence and constructive activity.

Also talked to many people—a few black guys from Colchester and Ipswich, others from up North, Ireland and the Midlands. I find I fit into this atmosphere here quite easily and am enjoying it thoroughly, both from the points of learning and new experience, but often from the sheer enjoyment. For some quirk of a reason our cells didn't get banged up this evening for a long time, so a few of us were out on the landing having a good laugh. There are a few real jokers here and they definitely make the place— highly intelligent and considered a bit crazy. This place is lot like a grown-up boarding school. I can see so many similarities in the way the mind is induced to work here as it did in Doon (when we were at school)—ways to get around petty rules. There is definitely a nasty side too, with headgames—but I've found the principle of 'do as you would be done by' works very well.

Most people here know what I am in for and have had a number of words in encouragement and support from many here. I was unsure about the reaction of other prisoners to prisoners of conscience earlier, but now I know it is nothing to fear. It also encourages many discussions on the nuclear issue which get extended into other areas. I feel very fortunate to have this experience in jail and wouldn't miss it for much. This must all sound a bit strange to you, when you must have seen my dilemma in making a choice to go to prison, also when your own concern was so great, so that I don't get hurt. Bhayya, to my surprise, I feel very strong here and free. My spirits are soaring, especially as I know of many outside these 'funny' walls are with me in spirit. For many others here, it's a different story. Many are suffering—the worst ones from guilt rather than just from the conditions. Others who don't see their crime in the same light as the State, feel it is unfortunate that they are here, but often they are the ones who make the best of it.

Many of the blokes here, if they were not so lonely on the outside, would not be here, and could do so much for the betterment of society.

It's strange writing a letter which the censor will go through, and so I feel I must think before I write, not to put down anything unwise. It feels like when I was writing to Mama and Papa at the time of the inquiry/emergency. It seems that the authorities try to breed a suspicious and distrusting atmosphere here. But it creates instead a strong bond between the prisoners, sharing what little they have (tobacco, soap etc.), co-operation and many smiles too.

I had a visitor today from the local CND group. She was more nervous and worried than I ever felt. It was really good to see her, though I spent the first 5 minutes calming her down. On the outside, we are made to feel that jail is a real hell and to fear it, but from the inside, I laugh when I think of how the State tries to call many of us criminals; when its own hands are dripping with the blood of exploitation, oppression and long term environmental damage.

Psychological damage to whole new generations brought up in fear of imminent nuclear annihilation, and the State put us in because, we want to see our kids and the court says 'no', we nick a duvet from Marks & Spencer because one is sleeping out in the cold, being done 15 months for one ounce of dope. Most of my co-prisoners are burglars, marijuana dealers, drug dealers, armed robbers, a few murderers—many sound ferocious and vicious. Instead many are the mildest people one could hope for. I feel, if they are genuinely dangerous to society then they should be given the opportunity to develop their skills and contribute to society in congenial 'prison' surroundings. Instead, governments thinking in terms of vote catching, choose to push the 'Law and Order' aspect, and emphasise punishment and harsh discipline, which only creates a deeper frustration amongst many and the deterrent of fear of returning affects very few. Instead, all that happens is greater alienation from State and society outside, especially with the added horror of Press shock-horror stories, portraying many of these men as ferocious beasts when their manner and ways are little different from ours.

In order to survive in prison, it's necessary to accept the discipline but somehow, without sinking into a passive sense of acceptance of injustice, bad food etc.

One of the unfortunate regulations is that I cannot go on writing beyond the end of the letter form, and I have spent my weekly allowance on paper already. I am not allowed paper to keep a record of my thoughts, so I'd like it if you could photocopy this letter and send it to me, as it is the only record I'll have of my feelings at the time, censored as they may well be.

With lots of love from Cell 20 on the '3's, locked in till 7 a.m. slop out.

Shantum

★

In the autumn of 1983, while she was in Delhi, Ma suddenly fell ill. One evening, I noticed that she was slurring her speech and was not able to open her mouth properly. I realized she was partially paralysed, possibly owing to a stroke. It was night and Aradhana and I were alone in the house. I spoke to Shama—Dr Jain—on the telephone and rushed her to hospital with the help of his driver, who knew the admission procedures. Ma was in hospital for a long time, but slowly made an almost complete recovery.

I had been told that a judge's dependent mother was entitled to medical treatment at government expense. But upon enquiry, I discovered that this applied only to male judges. When I persisted and asked why there should be this discrimination, I was told that sons were supposed to look after their mothers. So would my entitlement go to my mother-in-law, I asked the defensive Registrar. Maybe, he said, but the matter would have to be examined. In any case, since I had brothers, surely it was their duty to look after her. That was the tradition. But I saw this argument as specious. I was the judge. She was my mother. She had no private means of her own. 'No, no it can't be done,' was the response.

But a year or so later, when Sunanda Bhandare was also appointed to be a judge of the Delhi High Court, we started to push for a change to be brought about. But my mother died a little later and I don't know what happened to the discriminatory regulation; I presume the matter has been rectified and male and female judges have been put on par.

I hope, however, that the High Court has not proceeded

in the quixotic manner of the Delhi Gymkhana Club. This club normally took in High Court judges as members soon after their appointment. When I applied, there was no response and other judges, who had applied after me, were taken in. I soon found out that I was not being considered because I was a woman. I felt that there was no purpose in being a part of a club that discriminated in this manner, but my family felt that I should take the club to task. So I made enquiries from the club officials, and they were quite sheepish. They said that they had a category for lady members, but it only applied to women who were single, separated, divorced or widowed. Was I divorced or widowed, the secretary asked—or even separated? I said thank God I wasn't. I told them that their behaviour was a clear case of discrimination. A few weeks later, they wrote to me to say that their committee had met and that it had been decided that they would make my husband a member. (Premo had applied a few years earlier and his turn would normally not have come for another few years.) I thought this was a strange kind of logic, but they explained that their rules bound them; changing them would take some time, so till they were changed, this is how they had sought to be fair!

★

In 1984 Ma said, 'I want to stay here with you, as I am reluctant to complain about anything to my daughters-in-law. With you I can complain and fight and know that it will be forgotten and forgiven.' I had looked after her through her long illness, and I now wanted my brothers to share in the effort, especially the eldest, Michi bhai. So when he offered to help, I sent Ma to Pune. Premo insisted that we buy her an air ticket and not let her travel by train as she had always done in the past. Michi bhai's wife, Mohini, received her and was very good to her. Ma was very happy there as she had a room and bathroom to herself; new tiles had been put in with her in mind. But some months later, Ma fell down and broke her hip and had to be hospitalized. Mohini took very good care of her, prepared the dishes of her choice and fed her with a firm hand.

I visited Ma in Pune at the end of October 1984. She talked about death and of meeting my father again. She was in a nice, quiet room and had good medical care; all of us contributed towards her expenses. When I returned to Delhi by plane on the night of 31 October, Mrs Chandrachud, the wife of the Chief Justice of India, was on the same flight. At the airport the Chief Justice came right up to the plane to meet her and take her home. She must have told him that I was also on the flight. So he very kindly waited at the airport terminal to know if anyone had come to receive me, for otherwise he would have taken me home. Mrs Gandhi had been assassinated by two of her Sikh bodyguards; rioting, arson and murder had broken out; and it was not safe for me to travel back alone in a taxi. Fortunately, Premo was there with someone from the High Court. As we returned home, we saw numerous vehicles burning by the roadside, the repercussions of blind mob vengeance on innocent Sikhs.

Ma died on 3 December 1984. She had not been told that her granddaughter Ira had died suddenly on 10 November in Bombay. It seemed unnecessary and cruel to burden her with that pain, as we knew she was dying.

Ma had a lot of love to give. She gave it freely and generously—though she always said she wanted to come back after her death to see who was grieving for her. I had assured her in my matter-of-fact way that we would miss her, but I didn't know then how true that would be. It is one of life's ironies that when she died, the Hindi-speaking pundit who was due to come didn't turn up, and the entire puja and prayers were conducted in Marathi, of which I understood nothing; nor would she have.

But I still remember seeing the last of her, covered in a light-blue sari—a colour Ma liked—which Mohini had put on her, and the hot flames of the incinerator around her before it snapped shut. All the corporeal substance of seventy-eight years of her life had gone in a flash. But we were there, my three brothers and I, along with our progeny of four boys—Michi bhai's two sons, Rajiv and Rahoul, and my sons Vikram and Shantum—and two girls—Michi bhai's daughter Anuradha and my daughter Aradhana—as well as Rahoul's little girl Shawna representing the third generation.

We were her legacy. All she had been to us, all she had taught us, all the values she had instilled in us and all the love with which she had enriched our lives, remained. After she died, I wished I had loved my mother more. I wished I had spent more time with her and not been so irritated when she cried for no apparent reason. I felt a deep sense of regret and guilt. And Vikram, thousands of miles away, as if reading my thoughts, wrote to me at just this time to say: 'You were a very good daughter. You took good care of Amma and gave her a lot of love.'

★

Vikram continued at Stanford, trying to complete his dissertation, but literary inspiration intervened, and he wrote *The Golden Gate* instead. This was a novel in verse, an unusual sort of book, for which he could not find a publisher. He knew it was good, so he decided to take a job as an editor at Stanford University Press, so that he could keep his head just above water and later self-publish, if necessary. The poetry department of Random House had rejected the novel, but when a friend of a friend of a friend, who did not know about this rejection, also sent the manuscript to a fiction editor at the same house, she joyously accepted it. It created a literary storm when it came out. Gore Vidal called it the Great Californian Novel and others a *tour de force*.

Of course, this meant that Vikram's thesis had been relegated to the back-burner. He achieved fame as a result of *The Golden Gate*, but did not make much money. We suggested to him that he take up a job with the World Bank as a young executive and serve for five years, after which he would earn a modest pension, sufficient for his needs in India, and could write without economic worries for the rest of his life. His reply was, 'All my creativity will be killed in five years and then I will be bound by chains of gold and not want to leave. You would have supported me through college for at least five years, which you did not have to do, so please support me now for that period. And let me write.'

His proposal had us worried. We had visions of him as a penniless poet, living in a garage and being supported by his younger brother Shantum, after we were dead. But of course we couldn't *not* agree to take him in now. And, needless to say, we looked forward to his company. So, in 1987, Vikram came back to India to stay with us and write, as he had decided he wanted to do. He started writing his magnum opus, *A Suitable Boy*, at 8 Rajaji Marg, a large house in the High Court housing pool which had become available and to which we had moved.

Shantum, too, returned to India in 1987, after I had a mild heart attack. He was now pursuing his search for an alternative lifestyle and a path of peace. After reading Masanobu Fukuoka's book *One Straw Revolution*, he scattered seeds in our back garden in the hope that we would soon have a natural harvest. He advocated health foods, he grew organic lettuce and broccoli, planted tree saplings and taught at Mirambika, an experimental school run by the Sri Aurobindo

Ashram, New Delhi. At the same time he toyed with the idea of going off to Bali to be with his friends.

The house in Rajaji Marg was double-storied, one of six houses on that road designed by Herbert Baker; he and Edwin Lutyens had been the architects of New Delhi. The house was set in a huge garden. All five of us had space to live and work. In fact, the children lived upstairs and I hardly ever went up as the chaos I found there was more than I could cope with.

Premo and I each had an office. Our furniture from the Calcutta days suited the dimensions and spirit of the house, especially after I had removed various recently added walls that cut out light and cramped the space. The children adapted the house to their needs. Aradhana got the fireplace in her bedroom functioning, and spent long winter evenings with friends there, chatting or working on her various film projects. Vikram, when he won the Sahitya Akademi Award for *The Golden Gate*, used the money to enclose and glaze part of the upstairs verandah. It became a small tree room, easily cooled in summer or heated in winter, where, while working, he felt as if he was perched among the branches of ficus and Sita ashok. Shantum built a mud hut in the garden and planted a bamboo grove where he meditated with friends. It was from here that he began his pilgrimage with the Vietnamese Zen master Thich Nhat Hanh, 'In the Footsteps of the Buddha'.

★

Our 37th wedding anniversary took place on 13 March 1988, one of the few anniversaries when all five of us were together. We spent the whole day by ourselves, drove to Panipat, and later had a quiet dinner. We enjoyed the usual family conversations, full of jokes and references. The children always teased me that I had a squirrel-like habit of locking up everything possible in my steel Godrej cupboard, including dried fruits, such as nuts and raisins. Aradhana always slept late because of her many admirers, who visited her at odd hours, and then resented getting up early in the morning. Shantum had his unusual ideas about gardening, and Vikram wanted—pronto!—a path made in the front garden so that he could walk around it and cogitate calmly. Premo was forever going to spend time with our friends, Asha and Shanti Jain, in Anand Lok. When I was upset about anything, the children—and sometimes even Premo—would try to turn it into a joke.

Vikram composed a poem for the occasion, which incorporated much of our family banter:

1

The mewa in the Godrej shrine,
The plaintive 'Wake me up at nine,'
The vacillating calls from Bali,
The farming schemes of our new mali,
The trendy jeep parked at the door,
The mushrooms sprouting through the floor,
The half-baked bread, the untilled beans,
The dinner tiffs, the breakfast scenes:
'You think that everything's a joke.'
'I've been delayed in Anand Lok.'
'The footpath must be made right now.
At once. Today. I don't care how . . .'
Where, but at home, at number 8,
The mansion of Ms. Justice Seth
(And spouse and issue) may one see
So rich a social comedy?

2

Although for many years apart,
The five of us are one at heart.

Beneath a single roof again
We see the seasons wax and wane.

The years will come, the years will go.
How long this lasts we cannot know,

But give thanks, piecemeal and sincere
For one more March, for one more year.

Vikram wrote the poem on Indian birch-bark paper. It was added to a collage which included a Ganesh, hand-crafted in silver wire by Shantum, photographs by Aradhana, dried flowers and leaves from the garden, including bougainvillea, pansy, eucalyptus, rose and marijuana. The collage was sprinkled with Holi colours and a little kite was stuck on. The children marked it with their thumb impressions, framed it with an old green and gold sari border, and presented it to us. It is among our most treasured possessions and hangs in our bedroom.

A poem written by my mother to us on an earlier occasion was also pasted on. It had been adapted from a rather sentimental greeting card. The italicized words were her own emendation:

There's a world of special wishes
In this greeting/*card* sent your way
To congratulate/*bless* you *very* warmly
On this anniversary day
And each wish for a future
That is filled with nothing less
Than the very things you hope for
And continued Happiness.

★

Some months later, Aradhana's close friend Dhiren Bhagat died in a jeep accident, shattering his parents' hopes and those of us who had occasion to come in contact with him or his writings. Aradhana was particularly sad. So when Peter Launsky-Tieffenthal met Aradhana at a party and tried to make contact with her later, she wasn't particularly interested. But he was persistent; he kept telephoning and eventually got through to her. He said it was more difficult to make contact with her than with the Prime Minister. He was a young Austrian diplomat, exceedingly good-looking and charming. His mode of greeting, if you were a woman, was to kiss your hand. Like others, I too was charmed by him, but my mind resisted the idea of a foreign son-in-law.

I kept warning Aradhana of the difficulties of adjusting to a different culture, but she was gradually drawn in. Suddenly, she was in love. Peter wanted her to travel with him to Vienna to meet his parents and sister and to see the place for herself. I didn't want her to go at all. It was against our culture for a young woman to travel alone with a man before marriage. What if they decided not to get married after the trip? What would it do to her reputation? What about my own colleagues, who were traditional in their beliefs and ways? What about my friends, who would think I was disgracefully lax in the matter?

A family council was held. But I was excluded, as I was too overwrought. (I had even threatened not to pay for the ticket.) Premo, who came from a much more traditional background than me, and the two boys discussed the matter with Aradhana. They were convinced that she needed to go before taking a final decision about marriage. The opinions of my colleagues and friends were not important—it was the happiness of my daughter that mattered. They insisted I should do things graciously and not make a scene, as Aradhana would go anyway. Reluctantly I saw sense in what they were saying. Aradhana went to Vienna, and she and Peter decided to get married. Once I knew the decision was final, I was fully supportive of it.

I even started to see the positive side. At least there would be no dowry demands or last minute hitches or requests for a large five-star hotel reception.

Arrangements went ahead for a wedding in late May 1990, by which time it would be a year since they first met. I wrote to Peter's parents and requested them to come. They wrote back and said that they didn't think the wedding was a good idea, especially as they were Catholics and Aradhana was not. This was a shock. The cards had gone for printing, a Madhubani wedding scene in gold on white Austrian paper. Peter insisted we should go ahead and that his sister Alexandra would be there. But the situation became more and more tense as his mother mounted telephonic pressure on him.

The cards were ready, the lists typed, the envelopes addressed, but we could not send them out. It was a difficult time. We should have been celebrating; instead, all of us, and Peter most of all, was beset by confusion and unbearable stress. Eventually, Alexandra too couldn't come, and a traditional Austrian sibling function, which had been planned, did not take place. Peter was torn apart by the pain, pressure and exhaustion of it all. Throughout all this, he was supported, advised and comforted by the Austrian ambassador and his wife, Christoph and Gail Cornaro, who were almost like surrogate parents in their affection, concern and care. Eventually, Peter and Aradhana decided the wedding should go ahead regardless.

Two days before the wedding we had a Ganesh and kalash puja, with seven happily married women blessing the bride. And the day before the wedding, a blessing was held in the chapel in the Vatican Embassy: a beautiful function, with Aradhana dressed in a white and gold sari and Peter in a blue suit.

On the morning of 20 May, after the necessary signings, swearings and witnessings, Aradhana and Peter were officially declared married by the Registrar of Marriages. Vikram wrote a poem for the occasion, which he read out soon after they had exchanged their vows:

An Acrostic to Aradhana and Peter

Poets, like diplomats, observe their norms:
Epithalamia, like protest notes,
Their force enhanced by their traditional forms,
Express far more than what one reads in quotes.
Registered male and female, man and wife,
Austrian and Indian, signed, sealed, stamped and wed,
Now far from forms, unduplicable life
Draws you by its own laws to board and bed.
A year ago you met; nor is it strange
Romance has turned so happily to rhyme.
A year from now much else may also change:
Daughters-in-law, like Rome, require some time.
Here may we wish you, starting from this day,
As wild or calm a life as you both please,
Nothing that curbs your hearts in any way,
And all the love of both your families.

But of course the 'real' wedding was to take place that evening. During the day it was hot and even—owing to freak rain a few days earlier—very humid, and we prayed that it wouldn't rain again. A daughter's wedding day is a day every mother dreams about, however modern she is. I was twenty when I got married, Aradhana was twenty-eight. That was Calcutta 1951 and this was New Delhi 1990. Even in the midst of all the last-minute arrangements, all sorts of memories were going through my head.

Evening came, and with it the Hindu ceremony of the exchange of garlands, circling around the fire and the seven ritual steps. Aradhana was dressed in the traditional red and gold sari and Peter in a Lucknow chikan kurta and pajama. He also wore a dupali topi—even though he felt it looked like a baker's cap. The ceremony was followed by dinner, to which many of Peter's friends and acquaintances and our friends and relations had been invited.

The large garden in front of the handsome double-storeyed house at 8 Rajaji Marg was filled with guests. Just as one friend, Aman Nath, had designed the wedding cards, so too another, O.P. Jain, had arranged huge old brass receptacles filled with water and rose-petals around the lawn. Sona, our gardener, had been getting the garden in order for weeks and was delighted when, according to him, the lotus in the pool opened at night as if by magic for this special occasion. (It was probably the heat from the spot-lights which had done this.) Little lights twinkled in the hedges. The wedding ceremony was conducted under a fragrant vedi of roses and rajnigandha beneath the branches of the huge laburnum tree whose drooping clusters of yellow flowers looked like golden chandeliers. Aradhana's friends, resplendent in their gorgeous saris and jewellery, stood behind the buffet tables to help serve the vegetarian food. The sound of the whirring of the fans formed a gentle backdrop to the melodious taped music of Bismillah Khan on the shehnai.

When a daughter leaves her parents' home after her wedding, it is a moment of great poignancy. Traditionally, she is now subject to her husband's and his family's control and can only return to visit her family home with their permission. Quite often in the past it meant a total break; the flower the parents had nurtured would spread its fragrance elsewhere or be crushed by the cruelty of custom or a mother-in-law's mockery. Though I knew that Aradhana's situation was different and that she was a free spirit, I could not help feeling the tug at my heartstrings and the tears welling up in my eyes as she left that night with Peter—a final severing of the umbilical cord.

★

Peter's term had almost expired and he was due to move from Delhi. Shortly after the wedding, he got a posting in Washington, DC. Aradhana was to follow later, after completing a documentary film focusing on women's work in the unorganized sector in India.

Aradhana decided to retain her Indian nationality. As a result, because of India's bar on dual nationality, she could not get a diplomatic passport as Peter's wife. She also decided that she would retain her surname. When she went to get her passport corrected to show that she was married, the Regional Passport Officer, Delhi told her she would have to apply for a new passport. She asked whether a man would have to apply for a new passport if he got married? The answer was, 'No.' She was annoyed and argued with him. She called me up from his office and inveighed against this gender injustice. I too asked him what was the reason for the differentiation. He had no real answer, except that that was the way it was.

At the time she was married, a child born abroad to an Indian mother—as opposed to an Indian father—would not automatically be an Indian citizen. But a couple of years later, Parliament ended this gender discrimination. Though the change was not retrospective, it was nevertheless a positive step in keeping with the United Nations Convention on the Elimination of All Forms of Discrimination Against Women.

Aradhana left for Washington in October. For weeks before she left, she was torn between staying back and working on a feature film, *Electric Moon*, or going to join

Peter. The director, Pradip Krishen, wanted Aradhana to work on *Electric Moon* from pre-production to post-production, and she thought it would be a great opportunity to get to know from the inside how a feature film was made. But pushed by me, with the support of the rest of the family, her brothers included, she went to Washington, carrying curtains and sofa covers for the drawing room there. Peter was waiting for her at the airport and drove her straight to the Volkswagen showroom, where he presented her with a small car. So she had no option but to drive immediately, before she could become fearful of right-hand driving.

Premo and I visited them the next summer and enjoyed the experience of being looked after by our daughter and son-in-law. They took very good care of us and we had fun together. The garden was full of the most glorious azaleas, and Aradhana had created a beautiful Austro-Indian atmosphere in her home. Peter invited the lone Supreme Court woman judge, Sandra Day O'Connor, to dinner, and we spent a very enjoyable evening. The International Association of Women Judges also invited me and we had a lively and rewarding time together.

★

In late September 1990 the Chief Justice of the Delhi High Court retired. As I was the next most senior judge, I was notified as Acting Chief Justice. The immediate effects were startling. A top-secret 'RAX' telephone was installed and I was told that no one, just no one but I could pick it up if it rang. I wondered which VIP would wish to speak to me, but it never rang except once, when it turned out to be a wrong number. I was now considered to be in need of serious protection. A horde of security personnel descended on us. They were loud-talking, back-slapping policemen, who spread themselves all over the grounds and completely took over our privacy. They also used up our water, so we were left with little to bathe in. Aradhana's numerous friends, who wanted to come and say goodbye to her were stopped and checked. We tried to curb the policemen, but without success. Aggression and bluster alternated with scraping and kow-towing.

In the meantime, in early October, Justice Ranganath Misra was sworn in as the Chief Justice of India. I received a confidential letter from him dated 4 November. It had quite clearly been sent to all the High Court Chief Justices. This is what it said:

> My dear Chief Justice,
>
> At the last Conference of yours held here, all of you had discussed the serious problem of judicial indiscipline and the growing dissatisfaction of the general public in the matter of functioning of the judicial process.
>
> Last month I wrote to you and to each individual Judge that immediate steps should be taken to improve our performance to ensure acceptability of the system by the society. You would perhaps agree with me that the conduct exhibited, the manner in which Judges function, the social rapport that is permitted to be developed, the lack of commitment to judicial functioning, want of control over the atmosphere in the Court and reasons like these have cumulatively led to the present situation.
>
> For quite some time on the basis of reports of the Law Commission and debates else where, the idea of inducting one-third of the Judges of every Court from outside is being attempted to be implemented. This necessarily involves transferring one-third of the existing Judges from their own Courts to other Courts

unless this is done at the time of appointment by posting Judges outside their own territories.

It is being reported that in some Courts the Judges do not commence work in time and they frequently rise before the scheduled lunch time; they do not reassemble in time and get up before the time for rising of the Court. This necessarily leads to curtailing the availability of manpower apart from bringing in indiscipline. Judges are expected to dispose of 650 main cases a year but there are several instances where the output is grossly low.

I have no intention of generalising these aspects. There are many Judges in the High Courts who are conscientious and are anxious to maintain the dignity of their own as also of the institution but there are others who do not have that perception. Experience of life shows that a few erring ones are sufficient to spoil any system. It is the Chief Justice's responsibility—both constitutional as also moral—to make his Court work appropriately. Therefore, the Chief Justice must exercise his powers, influence, moral bearing and personal contact to improve the working in his High Court.

It is proposed to initiate proposals for the shifting of some Judges from their Courts to different Courts with a view to implementing the recommendation of the Law Commission. It maybe that certain Judges in your Court do not find the atmosphere congenial and would like to be posted out. There may be instances where close relations of Judges are practising and, therefore, to avoid embarrassment such Judges may also like to be posted out. We have come across instances recently where Judges have started litigating in respect of their properties in Courts subordinate to their own or even in their own Courts. This certainly gives rise to a very unhappy situation. There are also instances where some Judges are not amenable to any discipline and their shifting to a different Court is likely to bring about some improvement. I look forward to an honest assessment of yours and to indicate such names as you think would be appropriate for inclusion in a list to be drawn up for such purpose.

It is also proposed to maintain a separate wing in the establishment of the Chief Justice of India where the performance of individual judges in the High Courts may be appropriately registered. This would be necessary for several purposes including taking up Judges appointment as Chief Justices in High Courts, elevating them to the Supreme Court and for special posts as and when occasions arise. I would like to inform you that Union Government have accepted the proposal of setting up an in-service institute at the national level where judicial officers from the States and such of the High Court Judges who would like to come when invited would undergo a few weeks' refresher courses or undertake research. We shall also require the capable section of the Judges in the High Courts to visit the Institute for brief periods for purposes of lecturing to the officers.

There are some particulars available about the Judges and their performance until they are recruited but no information is maintained relating to specialisation, authorship of books or contributions to journals and the like once they are elevated as Judges. It is necessary that such information should also be available in the records to be maintained. Information regarding Judges' disposal per annum is also necessary to be maintained for assessing judicial efficiency for the purposes indicated already. Your Registry should, therefore, be directed to forward to the Registrar-General of the Supreme Court every month the record of disposal of main cases per Judge by name to enable the record to be complete and updated. This may start from December of 1990 when the information for November may be sent.

I would request you to kindly respond to the letter at your earliest.

With regards,

Yours sincerely,
Ranganath Misra

Hon'ble Smt. Leila Seth,
Chief Justice,
High Court of Delhi,
Delhi

[The word 'Acting' had been scribbled in by hand before the typed words 'Chief Justice'.]

I appreciated Chief Justice Misra's anxiety and sense of urgency in trying to get to grips with the problems facing the judiciary, especially those pertaining to delay and indiscipline. But I was surprised at some of his proposals, especially those pertaining to keeping a record of the work of High Court judges in the Registry of the Supreme Court. Under the Constitution of India, whereas the High Courts have supervisory or disciplinary control in administrative matters over the subordinate judiciary, the Supreme Court of India does not have such control over the High Courts. In fact, the Supreme Court's function regarding the High Courts pertains to hearing appeals and special leave petitions and laying down the law, which is then binding on all courts within the territory of India.

The letter was confidential and came in a sealed cover. As is apparent from its contents, it required some information about judges whose relatives were practising in the High Court, as also those who were litigating in personal matters. This information would have to be procured from the High Court Registry. I was very careful not to disclose the contents of the letter nor even the fact that I had received such a letter. I decided instead to start collecting the information very cautiously and in a circumspect manner. But even before I could do so, the letter and its contents seemed to have become public knowledge. Judges from Punjab and Haryana started talking about it and it became the subject matter of constant debate among the judiciary, in the legal profession in general, and in the press. Almost all judges felt that sending monthly particulars about their disposal rate to the Supreme Court Registry impinged on their authority and independence.

In fact, in an article written in the *Tribune* on 26 November 1990 by a former Chief Justice of the Delhi High Court, Justice Rajindar Sachar, the entire contents of the letter had been discussed. How he got hold of this confidential letter is not known, but he strongly deprecated the particular proposal mentioned above as being outside the Constitution's provisions and deeply demoralizing.

Over lunch in the lounge, all the other judges discussed the letter agitatedly. They said that judges should be appraised on the basis of their impartiality, their independence from any outside influence and the quality of their judgments, not by the number of cases they disposed of each month. In any case, work was allotted by the Chief Justice, and heavy cases, which took a long time for hearing, were often given to the more competent judges, but this would affect their disposal rate; also, while sitting in Division Bench, a junior judge might be paired with a senior judge who was over-thorough and slow, and thus failed to dispose of cases expeditiously. I listened to the discussions, but had to remain tight-lipped. I thought that since I was only an Acting Chief Justice and a new Chief Justice would be taking over soon, he would have to deal with the matter. But on the evening of 15 November, I received an extraordinary phone call from the Chief Justice of India. I was not surprised that he called, since I had requested a date to meet him in connection with work involving the International Law Association, of which I was the secretary. But the conversation took an astonishing turn. I took notes during the course of it. This is how it went:

He : 'Hello?'

I : 'Good evening, Chief Justice.'

He : 'Yes.'

I : 'I requested an appointment with you pertaining to the International Law Association.'

He : 'Yes. I am going to Calcutta on Friday and will give you a confirmed time by Monday, for next week.'

I : 'You might perhaps know that the Chief Justice of India is normally the President of the Indian branch of the International law Association—so Mr B. Sen and I would like to come over and request you . . .'

He cut in gruffly: 'That will be alright.'

After a short pause, he continued the conversation in an angry manner and started shouting loudly. He continued in this tone till the end. I held my temper in check.

He : 'I am informed that many of the judges of your Court don't sit in the afternoon.'

I : 'Chief Justice, I don't think that is correct; there may be the odd judge who is not sitting, but this may be for a variety of reasons.'

He : 'Why should there be even one who doesn't
sit. I know that there are a number. I know
that you sit the whole day. Send me their
names immediately. I will transfer them. How
dare they not work, sitting in Delhi, while
judges of the Supreme Court are slogging
from morning to evening. Send me the names
at once. I have written to you. I will transfer
them.'

I : 'Chief Justice, when I came to Delhi in 1972,
there was a practice in the Delhi High Court
of judges rising for coffee after admissions at
about noon. I found this very strange. But
there is no such practice now.'

He : 'No. No. No. Send me their names. I will
transfer them.'

The conversation ended with his banging down the receiver.

I was taken aback and totally nonplussed by this behaviour.
I wondered if he spoke to other Chief Justices like this—or
was it only because I was a woman and he thought he could
bully me? Or was it because I was just an Acting Chief
Justice? Well, I wasn't going to be browbeaten, but I was
certainly upset.

About half an hour later, the phone rang again. I picked
it up expectantly, thinking it might be the Chief Justice
calling to apologize after he had cooled down. Instead, it was
my friend and colleague, Justice Sunanda Bhandare, on the
line. She said, 'What happened between the Chief Justice and
you?' I kept quiet, as I didn't know what and how much I
should say. After all, I was in the position of the Chief Justice
of the High Court and should not really discuss matters that
were supposed to be confidential, with other judges. Sunanda
continued: 'I met the Chief Justice of India at Justice Sawant's

house. Murli and I had gone to visit him, as he is not well. Chief Justice Ranganath Misra also came to visit him. As soon as he saw me, he said, "I have fired up your Chief Justice just now." '

I was surprised at the impropriety of Chief Justice Misra telling a colleague of mine, and that too in the presence of a practising advocate, that he had shouted at the Chief Justice of the High Court. So was Sunanda.

In any case, I had decided to write to him, and that was what, on 19 November, I did.

Dear Chief Justice,

Thank you for your letter of 4th November, 1990 which I received on the 7th. I was planning to reply after collecting all the information and collating the material and making an assessment. But in view of your telephone call on the 15th November, 1990 I am sending an interim reply.

I agree with you that there is an urgent need to improve our performance to ensure acceptability of the judicial system in society.

I have made some enquiries and I am informed that normally, now, all the Judges of this Court commence work in time and adhere to the time schedule of the Court. It is only if a Judge is not feeling well or the list suddenly collapses and no lawyers are available that Judges are sometimes forced to rise.

I am not aware of any Judge of this Court who does not find the atmosphere congenial and would, therefore, like to be posted outside Delhi. However, there are a number of Judges whose relations are practising in this Court and the subordinate courts in Delhi. I am not aware of all the relations of the Judges who are practising but as far as I have been able to ascertain, I am listing below the name of the Judge; names of the practising Advocates and the relationship:

[The names of 12 judges and their relations, who were practising advocates, were then set out.]

It will take some more time to ascertain which of the Judges are litigating in either this Court or the subordinate courts. But, for the present, I know that there is a partition suit pending in this Court pertaining to the property of Mr Justice Mahinder Narain as also a rent matter pertaining to Mr Justice B.N. Kirpal.

Before ending, I would like to touch on a matter arising out of our telephone conversation on the evening of the 15th November, 1990, which has been troubling me since then. I have the highest respect for the Chief Justice of India and I expect that the Chief Justice of India also respects the Judges of the High Courts. Consequently, the manner in which you spoke to me on the telephone surprised and dismayed me.

I am not used to being shouted at or spoken to in an offensive tone; nor am I used to being spoken to in a manner that implies subservience on my part; nor do I appreciate the intemperate tenor with which you spoke about the Judges of the Delhi High Court. I would like to register my protest. I expect both to give and to receive a modicum of courtesy.

With regards,

Yours sincerely,
Leila Seth

Hon'ble Mr Justice Ranganath Misra,
Chief Justice of India,
5, Safdarjung Road,
New Delhi

Though Chief Justice Ranganath Misra did not reply to this letter, I know that it reached him because it was sent by the peon book. Also, when I went with B. Sen to his house for a meeting in connection with the International Law Association, he was very courteous and cordial and went out of his way to be over-hospitable and pleasant. When B. Sen remarked afterwards on his unwonted affability, I said something mild in response and deflected the conversation.

Very soon thereafter, at a seminar of the Brahma Kumaris, Chief Justice Ranganath Misra thought nothing of telling working women that they 'should go back to their homes . . . God has not created man and woman as equal . . .' Women and women's organizations were outraged by his remarks and referred to him as a male chauvinist. They wondered how someone like him could possibly protect their human rights and dignity. I wondered how much angrier they would have been if they had known about the undignified manner in which he had talked to me. But my lips were sealed at that time.

I often ponder how many men are even aware that they are being partisan when they expect women to play second fiddle. Their belief that women should not compete with men but should stay at home and take care of them, is part of their fixed mental wiring, brought about by their environment and upbringing, at least in India. I wonder when that will change. Years later, when, as a member of the Law Commission of India I suggested that marital rape should be treated as a crime, my colleagues, who were men, were thoroughly alarmed. In fact, a male judge in another context in a particular matrimonial case pronounced: 'The introduction of law in the home is like introducing a bull in a china shop . . . It will be a ruthless destroyer.'

First Woman Chief Justice

In late 1988, when I had been a judge for about eleven years, I received a telephone call from Chief Justice Pathak of the Supreme Court of India. I was a bit surprised at the call, as I was in Bombay at the time to attend a family wedding. He asked me whether I was alone and could talk freely. I was in the small passage of my brother Michi's flat where the telephone was kept and doors opened to all the other rooms, but since I was standing there on my own, I said, 'Yes.' One of the senior members of the International Law Association was coming over from Russia. I thought it was in connection with this visit that the Chief Justice wanted to talk to me, though I did wonder what was so secret about that.

I was therefore completely surprised by what he had to say. He told me that he was intending to make a recommendation that I be elevated to the Supreme Court of India and asked me if he had my permission to do so. My heart gave a little leap, but I replied quietly that it was kind of him to consider my name. The conversation ended there, with him adding that this was a matter of the utmost confidentiality. My brother, who had originally picked up the telephone and been told that the Chief Justice of India wanted to speak to me, was naturally curious. I passed it off as a matter concerning the International Law Association.

I was inwardly very excited. I was fifty-eight years old and would be the first woman judge in the Supreme Court of India. I had no patron and was totally non-political. I had made it so far on my own and this was to be the crown of my career. I meant to prove myself worthy of the trust reposed in me by the Chief Justice and be a competent member of the court.

When I returned to Delhi, I wondered whether I should call on the Chief Justice, as our conversation on the telephone had been so brief. On the other hand I didn't want to appear as if I was pushing him. The visit of the Russian member of the International Law Association gave me an opportunity to talk to him; he asked me to come over to his house. He said that there were six vacancies in the Supreme Court, but that he was thinking of recommending only two names at present; he would send another four names after the first two had been cleared. He added that he planned to recommend Chief Justice Verma of the Rajasthan High Court and me in the first instance, since everyone was very keen that there should be a woman in the Supreme Court soon.

He asked me whether I knew of any reason why the government would oppose my appointment; I said I was not aware of any. He also wanted to know about my family background. I told him about my upbringing: my father's early death, my widowed mother's determination to educate us, my husband, my children, my career. He then asked me whether I knew any people in high places; I replied that I did not. It was a quiet, friendly chat and I came away content except that I was left wondering why he had asked me whether I knew people in high places and whether there was any reason why the government might turn my name down. Was it because a distinguished and independent judge like Justice Lentin of the Bombay High Court, who had been recommended repeatedly by Chief Justice Pathak, had not been acceptable to the government?

In early June 1989, during the summer vacation, Justice Verma was sworn in as a judge of the Supreme Court of India. I wondered what had happened to my appointment and whether I had been struck off the list. Soon I learnt from the grapevine that Chief Justice Pathak had eventually decided to send all six names together and, being the juniormost, I was at the bottom of the list. For some unknown reason, only one name had been cleared by the government; the others had been kept in abeyance. This is called destiny.

Normally, Chief Justice Pathak would have retired from the Supreme Court of India in late November. But in mid-June, he was appointed a judge of the International Court at the Hague: the Indian appointee had died, there was an unfinished term, and Justice Pathak, when asked, had opted to go there. As a result, Justice Venkataramiah, who would normally have been Chief Justice for about twenty-three days at the end of Chief Justice Pathak's term, was now suddenly hurtled into the position. When I called on Chief Justice Venkataramiah to congratulate him, he brought up the topic of my appointment himself. He told me that he had read many of my income-tax judgements and that they were good. He said, 'Your name was jointly suggested by Chief Justice Pathak and me.' I was pleased by this and thought that I was through—but did not discuss the matter with anyone except Premo.

However, the appointment of a new Chief Justice meant that the names suggested earlier, even though they may have been discussed informally with the senior judges of which he was one, would be sent back by the Executive to him for reconsideration. (This was before the Supreme Court had judicially determined the legal force of the word 'consultation' in this connection.) Unfortunately, Chief Justice Venkataramiah fell ill in Calcutta a few weeks later. He was then advised to go for follow-up treatment abroad, which the government kindly arranged. Before he left, he wanted the six existing vacancies on the Supreme Court filled. The names that had been sent up by Justice Pathak and not cleared by the Executive for a long time were now set aside and an entirely new list prepared.

Instead of the two Reddys, there were now two Ramaswamis, instead of S.C. Agarwal there was N.M. Kasliwal, and instead of C.S. Dharmadhikari there was M.M. Punchi. M. Fathima Beevi had replaced me.

Justice Fathima Beevi had been in judicial service since 1958 and had been elevated to the Kerala High Court in 1983. She had retired in April 1989 at the age of sixty-two. Since she had already retired more than five months earlier, it was quite unusual—perhaps unique—that her name should have been put up for the Supreme Court. A couple of Supreme Court judges told me that she had lobbied for the position on the grounds that she would be the first Muslim woman in the world to be a judge of a Supreme Court, and that there was at the time no Muslim judge in the Supreme Court of India. When it was pointed out to her that Justice Ahmadi was a Supreme Court judge, she had responded that he was not a Muslim, merely an Ahmadi—and that even Pakistan did not treat Ahmadis as Muslims.

Many people knew that her brother-in-law was a prominent local politician and believed that the Congress government had been assured that they would get the Kerala Muslim votes in the forthcoming elections if she were made a judge. The Law Minister at the time, Mr Shankaranand, had been pressing for either Justice Fathima Beevi or Justice

Padma Khastgir for some time. Chief Justice Pathak had written back to him to say, 'I find myself unagreeable to their appointment to the Supreme Court,' and that I was the appropriate choice among the women judges of the High Court at that juncture.

Though I had heard some stories and gossip about Justice Fathima Beevi being appointed to the Supreme Court, I didn't give them much credence. As a result, when her appointment was actually announced and she was sworn in on 6 October, I felt terribly upset, both for the system and for myself. It showed that lobbying worked. It showed that politics worked. It showed that the misuse of religion worked. Above all, it showed that every decent convention could be broken and that merit was no consideration.

Her judicial record was quite ordinary. When some people pointed this out to Chief Justice Venkataramiah, he openly stated that she was going to be a very junior judge in the Supreme Court, would retire in two and a half years and would therefore not be heading a bench, so it didn't really matter. When his words were reported in the newspapers, lawyers and judges were shocked. Women lawyers were particularly dismayed, as she was the first woman judge of the Supreme Court and this was adding insult to injury—first by appointing a retired and not so competent woman judge, and secondly by making such disparaging remarks.

Justice Sabyasachi Mukharji became Chief Justice in December 1989. Two months later, Justices K.J. Reddy, S.C. Agarwal and Ram Manohar Sahai were brought to the Supreme Court; and so was the other Reddy, Justice Jeevan Reddy, a little later. Justice C.S. Dharmadhikari had retired in November 1989. The only person left out from the two lists was myself, as it was felt that the Supreme Court now had its token woman.

★

A few years earlier, a convention had been introduced that a judge should not normally be made the regular (as opposed to the Acting) Chief Justice of the High Court in which he had been a judge unless he had less than one year to go before retirement. That was why (though I was Acting Chief Justice in the interim) a judge from the Rajasthan High Court was brought in to head the Delhi High Court. Though I was now the seniormost puisne judge, and therefore in line to become Chief Justice somewhere, I was held back by another convention: that there could not be more than one judge from a particular court as a chief justice anywhere in India. Justice Yogeshwar Dayal from the Delhi High Court was at the time Chief Justice of Andhra Pradesh, and it was only when he went to the Supreme Court in March 1991 that a judge from Delhi could be made a chief justice.

I did not want to leave Delhi, since my husband's and sons' work and activities were located there. Unlike male judges, whose families could more easily follow them to their places of transfer, my family would not be able to give up their assignments and follow me. Chief Justice Sabyasachi Mukharji of the Supreme Court (who had succeeded Chief Justice Venkataramiah) had given me to understand that he would keep me in Delhi as Acting Chief Justice for some time; then, when there was less than a year for me to retire, I could be made the regular Chief Justice. But Chief Justice Mukharji died very suddenly in September 1990, and Justice Ranganath Misra became Chief Justice of India. He had other ideas. When, in late July 1991, Chief Justice Jain of the Delhi High Court retired, he decided that Justice Mital of the Punjab and Haryana High Court should be brought to Delhi and I should be made Chief Justice of the High Court of Himachal Pradesh in Shimla.

My feelings were ambivalent. I could have opted not to go and to remain a puisne judge in Delhi, but I was going to be the first woman Chief Justice of a state in India and that was something I did not want to pass up. I knew it was going to be hard without my family but looked forward to the new assignment with a great deal of excitement and some apprehension. I had no experience of administrative work except as Acting Chief Justice in Delhi. I knew that, being a woman, I would be critically watched and that any mistakes or misjudgments that I made would be highlighted and would reflect on other women who followed. I needed to be especially conscientious and diligent.

Before I assented to the appointment, Chief Justice Ranganath Misra assured me that, owing to the suddenness of the move and the difficulties that this would create, I could retain the house at 8 Rajaji Marg for six months. This would enable my family to find accommodation and me to return to Delhi in the winter vacation to pack up the place. In fact, the move turned out to be even more sudden than anticipated. On Friday, 2 August, I was informed that a notification had been issued and I had to move to Shimla immediately, as Justice Mital was to be sworn in as Chief Justice of Delhi High Court at 10 a.m. on Monday the 5th. Premo and I left at 6 a.m. on Sunday the 4th, in a car sent by the Himachal Pradesh High Court. I had practised in Delhi for seven years and had been a judge for thirteen. It was a great wrench to leave after twenty years. But there was no time for farewells or good-byes—not even for a party by the Bar.

The journey to Shimla was unusual. The Registrar of the Himachal High Court came to Delhi to accompany Premo and me. He brought along a liveried attendant and a personal security officer (or PSO). The gold on the livery of the attendant, especially on his resplendent belt, his splendid turban and the red cloth shield on the dazzling white front of his tunic quite outdid anything I was used to in the Delhi High Court! We stopped at Panipat for a sumptuous breakfast of puri, aloo and halwa with Premo's family. As soon as we entered the state of Himachal Pradesh, a guard of honour was presented and I had to take the salute—an experience I was entirely unprepared for. I did not know what was expected of me, but managed to get through it somehow. (My PSO later taught me how to take the salute correctly.) We got to Shimla quite late in the afternoon. Despite the rain, it was exhilarating to be in the mountains. Because the Chief Justice's official residence was undergoing repair, we were lodged in Hotel Holiday Home, which was just below the High Court. I was sworn in the next day by the Governor of Himachal Pradesh.

I knew no one in Shimla. Apart from Premo, there was no one to share my joy with: joy which was mingled with sadness as I realized that for the next fifteen months—that is, until I retired—I would be living on my own, without family or friends. As Chief Justice I could not make any new friends in Shimla; one never knew whose case might come up before the High Court and who was related to whom. But I have to say that the people of Himachal Pradesh were, in general, very welcoming and friendly, the members of the Bar respectful, the High Court Registry helpful and my colleagues caring.

After spending a few days in the Hotel Holiday Home, I shifted to the small rooms and meagre facilities of the High Court guestrooms in the High Court premises. The Government of Himachal Pradesh had been more than willing that I stay on in the hotel or move to more lavish accommodation until the Chief Justice's house had been repaired and repainted. But I didn't want to enjoy the State's hospitality for even a day more than was absolutely necessary, since the State is a major litigant in the courts. The guesthouse became my home for more than a month. It was cold and sunless, and—having been newly set up—somewhat bleak and uncongenial. It was the time of the apple harvest and trucks were being driven to market all through the night. They would have to negotiate the steep gradient outside the guesthouse, and the whine of their engines as well as the pollution were a constant irritant. It rained most of the time and everything was musty and damp.

The contractors and workers who were repairing the Chief Justice's house were taking forever. Their excuse was the rain. Repainting the bright green walls of the house a sober cream took more that a month. Finally, more than six weeks after I arrived in Shimla, I could wait no longer, and decided to shift, even though the work was not yet complete.

Armsdell—for so it had been named by the British who built it around 1860—was a beautiful little house nestling on the hill below the far grander Peterhoff (which was to burn down in the 1980s). The Viceroy had once had his regal perch at Peterhoff and his private secretary his humbler one at Armsdell. (Later, in 1884, the Earl of Dufferin moved to the newly-constructed Viceregal Lodge, a large grey stone edifice, now the Indian Institute of Advanced Study.) After 1947, Armsdell was used by Pandit Jawaharlal Nehru as a summer retreat. It became the Chief Justice's house in 1971.

The house has a long, narrow driveway with an elongated triangular garden with lovely deodar trees. There is a drawing room and a dining room and an office downstairs and three bedrooms on the first floor, but the life and soul of the house is a fully-glazed verandah room on the first floor built by Chief Justice Pathak when he lived there in the seventies. The downstairs drawing room was both dark and cold, so the upstairs verandah room, full of sunshine and warmth, was where I entertained the few non-official guests I had. This was also where I worked, ate when alone, lazed and read and watched the valley and the distant mountain ranges. In the summer I watched the antics of the monkeys jumping from branch to branch and tree to tree. In the winter I watched the snow falling silently and being held like a child in the arms of the tall deodars standing near the front entrance of the house. Two wisteria creepers, one white and the other mauve, covered the front of the house and, for the brief period they were in bloom, were a joy to behold. There were lilies growing on the hillside and nasturtiums creeping out of the supporting stone wall. There was even a small ginkgo tree in the garden.

I lived and slept all alone in this house. There was, however, a bell connecting my bedroom to the servants' quarters and another to the security staff outside, by the far gate. A few nights after I had moved in, I couldn't sleep; I kept hearing noises in the roof above me. I was reluctant to alert the staff, as they might think that I was a foolish female frightened by every sound. But the next night, when I went to the toilet, I heard a mouse scamper across the room. I was traumatized. I clambered on top of the bed and rang both bells with all my might. No one came. I wondered what would have happened if a burglar had come in, though this seemed almost as bad. I tried to scream but couldn't. I rang the bell again, this time continuously; and finally the cook arrived. He had a key to the house and let himself in. He was amazed at my conduct. Here was the mighty Chief Justice, whose fiats and orders were law in the State, and in whose presence people quaked in court—terrified of a little mouse!

He soon enlightened me about the situation: a family of mice had been living in the wooden roof above me for quite some time. They could not be got rid of unless the sloping tin roof above it was removed and the whole area reconstructed. The family seemed to be comfortably ensconed. That was their territory. What they ate and where they got it was a great mystery, but no concern of ours. If a baby mouse escaped and entered our territory, I should not take too much notice of it, as it was harmless. I accepted this advice and tried to remain calm until one day I discovered a large mouse swimming in the loo.

★

I loved the mountains, and used to walk to court from Armsdell, unlike previous Chief Justices, who used to drive in. I felt it was one of the joys of being in a hill station. My PSO used to follow me unobtrusively. One day, however, I noticed that, apart from my PSO, an armed guard in uniform, carrying a gun—an AK-47—was trailing along behind me. As soon as I got to court, I asked the Registrar what it was all about. He said, 'There had been a red alert, and the Inspector General of Police has designated a special guard for you.' I told the Registrar that hardly anyone noticed me trundling along in my usual way, but that with the AK-47 armed guard behind me, I would be a walking target for any terrorist. Not many people in Shimla knew who I was, and quite often busy shopkeepers would exasperatedly thumb me over to another counter. I liked to be in a position where I was treated as a common citizen, so that I remained in touch with people and things.

The Registrar informed the Inspector General, but it was a couple of days before I finally shook off the gun-toting guard, as the IG wanted me to indemnify him in writing with my signature appended, so that he would not be held responsible if anything happened to me.

★

I soon fell into the stride of court work and administration, but there was a ticklish human problem. Justice Vijay Kumar Mehrotra was the seniormost judge in Himachal Pradesh: he was just one day older than me but about four months senior to me as a judge. He had twice acted as Chief Justice, once when an earlier Chief Justice had been elevated to the Supreme Court and again when another one retired. I was told that he was hoping against hope that I would not be brought to Himachal Pradesh and that he would continue as Chief Justice. He had heard a rumour that I was refusing to come away from Delhi and he prayed that this was true. On the other hand, he knew that he had been transferred at his own request to Shimla from Allahabad on the clear understanding that he would not demand to be made Chief Justice when he became the seniormost judge. He had hoped that he would be elevated to the Supreme Court, but that didn't happen. He was strict, hard working and sober in his ways, a man of integrity, but obviously bitter that someone junior to him had been made Chief Justice—and a woman at that. I understood his feelings and realized how hard it must be for him. I tried to involve him in all the decision-making and never constituted a bench in which we would have to sit together and our relative positions become apparent. He, too, was basically cooperative.

I think it was hard for some of the other male judges too, particularly for those who came from feudal backgrounds and were not used to the idea of a woman being the decision-maker. At Full Court meetings I made a conscious effort to be gentle but firm. I was interested in achieving the best for the administration of justice rather than showing my prowess. So I tried to work by consensus. But when that was not possible or it went against the grain of what I believed to be right, I put my foot down.

During my term as Chief Justice, I had to deal with a strike in the High Court Registry, and I tried to handle it by applying the same principles and attitude. Before 1966, the hilly area of Himachal—literally, 'the land of snow'—was a part of the state of Punjab. When the state of Himachal

Pradesh was finally carved out, a portion of the plains of Punjab was also included in it. The hill people felt that they were the real, the old Himachalis, and that the Punjabis from the plains—dubbed the 'new Himachalis'—were not really acceptable. In June 1990, thirteen people had been appointed as clerks and restorers in the High Court for a limited period; they had been appointed on an ad hoc basis, without going through the standard open processes that should have been followed. They were now pressing to have their appointments made permanent. Ten of them were close relatives of people already serving in the High Court as readers, registrars, the private secretary to the Chief Justice, and so on. Other employees, who had been working for many years, objected to this. Why, they said, should a regularly appointed peon, for example, be prevented from being promoted to clerk, simply because an irregularly appointed clerk was taking up that slot—and was now making matters worse by seeking to get the irregularity regularized? There was a general feeling of ill-will, and it was unnecessarily being made into an issue of new Himachalis versus old Himachalis, since most of the people appointed on an ad hoc basis were old Himachalis. A decision had to be taken about these appointments. There was something of a rift even among the judges about this issue, as some were old Himachalis and some new.

Both groups filed writ petitions in the High Court, and these were heard by a Division Bench. In January 1992 Justice Bhawani Singh allowed the petition of the ad hoc appointees whereas Justice Devinder Gupta dismissed it. Since there was a difference of opinion between the two judges, the matter was referred to a third judge. Justice Kamlesh Sharma's view coincided with that of Justice Gupta's. In view of the majority opinion, the writ petition was dismissed on 26 May 1992. As a consequence of this judgement, on 27 May I was cloistered with the Registrar till late at night. A decision was taken on the file to terminate the ad hoc appointments, on the basis of 'last to come, first to go'. The orders were issued on 28 May. There were speeches and demonstrations in the vicinity of the High Court and a lightning strike of indefinite duration was threatened. I had a sleepless night, but I comforted myself with the thought that it was only a threat and that no notice of the strike had been given. But on 29 May at about 11 a.m. the employees of the Registry suddenly and without any notice went on indefinite strike.

As the court was in session, the Registrar apprised me of the situation at 1 p.m. at the start of the lunch break. I discussed the matter with my colleagues, guided the Registrar as to how to proceed, and authorized him to talk to the striking employees. The strike appeared to be inspired by the ad hoc appointees whose services had been dispensed with consequent to the judgment, though some other issues were also raised. The Registrar discussed the matter with the employees and they admitted that they should have brought their grievances to him or me before going on strike. In his amiable manner he explained that the High Court had nothing against any of them, but that recruitment and promotion rules had to be followed. He also told them that the strike was illegal and unjustified and that the consequences could be serious. After some persuasion by him, most of the people trickled back to work and the strike was called off. It had been touch and go. An indefinite strike had been averted and the administrative reputation of the first woman Chief Justice saved. I decided not to make a big issue of finding out who had tried to instigate the strike. I thought it wiser to let the two-year-old tension just fizzle out.

The Registrar, Mr Kuldip Sood, who—after my time— became a judge of the High Court, had sensitive antennae and a good deal of tact. I usually—though not invariably—

took his advice. One day, when concentrating on a case, I heard loud music floating in through the windows of the courtroom. I made inquiries and learnt it was coming from a gurdwara. I asked the Registrar to request that the sound be lowered. He said it was not possible; it could cause all sorts of trouble if one demanded authorities of a religious institution to be quieter. I looked up the law myself and asked him to write a letter, quoting chapter and verse, stating that they were welcome to play music for themselves, but could not inflict it by way of loudspeakers on all of us, especially hospitals, courts and so on. The Registrar then personally spoke to the gurdwara authorities and, in his diplomatic manner, obtained the desired result without writing the letter.

★

As Chief Justice, I travelled the whole state, either for administrative reasons or in order to popularize so-called Lok Adalats as an alternative forum to courts for the resolution of disputes—one that was speedier, cheaper and less adversarial. Some years earlier, Chief Justice P.D. Desai had tried to get magistrates and district judges to do reconciliation work among disputants: that is, to try and get them to sort out their differences instead of continuing to battle it out in court. He took pains to give the judicial officers credit for this work, since otherwise nobody would have been interested in doing it. Because of this background, introducing Lok Adalats was much easier in Himachal Pradesh than elsewhere.

Himachal Pradesh is a most beautiful state. Though some districts such as Lahul and Spiti are not easily accessible, the people there are particularly simple and charming. Many of the areas are tribal, and customary personal law has been preserved there. Practices such as polyandry prevail even today. Often, like Draupadi, a woman is married to a family of brothers. By tradition, the progeny are all shown to be the children of the eldest brother, though the mother more often than not knows whose child it very likely is. In order to avoid jealousy and heartburn in the family, it is customary for the woman to spend time with each brother, in rotation, for a fixed period of time. Before I went to Himachal, I did not even know that this form of marriage still existed and was therefore very surprised to talk to a woman who actually practised it. She told me that it worked very well for her!

23 March 1992 was a very special day. Justice Kamlesh Sharma, who was an additional judge of the Himachal Pradesh High Court, was appointed as a permanent judge; I had the honour of giving her the oath of office—a woman Chief Justice swearing in a woman judge. This had not ever happened in India before. The swearing-in was held in the large courtroom of the Chief Justice and was attended by a number of ministers, including the Chief Minister, who came because he appreciated the importance of the moment. The ceremony took place between 9.50 and 9.55 a.m., so that court work could start on time as usual.

I was particularly happy, having got to know Kamlesh in the eight months I had been there; I found her to be a person of great sensitivity, sincerity and integrity. We had travelled together to various places in the state, sometimes through difficult and even hazardous terrain, to hold Lok Adalats and legal aid and counselling camps. She really appreciated the problems of the people and had a wonderful way of relating to those who were in need.

The sanctioned strength of the High Court at that time was five permanent judges and three additional judges. It was a good feeling to know that out of the five permanent judges, two were now women. This was quite unusual, considering that out of about four hundred permanent High Court judges in all of the eighteen High Courts at that time, only about ten were women.

Being Chief Justice, I came in contact with the Governors of both Himachal Pradesh and Punjab. The Punjab Governor had a beautiful summer home in Mashobra, called Hem Kunj, not far from the President of India's summer home, The Retreat. One evening in early June, Governor Surendra Nath and his wife hosted a small dinner for nine people: the President of India, the Governor and Chief Minister of Himachal Pradesh, their respective spouses, and myself. His nonagenarian mother also put in an appearance and it was a particularly pleasant evening, informal and relaxed. The food was vegetarian but interesting and the company and conversation both friendly and free, though there was no alcohol to loosen our tongues. Ten days later, the President, R. Venkataraman, himself hosted a tea, as was his wont, in the beautiful gardens of The Retreat. But it was a large gathering and, though set in charming surroundings, lacked the personal touch and pleasure of the earlier evening.

As far as his or her judicial duties are concerned, the Chief Justice is merely another judge. But apart from the heavy and very time-consuming administrative duties and pressures, certain other roles and responsibilities devolve upon whoever holds that office. I will touch upon three of these— liaising with the State Government where necessary; representing the court, for example at the annual Chief Justices' Conference or when expressing our condolences on the death of a colleague; and helping to advise, guide and encourage judicial officers, such as magistrates and district judges.

Mr Shanta Kumar was the Chief Minister of Himachal Pradesh throughout my time in Shimla. Before becoming a politician he had been in the education field; he was a man of some sensitivity and decorum. I had to discuss matters pertaining to housing for the judges, appointments both in the High Court and to various tribunals, and other such issues with him. We didn't always agree, but there was respect and dignity in our relationship. He was a man of some courage and insisted on maintaining the principle of 'no work, no pay'. The government servants who were used to getting their own way and being pampered politically threw him out at the next elections as his regime did not suit them. They were continually striking and then demanding to be paid for that period.

In September 1992, two retired Chief Justices of the Supreme Court, M. Hidayatullah and S.M. Sikri, both of whom I had known and admired, died suddenly. As Chief Justice I was called upon to speak at the Full Court Reference and to send the Himachal Pradesh High Court's condolences to the bereaved family.

I said that since Justice Hidayatullah had been Chief Justice of India from 1968 to 1970, before I came to Delhi, I had never seen him in court; but I had read many of his judgments and been very impressed by their lucidity and fairness. Another fact, which had made a great impression on me, was that when he was called upon to be a prosecution witness in a case, where a person had physically attacked Justice Vaidyanathan, Justice Grover and him in open court, he refused to be examined 'on commission' and had gone to the Court of Session in person to give evidence and be cross-examined, like an ordinary witness, even though he was the Chief Justice of India. As Acting President of India for a short period in 1968, and later after retirement, he conducted himself with decency, dignity and decorum. He loved both literature and the law, as was apparent from his speeches. He was friendly and genial, as I could personally attest, and a family man.

About Justice Sikri I mentioned that he had the unique

distinction of being the first member of the Bar to be appointed directly to the Supreme Court in 1964, a very rare event to this day. He was Advocate-General of Punjab and a brilliant lawyer when he was so appointed. The landmark judgment in the case of Kesavananda Bharati was given a day before he retired; there it was held by the majority that the power to amend the Constitution did not include the power to alter its basic structure or framework so as to change its identity.

I pointed out that Chief Justice Sikri had been closely associated with the birth of the Himachal Pradesh High Court. In April 1971, when he presented the emblem of the High Court to the Chief Justice of Himachal Pradesh, he had observed that the emblem included the scales of justice, both sides of which were equally balanced and that it was the duty of the High Courts to strive to strike a just balance between the demands of the State and the precious rights of its citizens. In striking this balance the judges had to take into consideration all the relevant facts of the case, including the overwhelming problems facing India and the urgent need to eradicate poverty and to establish an egalitarian society. He was the Chief Justice of India when I first came to Delhi. I remembered him as a pleasant man, courteous to the Bar and particularly encouraging to junior lawyers. He had combined the learning of a jurist with the wisdom of a judge.

Appraising the contributions to the law—and to the atmosphere and environment of the exercise of the law—of judges whom I had respected helped me formulate my own views on the functions of a judge. At a refresher course for the Himachal Pradesh Judicial Service organized by the High Court, I shared my thoughts with the young officers. I said, perhaps partly stating the obvious, that a good judge was one who behaved well both inside and outside court, whose reputation was beyond reproach, and who gave balanced and unbiased judgments. He should not be overbearing; this held particularly true for a magistrate, the first and most visible rung of the judiciary with whom the public came into contact. The cases before him should be disposed of as clearly and as quickly as justice allowed; it was important not to grant too many adjournments or to dawdle over one's judgments. These judgments should be clear, logical, well-structured and untrammelled by inessentials, so that justice could be seen to be done—for nothing hurts as much as injustice, or even justice misunderstood. Finally, a judge should cultivate a creative and conciliatory approach, so that conflict between parties could be avoided if possible and minimized where not.

These refresher courses and the enthusiasm of the young officers reaffirmed my faith in the inestimable value of education—at any stage of one's life. I had often repeated the adage, 'If you plan one year ahead you grow rice, if you plan ten years ahead you plant trees, and if you plan a hundred years ahead you educate children.' But who are the best teachers for small children other than their parents? A case came up in the Himachal Pradesh High Court where this was indirectly the issue.

Lalima Gupta and a few others challenged the district-wise reservation to the Junior Basic Training Course for teachers as being violative of Articles 14 and 15 of the Constitution of India. Justice Devinder Gupta and I heard the matter. We both felt that the education of young children was one of the most important factors in the development of the nation and that a strong foundation of universal literacy was necessary for poverty, ignorance and superstition to be done away with. We were of the opinion that the district-wise reservation in the training course for teachers of small children was not violative of the Constitution because in a state like Himachal Pradesh, especially in rural areas, where children were normally first-generation learners, it was essential that the teachers should be able to communicate with them effectively. This was far more likely if the teachers belonged to the same or an adjacent area and were therefore familiar with the local customs and language, especially since there were so many dialects in the state. We felt that such teachers in general would be more approachable, and that a greater affinity could therefore spring up between the teacher and the taught.

★

Living in Shimla on my own as Chief Justice, I found that the household revolved around my needs. The staff at home was there to look after me and to ensure that I was comfortable. This was a new experience for me. In the morning, the newspapers were at my sole disposal, the bathroom available at my convenience, breakfast served at a time of my choosing, and the car ready at my command. In the evening, the fire would be lit, and the room heated and cheery for my return. In my earlier homes, my needs had always been considered last. The man of the house, whatever his job, was treated in a special manner; everything revolved around his needs, and it was accepted that he could never be disturbed when he was working. On the other hand, I, as a working woman, was treated differently. The servants thought nothing of coming and disturbing me for every domestic enquiry and problem. The children felt they could walk into my office at home and complain about some triviality, even if I was in the middle of writing a judgment. At Shimla, for the first time, I felt like a person in my own right—and this attitude of the staff somehow also rubbed off on my family when they came to visit.

But this state of affairs did not last too long. Vikram

arrived with his books and papers. He was completing his revision of *A Suitable Boy*. He took over the whole of the glazed verandah room on the first floor and all the table space he could find. I kept a small bridge table covered with law books to prevent its being taken over completely. When I wanted to work, I removed them, and quickly put them back when I finished. One day, when I came home from court a little earlier than usual, Vikram objected. I said to him, 'I thought it was my house.' He replied, 'When you come home, my characters run away.' So that was that! I quietly sneaked in. I was being put in my place once again by my demanding children.

I did not have many visitors during my stay in Shimla. One visit that I will never forget was that of my friend Rosalind Wilson. She came to spend Diwali with me and Vikram. She was ill with cancer and wore a neck brace; even the jolty journey to Shimla was agonizing for her. But once she was there, she found a sort of peace and joy. She sat in the sunlit garden by herself or with me or Vikram; she had always loved music, literature and nature, and she was as perceptive and articulate as ever. Even her constant pain did not dampen her sense of humour or dim the radiance of her smile. It was her last Diwali. She died in Delhi in July 1992.

★

High Court judges retire at the age of sixty-two. As 20 October 1992, my sixty-second birthday, approached, time seemed simultaneously to speed up and distend.

27 September, a Sunday, was the fiftieth anniversary of my Father's death. I spent a long time lost in thought. I recollected that Daddy and I had had less than twelve years together, of which a large time was spent away from each other, but I realized how much he had helped to mould me and make me what I was.

The next day too brought back memories of the past. I was the Chief Guest at the centenary celebrations of Loreto Convent, Tara Hall, Shimla. A year earlier, I had also been their Chief Guest. On that occasion, I had been called upon to say a few words. I had told them that I was honoured to be there especially as I myself was a Loreto girl—though from the other end of the Himalayas, that is, Darjeeling, and thereafter in college in Calcutta. I recalled my school days and the affection and camaraderie of friends and the dedicated and devoted nuns who took care of us and instilled in us a value system that had lasted through the years. One of the teachers, Romola Lahiry, who had taught me at college and whom I admired, was known to the girls of Tara Hall as Mother Stella. In a wonderful, manifest way this strengthened our common bond.

Before ending, I shared with them what an eighty-year-old American woman, Welthy Fisher, said when she saw the huge problem of adult literacy in India, which resulted in such great ignorance and poverty. She realized that one of the reasons it was not being tackled was because everyone felt that the problem was too large and did not know where to begin. She spoke to Gandhiji and at the age of eighty learnt Hindi, started an adult literacy class near Lucknow, and tried to persuade people to attend. At first it was difficult to attract even five people. But later, when people realized that they could write their names and read a little, it made them feel good and many more joined. It became a movement. People began to call her Akshardhari Ma, the carrier of the alphabet. She quoted an old oriental proverb, 'It is better to light one candle than to curse the darkness.' I encouraged the girls to go and light their own candles.

★

The Chief Minister of Himachal Pradesh, Mr Shanta Kumar, wanted to give a farewell dinner for Justice Mehrotra and me; we were due to retire almost simultaneously. The Chief Minister had on earlier occasions given a dinner and even a gift to a retiring Chief Justice. As we were both retiring, we felt that it was in order for us to accept his hospitality, but we made it abundantly clear that we would not accept any gift. Later, Justice Mehrotra had second thoughts even about the dinner and said that it might not be proper to attend. I did not agree with him and felt it was churlish for a retiring Chief Justice not to accept a dinner by the Chief Minister a few days before retirement. After all, at that stage there were no important cases to be decided in which the State was a party.

I consulted my colleagues and the majority view was that, despite the precedents, we should not accept the invitation. So at the eleventh hour I had to request the Chief Minister to cancel it. He was surprised and hurt, and it was a bit embarrassing all around.

15 October was Karva Chauth and, as always, I fasted till I had caught sight of the moon. This was the one fast that my mother-in-law had requested me to observe for my husband's health and, though I didn't believe in it, I always kept it out of respect, at first for her and later for her memory.

On the 16th there was a farewell dinner given by the Bar at Hotel Holiday Home; and on the morning of Saturday the 17th, I left at 5 a.m. by car for Dehra Dun, a beautiful drive at dawn. Vikram was to be the Chief Guest at the Doon School Founder's Day and I wanted to be there. He was just forty, and it was a great honour. He spoke, among other things, of the loneliness in boarding school of boys who were not interested in team games. He even wondered if in certain respects day schools were not more suitable in general. But he did emphasize strongly how much he owed to Doon School in terms of the breadth of non-academic interests it encouraged, the ethos of independence it sought to instil, and the inspiration of some remarkable teachers.

Vikram and Premo drove back with me to Shimla on the 18th. The next day was my last day in court.

After court was over, I sat in the Chief Justice's chamber and watched the sunset. The sky had a beautiful reddish glow and the clouds were scattered around. A turreted building was silhouetted against the sky. I thought about the curious paths that had brought me such a long way from being a student in Darjeeling in the eastern Himalayas to being Chief Justice in Shimla in the western Himalayas.

Slowly my thoughts came back to where I was—to the very building I was in. In just fifteen months, I had grown to love it. In the winter the large courtroom of the Chief Justice was very cold, but the small chamber was warm. I often thought that instead of having a fire at the back of the courtroom, some sort of central heating should be installed. There were some murmured suggestions about pulling down the old building and putting up a totally new one. The lawyers' library and the administrative offices of the court were housed in Ravenswood, a beautiful 'heritage' building. I had had it repaired and a plaque installed. In keeping with the structure and ambience, another courtroom had been built so that now there were eight courtrooms—more than enough for the Himachal High Court's needs for some time. I felt good that this had been taken care of.

But a few years later I was to learn that there was a plan to pull down Ravenswood and build a seven-storey structure for the High Court. I was aghast—a seven-storey building in a hill station—surely it was against the rules. What about the road tunnel underneath? What would happen to the skyline? What would happen to the heritage building, Ravenswood?

Recently, I received an invitation for the opening of the new seven-storey High Court in Shimla on 13 June 2003. I

With Jayaprakash Narayan at
White Pillars; Asha Jain in the
background.

Off to the Patna High Court
in the black Plymouth.

Ira, Usha and Sashi bhai.

Koly with a Nepalese baby.

Romola Lahiry.

Sarla and me.

Yolande and me with our spouses.

Sunanda Bhandare.

In the judge's chair—Delhi High Court.

Only woman at the Chief Justices' Conference 1991.

The seven of us in Delhi—with the leaves of the champa.

Graciela Iturbide

had neither the time nor the heart to go. I heard that a foreigner, who often stayed at the Clarks Hotel nearby had threatened to shoot the architect if he came within his sight. I too was deeply saddened by this desecration. Of course, the old order must change, yielding place to new, but not in such a manner as to damage so wantonly the very fragile ecosystem and what little visual beauty survives of a historic hill station.

But I am getting ahead of my story. As I was ruminating in my chamber, Premo came to fetch me to have tea with the Chief Minister and his wife. There was a farewell dinner given by the judges that night in the High Court premises. On the 20th Premo and I went to have tea with the Governor. Since it was my birthday, Vikram, Premo and I went to have dinner at a restaurant called Fascination. In all the time I had been in Shimla as Chief Justice, it was the only time that I went to a restaurant there. I was now a free citizen again and there was no need for my glorious isolation.

part three

❧

A Sense of Freedom

A Home at Last

I left Shimla by the small train on the narrow gauge line which connects it to Kalka. This railway is now a hundred years old. During its journey of over four hours, the little engine chugs its way through more than a hundred tunnels and over more than eight hundred bridges—and so one is, for quite a part of the journey, either burrowing under the earth or hanging in the air. The rest of the time one enjoys spectacular views of the Shivalik hills. Shifting to the broad gauge railway line at Kalka, I arrived in Delhi the next day.

Premo and I were lucky to have built a house of our own in Noida, across the River Yamuna from Delhi. I was almost sixty when we did. It was made for our retirement, keeping in mind the children who were grown-up. Our house is two-storeyed, and has a barsati. The rooms are small: having lived in government housing in Delhi for thirteen years, we knew the difficulty of cooling large rooms in summer and heating them in winter. But we made sure that the drawing room was just large enough to accommodate our crushed-strawberry pink carpet. We also arranged our doors so that we could move in our grand old carved mahogany 'Bangla khat' double-bed.

Our house has a tiny garden, which is my great joy. The bedroom faces it, so I can lie in bed and enjoy the greenery. The garden runs along two sides of the long-windowed drawing room. A pomelo tree stands in one corner of the garden, flowering in March and spreading its sweet white-flowered fragrance all around. Then its fruit appear and very slowly, over several months, turn into large footballs with juicy pink bitter-sour-sweet citrous pulp within. It's not a tall tree but it spreads its branches outwards; our swing-seat for three is placed under it so that we can enjoy the light fragrance and the shade. Close by, a small magnolia tree struggles to grow and flower in the Delhi heat. In the other corner is a gardenia, which gives us white flowers of exquisite beauty and texture and a delicate freshness and fragrance, especially in May. The white jasmine bush scents the air, and the bela creeper flowers from April right through the summer, spreading its perfume through the garden and giving me flowers for garlands to twine around my chignon.

But apart from these fragrant white-flowered plants, there are many others in the garden—a red pompom tree, small crinkled red poinsettias, a rose-bush with a thousand pale pink flowers, the dark crimson 'Happiness' rose that our gardener Sona gave my husband for his birthday, the rare red-flowering champa tree, the bottle-brush, the double-flowered red hibiscus, the orange rondeletia . . . Outside our gate, two mauve lantana bushes in the shape of elephants stand as welcoming sentinels. Near them is a small tulsi bush; Vikram likes to place a tulsi leaf in his mouth when thinking. We also planted by the roadside a harsingar tree, three orangey red-flowered Sita ashoks, which Shantum loves, partly because of the myth that the Buddha was born under such a tree, a copper-pod, a saptaparni and a glorious yellow laburnum—the last planted at Aradhana's request on Dhiren Bhagat's birthday, after his death.

I have loved orchids ever since I first saw them in childhood at Loreto Convent in Darjeeling. 'Parlour number one' at school often had exquisite orchids on display; it was a great temptation for us girls to creep in there and have a look. Otherwise, we only got an opportunity to go there when we had visitors who came to see us and the nuns allowed us in.

When I went to the North-East in 2000, I brought back many varieties of orchids from Sikkim, Manipur, Mizoram and Arunachal Pradesh. Everyone told me that it was no use taking them back to Delhi, as they would never flower there. But I was determined to try. I carried some of them back in a basket and some like a baby in my arms. I tied them to the pomelo tree and the champa tree, and lo and behold—first one, and then another flowered. The first had lupin-like flowers on a stem bending downwards, pale-pinkish, onion-mauve; the second was a purple single flower; the next sprouted a vertical stem with brown and white flowers; yet another had a beautiful white spray, each flower looking like a swan with a small tongue-like pink marking. As you can imagine, I am ecstatic. It is a wonderful feeling when things grow so beautifully and respond to one's tender care. But I also brought a purplish pink Cattleya hybrid orchid from Sikkim in a pot; it was flowering, and looked exotic and beautiful. But though the plant is still alive, it doesn't flower any more. Sad. Maybe I shouldn't have brought it to dry and dusty Delhi.

Why did we make a house in Noida? Why not in Delhi? Many of our friends have asked us this.

The reason is very simple. Land in Delhi was very expensive and we did not have that sort of money. I sold a piece of land that I had bought in Lucknow thirty years earlier. With the proceeds, together with our accumulated savings, we bought the land from the Noida authorities by instalment and built the house. But when it was complete, I could not get a completion certificate from the authorities. They wanted a bribe and told my architect so, in no uncertain terms. And if they got one, they were willing to forgo even an inspection of the house!

While building the house, I had requested my architect to build strictly within the rules, so that there would be no difficulties later. He assured me he would do so. I therefore confidently put my foot down and said 'No bribe.' I also quietly let it be known to the demanders of the bribe that I was a sitting judge of the Delhi High Court and would not stomach their nonsense. Do you think they were scared? On the contrary, they sent back a message, saying: 'Who does she think she is? We have extracted money from cabinet secretaries, high commissioners, ambassadors and other bigwigs. And in any case, this is not Delhi but Uttar Pradesh.'

I held out for months. Eventually, they came to inspect the house. They examined it from every angle and could not find anything they could take exception to. But upon re-measurement, they found that the area of a large vertical shaft, several feet across, was smaller than stipulated by three and a half inches. They now had a stick to beat me with. I was annoyed with my architect. He assured me that this was not a serious matter and was known as a condonable item, for which a small penalty was prescribed; he would get it calculated and paid, and all would be well. But the officials from Noida said that it might be condonable in Delhi, but was not condonable here. They said that I would have to break down the wall; of course, they added, the other option was always available to me: to pay the bribe that they saw as their due. I was furious. I decided that the wall would have to be brought down and four more inches of shaft space created.

My architect told me that the venal officials were asking for five thousand rupees, and that it would cost twice that amount to bring down and reconstruct the wall. He suggested that he would pay the lesser amount himself and bill me for 'miscellaneous expenses', so that I did not have to deal with the matter myself. I naturally did not agree. The wall was promptly brought down and a new one built. But the officials refused to come for another inspection. It took months before they were cajoled into coming. I finally did get my completion certificate. But the whole procedure took more than a year. Can I blame anyone for paying the money demanded and getting it over the counter?

★

The oppression of a heedless bureaucracy brings to mind a distressing and irksome business which dogged me throughout my otherwise pleasant stay in Shimla—and even in Noida after I had retired.

The Chief Justice of India had, as I mentioned in passing earlier, assured me that owing to the suddenness of my move to Shimla and other circumstances, I could continue to keep the house at 8 Rajaji Marg for a few months more, until December 1991. Later, the new Chief Justice of the Delhi High Court had, in my presence, acquiesced to this. But barely a couple of months after I moved to Shimla, the Directorate of Estates, at the behest of the Delhi High Court Registry, cancelled the allotment of the house with retrospective effect. My family in Delhi, facing eviction proceedings, phoned me in a panic. I was angry and worried: the word of both Chief Justices was being ignored, my reputation for scrupulousness was being besmirched, and the family was frantic. I telephoned the Chief Justice of India, reminded him that I was in authorized occupation and asked him why this was happening. From his reply it appeared that his discussions with the concerned authorities and their assurances had all been verbal. Finally, I persuaded him, as he was shortly to retire, to write to the minister concerned.

This should have sorted out matters. Not so. In November 1994, two years after I had retired and moved to Noida, I received a huge claim from the Directorate of Estates for payment of damages at the rate of more than Rs 30,000 a month—which included, for good measure, a period of three and a half months after we had actually vacated the house, with an endorsment to the Registrar, Himachal Pradesh High Court and the Registrar, Delhi High Court, 'to enforce the recovery of outstanding government dues from Ms. Justice Leila Seth'. I was both livid and in despair. Where was I going to find such a large sum? How could I fight this idiotic and illegitimate claim? I wrote back strongly to the Estate Office, reminding them that they had assured my husband that the matter was closed and reiterating my explanation afresh. Everything fell on deaf ears. Three months later I received a notice to show cause why an order requiring payment of interest should not be added to the claim already made. I saw not only my commuted pension but also my death-cum-retirement gratuity disappearing. It was the last straw.

As a judge, I had been reluctant to write to people in positions of power. I was now an ordinary citizen and did not have compunctions about complaining to them and getting my just dues. I wrote to all the concerned ministers, to the Chief Justice of the Delhi High Court, and to the Secretary, Ministry of Urban Development, sending copies to others, including the chairperson of the Cabinet Committee for Accommodation. This last minister, N.K.P. Salve, bless him, immediately took up matters with the minister directly concerned. This, together with my letters and my meetings with the Estate Officer and the Deputy Director, Litigation in response to the notices I had received, finally put the matter to rest.

Speaking of litigation, Shaw Wallace & Co. at one time owed Premo a substantial sum of money and were not paying, despite repeated reminders. He was angry and wanted to sue them. I begged him to settle. I said: 'Take half, take one-third, even take one-fifth, but settle. You have a good case, but if you take them to court, you certainly won't get anything now; if you have grandchildren, they might. Apart from that, you will lose sleep and get high blood pressure when you hear lies being treated as truth and frivolous adjournments being taken by the other side to delay the matter. I know that I will have to bear the brunt of it, as you will keep telling me what a frustrating and useless exercise the whole process is.' I badgered him to settle and settle he did. It was over in a few days and, though he got a mere fifth of what he should have, he had it to call his own. It was practical, 'tatkaal' justice—if very imperfect.

I often think about how litigation or the threat of litigation affects people. It takes over one's whole life. The fear of the lawyers and the courts, the delay, the tension when you have to appear and—all too often—the complete lack of reasonableness of the prosecutor or opponent are horrible realities. It is time-consuming, expensive and nerve-racking. And the result is so unpredictable. You can be called upon to pay damages even for something for which you are not responsible. If that is what I faced as a judge owing to an obdurate bureaucracy, if that was what I, as a judge, advised my husband to do rather than battle an obstructive large company, what must be the lot of the common man, who is totally bewildered by the language and trappings of the law, has no access to the levers of power or even the ears of the influential, has little to fall back on during the years of expense and delay, and lacks even the knowledge of what he should do or to whom he should go in order to redress an injustice or assert a just claim.

★

I had looked forward to my retirement and thought of all the things I had wanted to spend more time on when I was so busy. Now they all seemed possible—my family and friends, my home and garden, letter writing and reading, travel and exercise, exhibitions and lectures, films and plays. The first few months were wonderful and I wondered why men found retirement so difficult; there was so much to do and to enjoy. Perhaps they had no interests apart from their work. I had made a conscious decision that I would not appear in court, and would only write legal opinions or act as an arbitrator, umpire, nominee or the like. I also wanted to do something to better the lot of women and children and, in particular, the girl child. This pent-up wish was all the more strong because, when a lawyer, I had consciously done mainstream work that was not particularly associated with women's welfare and, when a judge, had been very particular about holding an even balance between men and women. But I didn't quite know what I should do and how.

★

Vikram's novel *A Suitable Boy* was launched in February 1993 in New Delhi by Penguin Books. He was very keen that the first publication should be in India. He had worked very hard on the book. When we were living in 8 Rajaji Marg, he used to walk to the Nehru Memorial Museum and Library regularly and read the newspapers and gazettes pertaining to the period. He also watched movies from the late forties and early fifties; he must have seen *Deedar* half a dozen times. He learnt Urdu from a teacher in order to understand the nuances of Muslim culture better. He met and interviewed our extended family, our friends, our acquaintances and many others whom he felt could give him an insight into understanding particular aspects of life or work or the psyche of the times. This included boxwallahs, bureaucrats, doctors, judges, lawyers, musicians, naturalists, politicians, policemen, professors, teachers, sants and gurus. He read all the land reform cases in the law reports, went—as Shantum had done earlier—to live with a Jatav shoemaker's family in Agra, stayed for a month at the height of summer in a largely Muslim village in eastern UP, tried to figure out how one visited a courtesan, and bathed in the Kumbh Mela at Allahabad.

But he didn't go out and socialize. And if a friend of his came over for dinner, we were often left to look after her or him, while he went off upstairs to sleep. When the writing didn't go well, he sulked and was grumpy and had to be placated with affection and ginger biscuits. He had set up a huge chart in his room indicating the ages and locations of his characters at various moments. He also carried a little notebook around with him, into which went all sorts of ideas and observations, including remarks made by the family; Aradhana called him 'Mr Notebook'.

One thing he did want to do was to spend time with the whole family. We each had our commitments and social obligations, and sometimes a week would go by without all five of us being together for a meal. So Vikram decided that Sunday dinner would be a family meal. For that one meal, we would not accept any other invitation, nor would we invite anyone else to join us. This was hardest for Aradhana, both because she was the most sociable and because Peter was not to be included in the home group, as he was not yet family. Vikram dictated that there should be no concessions and this rule was sacrosant. Once we had accepted this regimen, it has to be said that these family dinners were wonderful occasions, which it is now difficult to imagine our not having had.

The strict observance of the rule led to occasional tension if there was an important social function to attend or person to meet, or if a friend of Shantum or Aradhana arrived on a

Sunday unannounced and had to be sent off quickly rather than be invited to stay on for pot luck, as was the usual practice. Once, when Vikram's friend Gopal Gandhi telephoned him to tell him that the writer R.K. Narayan, then in his eighties, was in town for a day, and invited Vikram to join them for a small dinner on Sunday, Vikram had to very reluctantly refuse. At breakfast, I noticed that he was in a pensive mood and a bit depressed. I asked him what had happened and he told me. I knew how much he admired R.K. Narayan's writing, how keen he must have been to meet him, and how disappointed he must be. I told him he should phone Gopal Gandhi immediately and accept the invitation. He said, 'If I do, how can I face my siblings?' I replied, 'Leave that to me; exceptions have to be made sometimes.' He was delighted to spend the evening with R.K. Narayan; that was the only time they ever met. It would have been a real pity if he had missed the opportunity. His siblings too were happy that 'strict' was not 'so strict'.

Though Vikram wrote the bulk of *A Suitable Boy* in 8 Rajaji Marg, its revision and some additions were completed in Armsdell in Shimla. During the long process—lasting many years—of writing, revising and producing the book, quite apart from the creative stresses and difficulties, he had many problems: with his hand, which at one stage he could hardly write or type with; with his computer and printer, which were forever malfunctioning; and later, during the typesetting process, with his cheerfully optimistic friend and publisher, David Davidar. Vikram, facing deadlines from his foreign publishers who were dependent on Penguin India's typesetting and film, and impatient with the slow and erratic progress which he could not control from distant Noida, moved with a bridge table and chair, clothes, bedding, papers and books into David's flat in Delhi. At night he would sit for hours through power-cuts and system crashes in the typesetter's small shop. By day he would sleep or correct proofs. Whenever he became too fraught, David offered him whisky. It was a rather turbulent time and tempers ran high. But when the book finally appeared, resplendent in dark red and gold and elegantly printed on fine paper, all was forgotten.

Raghu Rai, commissioned by the *New York Times Magazine*, came and took a family photograph of the four of us (Aradhana was now in Washington with Peter) in our home in Noida. Journalists and photographers descended on us and wrote and shot what they liked.

The launch was a big occasion for all of us, and it was held at the Oberoi Inter-Continental Hotel. Family and friends gathered and toasted Vikram, who said a few words. The book was dedicated 'to Papa and Mama and the memory of Amma'. He now thanked Premo and me for giving him the space to write. He wished that his grandmother, his beloved Amma, had been alive to read the book, as it was about her times. It was an informal occasion, very different from the elaborate and media-dominated book launches of today. I was relieved and happy that *A Suitable Boy* was finally born and kicking. The excitement and tension were over, and normal life resumed.

★

About six months after retirement I found I was missing the routine of getting out of the house and going to work. Somehow, sitting at home exaggerated all the household problems, and a minor staff misdemeanour seemed harder to resolve than a complicated labour case. I loved reading, but when I had all the time in the world to read, it was difficult to focus on it. I had the whole day to enjoy my home and garden, but instead I only saw the dirt and the dust, and kept dwelling on the fact that the new plants took so long to grow, the geyser needed repairs, and the lawn-mower was out of order. I realized that going out to work, and being away from home, I could temporarily forget about my household chores and domestic problems. These sooner or later got sorted out without becoming my major concern. Of course, while I was in office, a whole infrastructure of staff and service had been available to me, which was now no longer there.

I started getting depressed; indeed, I went into a serious depression. Things lost their savour, and I could find no sense of purpose. At the same time, I could not believe it was me who was feeling this way. I had been so confident that I would be fine after retirement because I had so many interests. I kept telling myself that I had to take myself in hand and be more disciplined and cheerful. But, having no schedule to keep, I started getting up late, wandering aimlessly around the house, bathing any time I wanted to, and being generally lethargic.

Finally, when I decided this could not go on—I went to see a doctor: Dr K.P. Jain—or Shama as we call him—my friend, philosopher and guide. He told me to relax. He assured me that these were very natural feelings. After all, I had been following a routine of study or work for the last fifty-five years, and it would take some time to adjust to a different and slower pace. He gave me advice and medicine and these helped cheer me up. Vikram, who knew my passion for reading but realized that I would not be able to tackle a large book, presented me *The Collected Short Stories of Roald Dahl* and wrote: 'For Mama the Mareez—in the hope that these sharp tales will boost your spirits.' The master of the twist in the tale certainly did. He was addictive. After a while, I went on to longer books. As time passed, I started analysing myself to try and discover the real reason for my depression. I began to see that my lack of routine and my 'house-boundedness' were both symptom and cause. I had to find something worthwhile to do, and it had to have a schedule for me to keep. That was the only way I could raise my spirits.

I saw a course on environmental law advertised in the newspapers. I had hardly any knowledge of the subject but I realized its importance, especially after having lived in Himachal Pradesh. I also felt quite interested in it. So I joined the nine-month course of study to do a diploma in environmental law at the World Wide Fund for Nature. It was the very first such course they were running; classes began in the heat of mid-July and lasted two hours a day from 3 p.m. to 5 p.m. Most of the participants were law students and young lawyers. Almost all of them were below twenty-six years of age; I was sixty-two.

Dr Chhatrapati Singh, the Director, was himself in his early forties, and did not quite know how to treat me. But I fell in with the students, started enjoying the quizzes and other competitions with my classmates and, though for some reason they expected me to know all the answers, made as many mistakes as they did. Being with these young people gave me a whole new zest for life. Besides, I now had a routine and no longer had the unsettled, 'What to do, what to do?' feeling that I had been getting in the mornings.

Since I was going all the way from Noida to the WWF to do the course, I often dropped into the India International Centre nearby for some interesting programme—some concert or lecture or discussion or exhibition—that was taking place there. I was soon nominated to their Executive Committee and started taking an interest in the running of the institution. After a couple of years, I was elected to be a member of the Board of Trustees and really enjoyed the experience. I was elected for a second two-year term. When this expired, the life trustees exhorted me to stand again, but I felt that it was time to induct some fresh blood, especially as there were only seven trustees, out of whom five were life trustees and only two were elected. When I was on the Board, there happened to be three women trustees out of a total of seven. Now they are all men, except for one life trustee.

I had not been able to go with the other students at the WWF to Rajasthan for a fieldwork trip, as I had already fixed an arbitration session for the same dates. So when Dr Chhatrapati Singh and some others went to Nasibali on Garimata beach in Orissa on a project to try and save the Olive Ridley turtles, whose life-cycle was threatened by damaging developments nearby, I joined them.

Though it was the time for the annual mass nesting, no turtles showed up; all we saw was the skull of a dead turtle. I was moved and wrote a poem to them.

> To the Olive Ridley Turtles
>
> Where do you come from
> Where do you go?
> Dear Olive Ridleys
> Do let us know.
>
> On January twenty-fifth
> We waited all night
> In treeless Nasibali
> In the bright moonlight.
>
> You didn't show up
> To lay your ping-pong eggs
> Were you diverted
> By the trawlers' dregs?
>
> Has the news of Talchua
> Reached you out there?
> Are you frightened of the jetty
> The nets and the snare?

Do know we are trying
To preserve your path and place
So don't lose heart
Just continue your race.

Keep coming in numbers
As you have all these years
Complete your mass nesting
In peace, without tears.

When I completed my diploma course with WWF, I was invited by the President, Dr Swaminathan, to be a member of the Board of Trustees. I was honoured and delighted, took a lively interest in the Fund's affairs and after a couple of years became its Vice-President. I oversaw in particular the growth of the Centre for Environmental Law.

Dr Chhatrapati Singh was an exceptional environmentalist and jurist, and a very good human being. I respected him greatly as my teacher. Unfortunately, some time later, I—along with other trustees—was forced to conduct an enquiry against him. As a result of this enquiry, his services were terminated. I was very sad at the whole range of circumstances that had brought about the downfall of a basically good and visionary human being. But such is life. A few years later, he died very young of a brain haemorrhage. It was a tragic end for someone with so much talent and imagination.

Standing Up

Premo's birthday is 7 December. In 1992 we decided to celebrate it a day earlier because the 6th was a Sunday. Of the children, only Vikram was with us at the time. We had a simple lunch with the family and a couple of friends.

We were all tense, wondering what was happening in Ayodhya. We knew that hordes of Ram devotees had descended on the city to try to build a temple where the Babri Masjid was, since it was believed by many that a Hindu temple had stood there earlier and that it was the birthplace of Ram—the Ram Janmabhoomi.

The desire to rebuild a temple on that spot had been revitalized by political and other parties eager to garner the Hindu vote. The matter had been under litigation for a long time. The Uttar Pradesh government, led by BJP Chief Minister Kalyan Singh, had given an undertaking to the court that everything would be kept under control and that no harm would come to the mosque. It was difficult to see, however, how he would be able to keep the agitated crowd in check. The Congress Prime Minister P.V. Narasimha Rao, sitting in Delhi and equally concerned about Hindu votes, did nothing either.

Late that afternoon, we turned on the TV to be faced with terrible news. Many of the mob, some armed with iron rods, had climbed on top of the Babri Masjid and brought down the old and revered building. In a few hours, the entire mosque had been reduced to rubble. There was consternation and fear among the Muslim community in India and a reaction in Bangladesh and Pakistan, where numerous Hindu shrines were destroyed. The demolition of the mosque was an act of wanton destruction, a display of Hindu prowess that was oblivious to, or in many cases deliberately intended to wound the sentiments of the Muslim community.

Nor was the fact that the structure represented our ancient heritage considered. It was truly tragic, and it divided people in a manner that was harrowing. Yet most people were reluctant to speak up and condemn this barbarous act that had been committed in the presence of senior leaders of the Bharatiya Janata Party and various fundamentalist Hindu groups.

There were, however, some concerned citizens who immediately swung into action. Professor Dharma Kumar, an economist of repute and a good friend, rang up and said she could not sleep at night just thinking of the trauma the Muslim community must be going through. She asked me whether I would sign a statement about the whole affair. I never signed statements—during my time as a judge it had not been possible anyhow—and was a bit apprehensive about doing so, not knowing how it would be worded. But Dharma assured me that the wording could be cleared by me personally before signing.

Having retired in October that year, I felt I had a certain freedom of action. I decided that I should be part of a movement to re-establish communal harmony. I therefore willingly agreed. Dharma also added that I would have to contribute Rs 1,000 towards an insertion of the statement in the *Times of India*. It was to be a full-page advertisement with

a thousand names. Later, she rang up Vikram and said that
she had been advised that the advertisement would be more
effective if it was on the front page, with just about twenty
well-known names from various spheres. Were Vikram and I
willing to stand up and be counted and to face the
repercussions, if any, she wondered? We agreed to go right
ahead. This statement eventually appeared in the bottom
right-hand corner of the front page of the *Times of India,* on
30 January 1993, the anniversary of Gandhiji's death. It was
printed in a large format, 14 cm by 20 cm, in white lettering
on a black background.

If you are a Hindu, read on.

Do you believe that the demolition of the Babri Masjid restored Hindu pride, enhanced national honour, strengthened India? If so, consider the possibility that the act debased Hindu culture, shamed the nation across the world, increased the tensions between all communities and so weakened India.

Bharat Ram
Industrialist

R.P. Goenka
Industrialist

Lalit Thapar
Industrialist

Nanubhai B. Amin
Industrialist

Raj Tiagrajan
Industrialist

Desh Bandhu Gupta
Industrialist

Pupul Jayakar
Chairman, INTACH

Ashok Advani
Publisher

Ashok Desai
Former Solicitor General

Lovraj Kumar
Former Secretary,
Govt. of India

Ved Marwah
Former Adviser to Governor of
Jammu and Kashmir

Air Chief Marshal
S.K. Mehra (Retd.)
Former Chief of Air Staff

Admiral S.M. Nanda
Former Chief of Naval Staff

I.G. Patel
Former Director,
London School of Economics

Leila Seth
Former Chief Justice,
Himachal Pradesh

Vikram Seth
Writer

Mantosh Sondhi
Former Secretary,
Govt. of India

Gen. K. Sunderji
Former Chief of Army Staff

M.S. Swaminathan
Scientist

Times of India, 30th January 1993

While luminaries from industry, law, the armed forces, science, public service and academia were all represented, my brother Sashi was unhappy and fearful because both Vikram and I had put our names to this advertisement. He felt that if there was some fallout, it would be especially concentrated against us, since we were both from the same family. Further, because Vikram was a writer, it would be presumed that he was the moving force in penning the statement. (In fact, of course, it had been Dharma, who was rather cross that an editor or typesetter had inserted an unnecessary 'the' before 'tensions'.) Sashi bhai had a point; besides, he knew what a difficult time we had gone through earlier owing to the CBI enquiry against Premo. He was also aware that political parties believed that if you challenged any of their actions or the foreseeable results of their actions, you were against them, and they could be quite vindictive.

Though I had no intention of going out of my way to put my neck on the block, I certainly felt very strongly about our composite culture and the freedom of minorities to practise their religion. I was appalled at the manner in which it was being destroyed by fundamentalists. When we were very young, my father, while teaching us the Gayatri mantra, had told us that tolerance and respect for the rights and beliefs of others was an intrinsic part of Hinduism, which was the most catholic of religions. I felt therefore that this was too important a matter to let pass, even if one were harassed or persecuted for it.

A few days later, I was pleasantly surprised to receive a letter dated 2 February 1993 from 12 Rajaji Marg, New Delhi, the house assigned to the Chief of Naval Staff. It was written by Lalita Ramdas, the wife of the Chief, in her individual capacity, and was very heart-warming.

Dear Ms Seth,

Along with many many other citizens, who have always been proud to call ourselves Indian and Hindu, I have agonised over the recent events across this land.

May I say how wonderful it was to see your name in the front page advertisement in several national papers, calling on Hindus to reflect on whether recent events brought glory and honour to the country and its heritage?

In the prevalent milieu of gloom, uncertainty, and growing alienation amongst people, it is heartening indeed to see that there are still those among the top echelons in our society who are fearlessly willing to stand up and be counted as Indians who are proud of and prepared to defend their secular polity and composite culture.

It is time indeed for all of us who think alike to join hands and speak out in every possible forum.

God bless You.'

Lalita Ramdas

Not long afterwards, however, I received a letter from Bombay dated 9 February 1993, addressed to each of the nineteen people whose names had appeared on the advertisement. It sought to justify or at least excuse the destruction of the mosque. It was signed by six people: Ashok Chowgule, Piyush Singhal, P.N. Amersey, Vikram Kamdar, Pranlal Bhogilal and Madhu Thakkar. In order to forestall any question of selective quotation, I reproduce its contents in extenso.

Pranam,

We have no intention of being argumentative. But we feel that you have not been presented the issue of the Ram Janmabhoomi movement in the right perspective. The question that you asked in the advertisement is really a rhetoric one, since the answer for any true believer in Hinduism has to be a resounding **NO**! Time and again history has clearly shown that whenever a Hindu king has driven away a foreign invader, he has made no forcible effort to recover usurped religious site. This is in complete contrast to what happened in Spain in the 16th Century when the Arab invaders were finally defeated by the Christians. All the old church sites, which had been made into mosques, were recovered back for Christianity.

We strongly believe that the Sangh *parivar* is a true believer in the Hindu ethos as exemplified by the *puranas*. We say this in all sincerity and on the basis of our interaction with the various organisations of the Sangh *parivar*. We also believe that the Sangh *parivar* is truly nationalist, as has been clearly exemplified by the positive role that it played to defeat the Emergency of 1975. Its role in various disaster relief, ahead of the mobilisation by the government, has been well documented for any unbiased observer to admire. We suggest that you should not be carried away with the propaganda that the media has been conducting against the Sangh *parivar*.

That the Ram Janmabhoomi is an important site for the Hindu psyche is quite clear from the evidence that the Vishva Hindu Parishad has presented to the government and the AIBMAC [All India Babri Masjid Action Committee] in December 1990. The occasion was the dialogue that the Chandra Shekhar government organised. The question that the VHP framed was,

"<u>Is</u> <u>there</u> <u>proof</u> <u>that</u> <u>an</u> <u>old</u> <u>and</u> <u>persistent</u> <u>tradition</u> <u>among</u> <u>Ram</u> <u>devotees</u> <u>has</u> <u>considered</u> <u>the</u> <u>site</u> <u>as</u> <u>the</u> <u>sacred</u> <u>Ram</u> <u>Janmabhoomi,</u> <u>and</u> <u>that</u> <u>Ram</u> <u>worship</u> <u>took</u> <u>place</u> <u>there</u> <u>in</u> <u>a</u> <u>temple,</u> <u>before</u> <u>and</u> <u>until</u> <u>the</u> <u>Babri</u> <u>Masjid</u> <u>was</u> <u>built?</u>" The AIBMAC agreed that if the proof was offered, they will shift the masjid.

On January 6, 1991, both sides were supposed to give the rejoinder. The government minutes of the time say, "The VHP submitted the rejoinder in which it tried to refute claims of the AIBMAC point wise. The AIBMAC did not react to the evidences put forward by the VHP. Instead it submitted photo-copies of more evidences in support of its claims. Since the AIBMAC did not give comments on the evidences put forward by the VHP, it is not possible for the government to decide the areas of agreement and disagreement." This clearly shows that the AIBMAC went about the negotiations with an objective of being obstructive.

Even then, the VHP agreed that the experts of both sides should meet and discuss the evidence. On the first meeting on 24th January 1991, the AIBMAC experts said that they have not had a chance to study the VHP evidence, and that they would need six weeks to do so. This is indeed strange since the presentation by VHP is based on historic records, and much of it had been published in the Indian media during the previous five years. And it is these experts who have been talking and writing about the issue, against the Ram Janmabhoomi. For the second meeting on 25th January 1991, the AIBMAC experts did not turn up, and the VHP team disbursed (sic) after two hours of wait.

It is thus quite clear that it was the AIBMAC that

broke off the negotiations. They knew that they would have to honour their word, which would be politically inconvenient for them. More reprehensible is the role of the government and the media, which acquiesced with the AIBMAC, and refused to ask it to honour its word. In February 91, when asked about the progress of the negotiation, Shri Subodh Kant Sahay, the then Minister of State for Home, said, "One of the parties did not turn up". He did not specify which the party was, nor did the reporter ask. In the atmosphere at that time, it was assumed that it was the VHP.

The role of the AIBMAC in the negotiations that were conducted in October 92 was no better. The whole approach was one of nitpicking, rather than looking at the evidence as a whole. The government could easily have come with a firm report whether a temple was destroyed to build the Babri structure. Based on the past track record, we believe that because the evidence was firmly in favour of the temple, they chose to hide behind the facade of the judiciary, putting the latter in poor light. The media, too, played a role in hiding the evidence from the people, and gave prominence to vague theories like the original Ayodhya is in Afghanistan.

Under the circumstances, is it any wonder that some of the kar-sevaks felt that the recovery of the site to the Hindus cannot take place in a peaceful manner? The Sangh parivar has already regretted the destruction of the structure, with Shri Kalyan Singh resigning, and the BJP and the VHP accepting the moral responsibility for the same. However, it should be remembered that the site rightfully belonged to the Hindus. The question whether temples are important in a modern society has been answered by Swami Vivekanand, when he said, "Your forefathers underwent everything boldly, even death itself, but preserved their religion. Temple after temple was broken down by the foreign conqueror, but no sooner had the wave passed than the spire of the temple rose up again. Some of these old temples of Southern India, and those like Somnath of Gujarat, will teach you volumes of wisdom, will give you keener insight into the history of the race than any amounts of books. Mark how these temples bear the marks of a hundred attacks and a hundred regenerations, continually destroyed and continually springing up out of the ruins, rejuvenated and strong as ever! That is the national mind, that is the national life-current. Follow it and it leads to glory. Give it up and you die; death will be the only result, annihilation the only effect, the moment you step beyond the life-current. I do not mean to say that other things are not necessary. I do not mean to say that political or social improvements are not necessary, but what I mean is this, and I want you to bear it in mind, that they are secondary here, and that religion is primary."

You also say that "the act shamed the nation across the world, increased tensions between all communities and so weakened India". If the truth of the site was made known to the people all over the world, then this would not have happened. We are sure that if the Muslims had been told that the structure was built after destroying a temple where, for thousands of years, Hindus believed that Lord Ram was born, then they would have come forward themselves, and pushed their so-called leaders aside, and handed the site to the Hindus. The confusion that has been caused is because of the truth has not been given due publicity.

We would like to place a few points before you. Our country has been independent for the last 45 years. The Ram Janmabhoomi movement has been on the top of the national agenda for the last five years. We hope you do not believe that for the first 40 years the country had achieved tremendous progress, which was destroyed in the last five. In many ways, the movement gathered momentum only because of the wrong policies of the first 40 years. We also believe that our international image is poor because of our so-called non-alignment policies, support for Saddam Hussein, and our poverty of the first 40 years. Further we believe that there is a deliberate programme by the politicians so far to keep the Muslims suppressed by pandering to their so-called religious leaders, who could then herd their folks to vote as a block during the elections. We would like you to get in touch with the BJP leaders like Shri Sikander Bakht, who is also the Leader of the Opposition in the Rajya Sabha, to find what the Sangh *parivar* really stands for.

Namaste.'

After I got this letter I wondered how responsible was the group of people who could justify parties taking the law into their own hands because of a delay in matters pending in court. I was distressed as to what would happen if others did the same, as delay had become endemic in our courts, with some cases taking over twenty-five years from start to final appeal.

Many felt that the secular fabric of India was being threatened. In open discussions, people spoke about trying to restore a semblance of communal amity and faith in the country. But many Hindu fundamentalists felt that their behaviour was justified because elsewhere in the subcontinent, that is, in Pakistan and Bangladesh, minorities were crushed and made to bend to the majority's will. What the Hindu fundamentalists failed to appreciate was that to be provoked by the inhumane policies of those they saw as their enemies into inhumane policies of their own was in effect to grant them victory. India is not a state that favours one religion, unlike Pakistan. To protect them against the possible tyranny of the majority, minorities have rights entrenched in the Constitution of India.

At one meeting in the wake of the destruction of Babri Masjid, I tried to explain how education could help to bring about communal harmony. I said:

> There is no magic wand by which the tensions created and brought out in the open as a result of certain recent events can be wiped out. The process of healing is slow. Confidence has to be restored and the composite cultural heritage, which has been the tradition of this country, put on a firm footing.
>
> The aim is pluralistic humanism; live and let live; tolerance and respect. How do we bring it about? By awareness and education. By education, I mean holistic education, not just literacy.
>
> But when does education start? In school? No, as soon as a baby is born. He or she comes into this world without a mindset, but soon thereafter starts imbibing the culture of the home; the lullabies, the language, the colours and smells, the closeness of siblings and parents; but most of all the child imbibes their prejudices. So if there is anger and hatred towards a person or group, a child takes it in intuitively; and similarly, if there is a spirit of tolerance and respect for each other, and for one's neighbour from

whatever community or caste, this will also get passed on to the children.

A mother's role is particularly important and that is why it is said, 'If you educate a woman you educate a whole family.' What is required is space, affection for others, enjoyment of each other's culture and festivities. If the songs that are sung and the words that are spoken treat Ram and Rahim as brothers, so will the children. Because, as Gandhiji said, 'Every home is a university and the parents are its teachers.'

★

Slowly, very slowly, the wounds began to crust over and heal. The brutality of Babri Masjid became a dimmed memory. Thus, ten years later, when the incident at Godhra and its aftermath throughout Gujarat took place, it came as a great shock.

I believe that women are a great healing and unifying force. Across castes and religions, they share similar difficulties—for example, their lack of economic independence, which leads to their subjugation and suppression. They feel the pain of others and empathize with them. They can sense the silent sorrow of another woman at the loss of a child, a spouse, a sibling, a parent, a relative or a friend; the utter agony of not having food for one's family or a home in which to shelter them. Women have an inner shakti and the strength to survive. But when they themselves become virulent leaders, encouraging mob murder and screaming for blood, then hope for even future healing subsides.

This was the greater tragedy of Godhra and Gujarat. Women were part of the movement for communal carnage and division; in some places, they were in the forefront. Inflamed by the burning of men, women and children in a train at Godhra, Hindu women shouted, 'Theek hai, salon ko maro,' as Muslims all over the state were beaten, burnt and murdered—often with the acquiescence or encouragement of the administration, and with the police standing by.

The bare facts of the incident that triggered the bloodshed are that on 27 February 2002, the Sabarmati Express, running some hours behind schedule, was set on fire at Godhra station just before 8 a.m. The train was carrying some kar sevaks returning from Ayodhya. Coach No. S-6 was burnt, killing 58 passengers including a large number of women and children.

What actually happened at Godhra is not clear and is the subject of a judicial enquiry. Several theories, including an accidental fire in the coach, have been put forward. But what was alleged immediately—and spread like wildfire through the state—was that a frenzied Muslim mob had attacked the train with stones and set the coach alight as an affront to Hindutva. The backlash was phenomenal and Gujarat burned with violence for forty days. There was an outpouring of fear and communal hatred all over Gujarat, but luckily—and because the administration of other states behaved more evenhandedly and firmly—it did not spread to other parts of India.

Millions of people in India and abroad were horrified by what happened. 800 people were killed. Women were molested and raped. More than 120,000 victims of both communities were made homeless through arson, destruction or fear. They had to be moved to relief camps run by non-governmental organizations, with some state aid.

The National Human Rights Commission and the Minorities Commission went to Gujarat to investigate what had gone wrong and why the retaliation to the Godhra incident had not been contained quickly. Many NGOs, including the Editors Guild, sent fact-finding groups to examine the role of the media in this matter.

The Commonwealth Human Rights Initiative (CHRI), of which I am the Executive Committee chairperson, also sent a team to help the Centre for Social Justice to document cases of violence and of violation of rights during the riots. This was to be used for research on police reforms. They documented many instances of the partisan and biased behaviour of the police and their inaction in filing first information reports or FIRs. The writers of the CHRI report, immediately before their proposals for action, stated:

> Given the poor track record of several governments in punishing perpetrators of communal and caste related violence, it is shocking to notice that a sense of despondency has already set in, in the context of Gujarat also. The team often came across statements such as—'Nothing will happen to the murderers and rioters. There is no point in following up the cases as none of the FIRs have been registered in a manner as to lead to conviction.' There is a sense of resignation among many victims whom the team met. Some of the complainants are willing to withdraw their complaints and make peace with their neighbours turned murderers. In some places like Dahod the team heard faint murmurs of a settlement being reached between leaders of both communities to hush up all cases as a move towards peace. As leaders of both communities had resorted to gunfire during the riots, they have arrived at a quiet settlement to save their own skins. It must also be remembered that any intervention by outside agencies to help victims access justice without the right combination of political, judicial, extra-judicial and legal support is bound to increase animosity between the communities. The fracture between the various components of the majority community on the one hand and the minority

community on the other is very real and palpable. Halfhearted attempts will only vitiate the already tense atmosphere in the riot-affected areas.

At a meeting of the Executive Committee at which we considered this report, we felt that one of the things we had to press for was police accountability and reform, and non-interference by political personnel in its functioning.

In October 2002, CHRI, thanks to a massive effort by its dynamic and extremely eloquent director, Maja Daruwala, organized a seminar on police reforms. It took place in the premises of the Federation of Indian Chambers of Commerce and Industry, with whom we collaborated. The Editors Guild also joined us. We took pains to invite people whose actions might subsequently make a difference, for example, the Vice-President of India, the chairperson of the National Human Rights Commission, the Home Minister, L.K. Advani, and high-ranking policemen from across the country. We hoped in particular that if Mr Advani made a commitment, it would very likely be implemented.

At the inauguration of the seminar, I referred to the many national and state reports on police reform that had been written over the years and said:

> I think there is no point in us wasting time in talking about this aspect. The time for reports is over. It is time for action now. How do we go about stopping this rot? How do we implement the reforms suggested in a time-bound frame?

The sessions of the seminar were intended to be working sessions. I set out what I saw as the three basic forces that stood in the way of many no doubt laudable reforms: the abuse of political superintendence, the unaccountability of the police to the people, and the forces that had a vested interest in the status quo. I said:

Consequently, the first working session deals with insulating the police from external pressures. Since section 3 of the Police Act of 1861 provides for superintendence of the state over the police, which was logical for the colonial government, this has resulted even after Independence in unlimited discretionary powers, directions and orders to the police under the guise of exercising superintendence. Officers and policemen have been implementing these orders as well as some totally illegal directions by politicians, in the fear of transfer or punishment or in the hope of promotion . . .

The second working session will debate mechanisms and procedures for police accountability. A colonial system required a police force that could suppress and subjugate the community at the command of its master. However, a democratic nation committed to the rule of law requires an efficient and effective police force that ensures the rights of citizens and the safety of life and property—a force that is answerable and accountable to law.

The final session will deal with how to overcome the resistance to reform. This resistance comes from many quarters: politicians in power; the police themselves, who want service conditions to be improved but are not so anxious about doing away with the semi-feudal sub-culture which subverts the rule of law and helps sustain the system of favours given and taken; and those who have learnt to play the system to their advantage, be they corrupt officials, crooked contractors or tax evaders.

But the silent majority feel a great helplessness against the might of the police and yet a desperate dependence on the force. Many policemen also feel constrained by what is happening and want to be freed from a system which does not give them self-esteem. They want to act responsibly and be rewarded for it.

So there is a crying need for change. The silent majority has to become vocal. And the politicians have to think of the long-term future of this country and not their immediate gains, and ensure that investigations are conducted without interference and that the police act without fear or favour.

Another kind of reaction to the events in Gujarat was that of the eminent and very well-respected journalist, B.G. Verghese, who was one of the authors of the Editors Guild Report on Gujarat and the Treasurer of CHRI. He brought together a group of concerned citizens to form the Forum for Fraternity and Reconciliation. The daughter of Ehsan Jafri, a former Member of Parliament who had been killed in the Gujarat riots, came from the US and met the Forum at the home of Inder Gujral, the former Prime Minister.

George Verghese, a Christian, spoke of the past genius of Hindu India in making space for everybody and accommodating divergent tendencies within a greater oneness. But after Independence, this sense of oneness, this concept of fraternity had not been given the importance it deserved. He made the point that labels such as 'minority' and 'majority' could be misleading: Christians are a minority in India but a majority in Mizoram and Nagaland; similarly, a Hindu is part of the majority in India but becomes part of the minority in the state of Jammu and Kashmir and again reverts to majority status in Jammu. Besides, we each have multiple identities; and certain labels, which may be difficult to detach, are not chosen by ourselves but pinned on us by others. They link us to a group, and make us easier to dismiss or to hate. As George Verghese said, 'Ehsan Jafri died not because of what he was but for what he was perceived to be by a frenzied and misguided mob.'

Leila Seth Commission
of Inquiry

Two incidents, separated in time by ten years, formed the basis of the previous chapter. I must now return to 1995, a couple of years after my retirement as a judge. After a period of uncertainty and some depression, I had involved myself in the environment and environmental law, in setting the house in order, in arbitration and other matters. Things were moving along at an even pace.

I enjoy sitting in bed and reading the newspapers, occasionally glancing up at the greenery outside my bedroom window. (Even now, Premo rebukes me gently from time to time for not going for a walk with him or getting enough exercise in general, but this doesn't seem to have much effect on me.) In early April 1995, I remember reading some rather sensational news about the escape from Singapore to Bombay of the 'cashew baron' from Kerala, Rajan Pillai. At the time it was just another item of news to me, one of hundreds in the papers each day.

Premo and I went to England, mainly to spend some time with Shanti Uncle, who was now widowed and longed for family and company. Vikram was in England too, and we celebrated his birthday with him and visited his old college. At the end of June we went to stay with Aradhana and Peter in Vienna, where Peter was now posted. We did the usual touristy things: went to the palaces, the museums, and the opera (where we heard Pavarotti sing), saw the Lipizzaner horses perform at the Spanish Riding School, and drank lots of coffee at the numerous cafes. Peter has a sweet tooth, so we were offered a great deal of Sacher torte. We also played a lot of bridge, which Peter, like me, loves; Premo and Aradhana too, thanks to their respective spouses, have learnt to enjoy the game.

We returned home on 8 July after having had a wonderful holiday. It was unbearably hot. I reverted to my daily routine, beginning with the newspapers. Now they were full of the sudden death of Rajan Pillai. He had died the previous day in judicial custody in Delhi. He was very well-connected, and there was a huge hue and cry. In response to this, the Lieutenant-Governor of Delhi felt that his death under unexpected circumstances was a matter of public importance and decided to institute an inquiry.

On 20 July, the Chief Justice of the Delhi High Court told me that the Delhi Government had asked him to make a sitting judge available to head the inquiry. He had replied that he couldn't spare any, but that he could suggest a good retired judge for the purpose. Would I consent to his putting up my name? I asked him about the subjects that the inquiry would cover, and was told that these mainly involved ascertaining the circumstances of the death of Rajan Pillai; whether the treatment he had received had been adequate and prompt, both in the jail and in the hospital to which he had been taken and where he had died; and whether there had been negligence on anyone's part. I told the Chief Justice that though I was deeply concerned about the circumstances of any person's death in judicial custody owing to possible neglect or negligence, what was also important was that it shouldn't happen in the future, and that medical care and medical procedures in jails should be improved for all prisoners. If the terms of reference of the inquiry could be broadened to include my examining this aspect of the matter and making suitable recommendations, I would be happy to take it on.

When I was a judge in the Delhi High Court, I had insisted, despite my colleagues' concern that I might find the experience unpleasant, on visiting Tihar Jail, the very jail in which Rajan Pillai had been lodged. This was because I felt I had to get a sense of what sort of life and what sorts of conditions we as judges delivered people to, every time we pronounced or confirmed a sentence. It had been an enlightening experience, but I had not thought I would visit Tihar Jail again.

I now visited it several times in my capacity as a one-person Commission of Inquiry. I also visited the lock-up at the Tis Hazari district courts where Rajan Pillai's case had been heard; and the Deen Dayal Upadhyay Hospital, in particular the Casualty Ward where he had died. I interviewed numerous prisoners who were with Rajan Pillai during his stay in jail, and others who I thought might be conversant with the facts including relatives, lawyers, doctors and officials. I also read the reports of Jail Committees that had recommended reform in the past.

Gopika Nina Pillai, Rajan Pillai's young widow, came to see me soon after the Commission was set up. She was attractive and beautifully-groomed, and wore an exquisite Tirupati Balaji gold-jewelled pendant. Under her composed exterior, she looked vulnerable. I felt sorry for her and sad at the senseless loss of her husband's life and the tragedy of her having to bring up two young boys on her own.

★

Rajan Pillai was an Indian national carrying on business in Singapore. He was born to affluence, being the eldest son of the biggest cashew exporter from India. In Singapore he lived in a house in Ridout Road; there was a swimming pool and a tennis court in the five-acre garden. He and his wife Nina entertained businessmen and politicians lavishly. Mr Pillai was also Chairman of the Britannia Group of Companies, which had operations in India and the Far East. But a business partner complained about him to the Singapore authorities, which started criminal proceedings against him for fraud and, though the original complainant had not been made available for the defence to cross-examine, the court convicted him on various counts on the morning of 10 April 1995. Before he could be sentenced, Rajan Pillai fled to Bombay on a Singapore Airlines flight. Non-bailable warrants of arrest were issued. Interpol, New Delhi was alerted. A formal request for extradition was made by Singapore. But Rajan Pillai was untraceable.

On 28 April, he suddenly surfaced in Kerala; he appeared before the Additional Chief Judicial Magistrate at Trivandrum and was, surprisingly, granted bail. The High Court of Kerala then took up the matter of its own accord, and called for the records of the case. Bail was cancelled on 26 June. But Rajan Pillai did not surrender.

The Central Bureau of Investigation, despite its best efforts, could not trace him. On 1 July, the designated magistrate, M.L. Mehta, issued a non-bailable warrant of arrest. Rajan Pillai was arrested just after midnight on the night of 3/4 July at Le Meridien Hotel in Delhi, where he had booked a room under another name.

He was produced before magistrate Mehta on the morning of the 4th and remanded to judicial custody. He was taken to Tihar Jail and lodged in Jail No. 4.

It was claimed before magistrate Mehta by Rajan Pillai's

lawyers that he was a sick man, suffering from severe liver dysfunction and cirrhosis with various complications. When Rajan Pillai could not remember what medicines he was taking, the magistrate was sceptical. But when his lawyers pressed for him to be examined by any medical expert, the magistrate sent a confidential letter to the Resident Medical Officer (RMO) at Tihar Jail, requiring him to send a detailed reply by 2 p.m. the next day. He also said that Mr Pillai should be examined with regard to his 'alleged ailments and possible availability of treatment for the said disease in Delhi.' In the meantime he should be provided the required treatment.

This was the start of a tragedy of omissions and errors. The confidential letter never reached the RMO. In my report I criticized the person in the jail administration who received the letter but did not ensure that it got delivered to the RMO, and I suggested he be reprimanded. The lawyer for the Central Bureau of Investigation, which had made its own enquiries with the RMO and knew that Rajan Pillai's particular illness had to be treated in a 'super-speciality' hospital, chose to remain silent and did not see fit to disclose the information to the court. In my report I commented on his behaviour:

> Though Mr A.K. Dutt might be well within his rights not to have shown the letter of the RMO to the court, a responsible officer is expected to act in a manner showing a level of high integrity considering the fact that his silence might result in depriving a person of proper medical treatment.

When Rajan Pillai had been remanded to Tihar Jail, he had (on the basis of the first letter of his name) been lodged in Jail No. 4. The entry formalities had been completed at about 2 p.m., too late for the mandatory initial medical examination. Though Jail Nos. 1, 2 and 3 were interconnected, Jail No. 4 was not. For the approximate nine thousand prisoners in all four jails at Tihar, plus the staff and their families who made up another four thousand or so, there were only six doctors. Since one or two of these were usually on leave or absent, usually about four doctors were available during the day. In the evening, there was only one doctor who was available for emergency duty, and he was located in Jail No 3.

At 7.15 p.m. Rajan Pillai was sent in a van to Jail No 3 hospital to be examined by him. Dr A. Venkatsubbaiah examined him in a cursory manner and found his condition to be 'within normal limits', as his pulse was normal and he did not have any fever or high blood pressure or dehydration. Rajan Pillai told him that he was suffering from hypertension and taking Propanol tablets. He also told him that he had had an attack of haematemesis in 1992, had been diagnosed as having cirrhosis of the liver, and had been treated by non-invasive surgery at the Escorts Hospital. He wanted the doctor to send him there as he had vomited blood on 3 July. But Dr Venkatsubbaiah gave him some medicines for one day and told him to consult the medical officer in Jail No 4 itself the next day; this medical officer could refer him to Escorts or other multi-speciality hospital in the city.

On 5 July, Rajan Pillai left for court by van, with the other prisoners in the morning and returned only in the evening, too late to be examined.

On 6 July, the magistrate adjourned Rajan Pillai's application for bail till the 11th. The CBI submitted that his application for medical examination and treatment was not made in good faith as at no stage had he as a fugitive mentioned his illness. The magistrate held that in the facts and circumstances of the case, he did not require immediate hospitalization or check up, but was permitted to continue his prescribed medication. He also observed that 'the professionally and morally bound doctors at the jail hospital and the easily accessible court will always be concerned about the permissible and required medical treatment as and when the situation warranted.' He could hardly have been aware of how totally inadequate this concern would prove to be.

Rajan Pillai was naturally dejected when he returned to Jail No. 4, Barrack No. 1, Ward No. 9, and was shown a cement platform to sleep on. The summer heat was insufferable and the fans in the locked ward ineffective. His feet were swollen and he had to walk barefoot to the bathroom, which he repeatedly frequented that night. The condition of the toilet was abominable. He was restless and could not sleep. The other prisoners did not call anyone; they did not realize the seriousness of his condition and thought he was disturbed because he was new to the experience of jail.

On the morning of 7 July, when the warder opened the barracks, he found that Rajan Pillai had high fever and swollen feet. A Malayalee prisoner was summoned to try and understand what he was murmuring. This prisoner urged the authorities to send Rajan Pillai to an outside hospital, as his condition was very serious. But he was taken to Dr Hira Lal, the doctor available in the observation ward in Jail No. 4. This doctor examined him in a cursory manner, prescribed a calmpose injection and recorded that his general condition was 'fair'. (Rajan Pillai was at the time just hours from death.)

When Dr Hira Lal left for the day at 1 p.m. he knew that there would be no other medical personnel available till the next morning, but he neither examined him again nor sent him to the hospital in Jail No. 3 where some medical personnel would be available. He also knew that the observation ward was locked from the outside between 1 p.m. and 3 p.m. and the keys kept in the foyer of the administrative block, some 400 metres away. If a prisoner's condition deteriorated, the only remedy would be for the other inmates in the ward to shout to the warder, provided he was near and could hear (there had been a case of a deaf warder) and, if the warder was satisfied that the condition was serious, he would go to the administrative block, fetch the key and then open the ward for further action. (There had been a case when the key could not be found and a patient had had to be injected through the bars of the locked door.)

At about 4 p.m. Mr Pillai's lawyer came to interview him and to get a power of attorney signed. Rajan Pillai was brought to the administrative block to meet him at about 4.45 p.m. In the blazing sun, on his grossly swollen feet, he walked the 400 metres on a day when the temperature was almost 41°C in the shade and his own body temperature was 40°C (104°F). When his lawyer saw his swollen face and feet and his 'sick look', and sensed his disorientation and raging fever, he immediately went and informed the jail superintendent.

The superintendent had two benches put together in the foyer, started to have the patient cold-sponged, and summoned Dr Venkatsubbaiah from Jail No. 3. He arrived at 5.35 p.m. He found Rajan Pillai unconscious and unresponsive even to painful stimuli. The doctor did not have any life-saving apparatus like oxygen or respiratory equipment. He directed that Rajan Pillai be taken to hospital. The lawyer wanted him to be taken to Escorts, but the superintendent said that under the rules he could only send him to the Deen Dayal Upadhyay Hospital.

The ambulance was summoned. It arrived at 5.50 p.m. Rajan Pillai was put on a sagging stretcher and lifted into the ambulance. During the journey he started frothing from the mouth—white froth with a tinge of blood. There were no facilities for medical treatment in the ambulance, which was just like a van.

At 6.20 p.m. they arrived at the Casualty Ward of the hospital. Rajan Pillai was lifted on the stretcher by the policemen and placed on the hospital bed. Dr Venkatsubbaiah gave his referral slip, which mentioned fever and unconsciousness but did not mention any of the other conditions that he knew about. By this time the patient's pulse rate was 120 per minute, breath laboured, pupils mid-dilated and light reaction sluggish. Oropharyngeal suction was done immediately to remove the froth, oxygen and intravenous fluid given, and cold sponging started. Dr Venkatsubbaiah told the attending doctor, that the patient was a 'known alcoholic', and left within a few minutes. He failed to inform the doctor who took charge that the patient had told him on 4 July that he had a history of cirrhosis of the liver and had been treated with non-invasive surgery for gastrointestinal bleeding in 1992 or that he had said he had vomited blood on the evening of 3 July.

Since Rajan Pillai was in a critical condition, all the senior doctors at the hospital came to examine him and gave him symptomatic and resuscitative treatment, but they were hamstrung, not knowing the full history of his case. On their prescription they mentioned hyperpyrexia, cerebral malaria, septic shock and 'not known'. His condition was so serious that he could not even be moved to the Intensive Care Unit; he was put on an artificial respirator and attached to a cardiac monitor in the Casualty Ward itself. He bled from his nose and mouth at 7 p.m. and went into cardio-respiratory arrest. He would, based on the cardiac trace, have been declared dead at 7.15 p.m., but because of Nina Pillai's personal request to the Medical Superintendent, they continued resuscitation measures till the arrival of his doctor from Escorts at 8.30 p.m.

The post-mortem, which was conducted by a team of three doctors, found that Rajan Pillai had died of asphyxia as a result of aspiration of blood in the respiratory airway consequent to bleeding from ruptured esophageal varicose— a complication of advanced cirrhosis of the liver.

★

In my report I stated:

> There is no doubt that Mr Rajan Pillai was a sick
> man, having a chronic disease like alcoholic cirrhosis
> of the liver. He had two life threatening episodes in
> 1992 and ten sclerotherapies till March 1995. As to
> how many years he would have survived is a moot
> point especially as he continued to drink. But he
> certainly was entitled to proper medical treatment and
> it was the duty of the State to have ensured that it was
> made available since he was in custody. Unfortunately,
> both Dr Venkatsubbaiah and Dr Hira Lal, the two
> doctors in Central Jail, Tihar, New Delhi who
> examined him were casual and careless in the
> performance of their professional duty, as outlined
> earlier. Their negligence eventually resulted in giving
> him hardly any chance of survival.
>
> The State has a duty to ensure that the medical
> facilities and services in Central Jail, Tihar, are
> improved and the number of doctors increased and
> the quality of doctors upgraded, so that incidents like
> this do not recur. Prisoners are in custody and
> consequently have no access to medical facilities and
> services of their choice, so the duty of the State to
> take care is even greater.

Out of the approximately nine thousand prisoners at that
time in Tihar Jail, eight thousand were under trials. If they
had been out on bail, they would have been able to have
medical treatment of their choice. Consequently, I
recommended, in keeping with Rule 91 of the United Nations
Standard Minimum Rules, that they be allowed to be visited
and treated by their own doctor or dentist if there were
reasonable grounds for their request and they could pay for
the expenses incurred.

I made many recommendations including those pertaining to overcrowding in the jail, increasing and improving the sanitation facilities and increasing both the quantity and the quality of the medical facilities and personnel. I began this chapter of my report with the Arab proverb: 'He who has health has hope; and he who has hope has everything'.

After making my recommendations I ended:

> It is hoped that the suggestions and recommendations made will bear some fruit and not lie with the other reels of recommendations being ignored pertaining to prisoners that have been made over the years. It has taken the tragic death of a well-known person to shake the sluggish lethargy of the administration and to realize that six doctors to look after and examine over 9000 prisoners with a regular turnover is nothing but a token of medical facilities. It is hoped that the Dr K. K. Jain Committee's recommendations and the suggestions made herein are implemented on an urgent basis to inject some hope and help and humanity in the life of the prisoner who is endlessly waiting for trial and freedom.

The Action Taken Report sent to me at the end of September 1997 did indicate that some steps had been taken to increase and improve the medical facilities and personnel.

Often, in the years that followed the Commission of Inquiry, my mind turned to its events and circumstances. What life has in store for us lies hidden behind a veil. Who could have guessed that a man who was used to living and entertaining like a prince in five-star hotel suites and luxurious homes, travelling in air-conditioned and spacious splendour and hob-nobbing with Prime Ministers and Presidents would spend his last night sleeping on a cement platform in a hot and humid ward among under-trial prisoners, walk barefoot to a slippery, slimy bathroom and take his last journey to hospital on a stretcher on the floor of a rundown van; or that he who lived in a fabulous house in Ridout Road in Singapore and possessed beautiful homes and cashew plantations should have his permanent address shown in the post-mortem report as Jail No 4, Tihar, New Delhi.

★

From the time of her husband's death on 7 July 1995, Nina Pillai made vague accusations that business rivals and politically powerful people had conspired to kill him. Her senior counsel urged me to examine the matter. I asked him what evidence he had; I had to know at least some of the grounds for her belief before I could proceed. He said that the circumstances of the conspiracy were 'highly incendiary' and could affect the security of his client. An affidavit, together with documents, would however be filed. No such affidavit was filed.

After a counsel for the Commission was appointed in March 1996, I asked that Nina Pillai be cross-examined on this matter. She wanted to postpone the date of this examination on the grounds that she was standing for election to the Lok Sabha; she was told that this was not possible. Nevertheless, she failed to appear on 9 April. I postponed the cross-examination to 30 April, but she didn't appear on that day either, or on subsequent dates that were fixed for her. She changed both her senior and her junior counsel in July. She was due to be examined by counsel for the jail personnel on 20 July, but did not appear. I gave her one last opportunity to appear in this context on 23 July, but neither she nor her counsel appeared. I declared her evidence closed, but her counsel later appeared with a faxed medical certificate on her behalf, and I rescinded this order. On the next day, for her cross-examination, 23 September, she did not appear, declaring herself jet-lagged. She was told this was not acceptable. When she finally did appear in the afternoon, the lawyer for the jail personnel questioned her with regard to these allegations of conspiracy, and she made some conflicting statements. Finally, she said that certain clarifications had come to her notice and she wanted to place them on record before being cross-examined. Despite the lawyer's objection, I allowed her to do so by 30 September. Her cross-examination would be postponed till 1 October. No documents or materials were filed, nor did she appear.

On 1 October, her counsel moved an unverified application on her behalf, stating that she planned to go to the criminal court regarding the conspiracy, that any statements made by her before the Commission of Inquiry would affect the course of the criminal proceedings, that the continuation of the Commission of Inquiry in parallel with those proceedings was not in the public interest, and that consequently the Inquiry should be closed. The various lawyers and their clients wanted time to file written submissions in response to this application; I said I would hear the matter on 23 October. Once again, she did not turn up. I heard what her lawyer, the lawyer for the jail personnel and the lawyer for the Commission had to say, and I reserved orders.

On 11 November I dismissed her application. I noted in the order that her prevarication regarding the material pertaining to the conspiracy meant that it was either not there or that she had no intention of disclosing it. Though her husband had died on 7 July 1995 and sixteen months had elapsed, no steps had been taken so far either to bring the material on record or to file criminal proceedings. I further observed that there was no hindrance or impropriety in an inquiry continuing even if criminal proceedings were pending. This had been stated clearly by the Supreme Court. The Commission was a fact-finding authority to search out the truth. The report could be the starting point of criminal investigation but not its conclusion. Its report was only recommendatory in nature.

I directed her to appear for cross-examination on 18 November. She did not appear. Her counsel stated that she would not appear. She did not want to participate in the proceedings. Her evidence was consequently closed. But an affidavit was filed before me that day stating that bias and prejudice was writ large in my order of 11 November, and that her faith in the Commission had been shaken. Further, she had been utterly shocked by an article dated 1 October that she had read in the *Daily*, Bombay, that I was related to the spouse of one of the jail officials. Consequently, the Commission was biased and prejudiced and should adjourn its proceedings. An indistinct photocopy of the article, 'The Good, Bad and Ugly' by R.K.B., was annexed.

This was a totally unfounded allegation. That I was anguished at her unwarranted remarks goes without saying. Despite being angry and exasperated at the manner in which she had tried to stall the enquiry, especially when she had had to face cross-examination by the lawyer for the jail officials, I had accommodated her to the extent possible in her demands for one adjournment after another. I was stunned at the lengths to which she was willing to go to frustrate the Commission's proceedings when I had nothing but sympathy for her in her sorrow and judicial objectivity in trying to arrive at the truth.

On 20 November the jail officials filed affidavits denying any relationship with the Chairperson of the Commission, either directly or through their spouses. As Mrs Pillai failed to furnish, upon direction, a copy of the newspaper, a letter was sent to the *Daily* for a copy of the paper and the complete name of the writer and columnist. No copy of the newspaper was sent by them, even when a reminder was served; nor was any reaction forthcoming from the newspaper.

Consequently, counsel for the Commission prepared a criminal complaint for contempt of court against Ms Gopika Nina Pillai as well as the publisher, printer and editor/writer/columnist of the said article for an intentionally calculated effort to bring the Commission into disrepute. It was filed in the Delhi High Court through the Secretary to the Commission on 24 January 1997.

In fact, Nina Pillai even went to the extent of writing to the Delhi Government to request them not to give the Commission a final extension of time in order for me to complete writing the report. But she did not succeed, and the report was completed on 25 February 1997. The report was submitted to the Lieutenant-Governor immediately thereafter; so also—but in locked steel trunks—were the voluminous records.

The report was a confidential document until it was tabled in the House. Many people, including the media, both Indian and foreign, were anxious to interview me both when the Commission's proceedings were pending and after the report had been submitted but I refused to be drawn in or even photographed. I could not and would not discuss my findings and recommendations. It was about seven months later, on 24 September 1997, that the Lieutenant-Governor of Delhi sent me copies of my report, along with the Action Taken Report signed by the Jail Minister and circulated in the House by the Home Department of the Delhi Government. I was pleased to note that some action had been taken on some of the recommendations.

I sometimes wondered what had happened to the matter relating to contempt of court, but since the counsel to the Commission, Madan Lokur, had meanwhile become a judge of the Delhi High Court, I was not in a position to know. However, about two years later, I received a letter from Nina Pillai from Mumbai (as Bombay was now called); it was dated 22 May 1999:

Dear Ms Justice Seth

You will recall that I was appearing as a party before the Commission headed by you which was inquiring into the custodial death of my husband Rajan Pillai.

Those were troubled times and overnight I found myself a widow with two orphaned children having to fend for myself in a cruel and heartless world. The sudden reversal of fortunes and the betrayal by friends was something which was very difficult to cope with.

As if living life without Rajan was not enough, as a mother I had to answer awkward questions of two little children about their departed father. Why was he in jail? Why did he have to die?

I could think of nothing but to protect my two children and to remove the stigma from my dear husband's name. I believe that my husband was put to death by certain people. It is only when I am able to expose these people, that his departed soul will find eternal peace.

It is in the light of these circumstances that I filed my affidavit of November 18, 1996. In the affidavit I stated that I was pained and anguished by the Commission's order of November 11, 1996. An article published in "The Daily" had further disturbed me.

I cannot but admit that it was most improper for me to use the strong words that I had used in the affidavit. I am also conscious that the affidavit must have offended you.

I can only say, that I have the greatest of regard for you and that it was not my intention to cause offence to you or to bring the commission into disrepute. In times of trouble often people end up doing things which they do not intend to do.

I had wished that I could personally meet you so that I could convey my deepest apologies to you for the offence my affidavit has caused you. However, as a complaint was pending in the High Court of Delhi, I was advised that it was not appropriate to personally meet you to convey my apologies.

In my reply to the complaint I have reiterated my high regard for you and the commission and I have conveyed my apologies. It was at the hearing on May 7, 1999, that the suggestion fell from His Lordship Hon'ble SN Kapoor that I do convey my apologies directly to you.

I therefore take this opportunity to convey must (sic) deepest regrets. I believe that a written letter of apology is not sufficient. I would really appreciate if you could kindly permit me to meet you at your convenience to personally convey my deepest apologies.

Yours sincerely
Nina Pillai

I read the letter a couple of times. The matter had come full circle and I felt that in this regard it was finally closed.

Law Commission

The function of a Law Commission is to suggest reform of the law (by repeal or amendment or the creation of new laws) or of the administration of law in order to maximise justice in society and promote good government under the rule of law. The 1st Law Commission in independent India was set up in 1955 and, like subsequent commissions, ran for three years. The Law Commission consists of a chairperson, a member-secretary (who also handles administration), upto three full-time members, and a number of part-time members or consultants depending on the nature of the topics given to the Commission to study—which can be very diverse.

I was busy with my arbitration work when, in October 1997, I received a phone-call from the Law Minister. He said that the Government had it in mind to appoint me as a full-time member to the 15th Law Commission, whose term would run from 1997 to 2000. I remember being surprised by this invitation. It was an honour, certainly, but I was somewhat wary of taking up a new assignment. I asked him who the chairperson would be. When he told me it would be Justice Jeevan Reddy, a former judge of the Supreme Court

whom I respected as a person of great energy and acuity, I
knew that we would be doing interesting and substantial
work, and I agreed to join.

I joined on 10 November, but there was not much legal
activity as Justice Jeevan Reddy was abroad at the time. But
the activity outside the office room allotted to me was
considerable. As I tried to settle down to read some of the
books and reports that I was interested in, the noise in the
corridor rose to a crescendo. When I rang the bell and tried
to ascertain the reason for the hullabaloo, I was told that the
peons and others were having tea. This was repeated many
times a day. When I asked whether it was necessary to be so
voluble when having tea, I was told that that had been the
practice among the staff for years, and that, after all, they
needed to relax. As I was soon to discover, I either had the
choice of hearing high-pitched conversation or being
submerged in total silence when they disappeared and were
unavailable, however often I rang the bell.

I also learnt soon enough of the rigid and almost caste-
like stratification and division of work that was typical of
government offices. The sweeper would clean and mop the
floor; the 'farash' or cleaner would dust the furniture; the
peon would carry my briefcase and books from and to the car,
bring me tea, and take out the food from my tiffin-carrier
which I brought in a hot case from home every day; and the
driver would drive me to and from home to work. No one
would do the work of the other, yet—with un-caste-like
conviviality—they all had tea outside my room in the corridor,
in the winter with a heater on and in the summer with an air-
cooler blowing. The peons considered themselves entitled,
while shouting out their converations, to sit on the broken
chairs placed near the door. It required a change of member-
secretary and a major upheaval before the chairs were replaced
with potted palms and the peons relocated in the private
secretary's room on the other side of the corridor.

The Law Commission was located on the seventh floor of Shastri Bhavan. There were no bathrooms attached to the rooms. The common bathroom had a leaking tap, a totally broken dirty green plastic bucket, a pink plastic mug with a damaged handle, and no toilet paper. The glass window in the toilet was filthy, as it was difficult to clean from the outside; one of the panes was broken and a cardboard piece had been stuck there to keep out the cold air. The cistern leaked, and did not flush. It took me weeks of constant requests to get it functional till it broke down again.

My room had a typical CPWD look about it. Numbers and information were painted prominently on the front of all the furniture in white so that there could be no dispute as to whom it belonged. The office staff insisted on placing a large pink towel adorned with big purple flowers on the back of the chair by my desk, to be used like an anti-macassar. I promptly had it removed, despite the objections and horror of everyone as to my iconoclastic ignorance of both hygiene and aesthetics. I moved the furniture around, put up posters and pictures, threw out the plastic flowers and replaced it with a fresh money-plant in a ceramic vase, got rid of all the plastic pens and pencil cases, and covered the ugly dark-green steel cupboard for storing confidential papers with pictures of Himalayan snow scenes from old calendars. I brought a duster cloth from home and cleaned the furniture, which had not been dusted because the 'farash' had not come that day. By doing this, I slowly shamed the peon into keeping the place clean even if the 'farash' was not there. By the time the chairperson joined, I was ready to work.

I was provided with a white Ambassador car, the staple vehicle for government servants. But when I asked the driver to put my luggage in the boot, he looked at me strangely and instead placed it on the front seat beside him. When I reiterated that I wanted it put in the luggage compartment at the back, he told me that he couldn't oblige me because Justice Kuldip Singh was sitting there. I was shocked at his remark and told him so. He then asked me to see for myself. When he opened the boot, I saw that there was a huge compressed-gas cylinder occupying all the normal luggage space. He explained that as a result of a judgment of the Supreme Court given by Justice Kuldip Singh, all the old Ambassador cars with the government had been converted to CNG in this ad hoc manner.

★

At first the full-time members of the Commission consisted of the chair, the member-secretary and myself. (Another full-time member was to join later.) Justice Jeevan Reddy and I would work in our rooms for much of the time, but have lunch at the large table in his room and informally discuss the projects and areas of law reform we wanted to deal with. Sometimes, the Government or even the Supreme Court would request us to look at a particular matter. Quite often we would take things up ourselves. But a final decision about whether to undertake a project was made at a full meeting of the Commission. If we decided to go ahead, we would collect data, do research, sound opinion, take expert advice and prepare a working paper, which we circulated to concerned individuals and interest groups, sometimes with a carefully-prepared questionnaire. We were assisted by a number of researchers who were attached to the Law Commission. Seminars and workshops were often organized to elicit ideas and critical analysis on the reforms we suggested.

Thereafter, a report was written by either the chairperson or a member and then subjected to close scrutiny by the full Commission. Often a draft bill was also appended with the report before it was submitted to the Government. The report was then considered by the Ministry of Law in consultation with the ministries concerned with the subject of the report. After this, a Hindi translation was made, and the texts in both English and Hindi were submitted to Parliament. All this often took more than a year.

After submitting a report to the Government, Justice Reddy would release it to the press and even invite the media in to discuss it. But almost at the end of the three-year term of the 15th Law Commission, we were told by the Law Ministry that though we could discuss matters with the public at large while cogitating our decision, we could not do so after the report was finalized as it was confidential till tabled in Parliament. We thought this strange, since we were not a fact-finding commission whose judgments and conclusions should not be prematurely revealed; the subjects we dealt with were general issues, often of widespread public interest. But the Ministry remained adamant, and the 16th Law Commission, which started from September 2000, was struck silent, even though it had the same chairperson as ours for part of its tenure.

The whole process outlined above took a long time, and those who had initiated a reform had long since left the Commission by the time the Government implemented any of their recommendations. At one point, I began to wonder whether any reform actually took place at all. But upon making an enquiry, I learnt that out of the 156 reports submitted by the earlier fourteen Law Commissions, 80 had been fully implemented, 17 had not been implemented and 59 were in different stages of consideration. This gave me heart and some reassurance that more than half of the recommendations made by us would hopefully become law one day.

In fact, when I pondered these statistics, I came to realize that being a member of the Law Commission was a very powerful means of doing good. I could, with the agreement of my colleagues, tackle any subject that interested or deeply concerned me; there was a better than even chance that, sooner or later—well, later rather than sooner—the report would be taken up by some Government or simply be extended through its long consultative process and land up on the legislative roster. As long as one was not concerned with immediate or even future credit or kudos, this was quite satisfying.

And yet, the Law Commission, this half scholarly, half social-reforming body, so many of whose recommendations had become law, itself stood, rather anomalously, on slightly uncertain legal grounds. Indeed, it does so still. It was not, like the Election Commission or Finance Commission, established by the Constitution. It has not even, like the National Human Rights Commission or the National Commission for Women, been established by statute. The 1st Law Commission was set up by the Prime Minister at the time, Jawaharlal Nehru, by executive order. That is how things have remained. Each successive Law Commission has to be constituted by an order. But the institution has proved itself useful, and is now sufficiently hallowed by convention after almost half a century to be expected to continue.

The eighteen reports submitted by the 15th Law Commission, like those of earlier commissions, covered a very wide range of subjects, from the Hire-Purchase Act, 1972 to the Corrupt Public Servants (Forfeiture of Property) Bill, from the Repeal and Amendment of Laws to the Patents (Amendment) Bill, 1998, from the Biodiversity Bill, 2000 to Amendments of Army, Navy and Air Force Acts.

My inputs on certain reports was substantial. Among these were the reports on the Code of Civil Procedure (Amendment) Bill, 1997, on Reform of the Electoral Laws, and on the Prevention of Terrorism Bill, 2000. With regard to the first of these, we made numerous suggestions regarding the elimination of delay in the judicial process with the objective of attaining speedy and effective justice.

Working on the report on Reform of the Electoral Laws was exciting and exhilarating. We looked at the laws of other countries and had detailed discussions as we grappled with questions of how to make our electoral system fairer, more representative and more transparent in order to strengthen our democracy; how to arrest and reverse the process of the proliferation and splintering of political parties; and how to introduce stability in governance. We suggested measures to reform the electoral system and make governance more accountable: for example, the obligatory declaration of every candidate's assets as well as those of any spouse or dependent relations, and the non-entitlement to seats in the Lok Sabha or the state assemblies of parties receiving less than five per cent of the total vote.

The Terrorist and Disruptive Activities (Prevention) Act 1987 (or TADA) had lapsed in 1995. The Government urged us to look into the matter urgently in view of the drastically changing security environment. They contended that suitable legislation to counteract anti-national activities and terrorism was essential.

I was basically opposed to the idea of a separate act for the prevention of terrorism. I felt strongly that the enactment of such legislation would not by itself subdue terrorism. At one stage I even felt I should disassociate myself from the discussions and the report. But, on balance, I decided that it was better to remain a part of the team and ensure that some of the really harsh provisions suggested were toned down, so that though various measures would be introduced to combat terrorism, adequate safeguards would also be provided to prevent abuse of power and to preserve human rights.

The Government was anxious and in a hurry and tried to

rush us into presenting our recommendations without delay. But we felt that the Commission had to follow the normal procedure. Consequently, a working paper was prepared and widely circulated, and a couple of seminars held. Diverse elements of civil society were consulted before we prepared the final report, and some of the points they raised were incorporated in it.

We thoroughly revised the Criminal Law Amendment Bill 1995 sent to us by the Government as the basis for a new bill, and suggested a new name and bill to be called the Prevention of Terrorism Bill, 2000. 'Disruptive Activities'— so prominent in the name TADA—was dropped from the roster of crimes; thus, a mere speech, no matter how offensive from the Government's point of view, would not trigger the anti-terrorism law. The bill also provided several safeguards and greater protection from torture than TADA did. This report was sent to the Law Minister in April 2000. Many months later the Prevention of Terrorism Act was passed. It incorporated some of the provisions suggested by us; the Government introduced others of its own.

One report in the discussion and preparation of which I participated with enthusiasm was called Free and Compulsory Education of Children. I passionately believe that providing free primary education to children should be one of the priorities of government. Only then can there be some semblance of a chance for equal opportunity. An educated, informed society is crucially important for democracy and good governance; it will lead to smaller-family norms, reduce absolute poverty and help to curb the horrendous practice of child labour. In our report, we emphasized the urgency of the issue by including a draft bill for introduction in Parliament in order to give effect to the right to education, without having to wait for a constitutional amendment. But, encouragingly, the Constitution has since been amended to make primary education a fundamental right, and steps towards compulsory primary education for all are, slowly but surely, being taken.

Three reports involving the rights and welfare of women greatly involved me. One of these was a Review of Rape Laws. We undertook this at the behest of the Supreme Court, who were hearing a petition filed by Sakshi, an organization interested in issues concerning women and children.

After hearing Sakshi and some other women's organizations, including the National Commission for Women, we recommended changes to widen the scope of the offence of rape and to make it gender neutral. We also suggested some changes in sections dealing with the punishment for rape and for other sexual offences, especially where committed by people in positions of power—whether in police stations or jails or hospitals. We suggested the inclusion in the Indian Penal Code of a section dealing with unlawful sexual contact, especially in relation to young people. We suggested other changes in the Penal Code, the Criminal Procedure Code and the Evidence Act. The whole objective was to prevent sexual exploitation in general and the abuse of children in particular through more stringent provisions; this was even more important in view of the increased incidence of custodial rape and the sexual abuse of young persons.

Our report on the Indian Divorce Act, 1869 took us into the realm of 'personal law'. It applied only to Christians, and was heavily weighted against women. Despite several reports— one as early as 1960—by previous Law Commissions, the law had not been changed.

Once again, we made suggestions with regard to the notorious Section 10 of the Act, which provided that a Christian man could be granted divorce on the ground of adultery by itself, whereas a Christian woman had to establish adultery plus an additional matrimonial offence such as cruelty or bigamy or incest or desertion. This was obviously discriminatory and we wanted it changed. We also suggested repeal of the provision making it necessary for a decree of dissolution of marriage by a district judge to be subject to confirmation by the High Court. We recommended that the anomalies and ambiguities be removed and the law be changed expeditiously in the interest of social justice and the Christian community in India. I was delighted when the new law came into force in September 2001.

We also took up an important matter in Hindu personal law relating to the property rights of women. The Mitakshara system of the joint Hindu family (commonly known as the Hindu undivided family or HUF), where devolution of property takes place by survivorship rather than succession, permits only sons to be members of the coparcenary and excludes daughters. We felt that the exclusion of daughters from participating in coparcenary property, merely by reason of their sex, was unjust, and we made some clear recommendations in this regard. Kerala had abolished the joint Hindu family in the state, Andhra Pradesh provided that a daughter would at birth become a coparcenar like a son. Tamil Nadu, Maharashtra and Karnataka followed the Andhra Pradesh model. After due deliberation, we decided to recommend a combination of the two models; we believed that the synthesis we arrived at was in keeping with justice, equity and family harmony. We suggested that these changes be brought about by an amendment to the Central Act by Parliament so that there would be uniformity in this regard throughout the country.

In May 2000, our report on Property Rights of Women: Proposed Reforms under the Hindu Law was sent to the Law Minister. This was the last report submitted by the 15th Law Commission, whose term was to expire at the end of August. The press reported it extensively. When some TV reporters

came to the Law Commission to interview me on the subject,
I said: 'Despite the Constitution of India having proclaimed
equality before the law as a fundamental right, a daughter is
excluded from participation in ancestral property under the
Mitakshara system merely by reason of her sex. It is my
fervent hope that if the changes suggested are brought about
and fully implemented it will be the death knell of the curse
of the dowry demand and will also improve the condition of
women.'

Discrimination against women enshrined in the law exists
just as acutely in the Muslim personal law in India. What is
worse is that here, attempts by the courts to improve their
position have roused the wrath of sections of the community.
In the Shah Bano case, an impoverished divorced woman,
denied maintenance by her ex-husband, was granted it by the
Supreme Court on grounds other than those of Muslim
personal law. The subsequent uproar compelled the
pusillanimous, vote-seeking government of the day to rush a
bill, the speciously titled Muslim Women (Protection of
Rights on Divorce) Act through Parliament in order to
nullify the judgment and deny Muslim women this protection.
It was a shameful capitulation.

The founders of the Constitution, in their section on
Directive Principles, wrote in Article 44: 'The State shall
endeavour to secure for the citizens a uniform civil code
throughout the territory of India.' This uniform civil code
means a uniform personal law on such matters as marriage,
divorce, maintenance, adoption, guardianship and succession,
regardless of one's religion—as exists in most countries and,
indeed, even in Goa, a legacy of Portuguese rule. To my
mind, the principles of equality, justice and non-discrimination
are far more important than unequal, unjust and discriminatory
personal laws associated with particular religions. When I
suggested to Justice Jeevan Reddy that we take up the

question and write a report on it, he looked thoughtful and said, 'This is not the right time.' And indeed, the timing—which of course will never be perfect—is a vexed question. It is difficult to get minority communities to accept such legislation if they are suspicious of the partisan motives of the Government that seeks to introduce it.

I bade farewell to the Law Commission from my bed. I tripped over a wire at a book launch at the beginning of August, sustained multiple fractures of the left ankle, and was immobilized for more than thirteen weeks. The office in Shastri Bhavan was packed up by others and vacated on my behalf. So ended my term as a member of the 15th Law Commission. I had learnt a great deal and, I hoped, been useful in bringing about some much needed legal reform.

Laid up by my injuries, I had plenty of time to meditate about my future, grumble a little about my present, and mull over my past, including my recent experiences in the remarkable world of the Law Commission. My doctors and nurses were good, my therapist wonderful, and Premo a gem. But I longed to bestir myself from my bed-bound state, and—doctor's orders or no—go for a jaunt into the outside world—yes, even if it meant going in the white Ambassador of the last three years, with Justice Kuldip Singh sitting in the boot.

Arbitration and Other
Activities

After I retired as Chief Justice of Himachal Pradesh in 1992, I took a conscious decision that I would not appear in court, neither in the Supreme Court nor any other High Court, even though I was entitled to practise in all the High Courts other than Delhi and Himachal Pradesh. However, I let it be known that I was willing to do arbitration work. This meant that parties, if their contract so provided, could choose me to decide their matter rather than go to court. Most building construction contracts had such a clause. The parties, instead of having a sole arbitrator, could also opt for a two-arbitrator tribunal, where each party chose an arbitrator and the two arbitrators chose an umpire before the hearing started; the umpire could cast a deciding vote in case of a difference of opinion between the arbitrators. Sometimes, there was a tribunal of three arbitrators, one nominated by each party and a chairman chosen by the Indian Council of Arbitration. The three heard the matter and the decision of the majority prevailed.

In early 1993, I started getting work and was quite

pleased. But I soon found that almost all the cases dealt with construction contracts, which, though lucrative, were boring. Then, sometime in early 1995, the Supreme Court of India sent me a matter to be dealt with as its Nominee. This was quite different, because it had a human interest angle as well.

A dispute was pending before the court about the division of family property and family business. Three brothers had been running their vegetable oil and other business in Jammu and Moga together. One of the brothers had died and his widow, Indu Puri, was now trying to run the business along with the two remaining brothers. The brother in Jammu was at loggerheads with his elder brother and with Indu Puri, who were both residing in Moga. The grown-up son of the Jammu brother was called Sanjay and Indu's son was called Vivek. These youngsters each had his own ideas about how to run the business and distrusted the other regarding accounts, the stock of materials, and other matters.

They had been a large, happy family when they were young and Indu had loved looking after her nephew Sanjay. But now there was a great deal of acrimony and anger. The only way out was to partition the property and business. Yet despite a number of efforts, it had not happened. Because of the difficulties involved in separating the various businesses, no solution could be found. Also, owing to their constant fights, the flourishing business was deteriorating.

The Supreme Court asked Indu Puri to divide the entire joint property and business into three equal parts (as far as possible). They told her that since she was going to make the shares, she would have last choice and the Jammu family would have the first. This was a very wise move, because it certainly ensured that the division was fair.

After the Supreme Court made the order about which package went to whom, they sent the matter to me to help work out the actual nitty gritty of the division. This was a delicate matter since the business was a running concern, and separation, unless carried out amicably, might result in the business itself being destroyed. There were numerous documents and licences and shares that had to be divided. The businesses were not easily extricable: the mustard oil was manufactured in Moga but marketed mainly in Jammu. Even the use of the family trademark was in dispute.

The brothers, wives, sons, daughters and daughters-in-law were all partners in the various businesses, and getting them together and to agree on the actual modalities of the division was a strategically, tactically and diplomatically difficult task. When the parties came to me they were hardly on speaking terms and it was quite a job to ensure that they were civil to each other while sitting in the same room. I called them on a number of occasions to arrive at a general agreement as to how the break-up should be done and then asked all the family members to be present at my house just after lunch on 23 May 1995.

They came from Jammu and Moga and various other places; they included the young children of Sanjay and Vivek and even a little baby. They, along with their counsel, overflowed from my chamber into my drawing room and dining room. But when it came to signing the numerous papers dealing with the various businesses, they started raising objections. Because they were so suspicious of one another, they did not want to let their documents out of their sight, so I had two large photocopying machines installed in front of our kitchen! I told them that I would not let them wander off until all the papers were agreed to and signed, because it would be difficult if not impossible to get all of them together again. They prevaricated but I persisted, and a large number of papers remained unsigned even at 9 p.m. Poor Premo, dispossessed from his rooms, busied himself by getting some food in from a restaurant and some milk for the baby.

Objections continued to be raised throughout the night to almost every document. But I did not want the momentum to be lost, and used cajoling, pressure and even a bit of exasperation to bring about a solution and end the family strife of so many years. It was 7 a.m. before the basic papers were signed; none of us had slept a wink.

Seeing a number of cars outside our house, people in the locality thought that someone must be seriously ill and started coming to the house in the morning to make sympathetic enquiries. By 8.30 the twenty or so disputing family-members and lawyers had left.

Some weeks later, when I returned from a trip, I found a letter waiting for me.

Respected Madam,

At the moment I am perplexed, whether I should take the liberty of expressing my heart-felt gratitude for you or not?

I had only heard that miracles happen in life and Saviour God himself comes through His own divine souls to take care and impact further, but I could realize this fact only on 23 May.

Words fail me to express my immense feelings of gratitude for all the pains and interest sincere efforts, your goodself had taken on that day to ensure that this long awaited settlement takes final shape. It looked hard . . . very hard indeed! But due to your unparalleled patience and insight, it was made possible and saved the family from further torture.

Again thanking you and seeking apology from you for writing this little note.

With deep regards,

Yours sincerely
Indu Puri

A few weeks later I received a letter from her nephew Sanjay.

> Respected Madam,
> Thank you once again for all the trouble you undertook to help resolve our family disputes.
> I cannot express how grateful we all are to you for patiently bearing with our arguments and the difficult positions we take due to our differences.
> Fortunately with your blessings all problems have come to pass and what remains shall also heal with time and your guidance.

I was really relieved that the basic interconnected documents had been signed, especially as I had learnt that a number of previous efforts at an agreement had resulted in failure. It took a number of years more to entirely smoothen out the arrangement of the division, but fortunately this was done and the Puri family saved from destruction.

★

Now that I was not active either at the Bar or on the bench, I had time to read about the history of law, particularly in India, and to view with greater perspective aspects of the system that particularly interested or concerned me. One of these was the question of judicial corruption; the other was women active in the law.

When I was a lawyer and later a judge, I never wanted to believe the stories people told me about corruption in the lower judiciary. Nowadays, some people say it is totally corrupt. I don't agree with them. I think that earlier there were a few officers who were corrupt and that the numbers have been steadily growing. However, it would be wrong to tar everyone with the same brush. But that there should be even one dishonest judicial officer is indeed a matter of great shame, for honesty and justice go hand in hand.

Worse, there has for some time past been a nagging feeling that corruption is slowly creeping into the higher judiciary. Though it is difficult to find absolute proof, circumstancial evidence is often clinching. But the process of the removal of a judge by something akin to impeachment is so difficult that it has just not happened.

I was brought up with the conviction that a totally unbiased attitude was a prerequisite to judging a case. I remember Justice Sunanda Bhandare once asking my advice as to whether she should hear the case of an acquaintance, which had been listed before her. I told her that even if she had the slightest hesitation that she might feel influenced because she knew him, whether in his favour or against him, or felt she might have to bend backwards to prove her lack of prejudice, it would be better if she did not hear the matter. I said, 'There are so many cases to be heard that if you refuse to hear a particular one, there is no dearth of matters that can be placed before you. Remember that justice has not only to be done but also to be seen to be done.'

I told her that I had not heard a case in which the writer Khushwant Singh was a party, though at the time I had met him only once, because he had lavished praise in print on Vikram after he read *The Golden Gate*. I had naturally been pleased, and though I knew that I would not allow this fact to cloud my mind, I still felt that it would be better that I not adjudicate his dispute.

When recently I saw on the front page of a number of newspapers the picture of a Delhi High Court judge (who had just resigned) being arrested, and read that the judge's files had been found in the house of a private person, I was shocked. I read that his house had been searched and was horrified when I discovered that it was the very house that had been allocated to me when I was a member of the Law Commission. I was also stunned when I learnt that a judges' committee had found that another judge, Mr Justice Arun Madan, had been soliciting a woman doctor in return for a judicial decision in her favour. Though everything was not perfect at the time that I was a judge, this was certainly a far cry from those days.

These cases appear to me to be the result of the faulty system of appointments. If there were transparency in the process, Mr Madan certainly would not have been appointed. The Bar as a whole was aware of Mr Madan's misdoings and misconduct as a lawyer, and brought it to the notice of the judiciary, but powerful connections prevailed and he was duly appointed. What is devastating is that a few rotten apples are spoiling the whole image of an otherwise basically honest and fair higher judiciary. I hope that the National Judicial Commission, if and when it comes into existence, will be more transparent in its process of selection. I think it will be a better method of appointing a judge, rather than leaving it entirely to the seniormost judges and the politicians. But the constitution of the commission must be a matter of careful consideration: 'Who will appoint the appointers?'

People sometimes ask me, 'Kya kisi ne kabhi kuchh kaha?' Did anyone ever try to influence you about a case? The answer is that in my more than fourteen years as a judge, I was 'spoken to' on only a couple of occasions. This was done once by someone who did not know better; he wanted me to speak to a brother judge about a case. I explained to him the process of hearing and judging a case, and asked him how he would feel if he thought that the other side could speak to a judge and influence him or her. Would he not feel that it was a denial of justice? He understood. He went home after telling me that he did not know it was wrong; rather, he had thought that if he did not speak to anyone, it would look as if he was not interested in the matter. The other time I was spoken to was by a person who certainly should have known better. Indeed, I am sure he did, but, being a politician, he probably felt that there was no harm in trying. I was outraged and of course immediately recused myself from the case. On a later occasion, he expressed his surprise at my action. I, in turn, implied my disappointment at his.

There are many kinds of corruption, and the Bar is no less to blame. When I started off as a lawyer in Patna, a number of sons, brothers, nephews and other relatives of judges were also practising there. I heard people talking about 'Uncle Practice' and 'Lal Jhanda'. I wondered what all this was about. I learnt that, since a son was not permitted to practise in his father's court, if you did not want the matter to be heard by that court, you briefed the son and thus stopped the matter from going before the father; you had put out a warning 'Red Flag'. This misuse of a rule that had been incorporated to prevent partisan decisions was apparently quite prevalent, and some young lawyers even managed to make a living out of it. It was also rumoured that certain judges favoured the sons of their brother judges, and so the 'Uncle Practice' thrived.

Both the Bar and the bench have to make a conscious and consistent effort to change their ways, and to wipe out corruption. It is the impartiality with which a matter is heard and decided that is the foundation of justice.

★

When I think of the difficulties faced by me when I entered the profession, I remember the women, both in other countries and in India, who built some of the steps on which I have climbed. I think of their courage and determination and feel grateful and humble.

In 1872, Myra Bradwell in the USA was denied a licence to practise law. The argument made against her was that the 'paramount mission and destiny of women is to fulfill the noble and benign offices of wife and mother. This is the law of the Creator.' She did not give up and a few years later her efforts resulted in the US Congress passing a law in 1879 permitting women to practise before the Supreme Court.

In 1914, in the UK, it was held in Bebb v. Law Society that a woman could not become an attorney. Basically, the reasons adduced by Cozens Hardy, the Master of the Rolls, and two other judges were these: Lord Coke had said (three centuries earlier) that a woman could not be an attorney, and he was the authority on common law. No woman had applied or attempted to be an attorney for a long time, and usage was the foundation of common law. Finally, though the word 'person' and not 'man' had been used in the Solicitor's Act of 1843, this did not expressly remove her disability. But five years later, the Sex Disqualification Removal Act 1919 paved the way for women to practise.

In India, Regina Guha applied to the Calcutta High Court for permission to practise law in 1916, after passing her Bachelor of Law examinations. Her counsel argued before the Full Bench that the word 'person' in the Indian Legal Practitioner's Act both etymologically and logically would include a woman, especially in view of clause 13 of the General Clauses Act 1897 which provided that: 'In all Acts of the Governor-General in Council and Regulations, unless there is anything repugnant in the subject or context . . . words importing the masculine gender shall be taken to include females.' But her enrollment was refused by the judges on the ground that women were not fit for the 'hurly-burly' of the profession and that, since no woman had ever been enrolled at the Bar, they were not willing to make an innovation.

In 1921, Sudhansu Bala Hazra applied to be enrolled as a pleader in the District Court of Patna, after obtaining a

degree of Bachelor of Law from Calcutta University. She was
in all respects a proper person to be enrolled unless debarred
by the disability of sex. The judges referred to the judgment
in Regina Guha's case and concurred with it. They said it
would be repugnant to ideas of decorum to permit women to
join in 'the rough and tumble of the forensic arena'.

But around the same time, the Allahabad High Court had
admitted Cornelia Sorabji to practise law and this anomalous
situation was pointed out to the Patna High Court. So one
of the judges specifically mentioned that their refusal was not
an aspersion on women's intelligence as such, but that they
required the legislature to intervene.

In 1922, Dr H.S. Gour moved an amendment in the
legislature of the United Provinces so that women could be
enrolled without any ambiguity. He made an impassioned
plea for women and also stated that the Inns of Court in
England had reversed their earlier stand and were admitting
women. It was a matter of human rights, and not a special
favour, to allow women to practise. He withdrew his
amendment on the assurance that the Government of India
would consult the local governments and the High Courts on
the question: 'Whether women should be as eligible as men
to enter upon a career as legal practitioners.' Thereafter, Act
XXIII of 1923 was passed and received the assent of the
Governor-General in April 1923, removing all doubts regarding
women's right to be enrolled and practise. This was only
eighty years ago.

One of the first women to practise law in the Bombay
High Court was Mithan Lam. After she enrolled, she did not
get any work. After a while, she received a brief from a
solicitor; she was pleased but surprised. When she asked him
why he had briefed her, he told her that his client had a case
that he could not possibly lose. But he wanted his opponents
to be further humiliated by the insult of losing to a woman.

Much has changed since then. At the time of present writing—2003—there have been several women Chief Justices of High Courts. There have been three women on the Supreme Court bench. One, M. Fathima Beevi, I have already mentioned. The second, Sujata Manohar, came from a distinguished legal family. She was a very well-regarded judge in the Bombay High Court and came to the Supreme Court after being Chief Justice of the Kerala High Court. The third, Ruma Pal, came from the Calcutta High Court. She is regarded by the Bar as one of the best judges presently in the Supreme Court. But it is interesting to note that there has never been more than one woman at any given time on the Supreme Court. I wonder how a male judge would feel and behave if he were the sole man among twenty-five women judges.

★

When I started practising, I wanted to prove myself as a mainstream lawyer, not follow the stereotype of a woman lawyer. I took up company, tax, constitutional, civil and criminal matters. I consciously avoided 'women's work', such as divorce, custody, guardianship, adoption, and so on. After I retired as Chief Justice of Himachal Pradesh, I felt that perhaps I had leaned away too much in this regard. I felt a great urge to try and help women and to look into their problems.

Some time before retirement, I read that a National Commission for Women was being set up and that the functions of the commission were largely legal. I felt that I would be ideally suited to chair the commission; I telephoned my friend Sunanda in Delhi and asked her to find out more details. She came back to me in a few days and said, 'Sorry, Leila, it appears that the chair will be a political appointment.' So I left it at that.

A political appointment was made. When her three-year term expired, my name was suggested. But there was an age limit of sixty-five, and that was what I was going to be in about a year. However, three years later, after the next person's term had expired, I suddenly received a telephone call on 14 August 1998 in London, where I had gone for a short visit. The caller was a minister, Murli Manohar Joshi. He told me that he thought I would be ideally suited to chair the commission; he had consulted the Prime Minister, had his concurrence to my name, and wanted to make the announcement immediately, on Independence Day. I told him that I was a member of the Law Commission of India and over-age for the job. He said, 'We don't care about age— we want you to take on the assignment.' I said, 'There are statutory provisions about age. I know this from experience. Perhaps you should check up on this; we can talk when I return to India.' I sensed the disappointment and irritation in his voice as he put down the telephone. But quite apart from the rules regarding age, I was happy as a member of the Law Commission and no longer wanted the job of chair of the National Commission for Women. I thought of Proust's words, 'Everything comes about just as we desired but only when we no longer desire it.'

But in fact I did get the opportunity to involve myself through an NGO in issues involving women and the law— as well as education, another abiding interest.

I wanted women to walk alongside men, not two steps behind or one step ahead. I wanted to help bring about legal literacy, so that women would become more aware of their rights. So when Dr Vasudha Dhagamwar, the founder and director of the Multiple Action Research Group (or MARG), invited me to become its chair, I was honoured and delighted. Through seminars, workshops, books and even a film serial, *Bol Basanto*, MARG has helped greatly to increase legal literacy among women. Vasudha, who is a practical, focused and very thorough person and an academic of repute, deserves enormous credit for what she and her organization are doing.

But despite legal literacy and the knowledge of their rights, women are often prevented from using them. Women—by law—now form at least a third of the membership of village councils or panchayats. But when we held a legal literacy workshop for women in panchayats in Haryana, we were told by them that the men often sprang a notice on them the very morning of a meeting, when it was too late for them to cook in advance or make other arrangements for their families. Naturally, they could not attend.

At other times, women are simply reluctant to assert their rights. When I was a judge in the Delhi High Court, I came across affidavits filed by three sisters, relinquishing all their property rights to their two brothers. I was thunderstruck. After all, it was at the time almost thirty years since the Hindu Succession Act 1956 had been enacted. In order to ensure that there was no fraud and to ascertain the reason why the girls were relinquishing their rights, I insisted that they come to court in person. After a great deal of protest by the brothers about distance and expense, they agreed to bring them to court.

When I questioned the young women, first in open court, and then in chambers, about whether they knew their legal rights, they nodded. When I asked them why they were not pressing for their inheritance and just signing it away, they replied that they wanted to preserve a good relationship with their brothers, because now, after their father's death, their brothers' homes would be the only place they could go to if they wanted a change or a refuge from their own. Their quality of life would be affected if they demanded the share they were entitled to.

Had there been five brothers, instead of three sisters and

two brothers, the question of dividing the family property so unequally would never even have arisen. I tried my best to persuade them to withdraw their affidavits; they would not. But slowly, very slowly, things are changing. More women are asking for their rights. Men are beginning to give them, sometimes with alacrity or even without being asked; sometimes after a bitter fight. The chain of awareness, assertion, attitudinal change and action is beginning to come full circle.

★

Education in general, not just women's legal literacy, has always been a great concern of mine. My mother made many sacrifices to educate her children. Premo and I, too have always felt that our children's education should be paramount, and spent much of our income on it. Education is the key to prosperity, to a fuller enjoyment of life, to the avoidance of easy prejudice, to being able to help people more effectively— and to not being bored!

In 1982 I was asked to be the Chief Guest at the silver jubilee celebrations of Welham Girls High School in Dehra Dun—a sort of sister school to Welham Boys School and the Doon School, to both of which Vikram and Shantum had gone. The school developed in its students a pride in their Indian culture as well as awareness of global issues. I was impressed by what I saw, and when the chairman requested me to join the Governing Board two years later, I did. He was trying to ensure that there were more women on the board. As the board was predominately male, old and with local vested interests, and people remained on it for years, he introduced the idea of a fixed term. I was happy to contribute my views and strengthen the school's secular character and value system. When the chairman resigned, I took over as chair.

A few years later, Saroj Srivastava, who had been a wonderful Principal for eighteen years, was due to retire. The task of finding a new Principal was very difficult. Despite the effort of the search committee, we did not come up with the perfect person.

Shanti Varma—a person of great charm, intelligence, vision and wisdom—was a very active member of the board, always willing to do whatever she could to help the school to achieve its ambitions. We eventually persuaded her to become Principal even though she didn't have the exact academic qualifications required by the Council of Indian School Certificate Examinations. She acquired these within a short period after joining. She was Principal for twelve years and did an excellent job both academically and in developing the campus. Soon after she was appointed, my term as chairperson came to an end. I made it clear that I would not extend it at all, even for the sake of continuity.

There is a tail to this story. In 1992 Shantum met Shanti's daughter Gitanjali (or Gitu) and they were married four years later. I was very happy about the marriage, but also relieved that my choice for Principal had proved so good. I might otherwise have been accused of futuristic nepotism.

In 1994 the Delhi Government appointed me as Chair of the Governing Board of Miranda House, a college for women. The college had been started in 1948 by Sir Maurice Gwyer who was Vice-Chancellor of Delhi University and had been Chief Justice of the Federal Court, the precursor of the Supreme Court. It had been named after either his daughter or his favourite actress Carmen Miranda or possibly the isolated Miranda of *The Tempest*. What I liked about the college was that it encouraged its students to express different points of view. The Principal was Kiran Datar, a very determined and devoted woman who led the college boldly and forcefully and with exceptional transparency and integrity.

But my experiences on the boards and suchlike august bodies attached to admired institutions have not always been so fruitful and inspiring. In 1997, when the Government of India appointed me as the Visitor's (i.e., the President of India's) nominee on the Executive Council of Visva Bharati University, Santineketan for three years, I was very happy. I had always thought of Tagore's abode of peace as a place of high ideals, broad vision and an open and refreshing approach to education. I was sorely disappointed. What had been a dream had now become a mediocre parochial university. I tried very hard to get the powers that be to prioritize their traditional strengths—to get the music and art departments to become areas of excellence once again, but without success. I was sad that most of our meetings were devoted to administrative matters, mainly the salary and perquisites of staff. There was no vision for the future—everyone was consumed by the effort of survival.

★

In 1995 I was invited to a conference in South Africa entitled—lengthily, though not superfluously so—'Towards the Final Constitution: A Critique of the Interim Constitution from a Gender Perspective—the Way Forward'. It was held in Cape Town in January, the middle of summer. It was the first time I was going to Africa and I was very excited. It was an exceptional experience to see how the women's movement had cut across class, colour, political parties and religion. I spoke on Social Action Litigation in India and how it had attempted to bring about equality and social justice. I met some very interesting South African women, black, white and of Indian origin. There was so much to experience and to see. There had been momentous changes. I went to see a play where blacks and whites were acting together and a black man kissed a white girl on stage: an unimaginable sight—indeed, a criminal act—a few years earlier. Before I saw Cape Town, I thought San Fransisco the most beautiful city in the world, but experiencing the ocean and the floodlit Table Mountain, I began to have second thoughts.

The second time I visited southern Africa was some years later. After I became Chair of the Executive Committee of the Commonwealth Human Rights Initiative (CHRI), I travelled to Harare in Zimbabwe. CHRI is an independent and non-partisan international non-governmental organization mandated to ensure the practical realization of human rights in the Commonwealth.

CHRI has produced a poster which says that the three monkeys who 'see no evil, hear no evil, speak no evil', in the words of the ancient Indian legend are not the best thing for democracy. A democracy demands that we know and speak about the bad along with the good. The poster exhorts people to 'Exercise your right to speak and express yourselves freely. This also includes your right to know about things.' When I saw this poster, I realized that the three monkeys given to me by my father so long ago were in some ways out of date. While we were in Harare, three journalists were arrested and there was a hue and cry by some local human rights organizations. We too protested, and members of CHRI went to visit them in jail. The signs of restrictions on civil society, and the direction in which Zimbabwe was going were becoming apparent even then.

At the time of the Commonwealth Heads of Government Meeting in 1999, I travelled to Durban in South Africa. CHRI was there to publicly launch its report on the proliferation of light weapons, *Over a Barrel*. While in Durban, I decided I had to visit Pietermaritzburg, the place where the young barrister Mohandas Karamchand Gandhi was thrown out of his train, despite having a first-class ticket, because he was not white; this incident had been critical in changing his way of thinking. While still in Durban, I visited Fatima Meer, who had been an associate of Gandhiji. There was a wonderful rapport between us. She presented me with a book written by her, inscribed, 'To Leila Seth—with feelings of instant sisterhood.' She also remembered meeting Shantum and Gitu a few years earlier and spoke of them with great affection. We talked of the difficulties Indians had faced when their settlements had been cordoned off under Apartheid, and what their future was in South Africa.

I then drove to Pietermaritzburg; for me it was a pilgrimage. Gandhi had been an icon since childhood. I went directly to the railway station. Dashrath Bandhu, a gentleman of Indian origin, who had been informed by the Indian embassy about my visit, took me around and indicated the spot. He also showed me the statue of Gandhi in the town.

Gandhi was a young man when he left South Africa. He used then to wear western clothes, so many people in South Africa felt that that was how he should be depicted. There was a big debate about this; eventually, it was decided that the statue should show him as he was when he came to be known as Mahatma Gandhi. So he is shown without shoes or shirt, wearing his dhoti.

Dashrath Bandhu told me that a young South African boy had pointed to the statue and asked derisively why Gandhi was not wearing any clothes. His father had talked to him about poverty and explained that Gandhi had taken a decision not to wear a shirt and shoes until all his countrymen could afford to do so. The little boy had been thunderstruck and his derision turned to immediate admiration.

★

I greatly admire those who, like Gandhiji, try to ameliorate the tragedies and injustices of the world through vision and personal courage, without resorting to violence. These activists, organizers, visionaries can come from any of a hundred fields: Mother Teresa of Calcutta, who took on the tremendous task of looking after the poor, the sick and the needy for the love of God; H.D. Shourie of Common Cause, who stands up and fights for others in court with integrity and without any personal interest whenever he can; Justice H.R. Khanna who, in the Emergency, raised his voice for freedom 'without fear or favour'; Sunderlal Bahuguna, who has saved forests through his Chipko Movement; Ela Bhatt of SEWA, who made credit available for the unorganized sector and changed the lives of cart-pullers and many others; Laila Tyabji of Dastkar, who has brought economic independence to hundreds of women doing embroidery in their homes; and others too numerous to list.

Because it is difficult to act alone, like-minded activists sometimes come together, like the seven young Indians who set up CRY—Child, Relief and You—twenty years ago, inspired by the wish to do something for underprivileged children. Today, marvellously, it has grown into an organization of over 80,000 people in seventeen states, and has collected and disbursed money to development initiatives that have changed the lives of 850,000 children all over India.

In moments of reflection, I sometimes feel my own inadequacy in the light of the courage and enterprise of all these people; for me, they are true heroes. But I can only do what is within my capacity; I would be no good to myself or anyone else if I acted against the grain of my character, which is not cast in an activist mould. Even when I attempt to do good, I have noticed that I become self-centred when unhappy—not a heroic trait. When I am sad, I am empty. I can only think of my own problems and have nothing to give. But when I am happy, I feel generous, and eager to care for others.

But then I force myself to remember that a country is great or a world is liveable not because it has a few great people but a large number of good people doing their own work diligently and well and in a spirit of service. To aspire to do good to the best of one's ability is, if not heroic, at least honourable. Justice Felix Frankfurter said: 'No office in the land is more important than being a good citizen.' (I tell myself this as I sit through certain committee meetings.) It is enough if the friendly postman delivers the mail promptly, the policeman is fair and impartial, and the politician acts honestly. As Romola Lahiry wrote in my autograph book when I was sixteen:

Small service is true service while it lasts.
Of friends, however humble, scorn not one;
The daisy, by the shadow that it casts,
Shelters the lingering dew-drop from the sun.

The Family Again

It is said that the only really unselfish love is that of a mother for her child. Perhaps this is because the mother perceives the child as an extension of herself, having carried the baby within her for so many months. In India there is a belief that love goes downwards, so that the love of the mother for the child is greater than that of a child for the mother; and the child in turn will give that motherly love to her child. A large part of a mother's life is spent taking care of her children; for many women it is their whole life. Parents see children as a reflection of themselves, and a mother, who has been the moulder of their minds and morals, sees their successes and failures as her own achievements and shortcomings.

My mother, widowed at thirty-five, with very little money and no training or ability to earn any, scrimped and saved to give us a good education. She spent all her time and energy on us and had no other real interest. Not having a home of her own, she lived with my brothers and me in turn. We tried to include her in our lives to the extent possible. But we had developed interests and friends and activities, and we needed our own space as well. She was very affectionate and emotional and felt left out and very lonely if she was not a part of all our outings and activities. She used to cry a great deal and say, to all of us but especially to me, 'I have given my whole life for you, and you have no time for me.' Whenever I saw her upset, it used to make me feel guilty when I went out and enjoyed myself. It was a heavy burden to carry, and I was determined that I would have a life of my own, in addition to my life with my children, so that they would have freedom from these feelings of guilt, and not be weighed down by my over-attention or great need that they should reciprocate. This did not mean that I did not give my children affection or time; it was just that it was not to the exclusion of everything else.

Colleagues at the High Court often asked me, 'When will your children settle down?' By that they meant, 'When will they marry and when will they get regular jobs?' They saw Vikram's writing (this was before *A Suitable Boy* was published), Shantum's anti-nuclear and peace projects and Aradhana's film-making as useless, unproductive, non-remunerative work. Some acquaintances even questioned our driver about what our grown-up children did. He dismissively replied: 'Nothing. One sits upstairs, just reading and writing and sleeping and eating and living off his parents. The other boy has built a mud hut in the garden and sits there staring into space or talking to friends or gets up and scatters seeds at random around the garden. The girl is constantly on the telephone to various artists and architects—she comes home late at night and sleeps till late in the morning.' At the time, Vikram, Shantum and Aradhana were not married and were, respectively, thirty-seven, thirty-two and twenty-seven. When I attended the weddings of my friends' and colleagues' children and sometimes even functions to celebrate their grandchildren, I wondered if and where I had I gone wrong.

Apart from my family life, my legal career was very important to me—and I wanted both to be equally successful. I also loved reading and gardening and travel and the company and laughter of friends. I therefore tried to balance and prioritize. The children had top priority. Their life was my life. Though I tried to give them space to grow, I still felt that what they did and were was a part of me. If I had not included them in this book, a whole chunk of my life would have been cut out. Vikram, Shantum and Aradhana, however, are also very much themselves—and very different from each other too.

While they stayed at home or were in school in India, their lives and plans were inextricably linked with ours, and my influence on them was quite strong. But slowly, as they grew up, it waned. And one by one all three of them left home for distant parts.

★

First, Vikram left for England at the age of seventeen. He did his 'A' levels at Tonbridge School, read PPE at Oxford, and became a graduate student in the Economics Department at Stanford University. We visited him in Oxford when he turned twenty-one, and again in Stanford, before he left for Nanjing University in China.

But it was in 1982, when I visited him in China, that our roles were really reversed. He came and met Shantum and me in Hongkong, and we flew to Shanghai together. He had got us our internal travel permits, which in those days were difficult to obtain unless you were part of a group. This was partly because of the language problem and partly because China was still suspicious of foreigners. (There were only four

Indian students in the Chinese universities, three in Beijing and one in Nanjing.)

Our plan was to travel from Shanghai, which reminded us a bit of Calcutta, to Suzhou, the garden city, by train.

In Suzhou we heard the erhu, walked beneath the wutong trees, saw the small but exquisite Master of Nets Garden with three moons, in the sky, the mirror and the water. We also saw the Humble Administrator's Garden with its plump fish, and many others.

Vikram was not happy to let us out of his sight, as he feared that, not knowing the language, we might get lost and not know how to return. If Shantum and I went for a walk and were a little late in returning, he would fret like an anxious parent. He was always ensuring that we had enough 'funny money' with us so that we were not stranded. (Apparently, foreigners had to use a special kind of currency for certain purposes.) It was all a most unusual experience.

When we reached Nanjing, I was housed in a room with Gabrielle, a close friend of Vikram's, in the women's section of the foreigners' hostel, whereas Shantum shared a room with Vikram. It was the month of June and very hot, but there were no fans. Gabrielle had a small table fan, which she very generously directed towards me. The toilets were communal. Though the lavatories were partitioned, the bathing area was not, so any woman could walk in and take a bath while you were standing naked at the adjoining shower. When I discovered this, I was a little reluctant to bathe, but I could not hold out for long because of the heat.

Vikram, Gabrielle, Shantum and I travelled to Qufu, where we saw the ancient cypress trees near Confucius's shrine and took in the essence of his wisdom and teachings. I was to discover much later that in Qufu, Vikram had wanted to share a room with Gabrielle, but, because she felt

I would be uncomfortable with the situation, she had dissuaded him. When we moved north to Beijing, we stayed at the residence of the Indian Ambassador, Shankar Bajpai, and Gabrielle stayed at the British Ambassador's. Vikram had just finished the first draft of his book about his travels the previous year through Sinkiang and Tibet, and I began reading the manuscript.

The night before his thirtieth birthday, he suddenly asked me where Gabrielle would stay if she came to India. I said she would share a room with Aradhana. He replied, 'But she is my friend. Why shouldn't she share the room with me?' Before I could answer, he asked, 'If I had a male friend visiting me, where would he stay?' I replied, 'He would share the room with you.' Vikram responded: 'So you are driving me into the arms of men.' I was a bit taken aback by his remark and the annoyed and sarcastic way in which he said it, but tried to remain calm and explained that in Indian society that was how things were done. I asked him what the staff would think if it were done any other way; even my colleagues, if they got to know, would be horrified. He declared aggressively, 'You are more concerned with the opinion of others than the happiness of your children.' I was upset by the remark, but told him, 'When you come to our home, you must observe our rules, and when we stay in your house, we will abide by yours.' He retorted, 'I thought that the house in Delhi was my home too.' I found the situation was getting tense, and I didn't want to get into a heated argument. I decided to go to bed quietly and ignore the subject for the rest of the trip.

We celebrated his birthday quietly the next day and met the young diplomat who had told him he was 'a damn foolish fellow' to undertake the journey to India via Tibet without proper permission. He now reiterated: 'The Chinese are

ruthless if you break the law. You have parents, you know.'
Vikram frowned. He said that a stamp in his travel pass—
however obtained—was permission enough. I think he was
still a bit cross about our altercation, and somewhat peeved at
being reminded to consider his parents' anxieties at every
turn.

At the time I didn't realize that Vikram was bisexual. This
understanding came to me much later and I found it hard to
come to terms with his homosexuality. Premo found it even
harder. I also knew it was considered a crime in India and was
afraid that someone might try to exploit him because of it.
But we loved him and accepted it without understanding it.
It is only now that I realize that many creative persons share
this propensity and that it gives them a special nurturing and
emotional dimension.

★

In May 1994, Premo and I went to Hay-on-Wye, on the
border between England and Wales, for the Literary Festival.
There we basked in the reflected success of Vikram's novel, *A
Suitable Boy*. Vikram did a reading from his book of rhymed
animal fables, *Beastly Tales*; it was a sell-out, and for three
hours afterwards, he was kept busy signing books for a long
queue of people.

In June, we drove with Vikram to Plymouth for a magical
performance of *Arion and the Dolphin*, an opera composed by
Alec Roth for which Vikram wrote the libretto. It had been
commissioned by the English National Opera, and was
performed in the vast drill shed of the naval facility, HMS
Drake. As a special gesture, Vikram's family and friends were
invited and taken across in a boat for the gala night dinner
and show. Apart from the superb professional cast, a large

number of children were involved in the performance; some sang, others played the part of the sea: they blew bubbles or—dressed in oceanic turquoise—swished water onto the stage to create the semblance of waves. The music was wonderful and the singing by the dolphin very moving. When she dies, pining and trapped in a cage, Arion sings to his only friend:

> I hear your voice sing out my name by night,
>   By dawn, by evening light.
>
> I mourn for you, yet, Dolphin, to my shame,
>   I never asked your name.
>
> Your element protected me, but mine
>   For you proved far too fine.
>
> Dolphin, it was from your marine caress
>   That I learned gentleness.
>
>
> May music bind the sky, the earth, the sea
>   In tune, in harmony.
>
> Dark sea, protect all voyagers whose home
>   Rests in your ring of foam.
>
> Warm earth, teach us to nourish, not destroy
>   The souls that give us joy.
>
> Bright stars, engrave my dolphin and my lyre
>   In the night sky with fire.

As Arion sang these last words, the constellations of Delphinus and Lyra appeared in the darkness overhead.

After the performance there was hardly a dry eye in the drill shed. We were all requested to go out quickly. We soon found out why: a magnificent display of fireworks lit up the night sky. I was enchanted and overawed by the whole experience, and felt extremely proud.

Peter and Aradhana had come to England in time to see the performance. All of us now drove to Oxford, where we stayed at the Old Parsonage, a very pleasant small hotel. On 20 June we celebrated Vikram's forty-second birthday just where we had celebrated his twenty-first, though the Bleu, Blanc et Rouge was now a Thai restaurant. That morning he had been delighted when a messenger had entered the hotel room with a bunch of festive helium balloons sent by a friend from London. But the best present was the news that he had just been made an Honorary Fellow of his old college, Corpus Christi.

★

A Suitable Boy was set in India and therefore launched in India. But *An Equal Music*, Vikram's next novel, which is told in the voice of the second violinist of a string quartet, was basically set in London, and he wanted it to be launched there.

We were all invited. Shantum and Gitu, Peter and Aradhana, and Premo and I arrived at various dates and times in London. But where were the six of us to stay? Vikram moved out of his small flat in Bayswater to a room in a friend's house nearby, and the six of us took it over. Premo and I slept on the sofa-bed and the rest of them on the floor. The seven of us had a marvellous time together for the next ten days, cooking and shopping and chatting and going for walks in Kensington Gardens. We celebrated Aradhana's birthday on 10 April by staying at home, playing bridge and eating Lebanese food; we celebrated Shantum's on the 15th by taking a boat trip on the Thames to Greenwich.

But it was the evenings of 8 and 9 April that were very special. On 8 April there was a large reception to launch *An Equal Music* in a venue where a scene in the book is set: the first floor of the Wallace Collection with old and precious paintings lining the walls. White wine and champagne flowed freely, but not red wine, whose accidental spillage would, I imagine, seriously damage the paintings. Critics and publishers mingled with writers and musicians, family and friends. Mr Miller, Vikram's headmaster from Doon School, came to the party almost from his sick bed, as he was most anxious to attend. Vikram was really touched. After the reception, Vikram took the family as well as Philippe Honoré (to whom the book is dedicated) and his parents and uncle and aunt, all four of whom had come from France for the occasion, to dinner at a wonderful restaurant nearby.

The next day was a reading and concert to celebrate the launch in another place central to the story: Wigmore Hall. I was told that the gentleman sitting next to me, whom Vikram had interviewed when researching his book, was almost completely deaf; I wondered what he was doing at a musical performance and reading. Vikram read well, with emotion and clarity. Each reading was followed by the performance of a piece of music mentioned in the book. One of these, the first movement of Bach's partita in E Major for solo violin, was played by Philippe. It was a difficult piece; he played it with dazzling virtuosity but deep feeling, and the audience exploded with prolonged applause. His mother was obviously as nervous for him as I was for Vikram. She knew very little English, but she turned to me and said with joy and relief and pride—'Our sons!' I saw the deaf gentleman smiling and felt sorry that he was missing out on the performance. But in the interval I learnt that Wigmore Hall was equipped with a 'loop' to help hearing-aid users receive the sound clearly and without background noise. No wonder he had been smiling!

★

Shantum was the second of our children to leave India. In 1975, at the age of eighteen, he went to Leicester to study Boot and Shoe Manufacture, the two-year course that his father had taken many years earlier in Northampton. Shantum did very well and got the same sort of medal as Premo had from the City & Guilds of London Institute. He then worked with a shoe firm called Eatoughs in the same city and later joined the well-known firm of Clarks. In 1980, when we had gone to Stanford to visit Vikram, we had wanted Shantum to come too, so that the five of us could be together after many years, but he could not get leave.

Shantum had had a horrendous car accident the previous year, and it had changed his way of thinking about life. Besides, he was, having participated in it, increasingly restless and unhappy with the capitalist system. He decided he wanted to study further, left Clarks and enrolled in the School of Development Studies at the University of East Anglia in Norwich. He stood for elections as a green candidate and became Vice-President of the Students' Union. Since he could suggest changes to the academic curriculum, he proposed that Peace Studies be introduced as a subject at UEA.

He lived in Argyle Street, where he and some friends were squatting along with other young people. All the houses in the street had been evacuated; Shantum and his friends were anxious to prevent the area from becoming a car park. When Premo went to Norwich on business, he used to stay at the Maids Head Hotel, one of the best hotels in town. Shantum, dressed in kurta and pajama with a gamcha tied around his head, arrived there and asked to see Premo. The receptionist telephoned Premo and said, 'Sir, a gentleman of sorts is here to see you.' Premo replied, 'The gentleman of sorts must be my son; please send him up.'

But when I went with Premo to Norwich to visit Shantum, we both stayed with him in Argyle Street, even though I was a judge. Shantum wanted us to stay with him and made a great effort to make us comfortable and we were happy to stay with our son—though Premo's business associates were rather surprised when he told them his address.

From a hedonistic approach to life, where he experimented with marijuana and magic mushrooms, Shantum now began to search for a path of wisdom. After he had completed his studies at Norwich, he travelled endlessly, looking for a spiritual teacher. We were worried about him and wondered where it would all end. But in 1987, after he met the Zen Buddhist teacher Thich Nhat Hanh, respectfully known as Thay, he felt he had found his path. Thay taught him that one had to 'be peace' rather than seek peace, a message that Shantum found compelling. Shortly after this, he came back home to stay with us at 8 Rajaji Marg.

I remembered at the time what my friend Koly, who had no children, had told me about letting go of one's children. She had said, 'Imagine holding a chicken on your open palm. If you try to enclose it with your fingers, the chicken will struggle to escape, and if it does manage to, it will be unlikely to return. But if it has the freedom to leave and return whenever it likes, then even if it goes, it is likely to come back. It is the same with children—and not only with children.' How right she was! Both the boys returned in 1987 to live with us in Delhi.

Shantum was searching for an alternative style of living. He stayed in a number of international communities. He

Vasudha, me, Kiran, Tony and Kumkum on my seventieth birthday.

Ira Chatterji and me in Patna.

Ruma, me and Lily in Calcutta.

Orchids in our Noida garden.

At Ravenswood, Shimla—with my colleagues (and our ushers) of the Himachal Pradesh High Court.

Aradhana and Peter pouring ghee as
part of the wedding ritual.

In London with Vikram on his
fiftieth birthday.

Aradhana and Peter with Michi bhai and Usha (on the swing), and Tuttu,
Neepa, Mohini and Sashi bhai.

Thay leading Shantum and Gitu to their Buddhist wedding at Plum village in France.

In Noida before our golden anniversary.

Nandini aged four weeks with Gitu.

Nandini aged two.

Nandini aged six months with me.

went to the Kumbh Mela and met many sants and gurus. He did some work to try to protect the Dzukou valley in Nagaland. Vikram based his rhymed fable *The Elephant and the Tragopan* on this research. Later, Shantum worked with Oxfam and then with the United Nations Volunteers on artisan development.

After Vikram gave his speech at the Doon School in 1992, Shantum, who had come from Delhi to be there, decided to stay on in Dehra Dun. Shanti Varma, the Principal at Welham Girls, offered to put him up for a few days. That is how he met her delightful daughter Gitu, who had just returned from studying law in the US and was interested in village development work and using her legal skills to support the under-privileged.

Shantum was looking for someone to work with him in the United Nations Volunteer Programme on artisans. They obviously had similar ideas and decided to try working together, though they kept their options open. Gitu shifted to Delhi and stayed in a barsati in Defence Colony. One of the projects involved developing a network of artisan organizations in sixteen countries, so that experiences could be shared and insights gained: a sort of globalization from below.

In 1993, World Wide Fund for Nature (India) started a Centre for Environmental Law and held its first nine-month course soon afterwards. I have mentioned before that I decided to join; Gitu too was one of the students. I enjoyed her company and was charmed by her manners. I thought she was a wonderful, sensible, sensitive and beautiful young woman and longed for her to be part of our family. But it was three years before Shantum and Gitu made up their minds— which they did somewhere in South America on one of their artisan voyages. Both sets of parents were very happy. Shantum was going to be thirty-nine and we were wondering if either of our sons was ever going to marry.

Shantum and Gitu did not want to get married in town. They decided to have the wedding by the Ganga, which they both loved, in the presence of their family and their very close friends, their 'chosen relations'. We travelled there together in buses and stayed in the tourist huts and tents on the banks of the river at Kaudiyala, above Rishikesh. Bob and Shanti Varma and their family and friends had gone to a lot of trouble to make all the arrangements in this distant place.

Gitu looked resplendent in a red and gold sari and exquisite jewellery. Shantum wore a simple light fawn sherwani and white churidar pajamas. His friends felt he didn't look festive enough; so Aman took off his own beautiful jamavar shawl and placed it on Shantum's shoulder and Tehmina put her gold and coral chain around his neck.

The wedding took place on the night of 4 March 1996. We sat under the stars and watched the ceremony in the light of the full moon of Holi. There was no vedi; the sky itself was the canopy and Ganga the witness. After the Hindu rites were over, we shifted to the sandy area and sat around in a large circle. My friend Asha sang a song to the Ganga to bless the bride and groom. Gitu's Jewish friend Eric blessed them and asked them to break a glass which he put under Shantum's feet. (It was quite a job to break it on the pliant sand.) This symbolized the fact that a disaster could occur even at a time of great joy. Gitu's Christian friend Monisha shared the teachings on love from Corinthians. Our Jain friend Shama gave a blessing, Cynthia performed a Buddhist rite, Minhaz read a couplet from the Koran, and then wedding rings were exchanged. Gitu's ring for Shantum fell and it was impossible to find it in the sand. So I took off my wedding ring and gave it to her to put on Shantum's finger, which she did. We told her not to worry about the loss—Mother Ganga was probably claiming her tithe. Then Vikram read a poem, an acrostic, which he had written for them that morning:

> So, after years, the hesitater
> Has made his choice (or so we think)
> And though he might regret it later
> No-one has snatched him from the brink.
> The girl, though far too brainy, pretty,
> Unfairly lovely, wise and witty,
> Makes chocolate cake (yes! by the batch)
> And *therefore* is a suitable match.
> Now under the full moon of Holi
> Down by the Ganga, let us bless
> GITU and SHANTUM, G & S
> In the sure hope that, swift or slowly,
> Their raft, from this high shore set free
> Unfettered makes the open sea.

Shantum and Gitu sat near the edge of the Ganga. Each of us did an arti and blessed them with lit lamps in leaf cups, which we floated down the current. It was an incredible sight to see all these little diyas making their way downstream, while Asha sang to the Ganga. Vikram's diya decided to go upstream into a creek.

The next morning, when Gitu woke, she found a shining gold ring on the floor of the tent in which they had spent the night. She was delighted and returned mine. She was very happy—she felt this was very auspicious! The ring must have been lodged in the folds of her sari and fallen down when she took it off at night.

Next morning we all played Holi with bright colours and the gentle yellow juice of the tesu flower. The young played vigorously, with coloured water, while the old, who had indulged in a little dry powder, sat by and watched the fun.

Some, like Vikram, even swam across the Ganga, though it was swift. It had all been so different from the usual weddings held in town, in five-star hotels or other places, with loud music and everyone talking through the ceremony.

When Shantum and Gitu went to Plum Village in the south of France, where Thay has his monastery, he offered to perform a Buddhist wedding ceremony for them. So, six months after their second wedding—they had, needless to say, also had the usual dull and dour ceremony before the Registrar—Vikram, Premo and I joined them there for their third. It was very special. Gitu wore a flaming orange-red sari, Shantum his light fawn sherwani. Thay was in his usual brown coat with a light blue scarf around his neck. His gentle manner and shy smile encompassed us all.

All the monastics and those who had come to Plum Village for the Retreat as well as the three of us joined Thay, Shantum and Gitu in a beautiful walking meditation to the hall where the ceremony was conducted. We walked silently, enjoying the bamboo and the green bushes swaying and the birds singing on this sunny September day.

One of the requirements of the ceremony was that Shantum and Gitu had to say something about their love and their commitment to each other in front of us all. I think they both found it difficult to say something so personal in such a public manner. But they worked on it the night before. Shantum spoke of how friendship had turned to love and how they should continue to be each other's best friend, and Gitu responded by saying that she looked forward to spending her life with her best friend. Many other tender and humorous sentiments were expressed. Then they took their vows to practice the Five Awarenesses in the presence of the Three Jewels—Buddha, Dharma, and Sangha—and received a Certificate of Marriage signed by Thay and witnessed by two of their American friends. They agreed to practise the Five

Awarenesses and to recite them each month on the day of the full moon.

The Five Awareness are:

1. We are aware that all generations of our ancestors and all future generations are present in us.

2. We are aware of the expectations that our ancestors, our children, and their children have of us.

3. We are aware that our joy, peace, freedom and harmony are the joy, peace, freedom and harmony of our ancestors, our children and their children.

4. We are aware that understanding is the very foundation of love.

5. We are aware that blaming and arguing never help us and only create a wider gap between us, that only understanding, trust and love can help us change and grow.

★

Thus began a new life. Gitu and Shantum continued to work together, while maintaining their individual emphases. Gitu set up the Ahimsa trust, which, in their words, is intended 'to work for a peaceful and just society adopting a mindful way of living—to be achieved by promoting an ecologically sustainable and individually creative model of development that is artisan inspired.'

Shantum, while still working with U.N. Volunteers, also continued with his two- or three-week winter pilgrimages, 'In the Footsteps of the Buddha'. I went with him on one of these, on the cusp of the millennium. (Premo joined us for a couple of days at Bodh Gaya.)

Since the journey was mainly in Bihar and Uttar Pradesh and I had already seen most of the places, I kept postponing a trip on one pretext or another. I had a bad back and was afraid that travelling in a bus on bad and bumpy roads would make it worse. But I was going to be seventy in the millennium year and I decided that if I didn't go now, it would be too late and I would be sorry.

The journey took us to the places where the Buddha was born, lived, gained enlightenment, preached, spent time with his disciples, and died. The whole trip was to be undertaken 'mindfully' with walking meditation, stories and interaction. Shantum had been taking people to these places for the past thirteen years and I had heard from many of the pilgrims who had been, how much they had enjoyed the trip, how it had transformed their lives, and what a wonderful teacher Shantum was.

I thoroughly enjoyed the trip, despite the crater-ridden roads, the long bus journeys, the illness of one of the pilgrims, and the endless waiting, chaos and corruption at the Indo-Nepal border. The discussions about what 'struck' each of us on a particular day were very invigorating; even though our perceptions were apparently so different—we were eight Indians and eight foreigners, to mention just one of many possible demarcations—there was a common link of love and understanding.

But my deepest pleasure was spending the millennium hour in meditation under the Bodhi tree in Bodh Gaya, and watching the mist suddenly descend, as if by spiritual command, at the stroke of the midnight hour, while the little candles shone in large numbers all around the temple. I loved the stories that Shantum told us in his quiet, engaging manner, his soothing of our frayed nerves, and the way in which he led our morning meditation, while teaching us to breathe in and out while smiling. I was very relaxed with this reversal of roles where Shantum, the teacher, took care of my material, mental and spiritual needs. At the end, after the journey, each of us composed a poem and a few words of comment. This was my offering:

When Shantum was a child
He followed in my footsteps.
Now I am following his
On the Path of the Buddha.

On the journey I am learning
To breathe deeply, to act mindfully,
To smile and to be aware,
To experience the freshness of a flower,
The beauty and clarity of a stream
And to be as free as a bird;

To feel the mother's love at Lumbini,
The childhood of Siddhartha at Kapilavastu,
The serenity of the morning meditation at Sravasti,
And the teaching under the neem trees at Sarnath;

To enjoy the candlelight parikrama
On the last millennium night in Bodh Gaya
Under the Bodhi tree where the Buddha gained
      enlightenment;
The beauty of the sunset at the Vulture's Peak,
And the tradition of learning at Nalanda—
      the Lotus-giver,
To appreciate life and its impermanence in
      Kushinagar
In the presence of Buddha's mahanirvan.

For this joyous journey, I want to thank you, Shantum and Gitanjali and all my fellow pilgrims, for the harmony and space for better understanding and peace that it has brought to me. As for the manner in which Shantum has conducted the pilgrimage, I cannot say it better than in the words of Thich Nhat Hanh (Thay) himself:

> With each step and breath the Buddha comes alive. Shantum's balance of knowledge, insight, and humour brings joy to those journeying with him in the footsteps of the Buddha.

I was proud of him and loved him—in one of Thay's favourite adverbs—mindfully.

But Thay had not found me to be particularly mindful. When he came to India in 1988, he visited our home at 8 Rajaji Marg. The telephone rang while he was there and I rushed to pick it up. Afterwards, he told me that I should use the telephone as a bell of mindfulness. That meant that when I heard the bell ringing I should relax my body and become aware of my breathing. I should do that naturally and with enjoyment and without solemnity. The ringing bell should bring me back to myself; concentrating on my breathing would restore my calm and make me free. With just three conscious breaths, he said, I could release the tensions in my body and mind and return to a cool and clear state of being. I should pick up the telephone only after the third ring.

For a few days after he had spoken to me I made an effort and did just that, but I soon went back to my old ways. Ten years later, when Thay returned to India, he came to our home in Noida. The telephone rang and I rushed to pick it up. He said quietly to Shantum, 'Your mother has not learnt anything.' But he did not know that I remembered him every day after my bath, when I wiped the taps and shower dry. In 1988, he had also said, 'Do your everyday jobs mindfully. When you wipe the taps dry, imagine you are wiping a baby's bottom and do it with love.' Unknown to him, I had been practising a little mindfulness—but in seclusion.

★

Aradhana was the last of our children to leave home. She left at the age of twenty-eight after she and Peter were married. Peter was posted in sequence to Washington, Vienna, New Delhi (again) and Los Angeles—this last posting as Consul-General of Austria. Pooh has a wonderful sense of colour, space and design, which she has used not only for her work in film but also while decorating her various beautiful homes, all of which we have visited.

She has, to our pleasure, kept coming back to India to work on various projects. She and Nadia Haggar co-directed an hour-long documentary film on Vikram for the Omnibus programme of the BBC. She also directed one of the documentaries—'Magnificent Ruins'—in the TV series 'Stones of the Raj' with William Dalrymple as narrator.

In the world of feature films, she has built up a good reputation as a production designer/art director. She first worked on Deepa Mehta's *Fire*, and later on *Earth*, both of which I found powerful and moving. *Fire* was about a lesbian relationship in a traditional middle-class family and *Earth* depicted the partition of India in 1947 seen through the eyes of a young Parsi girl in Lahore. Aradhana managed to create just the right ambience in both cases. While watching the movies I kept noticing Aradhana-like touches of colour contrast or co-ordination and even spotted my cream-coloured four-seater sofa covered in Parsi pink.

The filming of *Water*, the third in the trilogy, a movie about the historical exploitation of young widows in Varanasi—not that it doesn't continue to happen to this day—was halted by a weak administration on the specious grounds that it presented a law-and-order problem. Thus did the Hindu militant bigots who swooped down on the set and partly destroyed it achieve their aims, even though the film team, for all their threats, wished to continue.

A short while ago, when I went to a multiplex in Delhi,

I noticed with pride that three films on which Aradhana had worked were showing: *Leela*, *The Guru* and *Everybody Says 'I'm Fine!'* Just as Vikram and Shantum have ventured into fields that no one in the family before them had made their own, so too Aradhana has entered and made a success of an area entirely of her choosing.

Aradhana has a way of delegating work and getting the best out of her assistants, who adore her. She has a social life which is something of a whirl; we wish we saw more of her when she comes to Delhi. Almost ten years on, Premo still remembers with amusement and pleasure the trove of gifts, selected with love and care, that she gave him on his seventieth birthday: seventy items ranging from a pullover to paperclips, with the result that she came to mind even more often than usual—whenever any of these items was used.

★

Premo and I celebrated our Golden Wedding on 13 March 2001. Vikram presented us with a large scroll that he had calligraphed with the Chinese characters, 'Gold and jade: harmonious union'; Shantum and Gitu presented us with an inverter, so that even in the midst of our frequent power-cuts, we should always have light; and Aradhana and Peter gave us fifty CDs, so that we wouldn't run out of music.

Four days later came the best present of all. On the 17th, a baby girl was born to Shantum and Gitu—our first grandchild. A few weeks after her birth, I wrote to her:

> Nandini, you are a very special child, as all children are to their parents and grandparents. You are precious as a pearl, born out of its own pain and love. You are a part of your ancestors and your great-grandmother would have celebrated your birth. So in commemoration of that link, I want you to have

something that belonged to her—an old kundan earring turned into a pendant and attached to a fine gold chain.

Isn't it fun that we girls can enjoy and share our jewels! We, your Dada and I, are really happy that you are a little girl.

Your Nana and Nani came back from America quickly to be present at your birth, as we thought you were coming early. But you took your time about it. Your Maama and Maami and Amaya were also present from Seattle for your birth. Your father returned in time from his travels and pilgrimages. Your Bua arrived from Los Angeles for our fiftieth wedding anniversary and was about to go back when you quickly showed up. Your Taoji was 'delighted' at your arrival and composed a fun poem for you. So you can see how happy we all are.

There were a number of names suggested for her: Diya, Deeksha, Uma and so on. But the hot favourite was Nandini, which means, variously: delightful; a daughter of the fabulous cow of plenty, Surabhi, owned by Vasishtha; another name for Durga and for Ganga. But Shantum and Gitu could not make up their minds. Vikram wrote a few lines to try and force the issue:

> No weepy babe—as full of fun
> As Ganga glinting in the sun;
> Name me, and name me now.
> Delightful, not to be outdone;
> In China, I'm a matchless nun.
> Now sing my praises everyone—
> I am a sacred cow.

Subsequently, on her Namkaran, the pandit whispered her name Diya Nandini into her ear.

Later, on her first birthday, Vikram composed rather a beautiful acrostic, in which he refers to elements in the names of Nandini's parents:

> No baby born of Peace and Song
> Arrives on earth without delight.
> No parents with a love so strong
> Deserve less than your voice all night.
> In limb and lung as you increase,
> Nandini, my beloved niece,
> I wish for you both songs and peace.

Happy birthday Nandini—And lots of love
                                      From your
                                      Taoji

★

In the summer of 2001, we went to Los Angeles to visit Aradhana and Peter. Peter's parents took the trouble of coming to meet us at Vienna airport, where we were catching a connecting flight. We were very happy. Premo and I spent a relaxed two hours with them; we chatted and ate lunch together in the airport restaurant, and the past tension was forgotten.

After a couple of weeks in London, we caught the long flight to Los Angeles. Premo drank a lot of coffee in the airport and a couple of whiskies on board. He did not get up much to stretch his legs. We were delighted to see Pooh and Peter again and we celebrated with a little wine. They had invited close family friends for dinner, so it turned out to be a long day. Knowing my love of flowers, Aradhana had placed some beautiful orchids in our bedroom. Premo seemed restless. Though he hadn't said anything at the time—and still didn't—I was later to learn that when he was pushing the trolley with our luggage to the car, he—normally so fit—had felt as if his right leg was dragging.

The next day we slept in and saw a movie in the evening. Once again, Premo felt uncomfortable; once again, he told no one.

The following morning, Premo felt some weakness in his legs and a slight dizziness. I noticed he was dragging his right leg, and I was worried by the symptoms. We had had strokes in my family before. Peter managed to get an appointment with the physician to the Austrian Consulate. He checked Premo thoroughly and said that, considering his age, he had found nothing seriously wrong with him, except that his blood pressure was a little high. He advised a baby aspirin and no alcohol.

Armed with this diagnosis, Premo felt much better. Peter had taken a week's leave to show us around, and the next day the four of us drove off to Joshua Tree—an area of stark natural beauty—as we had planned. But in the car Premo started feeling a numbness on the right side of his upper lip and in the fingertips of his right hand. He also felt weak, dizzy and exhausted. We drove back as fast as we could. The doctor, whom Peter had finally got through to on the phone, advised us to go to the UCLA hospital, as it was the best for stroke cases. We got there at 10 p.m., having lost our way. The doctors in Emergency took Premo into the intensive care room and started checking him. We were not allowed inside. After a while, a specialist emerged, and spoke to me in medical abbreviations: they suspected a TIA, had ordered a CAT scan and wanted to do an MRI. We should go home; there was no cause for alarm—his blood pressure was 146/78—and no point in hanging around.

Peter, Aradhana and I went home, tense and tired. At 3.30 a.m. Peter woke me up. I was startled and afraid. He said that there had been a phone call from Premo. He had been asked to sign a paper that stated that an estimate of the expenses for a three-day stay with treatment was likely to be in the region of fifteen thousand dollars! He was totally bewildered and his blood pressure had shot up to 190/90. He had visions of being detained in hospital, even after he had recovered, until the amount was paid, while the bill rapidly mounted. We certainly didn't have that sort of money, nor did Peter and Aradhana. We had taken out travel insurance in India, thank God, but it was not clear if this would be accepted by the hospital authorities. We eventually located Vikram at a friend's place in London. He immediately began to make arrangements to bridge the gap. After no response from so-called twenty-four hour service numbers, the insurance contacts in the USA finally responded, and cleared things up with the hospital.

Premo had had a very minor stroke. He was soon playing bridge again, and became his usual optimistic, go-getting self. But it had been a great shock. And had we ignored the symptoms or delayed much longer, or had less competent doctors it could have been a great deal worse. We knew this from painful family experience. Ma had suffered a stroke a year before her death. And a couple of years before Premo's stroke, my younger brother Tuttu had had a severe stroke. He had been paralysed and had still not recovered. He lay in bed in his home in Calcutta, and needed nursing night and day. He was cared for—and still is—with the most wonderful devotion by his wife Neepa.

★

On 10 September 2001, two weeks after Premo's stroke, the entire family was enjoying Aradhana and Peter's hospitality in Los Angeles. Shantum, Gitu and six-month-old Nandini had come from Plum Village, and Vikram had just arrived from

London. We swam in the beautiful pool, admired the bird-of-paradise flowers in the garden, played bridge together, chatted with friends, and enjoyed Nandini's innocent and delightful ways. After our recent scare, we were grateful that everyone was well.

But early the next morning, Peter, who is a radio buff, heard the news of the first attack on the World Trade Center, and woke us up to watch the television; we saw the next attack live. The images of the attacks were shown over and over again during the day, until the harrowing image was embedded for ever in the mind. We were constantly on the telephone trying to make contact with loved ones: Gitu's sister and her family were living in New York. In the hours that followed, we were very grateful to be together as a family. As three of the four planes that went down that day had been bound for Los Angeles, the city was particularly affected.

The mood was one of anger, anguish and fear—anger at the perpetrators of the crime, anguish for those who had lost loved ones and those who were injured, and fear at the enormity of the destruction and the fact that the enemy was not conspicuous and could attack anywhere again.

Little family skirmishes and quibblings seemed so insignificant in the face of all that had happened. We constantly reminded ourselves how lucky we were to be together, and Premo and I counted our blessings. The world has changed since 9/11—for the ill much more than for the good—and somehow, in the rapid flux of events and anxieties, the family seems even more precious. After the terrible events of September 11 and his own recent stroke, I found the sound of Premo snoring beside me at night comforting if not exactly calming.

★

I can hardly believe that I have known Premo for more than fifty-three years, of which we have been married for fifty-two. On balance, it's been a pack of lucky cards that I have been dealt. Premo is not like other men I know or meet, who are apprehensive of their wife's success. He takes pride in it because he is confident of the merit of his own work. He has given me the space to grow and not held me back; rather, he has encouraged me. I am so glad I married him despite the warnings of my elder brothers; one said that he was not sufficiently anglicized to fit into the family and the other raised unfounded doubts regarding his parentage.

When I have been diffident, Premo has pushed me forward. Soon after we were married, I slammed our car into the gate of Colony Number 1 at Batanagar, and said that I would never drive again. Premo persuaded me to drive again at once. He said, 'Uneducated people drive cars, and there is no reason why an educated young woman like you won't be able to drive well.'

When I have been afraid, he has held my hand. I was pregnant with Vikram when, one evening, he discovered that a steel trunk that we kept upstairs had been broken into, the leather suitcase inside hacked open, and what little jewellery I possessed—apart from what had been lying in an open cupboard—stolen. Things lay scattered about the room. His face, when he came downstairs, had grown pale. But he took great pains to prevent me from going upstairs—and, when it was unavoidable because I wanted to go to bed, he was loving and protective in a way that soothed my natural reaction of shock.

Premo has been a true friend, not a male chauvinist—maybe because he was an orphan and had to fend for himself and earn the love he got, or maybe just because of the generosity of his being. This generosity, however, does not prevent him from getting a kick out of the discomfiture of certain kinds of people. After I became Chief Justice of Himachal Pradesh, sometimes at a function or a party someone would point towards us and say, 'She is the Chief Justice.' But the men who were told this would not hear the 'she' and would automatically presume it was Premo. They would come up to us and start talking to him about the law; quite often, they would turn their back on me. He would smile and let them continue for a while before quietly directing them to me. They would be so shocked and embarrassed that they would edge sheepishly away without even acknowledging me. We would have a good laugh later.

Premo loves fresh air and believes that a brisk outing is the solution to most ills. He comes whistling into the house after his morning walk, bringing in the spirit of sunshine and good cheer. He is a great optimist and knows how to turn love into laughter. But he is also a great organizer and will sometimes not let you relax because he has his own agenda to complete. He loves making lists of things to do, as he believes in the old saying, 'The faintest ink is better than the best memory.' But even more than making these lists, he loves ticking off an item when the job is done. So as soon as he lists a point for future action, I am constantly badgered either to do my part of the job or to make a phone call in order to initiate action. I have named him Mr Tick-off. I sometimes don't tell him I need something done, because I know that this enthusiasm to tick it off his list will just irk me.

A good marriage is a wonderful thing—you are always there for each other. When I look back over more than fifty years, I wonder what the secret of our marriage has been. We were so different. I was brought up to eat everything on my plate, so that there would be no waste. Premo was brought up to leave food on his plate, to show that he ate like an aristocrat and not a pauper. He liked sweets and bland food, but plenty of ghee and butter. I liked fruit and spicy food but a minimum of ghee and butter. If we went to a restaurant, he never wanted to try a new dish; I always did, whether it was oysters or snails or frog's legs.

Thanks to something known as the leave travel concession or LTC, I have managed to travel extensively throughout India. When I became a judge, we were allowed one LTC every four years. After a few years, we learnt that the number was likely to be increased to once every two years. But the word actually used was 'biannual' rather than 'biennial'. This meant that we became entitled to two LTCs every year. I took full advantage of this. Premo was dragged unwillingly along.

We travelled all across India, from the Andamans to Arunachal; from Kerala to Kashmir; Manipur, Madhya Pradesh, Mizoram, Maharashtra, Gujarat, Goa, Sikkim and other wonderful places too numerous to mention. Justice Sunanda Bhandare and I even managed to go to Bhutan, covering the Indian part by LTC, and persuading our husbands, Murli and Premo, to pay for the Bhutan sector and the hotel! Premo, a reluctant traveller, heaved a sigh of relief when I retired as Chief Justice. But he didn't know that he would be faced with another spate of LTCs when I became a member of the Law Commission.

But in other ways, where I was cautious, he was adventurous. He wanted to go into business for himself and had grandiose ideas about what could be done. He even had a large portrait photograph taken so that he could hang it up in his future office. I held him back to the security of a salaried job. He was free with money (even when he had very little) while I was thrifty. He was confident while I was diffident. He would not suffer fools gladly while I was constantly looking for excuses for them. If he believed in something, he would fight for it openly, even to the extent of making enemies. If I believed in something, I would work at it quietly and diplomatically. If he cast a secret vote, he'd have no qualms in disclosing whom it was for—I'd keep silent. He was enthusiastic to a fault; this extended to showing off sample shoes and sandals on the dining table. I kept my enthusiasms under control, letting them emerge slowly. I loved meeting new people and going to new places but he wanted to spend time only with a limited group of friends and relatives and go for outings with them to familiar places; that was why he cried off going to China with Shantum and me. Premo has small eyes, which disappear when he laughs. I have large eyes, which become bigger when I am serious.

But we had things in common too. For a start, we were both short. We both loved English literature and studied it at university. In our childhood, we had both been nurtured and given a great deal of love from unexpected sources, he from his foster family, the Khannas, and I from the Dutts. We both had a great sense of loyalty to our friends and family, and gratitude and forgiveness moved us. Premo would go out of his way to help people and was generous both with time and money. I was with him in this, except that I made the occasional complaint that the family too needed his time. Both of us believed in hard work and strove for excellence in whatever we did. We had faith in each other, cared for, loved and understood each other, and took pride in each other's achievements and successes.

When Vikram wrote *A Suitable Boy*, almost all the characters were composite except for those of Mrs Rupa Mehra, who was based entirely on my mother, and Haresh, who was largely based on Premo. After the book was released, he received a lot of fan mail, but many women were upset that one of the characters had decided to marry Haresh. One American woman, in fact, was so distraught that she wrote that anyone who would choose him didn't deserve any better! Well, all I can say is that I couldn't have done any better. As some wise person once said, love isn't about becoming somebody else's perfect person. It's about finding someone who helps you become the best person you can be.

I have tried to follow the advice my mother gave me when I got married: 'Never sleep on a quarrel, it gets exaggerated in the darkness of the night.' So we always talked things over, even if it meant waking up a sleeping partner. And over the years I became more confident and he started eating fruit and 'licking the platter clean'. We started looking and behaving more like each other and borrowing each other's gestures. After fifty years of togetherness and three wonderful children, we felt that our life had been golden and that it was an occasion to celebrate. I would have liked to invite a hundred couples, Premo five. We settled for fifty people, numerically appropriate for a golden wedding.

At Premo's seventy-fifth birthday, a couple of years earlier, all four of us siblings—as well as Usha and Mohini—had been together. When I look at those photographs, I am overcome with sadness. I give thanks that Sashi bhai and Usha are in good health. The fact that they live so close to us is a very large part of our happiness. But Tuttu suffered his stroke just a few days after the celebration. And Michi bhai died within a year of it. Two years younger than Premo, he did not live to enjoy his own seventy-fifth birthday.

★

At the very end of August 1999 I flew to Dhaka to attend a conference; I had hardly arrived when I got the news of Michi's death in Pune. I was filled with sadness. The conference was to start the next morning. I spent the evening by myself. I thought about Michi bhai, well-dressed and suave and fond of good food and wine. I decided to go down to the restaurant in the hotel, have a good meal and be with him again as I brought to mind the last few days we'd spent together. Less than a week earlier he'd been in Delhi; usually, I sent a rakhi to him, but this time I had been able to tie it on his wrist myself. He had had a very good time in Delhi meeting friends and eating and drinking; he had looked happy and relaxed.

By some strange chance, Michi bhai and I had flown to Pune on the 27th, the day after Rakhi, he to go home, I to attend a seminar. We had arranged to have dinner together the next day. But Mohini called me to say that instead of coming to the house I should come to the hospital first as Michi bhai had been admitted for a check-up. I went there and found him very cheerful, eating chips and biscuits. I had been given a large bouquet of flowers at the inauguration of the seminar that morning and presented it to him. He jokingly asked me, 'Why have you brought only white flowers? Not for my funeral, I hope.' We laughed together. Little did I realize that it was the last time that I was going to see him.

Mohini and I went home and spent a pleasant time chatting and eating dinner. The next morning I called; he seemed to be fine. I checked out of the hotel, went to the seminar and from there straight to the airport. On the 29th, I telephoned from Delhi. It appeared that he was not feeling good. The next day he was dead.

Mohini is a beautiful and gutsy woman. When she married Michi bhai, she had three grown-up children of her own: Rohita, Nikhil and Gayatri. Michi bhai also had his own three.

Rohita lived in Bombay and helped Mohini to sort out her affairs. Gayatri lived in Uganda. In response to our letters and telephone calls Mohini wrote to me a month or so after Michi bhai's death:

Thanks for your letters and concern. I am learning to cope on my own and have begun tackling the paper work [. . .]

I am going to Uganda on 9 October because Gayatri and Rohita feel I need a change of atmosphere. I should not be here at Diwali so I feel I may as well go, I love the calm stressless life.

All of you must come whenever you wish and stay with me. It is still your elder brother's house and you are all welcome. I love meeting every one of you. I have so many letters to reply, Michi really had a great fan mail. The women in Pune really miss him. Its amazing as bossy as he was they loved him.

★

The meeting in Dhaka to which I had gone was called the Asian Parliamentarians' Conference for Peace and Cooperation, but others, like me, who were not parliamentarians, had also been invited. While we were going up in the hotel elevator, a gentleman introduced me to some of the Bangladeshi participants as Justice Seth. They nodded formally. But when he added, 'She is the mother of Vikram Seth,' they smiled broadly and even hugged me as their response to his spirit of understanding and tolerance in *A Suitable Boy*. I thought, truly, peace is brought about by cooperation and empathy, and these in turn are brought about by literature and culture and the intermingling of people.

Vikram has always had a thirst to understand and enjoy not only the culture he was born to but those of others. He is something of an obsessive when he is gripped by something—whether it is classical Chinese calligraphy or the songs of Schubert. At present, he is writing a double-biography of Shanti Uncle and Aunty Henny; in order to be able to read certain letters sent to her after the War, he has gone to the extent of learning to write in the old style of German handwriting—something few Germans today can do, or would even bother with. But this sort of thing helps keep him busy and fascinated with life—and, I hope, happy.

★

Shantum and Gitu are making a conscious effort to live a simple life in harmony with their surroundings and in a spirit of helpfulness to others. I was at Plum Village on the beautiful snowy day in December 2001 when Thay, in a very moving ceremony, ordained Shantum as a lay teacher. Shantum read an insight poem he wrote for the occasion:

> Circumambulating the stupa
> There is no beginning and no end.
> Smiling through the dance of birth and death
> The True Path reveals itself.

True Path is the name given to Shantum by Thay. After reciting the poem, Shantum offered to be a disciple and Thay accepted him. Thay recited, first in Vietnamese and then in an English translation, a poem he had specially composed for Shantum:

> Visualizing the true Mark of the Mind
> As a full moon, you will see
> That not only the Path is your mind
> But also the Object of Mind
> (Visaya) is your mind.
>
> Who is the One sitting there
> On the bank of the Ganga river
> Counting the white sand?
> Look at your lovely innocent child
> Smiling happily in the heart
> Of the Bamboo Grove.

He then transmitted the lamp to Shantum and also handed over the certificate or lamp transmission gatha. Shantum had two friends by his side—one carried the certificate and the other the lamp. Shantum walked to the side, sat down and delivered his first discourse as a teacher. He also thanked Thay and said something about himself and the reason for his joining Thay.

For Shantum, as he told me, his ordination at Thay's hands was the third most important event in his life, the first being his wedding to Gitu and the second the birth of Nandini.

★

When Nandini was a year old, Shantum and Gitu took her to Calcutta, so that Neepa and my brother Tuttu, who had been paralysed for more than three years, could see her. Tuttu had been very fond of my children—especially Shantum— who as a child had loved his sense of fun and the fabulous breakfasts to which he invited the family. Shantum, at six, whenever faced with a novel item of food, would seek assurance from Tuttu and say, 'If Tootoo Maama can eat it, I can eat it too.'

Tuttu and Neepa were very touched with Shantum and Gitu's gesture of bringing their child all these hundreds of miles so that they could see her. They handed over to them a letter for me together with a gold medal—one of two that my father had won at his engineering college, and which, ever since I was a child, I had wished to have. When Tuttu and Neepa were getting married in 1974, I had offered to buy one from Ma, so that she could give Neepa a piece of jewellery instead. But she had insisted that they were both kept for Tuttu. She had one of them made into a pendant for Neepa. I was really touched that, twenty-eight years later, Tuttu and

Neepa had given the other one to me. The letter read:

Dearest Leela Bahain,

At last your brother Tuttu has consented with a happy mood to present (The Gold Medal) of your father, to Santam and Geetanjali's—first born Daughter (child)

We are both delighted to hand it over to you (The Gold Medal) of your father, it is a Pride to the Seth family; and Brilliance and Excellence of Late Shree Raj Behari Seth—we feel that, you are the most elligible child of My Father-in-law—This was Presented to me by my mother-in-law Late Mrs Chanda Seth—on our wedding—as a family Heirloom—

There is one clause from our side, for this gift, that,

1. It should only go to Nandini Seth, Geetanjali and Shantam Seths First born child daughter.

2. 2ndly, under any circumstances, (The Gold Medal) should never be melted or sold to any body—

These are our and my sincere request to you and to its Recepient—

With love and regards to Both Premu Bhai and You

Neepa

Tuttu had scrawled at the bottom, as he could hardly write owing to his paralysis:

Dearest Leila Behen,

With my love I am sending you this medal. Ma always said, Daddy used to say that our family was really blessed because they had a child like Leila.

Love to you and Premo bhai,

Tuttu

★

Aradhana continues to balance work and home, no easy task when, as a diplomat's wife, she has to move house every four years. Peter is a loving husband and son-in-law, who goes out of his way to be helpful to those he meets in the course of his work—which he greatly enjoys. He gives Aradhana space and encouragement.

Recently, she directed a short film commissioned by BBC 4 on Arundhati Roy and the protests over the dam on the Narmada river that has dispossessed and will dispossess tens of thousands of villagers. It was called *Dam/Age* and won the One World Media Award.

Though Aradhana does not have children of her own, she has a wonderful rapport with Nandini, and with the children of her friends. When she heard that Rachna's young son was fond of tennis, she filled her suitcase with dozens of hardly-used tennis balls, which the exacting Peter had rejected in favour of new ones after a few games, and gave them to the delighted youngster.

Busy though she is, she rarely forgets to send her brothers a rakhi. Vikram received this year's rakhi accompanied by a drawing of a fish—one of Aradhana's motifs—and the lapidary message: 'dearest vikram bhaiyya—fishy love and rakhi thoughts—xxx—a.' We, on the other hand, received a long e-mail a few days earlier, after she had read the manuscript of this book:

> Dearest Mama and Papa—
>   a few fishes and a little note
>   While walking in the garden this afternoon among the 'banana tree' like birds of paradise I was transplanted back to the gardenia tree outside my bedroom window and the sita ashok in bloom. The many evening walks around Vikram bhaiyya's stone path and Shantum's papaya plantation. Your orchids

and cacti that travelled with us M and your little jibes
that went along P.

It continues to make me very thankful that I can
enjoy and feel thrilled about the little things—the
afternoon sun, the inside of a kiwi fruit, a shadow on
the wall, architecture and a thoughtful gesture. I
realize now that it's you who opened my eyes, while
I was growing up, to notice much of this. You led me
to it with a sense of freedom—allowing me to discover
it for myself.

In a similar way to you Papa who takes Nandini
for a walk every morning introducing her to the
flowers and trees.

Much of what you've given has become a part of
our daily life. Everyday I am reminded of walking
down the steps in Rajaji Marg to find you reading the
morning papers—drinking orange pekoe and freshly
ground percolated coffee.

Interesting conversations at a dinner table always
take me back to the ones we had at ours (very few can
really beat them!!) Politics, prose and poppies while
chillies in vinegar were being munched on! I feel
happy that we spent those many Sunday nights (family
only dinners instituted by Vikram bhaiyya). Despite
the fact that I sometimes wanted to escape to work on
a film—or see a friend.

And of course there were the other days when all
the communication we had was scribbled notes—in
the book by the phone.

Either way I always knew we were there for each
other and continue to be.

It's an unbelievable source of strength. To know
that I can wander and always have a place to come
back to.

An open home for all three of us all ways and always.

Growing up I always took this as a given. However I soon realized (and continue to) how fortunate we are to have each other while simultaneously letting each other be free—spread across three, sometimes four continents.

To be—

or not to be?

Okay now—enough. off to film Dom

Lots of love

hugs and fishes xxxxx

aradhana

★

One should be careful when naming one's children—often enough, they live up to their names. My sons have lived up to theirs, and Aradhana has certainly been the answer to a prayer.

My granddaughter too could not have an apter name: she is certainly delightful. As I watch Nandini grow, I am filled with pleasure. When she calls out, 'Dadi Ma!', my heart overflows. She likes to sing and dance and have storybooks read out to her. She has started going to a Play Club and enjoys the company and fun of other children enormously. Her love is very inclusive, because Gitu has taught her to be generous. Gitu has also, with love and laughter, instilled in her an affection and respect for the larger family. We are fortunate to have such a caring daughter-in-law and Nandini too is blessed to have a mother like her. She has taught Nandini, who is two years old, that her full name is Nandini Seth, who resides at such-and-such a house in such-and-such a sector in Noida.

Nandini loves to be in the garden, and I am trying to inculcate in her both a love and a knowledge of trees, plants and flowers. She has learnt the names of many, including some difficult ones, like poinsettia and rondeletia. Her Nani brought me a plant from Dehra Dun called Nandina Domestica; it has delicate green leaves, which turn red and look very attractive. Nandini is especially fond of the plant. She touches it tenderly and waters it regularly. When Gitu asked her, 'What is your name?' she promptly replied, 'Nandini.' Gitu said, 'I want you to tell me your full name.' She thought for a moment and then replied, 'Nandini Domestica'.

Why is one's grandchild so precious? Nandini, is it because I feel that when I die a part of me will be alive in you? Or is it because I have the satisfaction of knowing that some of my treasured possessions and family jewellery, whatever little there is, will be passed on to you and looked after by you with love? Is it your daily sense of delight and wonderment which brings me such pleasure? Or is it, as we Indians are fond of saying, that 'interest is more precious than capital'? Is it because I feel that the values and ideals I hold dear will be carried on by you, and that this will help lead to a happier and more peaceful world? Or is it all of these? I hope you read this book when I am gone, and that it repays you a little for all the joy that, in the autumn of my life, you have given me.

On Balance

I have now completed the age of threescore and ten. Though I feel young, and think that old age is ten years ahead of me, I know I am living on borrowed time.

I began writing this book after lighting a diya before a statue of Ganesh at 20.02 hours on 20.02.2002. I will not be here for the next such palindrome, when all the zeros have been replaced by ones. Nor probably will Nandini, for whom in the first instance I have written this book. But, as long as we have not messed up our world, very likely her granddaughter will.

The process of writing has been one of contemplation—about words and the nature of language, about the history of my times, about my chosen or chance profession of the law. It has also been one of introspection, of trying to understand how I became who I am. From a shy and somewhat frightened girl, who neither felt fully at home in the world nor comfortable about trying to change it, I am now someone who is willing to fight for change, though in a quiet manner.

It was Premo who gave me the confidence that I was as

good as anyone else and should not be afraid. Or perhaps I should say, it *has been* Premo, for in many ways this has been a long and even continuing process. Premo is a doer and a fighter, and courage comes to him naturally. He is practical (except in money matters) and knows how to use knowledge to his advantage. I am often deluged by the vastness of a problem or a project and don't know where to begin to think or write or act. From Premo too I have learnt not to fear change, in fact that change is essential to growth. Indeed, I have since come to believe that learning itself is a form of change. The day I stop to learn, I will truly be old.

I suppose I had potential but no confidence; I flowered after marriage. But many women wither after marriage, exhausted by cruelty, dismissiveness or the daily grind. Though my marriage has been happy, and though when I look back I can see that I did put some pressure on Aradhana to get married, I still cannot claim that marriage is invariably a good thing. My mother would not have had such doubts. She was educated in an English-medium school, and had what was then thought of as a modern outlook, but she could not have conceived of a life without marriage. It was mandatory, especially for a girl. My parents believed in a good education for me, and my father repeatedly told my mother that no dowry would change hands at my wedding. Nevertheless, my mother, as a widow, dinned into my head the admonition that I should learn to be submissive in character, as I would have to adjust, in time, to my husband's family.

I can see how much, for better or worse, I have been moulded by my parents' views, and I wonder how much my own views—stated or unstated—have affected my children. I have brought them up with certain values, which they have absorbed as much by osmosis as by actual teaching. As a result, I often used to feel they were misfits in the present culture of consumerism, corruption and fundamentalism. I wondered how they would face life, impractical as they seemed to be. Once, despondent, I turned to a kindred soul and friend, Meenakshi Mukherjee, and asked her, 'Have we made a mistake?' Her reply gave me the answer: 'If you had a second chance, would you bring them up any differently?'

Now, as I look at my children and those whom they have chosen to spend their lives with, I feel a sense of happiness; I am freer of doubts. Of course, as the Moroccans say, in the eyes of a mother, every beetle is a gazelle. I am trying, however, to be objective. In many ways, things have not come easy for any of them.

I suspect, children being more unsparing than parents, that they see me as a cross between a beetle and a gazelle. However old they are, when they are at home, they revert to some extent to their roles as children, and are delighted and irritated by the same things as before. One trait of mine that particularly irked and irks them is what they call my negativity. By temperament, I am cautious. And as a lawyer, I would try and see every question as a whole, taking in the viewpoints of both sides, so that I could meet the arguments of the opposing side. So when my children asked to do something— or asked me to do something—my first reaction would be to point out the difficulties and the drawbacks. Premo, on the other hand—unless of course he was so busy with work even to entertain their request—would plunge headlong into things. I can see now why my negative attitude bothered my children. I still tell them the problems involved in a particular course of action, but I try to be enthusiastic about it first.

What my children call my *Reader's Digest* kind of morality, my 'What will people say?' stance, also comes in for its share of criticism. Over the years I have learnt—or, rather, I have been trained—to be more broad-minded, and to examine my prejudices and preconceptions from a more objective and humane point of view.

As I established my legal practice, there were times when I had to choose between giving priority to work obligatons or to family commitments. I juxtaposed, manoeuvred and adjusted, but the flow of neither stream ever stopped. Luckily I never had to make the dreadful choice of following one to the exclusion of the other. I always knew in my heart that it would be very hard if I had to choose, but that of course my family would come first.

The balancing act has not been easy. Two considerations have, however, helped me. One thing I realized quite early on is that if you are sincere with your work and love your family, you can share your problems and difficulties with them. It is surprising what solutions emerge through consensus. Even small children, who want as much as they can get of their mother's time, make suggestions that show their selflessness. For one thing, they can get into the shoes of someone in desperate trouble who needs their mother's help in her capacity as a lawyer or other professional. For another, just as a mother feels good about helping her children sort our their problems, they too feel good helping to sort out hers.

The second consideration is that in some ways doing two different kinds of work is less stressful than doing only one. When I felt stressed by my legal work, I could switch to housework, and vice versa. This change of occupation was itself a form of relaxation.

Work has brought all sorts of concomitant rewards. As a child I longed not for money or power but, for some reason, to see my name in a newspaper. Perhaps this was because I was enamoured of the written word, perhaps because I saw it as an acknowledgement of merit and achievement. The first time I saw my name in print, which was in the *Times* after

I did well in the Bar Examinations, it gave me a quiet thrill. Since then, my reaction has varied. Sometime in 2001, late at night, a lawyer friend phoned me to say, 'Leila, you have caused someone a huge financial loss.' I was dumbstruck; what had I done? I had visions of being sued, of endless court hearings and adjournments. It emerged that that evening, in 'Kaun Banega Krorepati?' (the Hindi version of 'Who Wants to be a Millionaire?') a participant had incorrectly answered the question, 'Who was the first woman Chief Justice of a state in India?' Such was the popularity of this programme that I got more messages of congratulations owing to this unfortunate man's error than I had received for the actual event ten years earlier.

When I first came to live in Delhi, a couple who were friends of ours were invited on Republic Day to Rashtrapati Bhavan for the President's annual tea party; he was the head of the Delhi office of an important company. His wife described the beautiful gardens, Moghul in style, with their emerald green grass and vast variety of roses, and in particular the sunken garden at the end with its profusion of flowers. I felt a twinge of yearning, perhaps even of jealousy, and wondered whether I would ever get to see it. Once again, as a result of my work, a small dream became possible. As a judge of the Delhi High Court, I had the good fortune of seeing and enjoying the gardens once every year for thirteen years. Indeed, when I was a member of the jury for an award, the chairperson of which was First Lady Usha Narayanan, I had the pleasure of a very private showing. She took us around and pointed out, with justifiable pride, the fabulous tulips she had grown.

In Rashtrapati Bhavan too, I was once introduced to the Queen of England. She appeared to be having rather a boring time, standing stiffly and nodding her head as a great many people, arranged in two long queues, Indians to the left and Britishers to the right, were introduced to her one by one. I spoke to her, and we exchanged a few words. I later discovered that this was quite a faux pas; I should merely have curtsied or bowed, and spoken to her only if I had been spoken to.

On another occasion, I was introduced to President Clinton. On yet another, at a small lunch, I had a long conversation with Hillary Clinton. I have over the years met a fair number of the great and good—or not so good. In a sense, the little fatherless girl with no connections has come a long way.

But this fame in print and on the air, this privileged access to places, this mixing in elevated circles or, for that matter, Delhi society—though I certainly enjoy them, I recognize them at some level for what they are. The pleasures are fleeting, and mixed with a good deal of ego-feeding. I bring myself down to earth whenever I can remember to, with a remark that Premo made to me when we were first married: 'It is better to spend time making something of yourself rather than socializing.'

There are two books by my bedside which I often thumb through. One is *Daily Strength for Daily Needs* by Mary W. Tileston, which came to me from Aunty Dutt, to whom it belonged. It was printed in 1905 and consists of readings from prose, verse and Scripture for each day of the year. It has helped to cheer me up whenever I have felt low.

The other, *Bhagavad-Gita, The Song of God*, translated by Swami Prabhavananda and Christopher Isherwood partly in prose and partly in verse, was given to me by my mother forty years ago. It has helped me to learn that I must work, yet be detached. Sri Krishna says:

He who does the task
Dictated by duty,
Caring nothing
For fruit of the action,
He is a yogi,
A true sannyasin.
But he who follows
His vow to the letter
By mere refraining:
Lighting no fire
At the ritual offering,
Making excuse
For avoidance of labour,
He is no yogi,
No true sannyasin.

I have tried to inculcate in myself a spirit of detachment as advocated in the Gita, but have not always succeeded in not caring for the fruits of an action performed to the best of my ability. I wrote a judgment dealing with extradition law in 1990; it went up on appeal to the Supreme Court and though they decided it in 1993, I only learnt of its fate in 1996—by pure chance, since I never consciously made an effort to ascertain what happened once I had decided a case. At a social occasion during a conference, I overheard a lawyer praise a Supreme Court judge on his judgment in a particular matter. The judge, seeing me standing nearby, turned to me and said, 'It was all your hard work. I fully endorsed what was an excellent judgment.' I was very pleased to hear this praise; any attempt to remain detached went by the board. One of the things most difficult to be detached from is the regard of those for whom one has regard.

★

Many of those for whom, through my life, I have had great regard are now dead. Some of my best friends are among these: the religious, regal and dignified Ira, the beautiful, warm-hearted and strong-spirited Maya, the generous and savvy and fun-loving Sunanda, the laughing, loving and caring Lily, and Rosalind, gentle, lovely and wise; two of my very good male friends, Akbar who seemed to me to fly through the air, being so childlike in his wonderment and open in his friendship, and Shanti Jain, who suffered throughout his life from breathlessness and lung dysfunction, yet remained so cheerful and courageous, hardly ever complaining, trying to live life to the full both at work and at home; and my Michi bhai, tall, good-looking, charming, affectionate, emotional, autocratic and intelligent. I miss them all.

I also think of Raja Khaitan, the widow of the former Chairman of Bata India, who had lived like a queen, decked in pearls and diamonds, fragrant with perfume, and cushioned by every comfort. She died alone, and was cremated with little ceremony. She, who had made almost a fetish of cleanliness and luxury, was carried on the top of an Ambassador taxi, wrapped in a dirty black tarpaulin because it was raining, from Dehra Dun to Kankhal. There were just four men, including the taxi driver, to shoulder her dead body and cremate her: the other three were her nephew Vinod, Shanti Jain and Premo, who had driven in from Delhi. More than two hundred young men were standing nearby at the bier of an old woman; each of them had brought a piece of wood for her funeral pyre. When Shanti Jain asked one of them, 'How were you related to her?' he replied, 'She is just a beggar woman from our neighbourhood whom we have seen around the place since our childhood.'

Can we expect something after death? Or is it in fact the end? I don't know, and I don't expect to get a clearer answer.

But I proceed as if it is, and try to live this life well.

One of my favourite bhajans by Kabir is the one about the potter and the clay. I have often watched fascinatedly a potter shaping a pot on his wheel. Almost magically his hands imbue an ordinary clod of earth with life. He kneads the clay, then swiftly makes it assume a perfect shape. In Kabir's bhajan the mud humbly cautions the potter: 'You are mauling me today; but a day will come when I shall likewise maul you.' As a Hindu I will be cremated, not buried, and my ashes will be mingled with the waters of the Ganga, but this poem still conveys to me more than anything else the impermanence of our life and our swift return to our elements.

★

Do I have a religion? Over the course of my life I have gone from believing whole-heartedly in God, to not believing at all, to now not knowing whether to believe or not. But more years ago than I can remember, long before I studied law or even had the intention of doing so, I copied the following passage and kept it under a sheet of glass on my desk. I do not know who wrote it nor do I remember where I found it but I have read it so often over the years that it has become a part of me:

> My religion is to love justice, to long for the right, to love mercy, to pity suffering, to assist the weak, to forgive wrongs and remember benefits, to love the truth, to be sincere, to utter honest words, to love liberty, to wage relentless war against slavery in all its forms, to love husband and child and friend, to make a happy home, to cultivate the mind, to be familiar with the mighty thoughts genius has expressed, the noble deeds of all the world; to cultivate courage and cheerfulness, to make others happy, to fill life with

the splendour of generous acts, the warmth of loving words; to discard error, to destroy prejudice, to receive new truths with gladness, to cultivate hope, to see the calm beyond the storm, the dawn beyond the night, to do the best that can be done and then be resigned. This is the religion of reason, the creed of science. This satisfies the brain and the heart.

It is a tall order, but acts for me as a sort of credo. However short one falls of it, it is something one can use as a guide, something to aspire to.

As I grow older (I am now almost seventy-three) I have not lost my zest for living. I am still thrilled to see the crocus bloom or the tiny sunbird flit in and out of the pomelo tree in our garden. A double rainbow or the sun setting into the sea still brings me delight. The heady smell when the parched earth soaks up the first monsoon rain sends me into raptures. And the tall deodar tree, holding the snow in its arms and looking upwards is as lovely as a poem. But what delights me most of all is the innocent love and laughter of children. That is why the injustice of so many children, and especially girls, not having proper food, clothing, shelter and education in our country is so galling, when money is readily, even eagerly, made available for armaments and war.

I would like to end with a poem I wrote for the girl child some years ago:

Where have all the young girls gone?
Some were aborted before they were born;
A few were buried or choked with coarse paddy;
Others were smothered, starved or drowned in a well;
Poisoned with berries of oleander till dead,
So that dowry need not be paid or in-laws fed,
Or daughters raped, beaten or burnt—
This is the sad story of a girl child's hell.

Father, why do you discriminate against me
When I can be as good as my brother?
Mother, nurture nourish and educate me and you will see
That I will not be a burden but will control my own destiny,
And you will have nothing to fear (if brother is not there),
I will look after both of you in your old age;
I ask only to be treated equally—will you not dare—
So that I have the freedom to choose and the right to care;
And am no longer the prisoner of my gender
Unable to retaliate against injustice.

Oh Father, give me a chance,
Just give me a chance.
Oh Mother, break the bonds of tradition
And let me into the sunlight to dance . . . to dance. . . to dance.

Happy Annive Mam

I.

The mewa in the Godrej shrine,
The plaintive "Wake me up at nine,"
The vacillating calls to Bali,
The farming schemes of our new mali,
The trendy jeep parked at the door,
The mushrooms sprouting through the floor,
The half-baked bread, the untilled beans,
The dinner tiffs, the breakfast scenes:
"You think that everything's a joke."
"I've been delayed at Anand Lok."
"The footpath must be made right now.
At once. Today. I don't care how..."

Where, but at home, at Number 8,
The mansion of Ms. Justice Seth
(And spouse and issue) may one see
So rich a social comedy?